E-BUSINESS FOR TOURISM

PRACTICAL GUIDELINES FOR TOURISM DESTINATIONS AND BUSINESSES

CONSEJO EMPRESARIAL **OMT**
WTO BUSINESS COUNCIL
CONSEIL PROFESIONNEL **OMT**

September 2001

Copyright © 2001 World Tourism Organization

E-Business for Tourism - Practical Guidelines for Tourism Destinations and Businesses

ISBN: 92–844-0459-2

Published by the World Tourism Organization

FOREWORD

For every tourism destination and supplier, large and small, electronic business on the platform of the Internet offers the opportunity to undertake their business in new and more cost-effective ways. Marketing across the Web and by e-mail is a key aspect. However, e-business is much broader than that. It impacts on all types of communication and business process, internally and externally, and requires new ways of thinking and working.

Thus Destination Management Organisations (DMOs) and tourism businesses have to deal not only with technological change, but also with organisational change, based on the principles of collaborative working and sharing of resources. Individual DMOs and businesses should become more integrated internally, whilst new partnerships and alliances are possible externally.

Those who choose to ignore e-business, or to regard it as a peripheral activity, do so at their peril, because their major competitors will certainly be exploiting the opportunities it presents to enhance their competitiveness.

As the first chapter of this report demonstrates, the Internet is the ideal medium for tourism and tourism is a key sector for Internet commerce. Indeed, e-commerce in travel and tourism has continued to expand at a dramatic rate, whilst other sectors have encountered difficulties. Many forecasts suggest that travel and tourism's share of e-commerce will continue its rapid increase, possibly reaching 50% within the next two or three years.

The World Tourism Organization Business Council is aware that, in this dynamic environment, DMOs and tourism businesses have a real need for practical guidance on how to embrace e-business. This report is intended to meet that need. It is in three sections:

- Part A lays the foundation, with an analysis of market trends and an explanation of the concepts of e-business and Customer Relationship Management.

- Part B focuses on e-business for DMOs. It starts with an overview of the changing value chains and the evolving role of DMOs. Then it provides practical guidelines (on a step-by-step basis) on how DMOs should respond to the challenges, by developing e-business systems, and more specifically, how to go about developing Web sites for consumers, intermediaries, travel media and tourism businesses.

- Part C focuses on e-business for tourism suppliers, particularly SMEs (small and medium size enterprises). It starts with an overview of the e-business applications and services that are relevant to each of the main sectors of tourism, and then goes into detail regarding the opportunities for four specific sectors Hospitality Services, Travel Agencies, Tour Operators, and Visitor Attractions.

This report follows an earlier one, published by the WTO Business Council in November 1999, under the title 'Marketing Tourism Destinations Online'. That publication included a wide range of background information on the implications of the Information Age for marketing by the travel and tourism industries. It covered the development and use of electronic distribution systems in travel and tourism - particularly Global Distribution Systems and hotel central reservation systems; the emergence and impact of the Internet as a distribution channel; and the emerging technologies (especially interactive TV) that will impact on distribution in the future. These subjects are not covered again here, so readers who wish to know more about them should refer to the earlier report.

Whilst this report draws some content and concepts from 'Marketing Tourism Destinations Online', it is largely new material. The guidelines for DMOs are greatly expanded; the case studies of Destination Management Systems and of DMO Web sites have been completely updated; and Part C, written specifically for tourism businesses, is completely new. This new title for this report, reflects not only the fact that it is largely a different publication, but also that its scope is substantially wider.

Martin Brackenbury
Chairman
WTO Business Council

José Antonio Ferreiro
Chief Executive Officer
WTO Business Council

Acknowledgements

Parts A and B of this report have been written by Roger Carter and his Associates of Tourism Enterprise and Management (TEAM) and Part C by François Bédard of the University of Québec at Montreal.

The WTOBC would like to thank the authors and also the other organizations whose material is quoted or illustrated in this publication : Computer Industry Almanac, Concierge, Datamonitor, eTForecasts, IDC, Jupiter Communications, Nykamp Consulting Group, Scottish Tourist Board, Travel Industry Association of America.

This report has been produced with the active support from the International Federation of IT and Travel & Tourism.

The WTOBC would also like to express its appreciation and thanks to our member MasterCard International as well as to Microsoft Iberica, whose sponsorship made the financing of this study possible.

CONTENTS

Part A – Introduction

Part B – E-Business for Destination Management Organisations

Part C – E-Business for Tourism SME's

PART A - INTRODUCTION

1   Setting the Scene

1.1   The Internet and tourism – a powerful combination.

The Internet and its protocol (TCP/IP) have created a universal platform for communication and presentation - a truly open, global network. Increasingly it will be accessed from different types of equipment - TV, mobile devices, in-car technology, terrestrial phones, kiosks, computer games consoles, etc - for a range of purposes. The cost of access is going down and the speed of access is going up. The Web is becoming more useful (in terms of functions and content) and more user-friendly. This is a powerful combination of factors driving increased usage, as shown in Section 1.2.

Tourism and the Internet are ideal partners. For consumers, when they are planning a trip to a new destination, they face the problem of making a costly purchase without being able to see the product. The Internet provides them with the means to gain immediate access to relevant information of greater variety and depth than has been available previously, about destinations throughout the world; and to book quickly and easily.

For tourism destinations and businesses, it offers the potential to make information and booking facilities available to large numbers of consumers at relatively low cost; it enables them to make large-scale savings on the production and distribution of print and on other traditional activities (e.g. call centres and information centres); and it provide a tool for communication and relationship development with tourism suppliers and market intermediaries, as well as end-consumers.

Tourism has a key difference from most other sectors of e-commerce – its consumer goes and collects the product at the point of production – i.e. the destination. Thus the tourism sector avoids the need to deliver products around the world - a task that faces real logistical problems that have been a major source of customer dissatisfaction.

These factors, taken together, have resulted in the travel and tourism sector taking a larger and larger share of e-commerce globally – as documented in Section 1.2. As a result, the Internet is revolutionising the distribution of tourism information and sales. Not only does it provide tourism destinations and businesses with direct access to end consumers, but also it is becoming the primary channel for business to business communication.

1.2   The importance of the Internet and Internet-based e-commerce

1.2.1   The growth in Internet usage

The dramatic growth in the number of Internet users over the past five years and projections for the next five years are shown in Figure 1 – a nine-fold increase over five years.   The top fifteen countries in terms of the absolute number of Internet users (predicted for year-end 2001) is shown in Figure 2, with the United States clearly dominating.   The world's top nine generators of international travel are included (except The Netherlands) and Pacific-Asia features strongly.

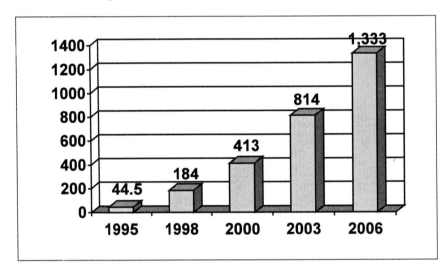

**Figure 1 – Number of Internet users world-wide (in millions)
[Source: eTForecasts, July 2001]**

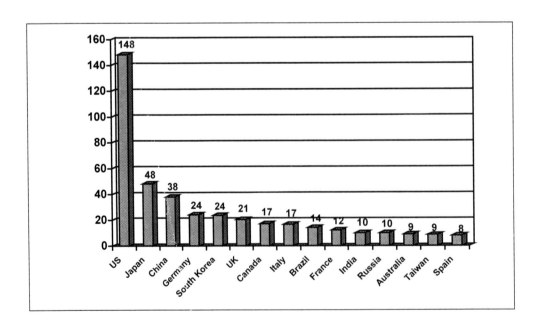

**Figure 2
Top 15 markets in terms of numbers of Internet users at year-end 2001
(in millions) [Source: eTForecasts, July 2001]**

Figure 3 shows a different pattern – the top 15 countries in terms of the number of Internet users per thousand population. On this basis, smaller countries stand alongside the larger ones, with Sweden having the highest rate of usage. Other Scandinavian countries and Australasia also feature strongly, as do the smaller Asian countries. Of the world's top ten major markets for outbound international travel, the following do not appear on this chart: Germany, UK, France, Japan, Italy, Spain and Belgium.

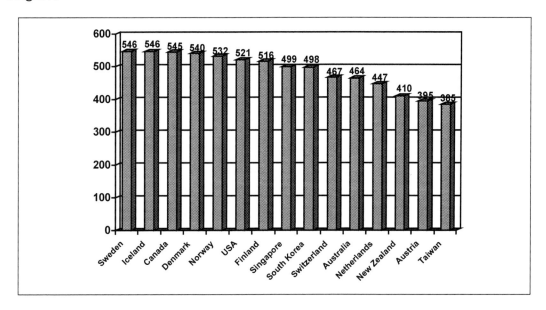

Figure 3 - Top 15 markets in terms of number of Internet users per thousand population at year-end 2001 [Source: eTForecasts, July 2001]

Future growth in Internet user numbers is expected to vary markedly between the different regions of the world. Jupiter predicts (Figure 4) that:

- North America will have a relatively slow rate of growth, but still remain predominant in 2003
- The largest growth overall will be in Pacific Asia
- The largest percentage rates of growth will be in the 'late adopter' markets, particularly the Middle East (from a low base).

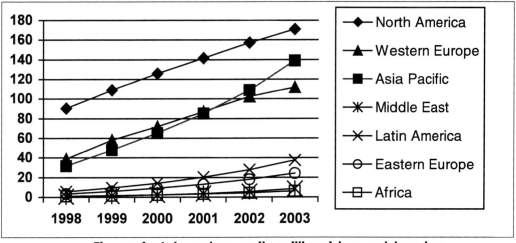

Figure 4 - Internet users (in millions) by world region [Source: Jupiter Communications, 2000, quoted by eMarketer]

Another company, eTForecasts (Figure 5), projects much stronger growth in Asia, to the extent that it will have overtaken North America by 2003 and will have twice as many users in 2006. The assumption of rapid growth in Asia is based on rapidly increasing use of wireless Web devices.

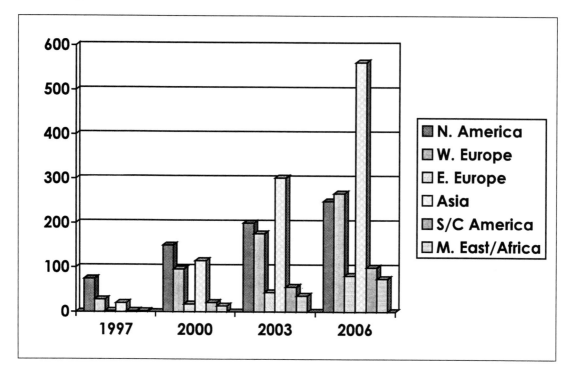

Figure 5 - Internet users by regions (in millions), 1997-2006
[Source: eTForecasts, July 2001]

1.2.2 Internet user profile

Internet users tend to be relatively:
- wealthy
- well educated
- interested in independent travel

In other words, they relate very well to some or all of the target markets of many destinations. However, as the number of Internet users grows, particularly through increases in the use of new access channels (especially interactive TV and mobile devices), the user profile will change, broaden and become less up-market.

In the United States, it is already the case that a very high proportion of people travelling internationally is, or will be soon, Internet users. The same will be true in other major markets within the next two or three years.

Thus, based on user profile, the Internet appears to be an ideal medium for marketing by tourism destinations and businesses. We shall see later in this chapter how this is, indeed, proving to be the case. First, however, we look at the key question of how far the Internet is being used as a medium for buying, as well as researching.

1.2.3   The growth of Internet commerce

Figure 6 contains a key analysis provided by Jupiter, showing how, in the US, the propensity to purchase increases directly with length of time as an Internet user. Those who have been Internet users for three years or more, are more than twice as likely to buy than a first year user.

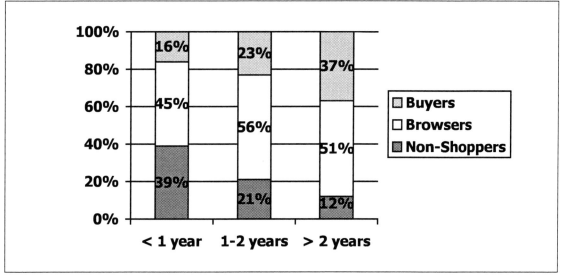

**Figure 6 - Browsing and buying, related to experience online - in US
[Source: Jupiter Communications 2000]**

Thus, as the market has matured, there has been and will be substantial growth in both the number and the percentage of Internet users who are buying – see Jupiter figures again in Figure 7. Figures 8 shows IDC forecasts of the number of Internet users and of Internet buyers on a worldwide basis.

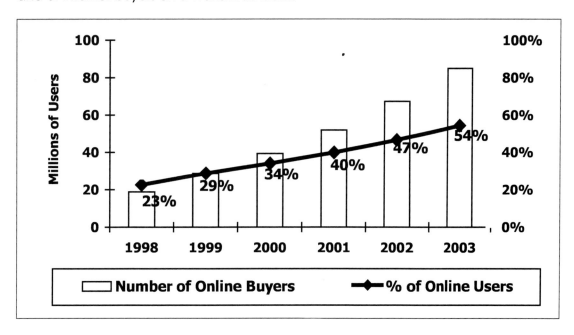

**Figure 7 - Online buyers increase as a proportion of online users in US
[Source: Jupiter Communications]**

5

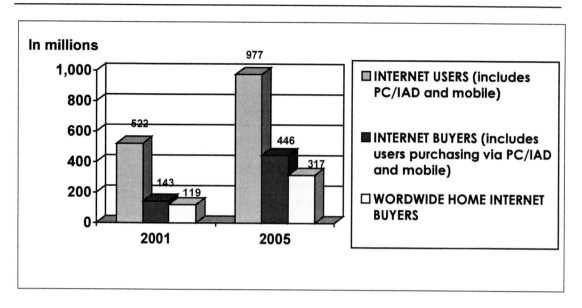

Figure 8 – IDC Internet Commerce Market Model – Worldwide (in millions)
[Source: IDC, 2001]

As a result of these factors, IDC forecasts that e-commerce revenue worldwide will increase approximately eight-fold between 2001and 2005, rising from $634 billion in 2001 to more than $5 trillion in 2005. The highest growth rates (percentage increases) are expected to be outside North America. As figure 9 shows, the US, Japan and the rest of the world are expected (by IDC) to have a reduced share of Internet commerce, whilst the share of Western Europe and the rest of Asia will increase.

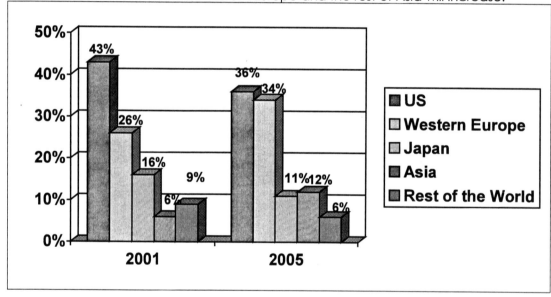

Figure 9 – Shares of Internet Commerce Revenue by Region
[Source: IDC, 2001]

1.2.4   Travel and tourism's market share

For the reasons outlined in Section 1.1, travel and tourism have become rapidly the single largest category of products sold over the Internet. In 1998, Datamonitor estimated that their share of Internet commerce increased from 7% in 1997 to 11% in 1998 and they projected an increase then to 35% by 2002. Other sources have suggested that this forecast may have been achieved already.

Jupiter has forecast that, as a result of these trends, US on-line travel industry sales will increase from $18 billion in 2000 to $63 billion in 2006, of which nearly half will come from the corporate travel market. PhoCusWright's projections for Europe are that online travel and tourism sales will increase from $2.9 billion in 2000 to $10.9 billion by 2002.

1.2.5   Travel products purchased

Travel Industry Association of America (TIA) research in 2001 has shown that a large majority of Internet using US travellers have bought air tickets and made hotel reservations online – see Figure 10. Because of the size and frequency of air ticket transactions, they have taken the largest share of the market, but that share is diminishing, from 80% in 1998 to a forecast 59% in 2003 (Jupiter).

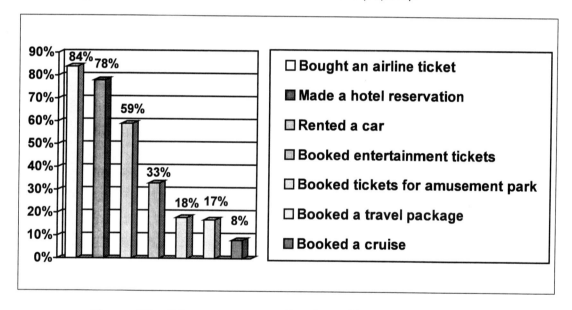

Figure 10 - US consumer on-line travel booking by sector
[Source: Travel Industry Association of America, 2001]

1.2.6 The impact of Internet use on traditional channels

A key question for DMOs and tourism businesses is the way in which the Internet is affecting the use of traditional channels of marketing. A number of recent surveys cast light on this:

- A travel & lifestyle survey for Concierge in 2000 (Figure 11) showed that, across the US population as a whole, the Internet had already become the number one source of information consulted when choosing or planning a vacation.

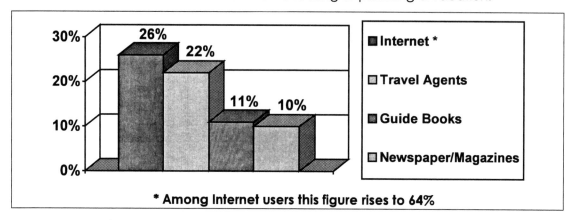

Figure 11 – First source consulted by US consumers for researching and planning travel [Source: Results of travel & lifestyle survey for Concierge, 2000 reported at www.hotel-online.com]

- Results from the "e-Travel tracker Survey", prepared by MORI on behalf of the Scottish Tourist Board, on the UK market, which tends to follow 18-24 months behind the US market, showed that in March 2001, the Internet and brochures were used in similar proportions, as sources of information for booking holidays or other forms of travel, by Internet using travellers- see Figure 12. In May 2000, when interviewees were asked which source provided the most complete information, the Internet was rated much more highly than brochures or any other source – see Figure 13.

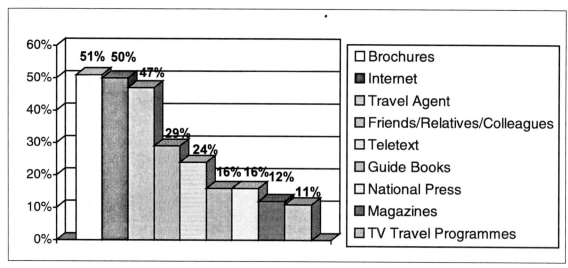

Figure 12 - Use of different sources of information for booking decisions – UK Internet users. [Source: Results from theE-Travel Tracker Survey from www.scotexchange.net, March 2001 Base: all who use the Internet (605) March 2001]

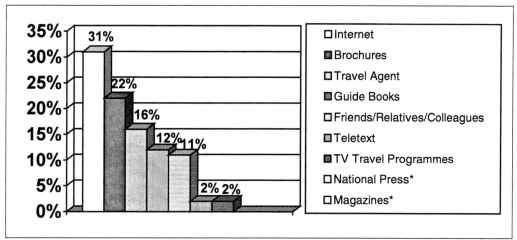

**Figure 13 - Most complete source for researching and planning travel
– UK consumers. [Source: Results from the E-Travel Tracker Survey from
www.scotexchange.net, May 2000. Base: all who have used any source of
travel information May 2000 (1,112)]**

- TIA research in 2001 (Figure 14) showed that about 70% of Internet using travellers were using travel agents and state tourism offices less often. A similar proportion was calling airlines less often, whilst nearly 60% were using other travel call centres less.

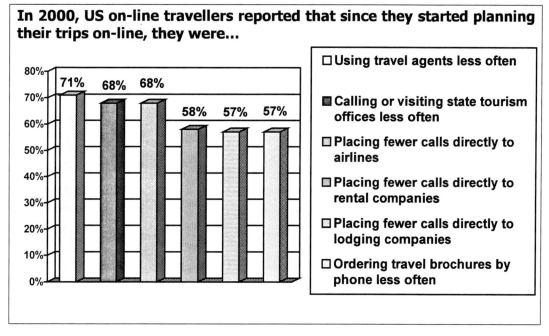

**Figure 14 - Consequences of increased use of Internet for traditional channels
[Source: The Travel Industry Association of America, 2001 (www.tia.org)]**

Thus, over a period of only five years, the Internet has become a primary source of travel information for the more mature markets of Internet users, which are also major tourism generating countries. At present, the proportion of travel booked through the Internet is relatively small (between 6 and 15% in the US, according to sector, and less elsewhere), but will increase substantially, as the number of Internet users grows and the propensity to purchase increases. It seems reasonable to anticipate that transactions across the Internet may account for 20-25% of all tourism sales in the main markets, over the next four or five years.

1.2.7   Summary of main market trends

- Usage of the Internet is increasing dramatically
- Increasing proportions of Internet users are buying online
- Travel and tourism will gain a larger and larger share of the online commerce market
- Ground products will gain a larger share of online commerce in travel and tourism
- User profiles relate well to the target markets many tourism organisations
- The Internet is having a major impact, relative to other channels, as a source of information for choosing and planning holidays and other forms of travel, and increasing importance as a booking channel.

1.3   The concept of electronic business (e-business)

E-business has been defined as "improving business through connectivity" (PriceWaterhouseCoopers[1]) and "the use of Internet technologies to improve and transform key business processes" (IBM[2]).   Taking these two definitions together, it is clear that for tourism destinations and businesses, e-business is about realising the opportunities of improved connectivity both externally, through the Internet, and internally, through intranets.

The external dimension is about transformation of the value chain, linking the tourism supplier (or service provider) to the customer, and of the supply chain, linking the tourism supplier with its own suppliers. This brings in e-marketing, e-commerce and e-procurement:

- **e-marketing** exploits the Internet and other forms of electronic communication to communicate in the most cost-effective ways with target markets and to enable joint working with partner organisations, with whom there is a common interest
- **e-commerce** is the sales activity undertaken through electronic distribution channels
- **e-procurement** streamlines the purchasing process by allowing a business to tie its inventory and procurement systems into the despatch and billing systems of its suppliers, or vice versa. Not only does this reduce costs through automation, it also facilitates identification of best value sources of supply.

Figure 15 illustrates diagrammatically how these three aspects of external connectivity fit within the envelope of e-business.

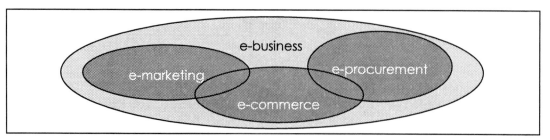

Figure 15
Components of the external dimension of e-business

---

[1] http://www.pricewaterhousecoopers.com/extweb/indissue.nsf/
[2] http://www.ibm.com/e-business/overview/28212.html

The internal dimension is about transformation of the way in which the organisation functions, enabling it to work in a fully integrated way, through the use of common systems. The transformed organisation should:

- Be fully networked for internal and external communication
- Use a common set of tools, protocols and standards
- Share product and customer data as a common resource
- Have staff operating as teams, focused on maximising the synergies of sharing resources.

In other words, the staff of a DMO or tourism business can work together more effectively, both to compile information and to use it - in effect, pooling knowledge and expertise. The tools (applications) that may be shared include content management, customer relationship management (CRM), financial management systems (sometimes called Enterprise Resource Planning – ERP) and operational control systems.

The internal and external processes are, of course, linked intimately. Most simply, the enhanced internal e-business processes enable the organisation to maximise the benefits of the external opportunities. Also, the boundaries between internal and external business processes become more flexible. Buying services in (or outsourcing) becomes a more practical proposition as external connectivity improves.

Thus the benefits of e-business may be summarised as:

- More cost-effective communication with target markets
- Making it quicker and easier for the customer to buy and thereby increasing conversion and levels of spending
- Improved customer service and retention
- Reduced costs through more efficient internal operations and purchasing processes.

Later chapters of this report look at the implications of e-business for DMOs (Part B) and tourism businesses (Part C). There is, of course, a direct relationship. The various categories of tourism business are key elements in the DMO's e-business network (see Section 2.1). The DMO has a particular responsibility to tourism suppliers – to act as the integrator of the many elements of the destination product and present them in the marketplace under the umbrella of the destination brand. E-business provides an ideal way of doing this more effectively.

1.4   The principles of customer relationship management (CRM)

A key aspect of e-business and of e-marketing is customer relationship management and/or marketing – normally referred to by the acronym CRM. CRM is a highly effective and cost efficient approach, some would call it a philosophy, based on the principle that knowledge of, and relationship with, customers is key to maximising sales opportunities, particularly through repeat purchase. It merits particular attention here, because it provides the basis for re-focusing and restructuring the whole organisation. The principles can be applied to customers of whatever type – whether end-consumers or intermediaries.

As for e-business generally, there are many definitions of CRM. The one used by Nykamp Consulting Group[3], "optimising all contacts with customers or potential

---

[3] http://www.eyefortravel.com/pastevents/crm/program.html

customers", picks up the essence of it in a few words. Nykamp has also provided an excellent conceptual model for the CRM cycle, set out in Figure 16. Perhaps the best starting point is the understanding of customer needs (lower right hand quadrant), followed by the differentiation between customers in terms of those needs and their potential value and the type of relationship that may be most effective.

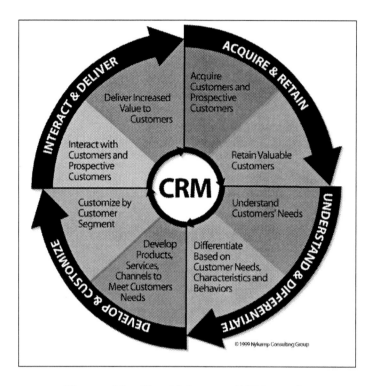

Figure 16 – The Nykamp CRM cycle

The cycle then moves through product and channel development and customisation for different segments, customer interaction and delivery of increased value to them, customer acquisition and retention.

CRM involves building up in depth information about customers or contacts. In the case of consumers, this information would normally include their socio-demographic profile, interests and activities, past and possible future requirements, etc. With this type of information, it is possible to be:

- Knowledgeable and efficient in servicing enquiries
- Pro-active in targeting best prospect customers with products specifically appropriate to their needs
- Establish the basis for a lifetime relationship with the customer, and maintain it even where transactions are not involved.

Relationships should be developed over time, as a result of contact through different channels, requiring that all customer facing staff have access to the same customer database. In the context of tourism destinations or businesses, the aim should be to maintain the relationship with customers before, during and after the visit, through the Web, e-mail, call centre, kiosk, Tourist Information Office, etc. – see Section 2.3.

CRM is not a module that can simply be added on to an organisation's activities. It must be integral to the whole ethos and method of operation, with customer (rather than product) focus to the fore. Marketing staff should be geared to addressing the needs of specific customer segments and their targets should be in terms of customer acquisition, retention, value and profitability, as well as satisfaction. This will require excellent monitoring systems, together with creative and focused market research. As it happens, the Internet provides a good means for instant research (through e-mail or surveys linked to Website usage) on customer requirements, interests, activities, attitudes, satisfaction, etc. This will need to be supplemented by market research through traditional methods from time to time.

PART B – E-BUSINESS FOR DESTINATION MANAGEMENT ORGANISATIONS

2   E-Business for DMOs - Principles and Concepts

2.1   Evolving value chains

As noted in Section 1.1, the Internet is revolutionising the distribution of tourism information and sales. The shape of travel and tourism value chains (taken here to include distribution of information as well as transactions) is changing in a fundamental way.   Figures 17 and 18 demonstrate this diagrammatically. Figure 17 [4] provides a broad representation of the 'traditional' chains, with the tourism organisation structure operating (in terms of information and transaction flows) to a large extent independently of the commercial sector.

In general, the commercial sector, particularly the airlines and major hotel groups, has made heavy use of ICT, whilst the DMO value chain has made only limited use of it. The commercial chains have been strong on transactions and weak on destination information. With the DMO chain, it has been the reverse. Generally, there has been little or no interaction between these two sets of value chains.

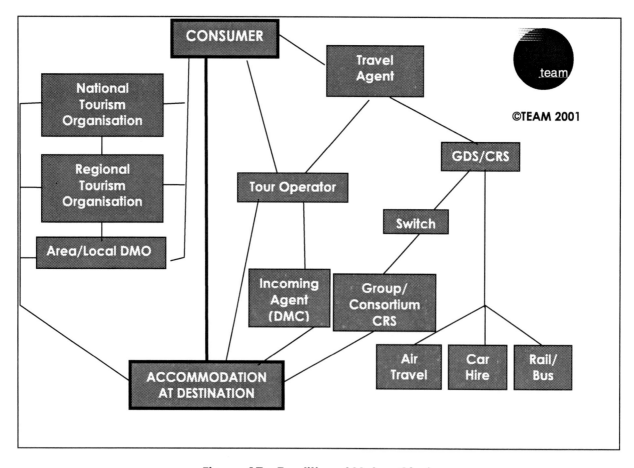

Figure 17 - Traditional Value Chains
[By TEAM - adapted from Werthner and Ebner]

---

[4] Hannes Werthner, 'Editor's Introduction', Information Technology & Tourism, Vol. 1 1998, p6. Arno Ebner, 'New generation of a DMS', Paper to Destination Management Systems Seminar, Madeira Tecnopolo, November 1998.

The situation is now changing, as the overall structure moves towards an Internet-based Value Net (or Value Star), as represented in Figure 18. Given the open, global platform of the Internet and the much wider availability of computers and good telecommunications, it is now realistic for any player within the system to communicate electronically with any other. Thus, at a general level, the opportunity exists for greatly increased business-to-business (B2B) communication; and for increased direct selling to consumers.

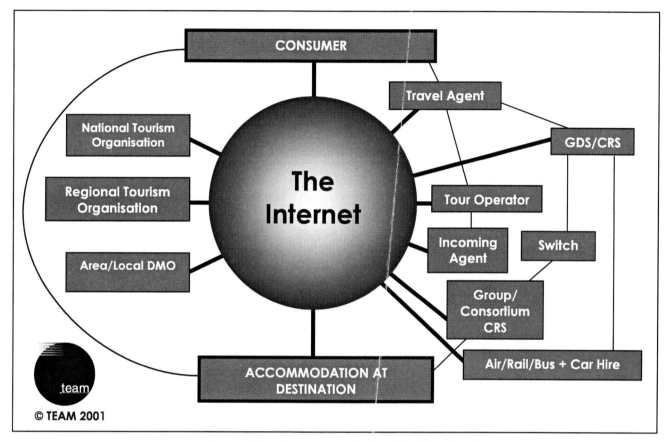

Figure 18 - Emerging Value Net (or Star)
[By TEAM - Based on a concept from IFITT Workshop, Sept 1998]

More specifically, the opportunity is opened up for DMOs to:

• Establish electronic links to tourism suppliers within their destination, to enable them to maintain their own product information and availability

• Act as an intermediary in consolidating the full range of destination products (particularly the small and medium size enterprises, which most need DMO support), and distributing it electronically to travel agents (online or otherwise) and other players in the travel trade – perhaps even to the GDS.

In neither case is this easy to implement, and may be seen as a medium to long-term objective. Also, distribution by DMOs to travel trade players may be more successful if undertaken on a joint basis, in order to establish a 'critical mass'. This subject is discussed in greater detail in the next sub-section.

2.1.1 The future of DMOs as intermediaries

The emergence of the Value Net naturally leads to the questions: If anyone can communicate easily with the end consumer, what is the role for intermediaries, including the DMO? Do they have a role at all?

The answer lies in the need to add value. DMOs certainly can add value, if they engage actively in e-business. They can add value for consumers, by providing:

- unbiased, high quality information based on local knowledge
- The facility to buy, including tailor made packaging
- Special offers - exclusivity, price, etc.

They can also add value for tourism suppliers, by providing:

- The destination brand, as an 'umbrella' for individual product offers. This is especially important for SMEs
- Information on the complete range of products within the destination
- Distribution, both to consumers and intermediaries, that would be difficult or impossible for the supplier to achieve on his/her own
- Facilities for secure, automated transactions.

Whilst DMOs have advantages, they also face threats. In a competitive global marketplace, destination organisations face threats from:

- Other destinations that have been quick to spot and exploit the potential - establishing their position in the new market place
- Commercial online players that have exploited new online opportunities to promote destination products. These players generally promote only a limited range of products – normally, the larger businesses that have the greatest commission or advertising potential; and their generic destination information tends to be very limited.

2.1.2 Positioning DMOs within the Value Net

How should destination organisations face up to the threats and realise the opportunities? The answer lies in establishing and exploiting a strong position within the new Internet-based Value Net. This is represented diagrammatically in Figure 19 (see next page).

As noted in Section 2.1, the Value Net potentially enables DMOs to link electronically:

- To their tourism suppliers (or vice versa) in order to maintain up-to-date availability, so that the DMO can implement electronic distribution direct to customers and to market intermediaries
- To travel agents, GDS and other 'traditional' players in the travel trade.

In addition, there is the opportunity to distribute destination products through the alternative distribution channels (ADCs), shown in the lower right hand side of the diagram. These are the new electronic distribution channels of the online travel agencies, the general search directories, destination portals and other successful online players. There are also online accommodation reservation services, with which DMOs may choose to partner.

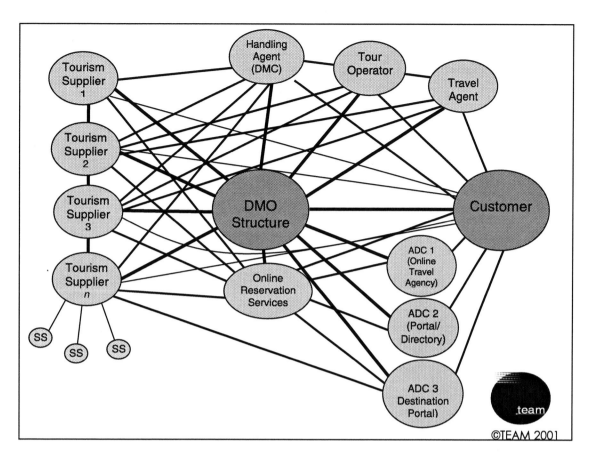

Figure 19 - DMO Positioning within the Value Net

Given that the web has become already a primary source of information for planning travel and tourism in several of the major markets, it is critical for DMOs to achieve maximum distribution of their online product. The first and most obvious task is to maximise the number of consumers and trade buyers coming direct to the site – the techniques for which are outlined in Chapter 3. The number of visitors achieved will depend on the skill with which these techniques are applied, the level of marketing resource available and the existing interest in the destination brand.

To maximise distribution, DMOs will need to give greater attention in future to achieving distribution through third parties online (mainly ADCs), who can provide access to large numbers of users. The first priority for most DMOs here will be to establish partnerships with leading online companies (media, telecom, ISPs, etc) that are active and successful within the DMO's own domestic market.

To attract international visitors, it will be necessary to establish partnerships in individual target markets abroad, or with global ADCs. To date, with a few notable exceptions, DMOs have not been active (individually or jointly) in distributing through global ADCs, perhaps reflecting a limited awareness of the opportunities and the difficulties or cost of achieving such distribution.

These ADCs do provide destination information, but, in order to achieve consistent global coverage, they have focused on drawing content from major publishers or linking to their sites – for example, Fodors, Lonely Planet and World Travel Guides (used by Travelocity); Fielding World-wide Inc and Moon publications Inc (used by Expedia). Most ADCs will supply links to DMOs only on the basis of payment for banner ads (or some other form of advertising) – except in the case of the general search facilities of the search directories, such as Google, Alta Vista, etc.

Only a few portals are dedicated to promoting the use of destination organisation sites - primarily those of the international tourism organisations. These portals tend to be relatively unsophisticated and to lack the ongoing marketing and distribution activity that is required to maximise the opportunities.

2.2   Integrated e-business systems for tourism destinations

2.2.1   Destination e-business system model

The challenge for DMOs is to provide the ICT systems that will enable them to fulfil the role within the Value Net, as outlined in the previous section – developing a wide range of e-business relationships with consumers, product suppliers and market intermediaries. In order to do this, they must think and act in an integrated way, as outlined in Section 1.3.

To fulfil this role, the ICT infrastructure for DMO business operations is changing from the vertically integrated legacy systems that were developed in some destinations during the 1990s to Web-enabled, modular, networked systems. With these systems, users require only a Web browser to enable them to access databases and functions across the Web or via organisational intranets.

Whereas, in the past, different departments with a DMO, and different DMOs within a country or region, may have maintained their own separate databases of information regarding tourism services and customers, now they can work together across intranets and the Internet, both to compile high quality information and to use it.

Figure 20 (see next page) provides a diagrammatic representation of a Web-enabled destination e-business system. This shows different categories of **users**, accessing the system through their own dedicated Web **gateway** or **interface**, using one or more **channels** (PC, handheld device, interactive TV, kiosks, in-car systems, etc). Having accessed the system, the users may select from a wide variety of **services** (or applications) that will draw, in turn, on the appropriate **database**.

Chapters 4 to 6 of this report discuss the development of interfaces for the main user groups:
- Consumers at home or in the destination – Chapter 4
- Travel trade, media and meetings/incentive buyers – Chapter 5
- Tourism suppliers and other stakeholders/partners in the destination – Chapter 6

Depending on the requirements of the DMO's marketing plan there will be a requirement for different gateways for sub-categories of user – for example, for consumers or travel trade from different geographical or language-based markets; for corporate meetings buyers, separately from international association conference buyers.

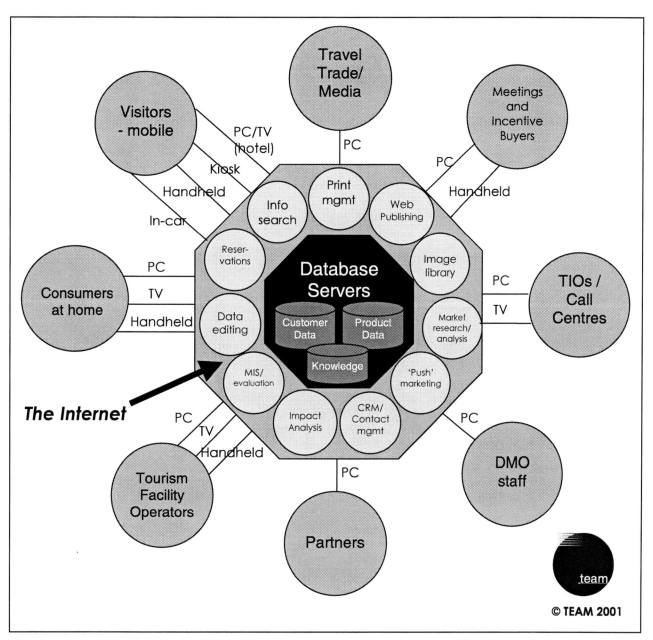

Figure 20 - The TEAM e-Business System Model

The core **generic services** may include:

- Information search - by category, geography (using GIS), keyword, etc
- Itinerary planning
- Reservations
- Customer/contact database management (which would cover registration, membership and grading management)
- Customer relationship management (CRM) functions – see Section 2.3
- 'Push' marketing
- Market research and analysis
- Image library
- Publishing to electronic and traditional channels
- Event planning and management
- Marketing optimisation and yield management
- Data editing and management
- Financial management
- Management information systems and performance evaluation
- Economic impact analysis
- Access to third party sources, such as weather, transport timetables and travel planning, theatre and event ticket reservations.

The way in which these services are designed and presented for the different user groups will vary significantly, of course. For example, accommodation booking will be structured and presented differently for conference organisers, than for consumers.

The services available through some of the gateways may be password protected, where the services are chargeable or the use of the information is restricted in some way.

This model sets out a menu of e-business opportunities. For each destination, the user categories, channels and applications may be varied, in order to meet local requirements.

How quickly the various services are implemented will depend on the level of funding available and the capacity of the DMO(s) and partner organisations to handle them. The latter is a key factor to take into account – not only in terms of the human resources available, but also the culture of the organisation(s) and their willingness to do business in new ways. In the right circumstances, it may be possible to implement such a programme within 12 to 18 months. In other destinations, it may take three or four years.

2.2.2 e-Business Partnerships for DMOs

DMOs do not operate in isolation. They are part of wider networks and partnerships. The networks through which information is distributed and received, and transactions undertaken, is extensive. As explained in Section 1.3, e-business is all about improving the operational efficiency and effectiveness of such networks, through seamless electronic connections across the Internet.

Most importantly, there is now the opportunity for DMOs within a country (or even between countries) to operate common e-business systems - perhaps with the medium to long term aim of establishing common, integrated network systems, linking local, regional/provincial and national level. This is a major task, requiring common approaches – ideally common software and data structures, but at least common technical standards and type of content.

In countries with limited existing systems, it will make sense to implement integrated systems as part of one implementation programme, not only to ensure a high degree of interoperability, but also to achieve potential economies of scale in system specification, procurement and implementation – i.e. as outlined in Chapter 3. Such initiatives will succeed only where there is both the environment and the will to work together.

Access to such networks can be extended to:
- Appropriate partner organisations in the public sector, which have some interest in tourism – notably, relevant departments in central and local government, economic development agencies, etc
- Strategic partners in the private sector – e.g. Chambers of Commerce, marketing associations or consortia, etc
- Community interests – schools, colleges, neighbourhood groups, civic societies, etc.

A specific e-business opportunity for DMOs is the networking of their Tourist Information Offices and call centres (also known as customer contact centres) within a country or region – to exchange information and bookings. The technology to enable such networking is becoming relatively straightforward. However, other issues can be quite complex - e.g. terms and conditions for trading, transmission/clearance of payments, legal liabilities, etc.

Another key partnership is with the tourism suppliers, especially accommodation operators, within the destination. There is the potential over time to develop a network (technically, an extranet) specifically for suppliers:
- To enhance DMO/supplier communications and working relationships generally
- To provide intelligence and services to tourism suppliers, to enable improved business performance
- To enable suppliers to access tourist information for guests
- To enable them to update product information and availability on the destination system, to facilitate real-time, online bookings.

Chapter 6 provides a detailed overview of how an industry network should be designed and established.

DMOs have the opportunity also to link with Web-enabled networks of other suppliers such as transport services (air, bus, rail, sea passenger services), operators of tours, event and festival organisers, theatres, etc. In the past, inter-operability of systems has proved difficult, but e-business networks and software are now making it a reality.

Finally, in establishing new e-business systems, there is potential for strategic partnerships with companies that may not be involved directly in tourism at the moment, but which have indirect benefit to gain – for example:
- Media companies, which often have substantial content assets and, in some cases, key electronic and traditional distribution channels
- Telecommunication companies, which are interested in network provision and system development and supplying ICT services to tourism businesses. In some cases, they can offer distribution through their own major Web portals
- Banks, which are interested in supplying financial systems and payment transmission/clearance to DMOs and tourism suppliers

- ISPs, which supply DMOs and tourism suppliers with Internet connectivity, hosting services and, in some cases, portal distribution
- Web developers and system suppliers, who may be willing to participate in joint ventures, etc.

2.3   The potential of e-marketing and CRM

2.3.1   The scope for e-marketing by DMOs

E-marketing offers DMOs the realistic potential to reach a far wider audience than ever before. It encompasses a wide range of activities, and there are many techniques in use. Examples of the most popular are outlined in the Section 2.3. The key factor is the cost-effectiveness of the Internet – the Web as a mechanism for publishing information and providing a transactional capability for customers; and e-mail, as a means of conveying information and offers directly, cheaply and at short notice to prime prospects. E-marketing must work in harmony with off-line marketing activities so that traffic can be driven in both directions, Web to brochures or telephone, telephone to Web and so on.

One of the key advantages of e-marketing is the ability for DMOs to engage with customers on a one-to-one basis (dealt with in the Section 2.3.1 below) but e-marketing can be used also to promote 'one-to-many' activities, where large numbers of potential visitors can be attracted to the DMO Web site(s). Techniques for this include:

- Reciprocal or paid links from other appropriate sites
- Prominent promotion of the site URL on every item of print and promotional material
- Sponsorship both on and off-line to raise the profile of the destination's URL.

2.3.2   Customer Relationship Management for DMOs

Section 1.4 provided an introduction to CRM, explaining that it is an effective and cost efficient approach, based on the principle that knowledge of, and relationship with, customers is key to maximising sales opportunities, particularly through repeat purchase. Reference was made to the Nykamp Consulting Group[5] definition, "optimising all contacts with customers or potential customers". How then do we apply CRM within the context of DMOs?

A starting point is to identify the potential points of contact that a DMO may have with its customers. A useful framework for this is the Communications Life Cycle (also called the Consumer Life Cycle) – CLC. Figure 21 (next page) summarises points of contact within a four-stage cycle. [N.B. The cycle could be extended to five or six stages.]

---

[5] http://www.eyefortravel.com/pastevents/crm/program.html

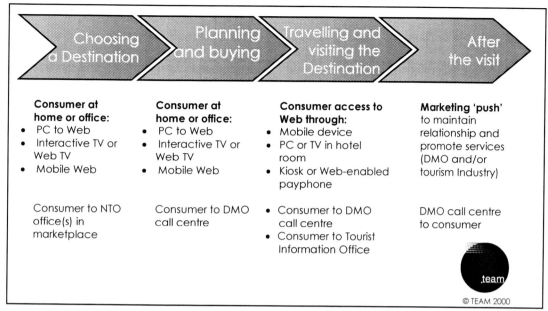

Choosing a Destination	Planning and buying	Travelling and visiting the Destination	After the visit
Consumer at home or office: • PC to Web • Interactive TV or Web TV • Mobile Web	**Consumer at home or office:** • PC to Web • Interactive TV or Web TV • Mobile Web	**Consumer access to Web through:** • Mobile device • PC or TV in hotel room • Kiosk or Web-enabled payphone	**Marketing 'push'** to maintain relationship and promote services (DMO and/or tourism Industry)
Consumer to NTO office(s) in marketplace	Consumer to DMO call centre	• Consumer to DMO call centre • Consumer to Tourist Information Office	DMO call centre to consumer

.team

© TEAM 2000

Figure 21- Customer Contact across the Communications Life Cycle

The application of CRM involves the use of sophisticated IT software and databases to maintain an interactive, 'one-to-one' relationship with customers or potential customers – through direct mail, e-mail, Web, telephone or personal contact – through the different stages of the CLC. Thus it involves:

- Customising the marketing and sales messages, ensuring a close match between a customer's requirements/interests and the types of product promoted to him/her. It is particularly appropriate for promoting niche products and special offers at short notice, to those with the highest potential to buy;

- Personalised service during the visit;

- Perhaps most importantly, 'closing the loop' through post-visit follow-up to stimulate the desire to come again or to visit a partner destination – or make a recommendation to friends and relatives.

In order to do this, it is necessary to:

- Build a customer database and capture as much information as you can about the lifestyle, travel and buying habits of your customers, through the different contacts through the CLC (see below)

- Develop and nurture a one-to-one relationship with your customers. Communicate by e-mail wherever possible, as it is personal and immediate, but less intrusive than the telephone

- Use database-filtering tools to ensure that proactive mailshots are really personal.

- Use competitions, auctions, chat rooms, feedback forms, quizzes to encourage your customers to tell you more about themselves

- Tailor your product offering more exactly to fit the demands of your customers

- Give your customers a reason to come back to your Web site and encourage them to buy on impulse.

CRM is normally applied in situations where customers may potentially repeat purchase on a regular basis. For many destinations, particularly those with substantial long-haul markets, this is not the case and people may be unlikely to visit more than once in five or ten years. Indeed, in a destination like Seychelles, customers may see their purchase as a 'once in a lifetime' event.

This does not immediately negate the relevance of CRM. Instead, it can be adapted to meet the requirements of the marketing strategy. Three possible opportunities are:

- Through the attractiveness of special offers, to persuade past visitors to consider visiting again, where they might not otherwise have not even considered it. The stronger the relationship that can be developed with the customer before, during and after the visit, the more likely such an approach is to be successful. Getting customers to buy in to the destination emotionally will be important.

- To encourage past visitors to make recommendations to friends and relatives – not just for the destination, but for special activities, events or offers about which they have been sent information by the DMO. It would probably be most effective if some form of incentive could be offered to the past visitor to pass on a recommendation.

- To obtain access to databases of people who have not yet visited the destination, but are potentially good prospects to do so, by virtue of their interests and holiday choices and aspirations. Such customer databases may be obtainable through commercial mailing houses or list brokers, or they could be accessed by forming alliances with other similar destinations. For these destinations, there is much more to be gained than lost through sharing of customer data.

CRM is enhanced by the ability to use e-mail, but it is not dependent on it, of course. Other methods of distribution can be used, although they may not be so economic or immediate.

As a technique, CRM is relevant also to contact with the travel trade media and conference buyers. Arguably, it will be even more important here, in view of the need to develop a close, continuing and productive relationship with a relatively small, manageable group of contacts. Such is the importance of developing these relationships that they merit a special mechanism, based on the concept of extranets – see Chapter 6.

Capturing Customer Data

From the previous paragraphs, it follows that it is important to capture as much data as possible about the customer, in terms of lifestyle, past holiday types and destinations, future holiday aspirations, etc, as well as accurate contact data, including where possible an e-mail address. Many DMOs collect a wide range of consumer data from different sources for a particular purpose, but it is not until you consolidate this data in a single database where you can manipulate it, that you really start to maximise the value of your customers.

There is a number of opportunities for collecting customer information that occur as part of your day-to-day activities. They include bookings, general enquiries and brochure requests, surveys, feedback forms and even complaints. In addition, there may be other opportunities that you can create, such as proactive telesales or telemarketing, visitor surveys, exhibitions or even competitions.

Once you have an online presence you open up even more opportunities for gathering information about your customers. As with all things, it pays to be subtle in your approach. Do not ask a lot of questions the first time someone calls with an enquiry or visits your site. Just ask a few things that only take a few seconds to answer. Next time the customer makes contact you can recognise him/her and will already know something about him/her. It is important to train your staff in the best techniques for this. Many enquirers volunteer a large amount of information about themselves in their first call, whilst others are in a rush and just want the basic information.

Data protection and privacy is an increasingly complex subject, particularly when it relates to organisations trading across the globe. It is important that due attention is given to the legal requirements of data protection laws, not just in the country of the DMO, but also for those of foreign countries. Recent changes in the law in Europe mean that consumers now have to positively opt in to having their data held and used by a DMO, rather than opt out as was previously the case. In general this should be viewed as a positive move as it ensures those receiving offers from a DMO are the most likely sales prospects.

2.3.3 E-marketing techniques

The following paragraphs provide some examples of e-marketing techniques.

Push marketing - e-mail campaigns

A push marketing campaign involves identifying specific customers from your database or a purchased list, and sending them an e-mail with a specific purpose. It might be notification of a special offer or it might be a monthly newsletter. Sometimes the message is contained within the e-mail itself, or it can be an e-mail alert, that encourages the reader to link to a particular page on your Web site.

There is a wide range of CRM tools that can help you manage your database, filter and clean your records and run queries to come up with your target audience. Producing the campaign itself follows a similar process to a traditional advertising campaign. You will need an offer, a mechanism to communicate it (e.g. the Web page or piece of print) and a method to get the offer to the audience – in this case by e-mail. It is essential to set up the response mechanism before the campaign goes live, as push marketing has a much shorter time window than traditional advertising or direct mail.

Dedicated e-mail list serving software is necessary if the number of customer records exceeds a few hundred. CRM tools are generally very expensive, around $75,000 for entry level systems, so it is worth considering using an agency, particularly if your record numbers are limited.

Online Clubs

Many destination Web sites offer the user a chance to join a special club that provides value added benefits. Registration is usually free, but involves the user in providing some personal details that are captured by the DMO for use in their CRM activities. Benefits include early notification of offers, regular news updates and fast track booking.

Customise your home page function

Some sites offer the user to customise their home page so that it can be tailored to their particular needs. Again this usually involves completing a number of questions about your interests, likes, dislikes and plans. This information is then used to filter data to ensure that items of particular interest are prominently displayed in future.

Send a greeting function

Many sites offer users the chance to send an e-postcard or greetings from the site to their friends and families. This involves selecting your choice of postcard (usually with an attractive image of the destination on it) and typing in the name and e-mail of yourself as sender and your friend as recipient, and a short message. The card is sent to the recipient in one of two ways. Either an e-mail with a link to the destinations Web site, or a notification encouraging the user to visit the Web site to collect the card.

E-greetings are very popular and provide the opportunity to invite friends and relations to submit their e-mail address to receive information about the destination. This raises data protection issues, of course. You need to ensure that all users get a chance to opt into your customer database, before you can target them with your CRM activities.

Travel stories and reviews

As travel is such a personal experience, it is fun to encourage visitors to write short articles about their trip and publish them on the site for others to read or to send in photographs of their recent visit. Some form of moderation is required to ensure that the quality of the submissions is reasonable, but it is a good way of creating ambassadors for your destination. This assumes, of course, that their experiences are good. Recognising that this is not always the case, the content will need to be moderated on a regular basis.

Bulletin board and chat rooms

You can create an online community on your site by hosting a bulletin board or chat room. This allows users to chat amongst themselves or to respond to specific topics. You might wish to animate this part of the site by establishing some themes and encouraging users to participate. Most sites ask you to register before participating and this provides another opportunity to capture data.

Feedback forms

Some sites ask users to provide feedback to the DMO about their visit or about the Web site itself. It is important to design any feedback form so that it captures a minimum amount of data, and enables you to respond to the correspondent with a thank you and any appropriate reply.

You can also publish a more proactive questionnaire, as an interstitial (a separate window that pops up at a specific point in the site visit) or as the user logs in or out of the site. All the data from responses should be captured in the customer database.

Enquiries and sales data capture

Many customers will contact the destination by telephone or make a visit to an information office, which also provides a further opportunity for data capture. Those making bookings or requesting a brochure should be recognised by the system if they are existing customers, or created as new customers if not, and then followed up a short time after they return home.

Text chat

Text chat is a feature that enables a user to contact an agent (usually within the destination) using an online text editor. The messages get passed over the Internet in just a few seconds, and while not as quick as a telephone call, the fact that it uses the Internet means that it is a very cheap way for the customer to make contact with foreign destinations.

Call me buttons

Some destinations have 'Call Me' buttons on their Web sites that request a call from an operator at the DMO's contact centre. This is usually configured to allow the user to specify a time he/she would like to be called e.g. now, or in 10 minutes, and in his preferred language. Both this function and the Text Chat feature help to bring the human touch to online processes, but it is essential that the DMO can resource the service satisfactorily. There is nothing more frustrating than asking for a Call Me, and then waiting 30 minutes until an operator is free.

Competitions, quizzes and auctions

Inviting users to participate in competitions or quizzes is another good way of encouraging them to log their personal data with you, as well as providing interest and encouraging users to stay longer and return often.

Auctions can provide special interest and can offer revenue raising opportunities as well as a chance to capture customer data.

Cookies

An excellent way of tracking users is the use of 'cookies'. A cookie is a simple data file that is sent to a user's computer when they access a Web page. Once the cookie has been sent it allows you to track the user - you don't know their name or contact details, but you do know that they've been to the page where the cookie was served before.

Cookies are generally used for things like enabling access to password-protected pages or managing 'my homepage' set-ups (see the next sub-section). Cookies are held in a separate cookie folder, and users can choose to delete them if they wish. Also it is possible for users to set up the security on their PCs to reject cookies or to be alerted to them before they are passed. Most people are happy to accept a cookie without an alert, especially as most offer useful functionality.

Homepage customisation

One technique for gathering information about customers is to include functionality that allows users to customise their homepage to reflect their interests. This can range from a simple greeting e.g. 'Welcome John' to a completely user defined page, with defaults to the content and functionality most relevant to the user.

Whilst the most obvious e-marketing applications relate to 'end-consumers', the principles are equally applicable to communications with market intermediaries, tourism industry suppliers and DMO stakeholders.

2.3.4 Critical success factors - for CRM and proactive electronic marketing

- Build a customer database and capture as much information as you can about the lifestyle, travel and buying habits, and information requirements of your customers over time. You can not expect to gain all the information on the first contact

- Develop and nurture a one-to-one relationship with your customers and recognise them when they make contact through all channels

- Use competitions, auctions, chat rooms, feedback forms, quizzes to encourage your customers to tell you more about themselves

- Communicate by e-mail wherever possible, as it is personal and immediate, but less intrusive than the telephone

- Use database-filtering tools to ensure that proactive e-mailshots are really well targeted and personal

- Tailor your product offering more exactly to fit the demands of your customers

- Give your customers a reason to come back to your Web site and encourage them to buy on impulse

- Encourage your customers to be ambassadors for your destination, for example through 'e-mail this page to a friend' type functionality.

2.4 E-commerce for DMOs

Many DMOs have offered an accommodation booking service to their consumers at tourist information offices and increasingly by telephone. More and more DMOs are now moving towards offering online booking of accommodation and other products via their Web sites.

The technical processes involved in establishing an e-commerce platform is relatively straightforward, but there are a number of difficulties on the business side that have acted as major inhibitors.

There are four main options for enabling accommodation transactions through a DMO Web site. These are summarised below with some comments on the pros and cons of each option:

E-mail enquiry direct to the accommodation establishment

- *You can set up your system so that any booking enquiries can be passed directly to the selected establishment, either as an online form or as a simple e-mail. If the provider does not have access to e-mail, the message can be sent automatically as a fax or it can be sent to the local DMO and handled manually by a telephone call to the provider. This is the simplest solution, and is often adopted by DMOs that have a large proportion of small-scale providers amongst their suppliers. This is not e-commerce, only an e-mail enquiry.*

- *The advantage is that the provider does not have to maintain his product inventory online or provide an allocation (or allotment) to the DMO. The draw back however is that the process is far from dynamic, and it can be frustrating for the visitor who has to wait to see if his request can be met, and may get a series of rejections particularly at times of peak demand.*

E-commerce through the DMO

*   *To provide users with an online, real-time booking function, the DMO will need appropriate software to run the reservations engine, a facility for processing the financial transaction, and most importantly a current and accurate inventory of stock availability or allocations.*

*   *Most of the leading destination systems incorporate reservation engines and increasingly the system suppliers are interested in joint ventures involving transaction revenue sharing.*

This last point is probably the most difficult. The traditional method of allocations works well for advance bookings of larger hotels, but is not good for short-term bookings or for smaller establishments.

There are various partial solutions to the problem:
*   Accommodation operators take the responsibility for updating their availability information to the DMO through a variety of methods - telephoning, faxing or e-mailing the data, which is then manually entered by DMO staff into their system, or by gaining access to the system through a password protected interface such as a Web browser or touch tone telephone. The difficulty with this method is that the DMO must rely on the accommodation operator to update his/her record. Many do, but some operators lack the motivation and so this method cannot be relied on to give the most up-to-date position for all stock.
*   Operators are supplied with a booking system that links to, or is part of, the destination system, which they access through a Web browser, so that effectively they are using the DMO's system to manage their entire inventory. This provides difficulties for those providers that already have their own property management system (PMS).
*   An interface is established between the destination system and accommodation's own property management systems, enabling automatic exchange of availability information. This is the best solution but is expensive to implement, as you may need to interface with a number of different PMSs.

It is likely that for the next two or three years, DMOs will need to offer options, allowing time for an increase in industry awareness and understanding of the benefits, in order to bring a majority of suppliers to a more sophisticated solution.

Outsourcing to one or more commercial agencies

*   *It is possible for a DMO to outsource its e-commerce function to a global player, such as all-hotels, HRN/TravelNow, Hotels Online or WorldRes or to a national or local reservations agency. This should be subject to a tendering process. There are advantages of going down this route - particularly the speed with which such a solution can be implemented and the extensive distribution that some of these partners can offer. However, there may also be potential problems, particularly in relation to splitting commission, retaining the customer data and the right to use it and incorporating the full range of the destination's accommodation products.*

Provider nominated agency

- *This option enables each accommodation establishment to nominate an online booking agency of its own choice, potentially from a list approved by you. This places the responsibility for maintaining the inventory with the provider, but does allow those who are motivated to do so, the best opportunity to sell their products online.*

- *For destinations that are heavily dependent on intermediaries, e.g. tour operators or travel agents, for their business, it is possible to drive customers to the booking engine of those intermediaries to undertake the transaction.*

Conclusions on e-commerce options

All of these options could provide an opportunity for you and your partners to generate commission income, but at a lower level, of course, where another agency is actually handling the business. You might decide that it is worthwhile forgoing such income in order to maximise the return for your accommodation operators.

DMOs do have a number of disadvantages to overcome when they seek to establish an online booking facility. It is important that the following factors are considered carefully before deciding on the best course of action.

- DMOs do not own the product they are selling and have no immediate control over it
- Many DMOs represent predominantly small-scale operators who are often reluctant to pay even quite reasonable commission fees and can lack either the business skills or the motivation to manage their inventory in a manner that would enable online booking
- Larger tourism operators are usually already doing significant business through their own Web reservation systems, Web-based reservation agencies such as those noted above, the Global Distribution Systems and sometimes find dealing with a DMO unduly arduous
- Travel products have inherent difficulties, as a customer can not try, or view, before they buy, and therefore the buying procedure is often quite protracted as more and more information is gathered by the potential purchaser
- DMOs often have a service culture, and both staff and management find it difficult to adapt to a more sales orientated culture
- DMOs often find it difficult to handle credit card transactions (particularly those operating within government structures)
- DMOs find it difficult to create terms and conditions which are acceptable to the visitor, the supplier and the DMO itself and under which all are suitably protected.

There are some good examples where DMOs are achieving high levels of enquiries and bookings from online sources, but there are many more for whom it has not really been successful. Much will depend on the business model of the DMO. Where a DMO chooses not to operate an e-commerce solution itself, the options to outsource the e-commerce, or to pass booking enquiries directly to the selected supplier will be the most attractive.

2.5   New ways for DMOs to do business

DMOs have the chance to exploit e-business techniques in every department, marketing , sales, information services, development, research, accounting etc. Whereas before each may have had its own data, specific to its purpose, now there can be a greater degree of knowledge sharing using tools that allow communication across the extended network.   Providing this kind of network opportunity can dramatically improve awareness, and in turn, performance and help to reduce costs through the economies of scale that can be achieved.

New services must be developed to replace those in decline. For instance, it is likely that demand for an annual destination guide will decrease dramatically over the next three to five years, to be replaced by use of new media, travel trade and conference manuals, etc, on the one hand, and by targeted, smaller print run publications and by personalised print produced at the point of enquiry, on the other.

Another example is a potential fall in demand for the services for tourist information offices, once visitors to a destination have access to in-depth information through mobile devices, Web TV in their hotel rooms, etc. DMOs must be ready to use the new channels to distribute their information and reservation services.

More generally, the opportunities for e-commerce have substantial implications. Whereas in the past DMOs have tended to be providers of information and facilitators of tourist/service relationships, in the future they are likely to become more involved in tourism transactions, directly or indirectly. As more DMOs provide or enable online booking functionality for their destination products and, where appropriate, receive commission, they will evolve into a new type of intermediary, where they can be judged more directly by easily measurable results. Regardless of this changing role, it is crucial that DMOs remain the guardian of their destination's interests and the main promoter of its worth as a place to be visited.

As the structure of DMOs move more towards e-business partnerships, management and staff have to adopt new ways of working. These are broadly based around standard business principles, but for some DMOs, particularly those well established in the public sector, these realities will take time to achieve. Key considerations are as follows:

- The planning and management of e-business systems cannot be done by individual departments in isolation from others. It must be an integral part of every manager's and staff member's day-to-day activity.
- Managers and staff must embrace a new culture for their organisation, based on sharing and teamwork. Central to this will be adopting the concept of relationship marketing, not just for consumers, but also with the travel trade, media, conference buyers etc and with the tourism industry suppliers.
- All staff, and indeed wider destination stakeholders, must view the common systems and databases as key assets for the organisation, the foundation upon which all activities are based, and ensure that the data content is used to its full potential throughout the organisation
- DMOs must be much more alert to the needs of their existing and potential customers. They must anticipate needs and be proactive in meeting them
- In many DMOs, management and staff are not well equipped to embrace the modern e-business techniques, so a large scale programme of awareness raising, training and development is a key challenge for the future. All stakeholders need to be engaged in the process and encouraged to participate in a proactive manner.

- DMOs should not assume that implementing new systems will automatically be very expensive. Increasingly it is possible to access services and databases across the Web, using only a Web-browser. Various suppliers of destination system software offer access to their services in this way already, avoiding the need for the DMO to buy expensive hardware, software or networks and support services. A simple PC, browser and Internet connections are all that is needed. It is likely that, over the next two or three years, the majority of system suppliers will offer this option, becoming 'Application Service Providers' (ASPs). The ASP model is ideal for smaller DMOs particularly.

There is no option for DMOs to retain the status quo. New online commercial players will be quick to move into territories where the DMO is not performing adequately, but without the DMO's commitment to the destination as a whole. All DMOs must make their investment plans and look upon their destination e-business systems, in whatever form they may take, as the key tool in their organisational armoury.

2.6 Strategic Challenges for DMOs

The advent of the Internet is creating both strategic opportunities and challenges for DMOs. We are seeing the rapid emergence of a major new marketplace for tourism. Over the past three or four years, the major commercial travel and tourism Web sites have reported rapid increases, not only in the number of visitors to their sites, but also, importantly, in the number and value of transactions. As noted previously, Internet market research companies, such as Forrester Research and Jupiter Media Metrix, are projecting dramatic growth, not only in Internet usage and commerce, but also in travel and tourism's share of this growing market. Importantly for many DMOs, the Internet is facilitating and encouraging the trends of recent years towards independent travel and special interest holidays and breaks.

Thus the Internet represents an increasingly important marketplace of consumers whose profile matches well the requirements of most, if not all, DMOs. In addition, however, the Internet will be used more and more by travel agents instead of brochures and guides to obtain destination information (generally from bookmarked sites offering quality information on attractions, events, weather, etc.) to back-up the sale of specific travel and tour products. Thus it allows DMOs to communicate directly and relatively cheaply with high yield consumers – and with intermediaries as well. The implications for the future role of DMOs are significant.

The essential challenge for tourism suppliers and destinations is to capture and retain attention in a marketplace with a strong conceptual resemblance to a bazaar, where there is a number of major players who have developed leading brands for travel and which have already built up a large customer base. Leading travel companies are now spending very large amounts of money on building attractive and effective Web sites and developing their online brands. In these circumstances, should DMOs try to compete directly and, if so, how can they gain 'voice' in the marketplace? Or should they seek to work with these major new players?

DMOs start with the advantage that many consumers actively look for destination information. However, using the search engines, it is often difficult to distinguish official DMO sites from other sites (usually in large numbers) providing tourism related information on one or more destinations. There is also the problem for DMOs of how to attract the interest of consumers who may not have a specific destination in mind, but have a clear idea of the type of experience they are seeking - for example trekking, bird watching, canoeing, etc.

At the outset, it is important that DMOs build up an understanding of the medium and the people who use it. The Internet is a relatively new medium, with distinct advantages over traditional media, but also, significant constraints, at least for the time being. The advantages should be exploited to the full, and the constraints acknowledged.

Where a DMO has identified target segments in a particular market, it will be important to analyse whether the Internet will provide cost-effective access to those segments. Internet user surveys have been undertaken in most major markets and should provide some guidance on this. This groundwork will enable DMOs to plan their use of the Internet with the same method and care that they would apply to their other marketing activities.

3 Implementing a 'Destination Management System' (DMS) as the infrastructure for e-business

3.1 Introduction

The term 'Destination Management System' came into use over the last decade to describe the ICT infrastructure of a DMO. Initially, different Destination Management Systems supported different functions, depending on the requirements of the destination concerned. Increasingly, however, DMSs have supported multiple functions, drawing on central product and customer databases.

Today, we are starting to see a move away from vertically integrated DMSs towards systems consisting of a set of 'browser-enabled' software modules, accessed across the Web from the remote servers of application service providers (ASPs - see Section 2.5) or internally through intranets. DMOs may still choose to buy their whole system from one supplier. Alternatively, they may prefer to buy different modules from different vendors and integrate them into a network.

Several of the traditional DMS suppliers have indeed sought to provide their products on a modular basis, but often they have been reluctant to facilitate integration with other software. However, this attitude is changing. There is now an influx of new players in the market, providing products to meet specific needs that are capable of being easily integrated into e-business networks by virtue of being designed for a Web-enabled, browser based platform. By the same token there is likely to be an emergence of specialist integrators and business analysts to advise and support DMOs in their e-business developments.

As DMOs aspire increasingly to establish integrated destination e-business systems, the term DMS may well become obsolete, but, for the moment, we shall it to describe the IT infrastructure required to support the destination e-business activities.

3.2 Step-by-step guide to implementing a DMS

The core components of a DMS are:
- The technical infrastructure of a computer network, hardware, software and communication links
- A database or series of databases, with a content management system which allows users to manage the data content within the database(s)
- The various applications i.e. the software that undertakes the functions to support the business activities
- The data content.

You will need to view all of these interrelated ICT components in parallel during your planning process.

This Step-by-Step guide provides a logical sequence of steps to help you through the complex process of designing and implementing your e-Business Strategy and DMS.

Step 1 – Secure specialist support

Depending on the skills available within your DMO, amongst your partner organisations or your existing suppliers, you may wish to buy in some specialist help. If your project is sufficiently large scale, you might want to recruit a project manager to lead the process from the outset. However, for many DMOs this is not practical, and employing the services of a consultancy for key elements of the work may be more efficient.

You may consider seeking external help for a number of elements. These include:

- Preparing an e-business strategy
- Helping to develop the brand, look and feel of your destination or to interpret the existing brand for digital use
- Building specific components of the DMS
- Organising the data collection and input of the products and editorial
- Hosting and maintaining the DMS and its various sites
- Project managing the implementation
- Registering sites with the search engines and optimising their visibility over time
- Providing analysis of users and their usage of all relevant sites and services
- Preparing the business case analysis

If you want support to help you work up the project in the first instance, let the contract in small stages so that you are not tied into a long-term deal before you understand what is really required.

The more specific you can be in your brief the easier it is. You may wish to work with just one agency that can deliver all the services you need, or with several each carrying out a specialist task. The latter is perfectly feasible, but will require you to ensure co-operation, with the dependencies between agencies clearly identified and documented - and penalties included in the contract where time is critical.

Step 2 - Prepare a draft e-Business Strategy

The next step is to prepare an e-Business Strategy, embracing the principles set out in Chapters 1 and 2 of this publication. Producing this strategy is the first, and most crucial, step in the whole process. If it is not done well, your ability to undertake the subsequent steps successfully will be considerably reduced and you could end up making costly errors along the way.

The e-Business Strategy should be set within the framework of the overall tourism strategy for your destination and your own organisation's business and marketing plans. These will help to determine the objectives and targets for the strategy.

The strategy is about defining the key components of the e-business programme (in terms of users, channels, applications and data sets); the priorities for implementation; the players involved in implementation; the resources required; and an outline programme for delivery. You may find it helpful here to refer back to the destination e-business model and related text, set out in Section 2.2.1. Work through that in a systematic way.

Start by thinking about your users, particularly your customers – what are their needs and what channels will they use to interact with you through. It is important to realise that potentially your system will have many different interfaces, for each category and segment of users and for each type of channel that they may use. Once you have assessed the potential requirements of your users and the types of channels they are likely to use, you will be able to consider what applications are needed and what data sets will be required to support those applications.

Based on your analysis, produce a version of the destination e-business model specifically for your destination. This will encapsulate the core of your strategy.

You need to consider your own organisation and how each department of could better achieve its goals, by realising the opportunities to communicate more cost-effectively with its customers or stakeholders; and to share resources and data content internally and externally across a browser-enabled network.

It is important to define some broad priorities in the Strategy, identifying the areas that will provide widespread benefit in the first instance. For instance your main priority may be to create and populate a Web-enabled product database as a common, open resource, or you might want to concentrate on developing a consumer facing Web site first. It is likely that you will have some existing systems and resources, so you must think about how they can be integrated into your new e-business systems.

There are a number of fundamental issues that you should address in your strategy:
- How will you create, maintain and share your core assets - your product, consumer and contact data?
- What common tools, protocols and standards will you need?
- Should you implement e-commerce and if so how?
- How will you adopt CRM principles and techniques to communicate to consumers and intermediaries in the most cost effective and targeted way?
- How will you partner with other organisations with which you have a common interest?
- How will your achieve buy-in from your staff and suppliers, so that they act together to achieve the objectives of the e-business strategy?
- How you will manage the changes in culture and working practices that may be required?

In addition to the fundamentals outlined above, you should also identify the local, regional and national context, in which you are working and identify opportunities for linking up with other initiatives.

The strategy must demonstrate clearly how e-business will make a real contribution to achievement of both the strategic objectives of your destination and improved performance of your organisation. In financial terms, it should identify potential cost savings and, where appropriate opportunities for increasing income. These potential benefits could be illustrated by reference to examples of good practice from other destinations.

The strategy should consider alternatives. You should not be tempted into a large-scale, complicated project if it is not the most appropriate thing for your DMO. Think about what you really need and whether it could be achieved more simply by building on your existing processes or by looking at outsourcing options.

Step 3 - Advise and consult key stakeholders

Your stakeholders will include a wide range of people and organisations that have a direct or indirect interest in your destination. These include your management, staff and funders, tourism operators, transport carriers, tour operators, entertainment and events organisers, residents, local associations, and commercial players such as telecom companies and local media.

It is important that you gain widespread support for your DMS initiative and involve the key stakeholders at an early stage, particularly if you need to raise money to finance the project.

Implementing an e-business strategy will require a significant investment of money, time and expertise, and will have a major impact on the way the DMO works and interacts with its various partners and stakeholders. It is important that they should be involved in defining their requirements as users.

Communicating the progress of the project at key stages is crucial. There are many examples of DMOs that have failed to engage effectively with their stakeholders and who have paid the price in terms of poor support and negative press. You can do this by holding regular progress meetings for the key players, providing reports to or attending association meetings or relevant committees, issuing press releases and newsletters or holding regular open fora.

Establishing good communications with your stakeholders at the beginning of the process will make training and animation at the end much easier. Ensure people understand what will be expected of them and how they can participate in and benefit from the new systems being established.

Step 4 - Prepare a draft specification of user requirements

Once you have established your e-business strategy and have effectively gained the support of your stakeholders, you need to move into a more detailed stage of planning, with production of a Specification of User Requirements (SUR).

The first task is to determine the detailed requirements of the various user groups and to identify which of these you want to be supported by the DMS. Start by getting together a group of colleagues and having a brainstorming session. Identify all the types of users and all your target audiences e.g. staff, suppliers, customers, intermediaries, community groups etc. Think carefully about those less obvious users, such as Government officials who require statistics, or students requiring information to help them undertake projects.

In this report, you should identity the users and list all their requirements and how they interact with or within your organisation. This will provide a well-structured list that you can use as a framework for discussions with your users.

It is important to think forward to how you intend business processes to be undertaken in the future, as some existing processes may disappear in the new way of working. Make sure you include a date and version number on your SUR as the document will be updated over time as you start to talk to your various audiences.

Once you have your draft SUR, ask a small, but representative, number of people from each of the user groups to consider the list and identify any requirements they might have that have not already been identified. Ask them to indicate the level of priority that they attach to each requirement. In doing so, they should consider, for each requirement:

- How many users will benefit and to what extent?
- How much work is involved in delivering functionality to meet this requirement?
- Does it rely on other features or functionality being in place e.g. a database or e-commerce solution?
- Can it deliver a quick win?
- Is it a major undertaking?

You will need to consolidate all the comments in your master SUR to give you a prioritised list of requirements.

The SUR describes what you require and forms the basis for your Functional Specification that describes how you are going to deliver what you require. See the example in Step 5 below.

Step 5 – Prepare a Functional specification

Your Specification of User Requirements (SUR) describes what you require and forms the basis for your Functional Specification that describes how you are going to deliver it. Functionality can be more or less sophisticated but includes for example, reservations, key word searches, bulletin boards, interactive maps. The following example shows the user requirement for managing customer data, and the corresponding functional specifications.

User requirement	Functional specification
Manage consumer data, including: • Contact information • Origin • Demographic profile • Activity history Record date, time and originator	Create a database with appropriate fields: title, first name, surname, etc Create interface for data capture via: • Manual input (e.g. via a keyboard) • Automatically during a transaction • Through an import routine • Restrict data entries of pre-define answers whenever possible to aid quality control, e.g. for title, origin, demographic profile and activity Automate date, time and user entries to the database drawn from the users login ID and the system's calendar/clock.

Step 6 - Build up your knowledge

At this stage it is often useful to build up your knowledge of existing systems on the market and the sorts of functionality that is available as an outsourced service. Talk to your own in-house IT staff (if relevant) about different approaches or hold some preliminary discussions with potential software developers and system suppliers. Most are only too willing to demonstrate their product, or you might like to visit another destination where their system is in operation. If your project is sufficiently large you might consider issuing a formal 'Request for Information' call, which will initiate structured discussions with system suppliers, as a pre-cursor to the final tendering process.

These discussions will also help you to get some indication of likely costs. It is helpful to create a cost table in which you can detail current expenditure and income on each activity to compare it with the costs of the same activity if it were to be delivered through the DMS. Comparing the two columns will enable you to see the net gains or costs attached to each component. It is worth splitting costs into one-off development investment and recurring revenue costs. Remember there are soft costs and benefits, such as savings in staff time, improvements to services as well as direct costs and savings like hosting charges and reduced print and postage costs.

Step 7 – Prepare an initial business case analysis

Based on your increased knowledge, and with specialist advice where necessary, you should now be much better informed about:

- The ways in which a DMS could help your organisation to do its job better
- The potential costs
- The implications for management and staff and the extent to which existing business processes will need to be changed
- The views of your stakeholders

You should now be able to review and finalise your e-Business Strategy, your Specification of User Requirements and your Functional Specification, adding in anything you missed in the first drafts and looking at what you can realistically afford and how it may be phased over several years.

All this information will help you to prepare an initial Business Case Analysis. This should detail the potential benefits and risks associated with operating a DMS and an estimation of the overall costs and additional income that you might expect, including:

Potential areas for generating additional income:

- E-commerce revenues from sales of tourism products via the Web and e-mail, especially accommodation but also transport, entertainment, services and merchandise
- Increased membership and participation fees from tourism suppliers
- Increased sales through tourist information offices and call centres, resulting from faster service, higher throughput, better matching of demand and supply
- Corporate funding and sponsorship in return for exposure on the destination Web site, kiosks etc
- Exploitation of the product, consumer and business databases

Potential areas for cost savings:

- Reduced costs of print runs and print distribution
- Savings in staff time, print production and distribution, enquiry handling, transaction processing, communications etc
- Reduced investment in traditional marketing and sales activity
- Reduced cost in staff liaison
- As well as the financial savings, there is considerable benefit in being able to provide information and services that were not previously available. One of the key advantages of a DMS is that it can be configured to capture a wealth of data automatically which can then be analysed to give valuable management information.

If you need to secure a budget for the DMS, look at the guidance set out in Section 6.3, Step 3 and consider how the principles set out there might be applied in this wider context.

Step 8 – Develop a technical specification as the basis for tendering

This is an area where you are more likely to need specialist support as it involves specifying the technical requirements for the hardware, software and communications you will need to implement your DMS. You can approach this in one of several ways:

- If you have confidence in one particular supplier, who can supply all or most of your requirements at a satisfactory cost, you might wish to move into a closer relationship with them and ask them to prepare the technical specification as a preliminary to tendering. It may be easier to pay them for this stage so that you are not committed to choosing their solution if a more appropriate solution is presented at the tendering stage.
- If you don't have an existing relationship it may be easier to seek independent advice from a consultancy. This would ensure a neutral proposal as they would not be aligned to a particular system. However, you should choose a consultancy with good experience in this area, or they may lack the understanding of the business sector required to do the job effectively.
- Alternatively, if your project is of a suitable scale, you might wish to employ or contract with a project manager who has the necessary technical skills to undertake this element of the work as part of a wider remit for the whole project. Under this option you would appoint this person early in the project so that they could effectively drive this part of the process.

You may wish to delay producing the technical specification until after you have recruited a supplier and require its production as part of the first stages of preparatory work for the contract. This can be an effective approach as the supplier will be well equipped to produce the specification and will have done much of the work in producing tender proposals. To enable this approach, the Functional Specification will have to be sufficiently developed to provide a suitable basis for tendering.

Step 9 – Undertake a tendering process

Depending on the size and scale of your project you may wish to approach the selection of a system supplier or software developer in different ways. If your project is large scale, you may wish to issue an open tender and advertise it widely. If you have obtained grant funding you may be required to follow a particular procedure. Local authorities are usually subject to specific tendering rules, as are projects that have to comply with national government and EU procurement regulations.

- *If, on the other hand, your project is small scale you may wish to appoint a company with whom you already have a relationship and are happy to work. It might be the company that built your consumer site or supports your office network.*

If you need to adopt the open tendering option you should seek specialist advice from a relevant authority to ensure you comply with the regulations. Using an existing supplier has distinct advantages in terms of speed of implementation and project management, but may restrict your capacity to take advantage of companies with greater experience.

Most DMOs opt for the middle ground and invite tenders from a reasonably small number of suppliers who they feel can meet the majority of their requirements. Identify relevant companies from your own knowledge and supplement it by talking to other organisations that have been through a similar process. You might want to approach each of them and ask for a simple resume of their company's experience and some examples of sites they have built for other clients. You will probably be able to gather a lot of information from their corporate Web sites.

It is always useful to speak with one or two of their clients as a reference point to gather information about the company's customer service levels and overall capabilities. A telephone call will often reveal more information than a letter or e-mail so it is worth the extra effort involved. From this information you should be able to create a short list. You may have already been through this process at the 'build up your knowledge' stage.

The number of companies in your short list will depend on the nature and complexity of your project. Three to five is a reasonable rule of thumb.

Prepare a Request for Proposals document. This could include some or all of the items below or be a document summarising the key points:
- Covering letter (see below)
- e-Business Strategy
- Specification of User Requirements
- Functional and Technical Specifications
- Initial Business Case Analysis

Use your covering letter to specify exactly what it is you want to know. Set out some guidelines for the companies to follow when responding to the tender. This makes a comparative analysis between the responses easier to handle. Examples include:
- Company contact details and legal status
- Length of time established – years/months
- Overview of the company's skills and experience, with references
- Number of employees, particularly developers and programmers
- Details of any sub contractors or freelancers
- Details of any third party software or services proposed
- Details of project management resources
- Overview of the approach they intend to employ on your project, noting any particular issues you wish them to address
- A proposed timetable for delivery
- A full breakdown of costs and proposed payment schedules
- Details of the company's trading terms, conditions and disclaimers
- Any exceptions, restrictions or penalties
- A closing date for submissions, a note of the acceptable formats and your reply address.

At this stage you need to think about how you will evaluate the proposals you receive. This should be done on a systematic basis, using your Request for Proposals as a point of reference. You will need to:
- Draw up an evaluation matrix or scoring chart listing all the key requirements and allocating weights to them according to their relative importance to you
- Seek independent technical and/or business advice if you do not have sufficient skills in house
- Involve key staff and perhaps some of the main stakeholders in the process, to review the tender responses and/or to sit on the selection panel.

Step 10 - Select a system supplier or software developer

Once you have your received all the responses, you should distribute them to those involved in the evaluation process. You may be able to make a selection immediately, or you may consider interviewing the most promising companies to gain further information. This can be done by a short telephone call, or through a more formal presentation process – depending on the size and scope of your project.

The following list provides some tips on what to look for in a software developer:

- Technical capability – you need to be sure that they have the capability to deliver against your Functional Specification and that they are fully conversant with the latest technological advances and able to exploit the best technical solutions in your system. This is particularly relevant to DMS suppliers whose systems are not fully Web-enabled.

- Design skills – look at examples of their work and consider whether they have a flair for graphic design and can adapt your existing brand for a digital application. Generally technical developers are not good at design, so, where design is important, you may wish to use a separate graphic design house for your 'look and feel' - perhaps your print designers.

- Demonstrations of relevant examples – assess the relevance and complexity of their examples and note how recent they are. Ring the client to discuss how well the project went, was it delivered on time, within budget, what were they like to work with?

- Project management support – how do they propose to support you throughout the project? Will you have one point of contact?

- Price – it is not as easy as saying the cheapest or the most expensive is the best. A more expensive programmer may be able to do the job in half the time. However, big companies often carry large overheads that push their prices up.

- Delivery timescales – can they deliver on time. Try to find out what other work commitments they have and compare that to the size of their team. Do not place unduly tight timescales on the project as it can push the price up considerably.

- Innovation – do they offer anything different, innovative or really adding value?

- Type and size of organisation and length of time established – companies established very recently may not have the experience you require. Small companies often try harder, but large companies can provide security against one-person dependency.

- Reliability – you can assess this best by talking to some of their existing or past clients

- Location – if your project is complicated you may wish to have regular progress meetings, so having a local company may be preferable.

You may decide to use several suppliers and integrate the various solutions. If you do this, you should consider appointing a single supplier to take the lead role and to co-ordinate the integration programme. Otherwise the responsibility will fall on you and you will need to have the technical capability to do the work.

When you have made your decision you need to take the following actions:
- Inform the successful company in writing
- Arrange for appropriate contracts or agreements to be drawn up between you and the successful company
- Make any payments due on commencement
- Inform your staff and partners of the appointment
- Arrange a project initiation meeting and agree a project timetable
- Notify the unsuccessful companies as a matter of courtesy

Step 11 – Finalise your Business Case Analysis

Once you have decided on your chosen supplier you need to finalise your Business Case Analysis that you developed in Step 7. Now that the scope and costs of the project are known, you may need to revisit and revise the analysis, possibly as the basis for the final decision to proceed with the project.

Step 12 – Organise project management

In moving into the implementation phase, it is essential that a clear project management structure be put in place. You will need to:

- Set up a Steering Group to oversee all aspect of the e-business strategy implementation. This must be led from the top with support from all parts of the organisation and its wider partners. It will have the responsibility of monitoring progress against deadlines, controlling budgets and evaluating achievements. The project management team must report progress to the Steering Group in an open and honest manner and will gain strategic support from them.

- Appoint a project team. The key role will be a competent Project Manager who will act as client on behalf of the DMO - the interface between it and the suppliers, including internal suppliers (e.g. of data, staff development, etc.). It is important that he/she is given sufficient authority to be able to make decisions on a day-to-day basis, while remaining responsible to the Steering Group for key decisions, such as the need to make major changes to the project plan. Ideally the Project Manager should be involved, even if only on a part-time basis, from the early stages of the project and possibly undertake most of the planning work involved.

- Set up the project management systems such as project plans, financial and milestone tracking devices, reporting mechanisms, supplier contracts etc.

Step 13 - Prepare an implementation plan

Your project manager should prepare an implementation plan for the project in conjunction with your lead supplier. It should cover the installation of the information and communication technology and everything that your organisation will have to do as an integral part of the programme to ensure that your DMS is used fully and effectively. In particular, this means ensuring that:

- Staff are fully behind the project, understand what is happening when and have all the skills necessary to do their future jobs in the most effective way

- The necessary data are available as and when required, and are of high quality.

Whether or not you are purchasing everything through a lead contractor, there will be one or more technology suppliers involved in each sector, hardware, software and telecommunications. Their work will have to be carefully planned with a critical path analysis. The more suppliers there are, the more delays are likely. Build in time for slippage.

The final plan should show, week-by-week (and day-by-day at key periods), what each of the suppliers and each of the key players in your own organisation should be doing. As a general rule, be very cautious about the speed of implementation, particularly where any significant software development is involved.

The agreed implementation plan should be reflected in the contracts with each of the suppliers. Where you have critical deadlines for implementation of specific elements of the DMS, you should consider writing penalty clauses into the relevant contracts.

Be aware of the possibility of 'specification creep', where more features get added to the specifications after work has begun. Try to finalise the specification and the contracts before work starts. Draw up a formal 'change control' procedure, so that changes can be accommodated in an orderly way, with both parties aware of the time and cost implications.

Allow plenty of time in your plan for thoroughly testing the system before launching it to your users. Ensure you have fully tested all the business processes and that they have worked successfully. Acting as trial users, make some deliberate mistakes, so that the system's error handling facilities work properly.

Step 14 – Prepare specific plans

You may need to prepare detailed plans for particular aspects of the project, for instance content management, training, communication or PR.

- The Content Management Plan sets out a logical path through the various stages involved in creating and managing a wide range of data on an on-going basis. Initially the range of data required for each product or item will need to be determined, and then mechanisms for collecting, verifying and quality assuring that data will have to be developed and communicated to the people who will be responsible. If you intend to update the data regularly it would be sensible to undertake the work in-house, as far as possible. This offers a far higher degree of flexibility and enables you to react quickly to emerging opportunities or to manage a crisis.

- The Training Plan has to identify the training needs for the various groups involved – both inside and outside the organisation. There will be a need for training at all levels – from senior officers involved in strategic planning and system exploitation, through management and supervisory levels with basic man-management skill requirements, to operatives and frontline staff with a need for customer-facing skills.

- The Communications Plan will identify your key audiences and set out what you need to communicate to them about and define which channels will be most effective. Methods might include meetings, workshops or conferences, newsletters, Web sites, press releases, road shows, printed brochures, CD-ROMs etc. It is likely that you will need a major programme of animation of your stakeholders. Some of this will fall under training, some under communication. Establishing and maintaining good relations with your stakeholders is something that should be woven into the fabric of the project from the very start.

Step 15 – Monitor, evaluate and review

Although this is the last step, it is another aspect that must be considered from the very outset of the Project. In order to evaluate whether the project has been successful in achieving the objectives and targets set out in the e-Business Strategy, monitoring systems must be in place from the outset.

There is often a danger that the key performance indicators become, in themselves, the objectives. For instance, attracting one million unique visitors to your consumer Web site is an activity target, not a business objective. It is important that your evaluation follows through to identify how much increased business has been experienced in the destination as a result of this.

It should be a regular part of the work of the project management and Steering Group to oversee the monitoring and evaluation and determine the action to be taken as a result. They also will have the responsibility for reviewing requirements for extending the specification of the project (see Step 13). Many of these requirements will be tactical, but others will be strategic – for example, the desire to publish data through emerging channels, like 3G mobile devices and interactive TV or to implement a major new area of functionality, such as itinerary planning.

3.3 DMS Critical Success Factors

- A DMS should be integral to the operations of a DMO and should be led by business needs. The project should not happen just because you have access to grant funds to support a technology project!

- You must gain genuine support from the highest level. Too many DMS/e-business projects have failed because the senior management did not fully understand the project or its implications.

- Setting up a DMS is not a 'once and for all' cost. There will be substantial revenue costs and additional capital costs on a continuing basis. Prepare your business case analysis (BCA) projections over three or four years. Undertake an initial BCA early on and a more detailed one later, when you have a clearer idea of the proposition and the costs. It is unlikely that in the short term a DMS will pay for itself financially, if ever. Do not assume that there will be a large increase in income immediately.

- Implementation of a full DMS should be phased in over a reasonable time period, starting by setting up the internal network, getting staff used to using the latest office software, etc. A number of small steps are a lot easier to take than 'one giant leap'.

- Staff understanding, buy-in and involvement is essential and requires specific programmes of consultation, discussion and active participation, backed up by appropriate training and development activity. This includes communicating to those at the highest level especially where there is a significant amount of change to manage. It is important to ensure in this way that the pressures that can be caused by the setting up of a DMS and by implementing new ways of working do not become de-motivating.

- When dealing with system suppliers, be sceptical and make sure to ask the key questions. Don't assume you have to buy all the components from a single supplier, but ensure that the lead supplier is happy to take responsibility for integrating those components that you buy from elsewhere.

- Go for proven, off-the-shelf software, wherever possible, but be aware that anything more than 5 years old is likely to be out of date and not making the best use of modern technology. Ask about the company's investment programme. Where it is necessary to develop new software, remember that a substantial investment of DMO staff time will be needed to work with the software developer; and the process may be a long one. Where deadlines are critical, include penalty clauses in supplier contracts.

- Thoroughly test your DMS before launching it to your users and when you do, phase it to involve your most experienced users first.

- Achieving and maintaining a high quality digital database is a substantial task, for which proper resources should be allowed.

- Set up a mechanism to drive implementation and to monitor and evaluate progress openly and honestly against deadlines and budgets.

3.4   DMS Case Studies

This section provides a summary of the DMS/e-business activities of five DMOs from around the world – DMOs which are well advanced in e-business development and implementation and which may be regarded as potential role models for others. They were selected to represent different types of DMO: Tourism Organisations from countries, cities and regions. Some have well-established systems that have been developed over many years, others have embarked on e-business recently, with the advantage of adopting the latest Internet based technologies.

3.4.1   British Columbia

Destination Overview

British Columbia is a Province on the western seaboard of Canada. It has a relatively small population, less than 4 million people, and is governed by a Legislative Assembly.

Tourism is worth Canadian $9.5 billion annually (2000) representing an estimated 22.4 million visitors and is the second most important industry sector after forestry in terms of GDP. 113,000 people are employed directly in the tourism sector and in constant dollars, tourism GDP has grown significantly over the past ten years, up 22.7%

British Columbia's major markets include Asia Pacific, North America and Europe.

Structure of the DMO

The DMO is called Tourism British Columbia. It is an independent Crown Corporation that reports to an industry-led Board of Directors. Liaison with the provincial government is through the Ministry of Small Business, Tourism & Culture.
Its prime role is as a tourism marketing organisation for the Province. It has international offices in California, London, Frankfurt, Sydney, Tokyo and Taiwan and is a partner in a new office in Beijing.

Tourism British Columbia is not a membership organisation and is funded by a proportion of the Provincial hotel tax.

The Board of Directors includes 15 members, 5 of which are Government appointees and 10 from the private sector. Hence the private sector has considerable power and influence in its affairs.

Within BC there are some municipalities that have set up local and regional DMO's which have mixed revenue streams including members dues and portions of local hotel taxes. These include Tourism Vancouver, Tourism Whistler, Tourism Nanaimo and Tourism Victoria.

Local destinations are responsible for running local Visitor Centres, typically as a function of the Chamber of Commerce. There are approximately 120 of these throughout the Province, and four are run directly by Tourism British Columbia.

Tourism British Columbia provides support and materials for the local Visitor Centres, and 30 on them use its reservations mechanisms to book accommodation online for their customers.

History of British Columbia's DMS development

Tourism British Columbia has been operating a legacy DMS for a number of years. This is effectively made up of several components that are currently integrated (mostly manually) to provide the wide range of services. They are:

- Product database – which was custom built
- Reservations platform – InfoRM, supplied by InfoCentre, which focuses on the call centre applications
- Contact management – Maximiser
- Web site – custom built on an Oracle database

In 2000, Tourism British Columbia appointed a senior ICT professional to look at the future of its e-business requirements. It was quickly recognised that the current system integration was performing inadequately and that much more efficient modern e-business systems were required.

The staff is currently working on a re-definition of what is needed. A policy decision has been taken that the DMO will work with mainstream e-business suppliers rather than embark on a bespoke development programme in house.

Current Status

There are 7000 products in British Columbia of which approximately 2800 are accommodation establishments. The vast majority of these are small scale B&Bs with very limited scope for online booking. Tourism British Columbia therefore approves only 800 accommodation establishments for online booking. However these 800 represent over 80% of the total bedstock.

Inventory clerks at the call centre gather availability data from the accommodation providers by fax and manually enter these details into the system. The main call centre operation is serviced by a company called Corporatel West. It employs between 70 and 80 agents at peak times to answer calls and the main marketing campaigns drive traffic towards the call centre (or online) to book.

The call centre is promoted as an information and booking service and Tourism BC pays by the minute for the calls to be serviced. It charges 10% of the full stay to the accommodation provider to help offset these costs.

In common with some other destinations, Tourism BC has seen a 20% drop in call centre business over the last couple of years, although its booking streams have gained ground. The reason for this is thought to be that more and more people are researching their travel plans on the Web and so have less need to contact the call centre with general enquiries. Whilst it may be seen as a good thing that the non revenue generating calls are declining while the revenue generating ones are increasing, it does provide a cause for concern that the overall volume of calls is dropping and therefore it is harder to attract volume rates from the call centre contractor. If this trend continues it may ultimately put the call centre operation under threat.

The www.hellobc.com is a comprehensive destination Web site with online booking and BC Escapes package offers. It has a link to a dedicated media section including story ideas, image bank and statistics.

Performance

Tourism BC has a well-established DMO operation and has been successful in creating considerable business for the destination. The Hello BC Web site is receiving 2000 unique visitors a day, of which 200 (10%) are making firm bookings. Additionally 400 bookings a day are made in the call centre.

Data management

Product data is collected at a Provincial level by Tourism BC and inventory is collected manually by clerks at the call centre. There is no mechanism for sharing data up the line to the Canadian Tourism Commission or down the line to the Municipalities. As previously mentioned, of the 120 local Visitor Centres, 30 are able to make bookings on the BC reservation engine (a system called InfoRM). They do not however, have any facility to manage the data.

Tourism BC maintains a consumer database, and runs some traditional direct campaigns from it. The staff has made a policy decision not to adopt e-mail marketing techniques at this time as they are currently concentrating their efforts on TV and print mechanisms for their inspirational marketing.

Distribution

Products are currently distributed through Tourism BC's own Web site. It has not embarked on any further distribution deals to date but is keen to develop a strategy to build up relationships with online travel players in the future.

They would like to develop partnerships whereby they provide private label product data, with accommodation, flights and car hire, to some of the major commercial players, possibly through a hook up with the GDSs for reservations.

Financial aspects

It is difficult to estimate the costs of establishing the Tourism BC DMS in the first instance, as it has evolved over time. Current annual running costs are in the region of Canadian $1.5m, but it is likely that a major investment will be needed to redevelop the existing legacy systems to meet the future requirements.

Tourism BC does not charge businesses a participation fee, but it does collect a commission charge on the bookings it makes, 10% of the full stay. Revenue funds for the whole operation are derived from a proportion of the hotel tax that is levied on businesses by the Provincial Government.

Specific issues

Staff at Tourism BC see a big challenge ahead in educating tourism providers to understand how the new business models will change the way they operate. Tourism BC is considering where it, as a DMO lives. What is their role to be in the future? It is hard for them to be more commercial without competing with their own industry.

Future developments

The pressing task now is to replace the legacy systems with new e-business systems that can meet the challenges of the future. Tourism BC is clear that it is a marketing organisation, not a technology company. Thus it does not wish to undertake a bespoke development project. It is keen, however to work in partnership with others, and perhaps to gain a suitable partner by merger or acquisition.

Conclusions

Tourism BC has a well-established DMO operation and so has the advantage of having many of its business processes already in hand. Because of this, its progression to a new e-business system should be relatively easy to manage. Tourism BC is questioning its role as a DMO, and it knows that its strategy and actions must be in the best interest of the private sector tourism players in the Province.

Relevant URLs:
www.hellobc.com
www.hellobc.com/media/index.jsp

3.4.2 Finland

Destination Overview

Finland is a Nordic country situated between Sweden to the west and Russia to the east. In 1999 it received nearly 3.4 million visitors, primarily from Sweden, Russia, Germany, Estonia, Norway, Great Britain, United States, Denmark, France, Netherlands. (Source Border Interview Survey 1999 / FTB).

In 2000, the room capacity was 63,400 of which nearly 55,000 were in hotels and serviced establishments. There are a total of 151,000 bed spaces (Statistics Finland).

Tourism accounts for 2.2% of GDP (1998) and employs 98,000 people. (Source: Tom Ylkänen: KTMFactcard /Mextra, SMAK).

Structure of the DMO

The Finnish Tourist Board is a government organisation marketing Finland as a tourist destination. The Finnish Tourist Board operates from a head office in Helsinki and has offices in 11 other countries.

Its major products are city breaks, touring and culture travel, family travel and winter holidays. Incentive travel and meetings are an important niche product and have gained a good reputation.

In line with its main markets, FTB are targeting visitors from the following countries in order of priority: Germany, Russia, Sweden, United Kingdom, France, Italy, the Netherlands, Spain, Norway, US, Estonia and Japan.

History of the DMO's DMS development

The Finnish Tourist Board (FTB) has developed and operated an integrated tourism-related networked services for use by the Finnish tourism or~ the industry since1992. The development has been an orgor: follows:

- 1992 - the development of a Market Information System marketing data. Initially this was an internal system for FT. soon extended to professional users within Finland. Lotus l basis for the system.

- 1995 – the development of an English language data bank of travel products and services, called PROMIS, covering the whole country in co-operation with the regional tourist offices
- 1997 – the development of RELIS, a research, education and library information system. Owing to strategic changes in FTB's activities, the RELIS system has not been used since 1999
- 1997 – digitisation of images was contracted to Comma Finland
- 1997 – launch of the first international Web-service including an 'Online Travel Guide' that used the PROMIS files.
- 1998-1999 – launch of 14 tailored country pages in local languages, extranets for press and international services for market segments (Christmas, Winter holidays, Nature holidays)
- 2000 – launch of second version of the international homepage including 'Finland Travel Guide' (new name for PROMIS files on the Web), new Contact Centre tools (Infoset and CIS) and browser-based data maintenance tools for SMEs to access PROMIS
- 2001 – launch of the WAP Service: 'Finland mTravel Guide' with national coverage including the PROMIS files for attractions, accommodation, events, tours and excursions, customer service telephone numbers. Finland was the first National Tourist Office in the world to promote its national database on a WAP service.

The strategy of the Finnish Tourist Board is to work together with the tourism industry and other interest groups that share common goals so as to maximise the country's reach and impact in the international marketplace. Information and communication technology is regarded as a powerful tool for this – not just to provide an electronic presence at the point of sale but also to foster collaboration between the different industry sectors.

An early goal was to improve the cost-effectiveness of the Board's work by simplifying and speeding up work processes, reducing duplication of activity and improving FTB internal and external communications. The successful implementation of the Board's ICT initiatives has also provided an effective technical environment for the Finnish travel industry to develop applications for their own use.

Specific emphasis is made in Finland's overall tourism strategy to 'the clear profiling of the nation's tourist image, the precise segmentation of customers and markets and the effective marketing and distribution of products'. The Market Information System (MIS) in particular, enables the FTB and their trade partners to manage and organise sales and marketing campaigns world-wide.

Current Status

The current applications focus primarily on information management and delivery to and from a range of users including the Finnish tourism industry as well as domestic and international tourists. Transactions are not handled directly by the Finnish Tourism Board but there are direct links from the Finland Travel Guide to the reservation services of individual companies or municipalities, as appropriate.

A range of country-specific pages for Belgium, Canada, Denmark, Estonia, France, Germany, Italy, Japan, Netherlands, Norway, Poland, Russia, Spain, Sweden, Switzerland and USA are available. These act as local language 'gateways' to the Finland Travel Guide and additionally have specific information on relevant products available in each market such as tours and transportation.

The Market Information System (MIS)

MIS is a data management and distribution system, which is used and maintained by all staff within FTB to manage and organise specific sales and marketing campaigns. It has eleven core MIS applications covering the whole range of tourist board and travel industry activity. For example:

- the Buyers and Media application contains tour operator and travel agency profiles together with contact information. It also holds basic data on major media in key markets. The application functions via the Internet to the Finnish Travel Trade.
- the RMS Marketing Plan application holds details on all marketing plans, promotional campaigns and their related actions from all FTB offices world-wide.
- the popular Mekkala application functions as an electronic notice board for the whole of FTB world-wide and for the Finnish Travel Trade via MeXtra on the Internet, providing an efficient platform for internal discussions and news, the posting of proposed presentations and other corporate communications.

Other MIS applications include information on statistical data, general information about FTB's offices and personnel as well as data on FTB working groups, projects and their status reports. There is a specific Events application to manage seminar and workshop documentation and correspondence (via the Internet for the Finnish Travel Trade and Tour Operators abroad) as well as FTB customer contact information. FTB offices use Lotus Domino tools for producing and updating their own Web service structure and content.

The Professional Marketing Information Service (PROMIS)

PROMIS is the national database of Finnish travel products and services. It provides all PROMIS, Mextra, Tradextra and MIS users with a wide selection of up-to-date information on travel products, services and contact information. In September 2000 a new browser-based interface was introduced and by May 2001 about 70 organisations and 130 SMEs were using it.

PROMIS is a data source for:
- Web and WAP Services: Finland Travel Guide, Finland mTravel Guide, data source for trade pages in Finland and abroad, theme sites sales manuals
- MEK Brochures
- Finland Handbook, Hotels
- Family Vacation, Winter Wonderland, Culture and Christmas
- MEK offices
- Call Centre Europe
- Data producers own brochures, Web services etc.
- Delivering some MEK-outside services by Publisher licences

FTB's Web site, the Online Travel Guide, draws on MIS and PROMIS applications. Currently the Web applications are text only so as to optimise browsing and printing speeds, though clearly there is the capacity for presenting multimedia data as well. Extranet applications MeXtra and TradeXtra are for professional use.

Country Presentation
- Open international consumer marketing tool
- Open for everyone, in English

Organisation Presentation
- Shows what MEK as an organisation is doing, in Finnish

MeXtra - launched in April 2001
- For trade in Finland, registration needed, Finnish
- Domestic extranet site for the Trade and Media (B2B)
- Market Information, Statistics, Sales Events, Contacts etc.

TradeXtra - launched in June 2001
- International extranet-site for the Trade and Media (B2B)
- Registration needed
- Sales Manuals of main product groups
- Events and Familiarisation Trip management tool
- eLearning (Arguments for selling Finland etc.)
- Marketing Tools ...etc.

Finland mTravel Guide – main menu
- Places to visit
- Places to stay
- What's on
- To do
- Questions (Call centre-numbers)

ICT Systems used by Contact Centre Europe
- CIS
- Managing system for brochures and orders
- Campaign and direct marketing mailings
- InfoSet
- PROMIS + files produced by MEK especially for CCE:n agents use
- Tailored country pages
- Bulletin board 'Mekkala'

Performance

Usage statistics for www.finland–tourism.com in May 2001

Total hits: 287,470
Total files: 254,306
Total pages: 255,150

Usage statistics for www.mek.fi in May 2001

Total hits: 292,068
Total files: 251,171
Total pages: 243,429

Data Management

The data is maintained by different parties, for example general information on Finland as a destination is maintained by FTB personnel and external PROMIS partners, such as regional and city tourism organisations, hotel chains and SMEs themselves. The database holds tourist information for the whole of Finland, though the quality and depth of information varies.

Updates to the PROMIS database by information providers are automatically converted into HTML and transferred to the common Internet server daily and from there to the relevant section in the Online Travel Guide. They are also available to all MIS, PROMIS, Mextra and Tradextra and WAP service users and to the Infoset for the contact centre agents' use.

Importantly, certain PROMIS information is copyright free and can be downloaded by PROMIS partners for use in brochures and other marketing publications. Similarly, the partners are able to use the data in their own ICT applications, such as Websites and CD-ROMs.

The Customer Information System (CIS) is a customer relationship management program developed especially for the Finnish Tourist Board to help them manage their relationships with end customers, trade and media representatives.

All brochure orders input by contact centre agents and from Web based brochure order application are stored into the CIS. At the moment, the system produces brochure order transfer files once a day to a mailing house. The file contains customer contact information (e.g. names and addresses) and information of ordered brochures (e.g. brochure item ID's and quantities).

Distribution

Finish tourism products are distributed via FTB's own sites, through partner sites, and by outside contract partners, who have publisher licenses.

Financial Aspects

The core MIS and PROMIS systems are funded by FTB and operate on a non-commercial basis. The majority of data within PROMIS is collected and maintained by PROMIS data producing partners who pay approximately 600 euros per year and by the SMEs themselves via browser based data producing forms. The PROMIS data producing partner generally provides the SME licence for free. Total set-up costs are not available but are cited as being 'surprisingly modest'. The whole operation was managed essentially by one executive until 1997. At the present there are six ICT employees.

Future Development

FTB have launched several new functions in 2001, which it will seek to consolidate over the next year.

Conclusions

The Finnish Tourist Board has in many ways pioneered the use of ICT as an integral part of a National Tourist Office's operations. The Board believes that ICT has been an effective tool for developing cross-industry co-operation within Finland, as well as for reaching a world-wide audience. FTB has demonstrated that, through effective management of the various projects, the use of industry standard software, the direct relationship and response of the projects to user requirements, it is possible to develop significant systems without massive financial investment.

As a destination Finland is relatively off-the-beaten-track, so it has to work hard to maximise its reach and impact in the international market place. It is not surprising that, as a country with the third highest levels of Internet and mobile phone usage in the world, Finland has adopted ICT so intensively as a tool to achieve this aim.

3.4.3   Seychelles Tourism Marketing Authority

Destination Overview

Seychelles is an island archipelago in the Indian Ocean, 1000 miles east of Africa. It attracts 130,000 visitors per annum, mainly from Europe. There are only 143 accommodation providers, spread across 13 of the islands. 80% of the accommodation is in 20% of the establishments. There are plans for four major resort developments currently under consideration and these would significantly increase the accommodation stock.

The majority of the business is delivered through major tour operators. Although the destination is not particularly seasonal, they do tend to have peaks reflecting the holiday taking patterns of their main markets, particularly Christmas and New Year, which is the time of greatest demand.

Tourism contributes 12.7% to GDP (US$70.2m) and employs just over 5,000 people, 16.6% of the working population. Tourism is the major source of foreign exchange - a critical issue for an island archipelago heavily dependent on imported goods.

Structure of the DMO

The DMO is the Seychelles Tourism Marketing Authority. It was established in July 1999 as a non-profit Government organisation, to market and promote tourism to the Seychelles. The scope of its activities includes implementation and co-ordination of international marketing activities through its various tourism offices and representative agencies abroad, research and liaison with Central Government.

STMA is responsible to the Seychelles Tourism Advisory Board, which is chaired by the Minister for Tourism, but also has strong representation on it from the private sector, including Air Seychelles, the national carrier.

STMA itself has a company board, 51 staff based at its head office in Mahé, and 21 staff based in their overseas offices in nine countries around the world. STMA operates three information offices within the destination, one on Mahé, one on Praslin and the other on La Digue. .

The Seychelles is ecologically sensitive, so STMA's key role is to market the destination sensitively and within the limits of its carrying capacity. It is unlikely that visitor numbers can be increased by more than 20%, so proactive yield management is the primary aim. STMA has a role in managing the product development programme, and is able to influence planning decisions to ensure that supply meets demand.

Seychelles is very remote from its core markets, which means there are high costs involved in reaching its consumers. The destination is high value, low volume, and many of its visitors will only come once in a life-time, meaning that STMA have to constantly be seeking new visitors.

History of the STMA's DMS development

The destination is mainly sold through intermediaries, so traditionally STMA and its predecessor has not had a consumer interface. Instead they have worked extensively through their overseas offices with tour operators and media, and directly with the local destination management companies.

STMA has been faced with costs of managing their overseas operations that have escalated beyond the resources of a small country. It recognised that a technology solution could provide a cost effective and joined up approach. It was also particularly relevant for STMA as they knew that there was a high propensity to use the Internet amongst their core markets.

Following a WTOBC seminar in April 2000 on the use of ICT and e-business in tourism, STMA initiated a project to create a suite of Web enabled products to manage and promote the tourism products and provide the best visitor and intermediary servicing in May 2000. The first stages involved securing professional assistance to help them prepare a strategy and business case, specify the user requirements, document functional and technical specifications and re-engineer their business processes.

The initial design and specification work was carried out between July and December 2000, followed by a tender process in March 2001.

Current Status

As the destination is heavily dependent on intermediaries, the DMS has been designed to raise awareness of the destination and drive traffic to existing mechanisms to book. STMA made a conscious decision not to compete in the booking market, but rather offers potential visitors five options to book:

- Through a tour operator in their own country
- Through a tour operator (DMC) based in the Seychelles
- Through a number of on-line tour operators
- Through the hotel's CRS, or
- Direct with the hotel.

Although these mechanisms are well established, they are not usually offered through the same interface, so there has been a challenge to manage the pricing structure in such a way as all parties are satisfied.

The primary aim of STMA is to attract more business to Seychelles but within the carrying capacity of the islands. STMA has therefore adopted a two pronged approach:

- Concentrating their efforts on raising the profile of the destination, through media activity and through direct relations with intermediaries, by providing focused Web sites and services
- Maximising the potential of existing customers, both as returners and as ambassadors amongst their friends and family. STMA are tackling this through the adoption and adaptation of CRM techniques.

The core components of the system are:
- Suite of databases to manage tourism products, editorial, multimedia, customers, intermediaries

- A Web enabled, browser based content management system enabling a wide range of users, both in Seychelles and in the overseas offices to maintain the data (in five languages), via secure password login
- A consumer facing Web site, in five languages, with emphasis on inspirational graphics to heighten the consumers desire to come
- A media Web site, again in five languages, to enable journalists from around the world to access a wealth of useful material, story ideas, press releases, a multimedia library etc (expected Dec 2001)

Performance

At the time of writing the System was only just launched, as so there are no performance figures available yet. The following figures are targets for the first operational quarter:

- New members to Seychelles Select: 675
- Number of unique visitors (by site):

Aspureasitgets.com	13,500
Media	1,350
Fishing	2,700
Diving	2,700
Sailing	2,700
Ecology	4,100
Romance	6,250

Total number of enquiries to:

Local accommodation	675
Destination Management Companies	270
Non local tour operators	900
Airlines	675
Registered journalists	540

Data Management

STMA has designed the DMS so that any authorised user can maintain their content. This applies to all audiences:

- tourism product providers can maintain their product data, particularly prices and inventory
- tour operators can maintain packages and special offers
- overseas staff can create editorial and news targeted at their own markets
- STMA staff in Mahé can maintain destination editorial, media stories, news, press releases and the multimedia library

Although STMA made a conscious decision not to become involved in e-commerce, they have designed their DMS to enable them to capture and exploit consumer data. Seychelles Select is a loyalty club, which consumers can join from the Web site. STMA plan to target these members with offers and promotions using sophisticated CRM techniques.

Distribution

The DMS is at an early stage, so there are no distribution partners at this time. The product data will be distributed via the aspureasitgets.com site. There is considerable interest from commercial companies, both on and offline, in destination content and there may well be deals forthcoming soon whereby STMA provide this content to operators who already sell Seychelles product.

Some large online travel intermediaries have shown an interest in offering split commission deals if STMA act as consolidator of the product data, particularly for inventory. However no firm commitments have been made at the time of writing.

Air Seychelles is the national carrier. It has plans to develop its own e-business systems and so it is working in close liaison with STMA to ensure that there can be an information exchange between the new Air Seychelles system and the DMS.

Because of the nature of the islands, there is a number of niche operators in the adventure travel and ecotourism sectors, interested in distributing data. Deals with these operators are being actively sought.

Financial

STMA's total annual budget is US$3m. This supports all their activities including running their overseas offices.

The DMS project has been funded by Government funds and is estimated to cost US$1m over 3 years, with approximately US$150,000 set aside for annual revenue costs.

At the present time there are no plans to raise advertising or participation fees from the private sector. As there are no e-commerce facilities, there are no commission charges.

Specific Issues

The size, location and nature of the destination are major challenges. STMA has set targets to attract 30,000 new visitors, which may seem modest, but in percentage terms this is a significant increase, 25%. Yield management is the major challenge.

There are challenges presented by publishing all purchase methods to the consumer in the same place and time. This process is reasonably transparent, so suppliers and intermediaries have to demonstrate integrity in their offerings.

The product is complex and it is not easy to buy individual components direct. The packagers have a role to play and it is important not to undermine them in the search for increased yield.

Perhaps the biggest challenge is the small scale of the community. Despite having an accommodation product base of just 143, STMA need a major investment to develop and run their DMS. Other countries, which have thousands of products, struggle to raise similar amounts of finance.

Future Development

There are immediate plans to develop five niche sites for sailing, fishing, diving, ecotourism and romance, for launch in late 2001. Research is currently being undertaken into the feasibility of a centralised or distributed customer contact centre. Issues under consideration include understanding the extent to which consumers make direct contact with the network of Seychelles offices now and whether improvements to this service is something which would facilitate a growth in business.

Conclusion

It is early days in the implementation of the Seychelles DMS, so it is hard to draw any firm conclusions. STMA has focused its attentions on the business case and designed the DMS solution around their core needs. The destination is very small scale and could be heralding a new model for destinations and we should watch this project carefully.

www.aspureasitgets.com

3.4.4   Singapore Tourist Board

Destination Overview

Singapore is at the heart of Asia, receiving 7.6 million visitors per annum, 70% of which are from within Asia, with other primary markets being the US, Canada and northern European.

Singapore is a premier destination for corporate meetings; it is an important economic and trading hub with a base of over 5,000 multinational companies. It has been the number one convention country within Asia consistently for the last 20 years.

It has 32,000 hotel rooms, a staggering 50% of which are 5 star. Tourism accounts for 5% of GDP.

DMO Structure

The DMO is Singapore Tourism Board (STB). It is an autonomous Government agency with 25 offices world-wide and approximately 350 staff. It is run by a board of 10 directors, and chaired by a representative from the private sector.

Singapore is a compact geographical area, a country the size of a large city, so it does not have a complex organisational hierarchy. STB is responsible for managing and marketing the destination and is keen to evolve Singapore into a Tourism Capital and a world-class destination, tourism hub and business centre.

STB's Mission Statement is:

'...to establish Singapore as a leading force in global tourism and a unique and attractive destination, offering an integrated tourism experience linked to regional development. We are valued partners and pioneers of new frontiers of total tourism business. We promote economic prosperity and enhance the quality of life in Singapore.'

Major infrastructure developments and initiatives attract direct Government funding, but the operational costs of running STB are met from a 1% tax levied on tourism suppliers.

History of the STB's DMS development

STB's first use of ICT was a consumer facing Web site developed in 1995. The initial site was just information based, and then in 1998, STB introduced some booking functionality through a partnership with WorldRes. Since then STB has created a number of different sites targeting specific audiences.

Current Status

STB is currently operating the following Web sites targeted at specific audiences:

Consumer site – www.newasia.singapore.com.sg

The main consumer site has also been tailored for the specific markets of US, Canadian, Chinese, Japanese and Nordic travellers, including translation into a number of languages.

The e-commerce module is provided by a link to www.stayinsingapore.com that is operated by the Singapore Hotels Association. The site promotes 21,000 rooms from over 58 hotels, offering real time bookings with instant confirmation.

The site is targeted at both pre and post-arrival markets: pre-arrival through the Internet, and for travellers post-arrival, through a kiosk network and a TIC service run by local partners.

A 'live chat' feature on the site enables users to link up with a Singapore specialist agent over a text chat service for assistance with enquiries and bookings.

Singapore Travel Exchange - www.ste.com.sg

This site is for internal tourism industry communications. It includes a travel agent directory, bulletin board, events listing and registration, classified advertisements and CTRS courses. Licensed travel agents and tour operators are able to renew their licences and complete performance statistics online at this site.

Tourism resource centre - www.cybrary.com.sg

The Tourism Resource "Cybrary" includes a tourism resource centre, tourism statistics, global tourism resources, Singapore tourism cyberstore and an online training section. There is a link to a Tourism e-business section and Tourism Resource Centre Slide Library, www.sms.stb.com.sg.

Corporate site – www.stb.com.sg

STB's corporate site offers a wide range of information about STB, its organisational structure, its roles and responsibilities, a version of its business strategy and plan 'Tourism 21', links to useful sites and a news section.

MICE site – www.meet-in-singapore.com.sg

The "Meet-in-Singapore" Web site is dedicated to business visitors including an event database searchable by dates, keywords, event subjects, event type.

Performance

The main consumer site is receiving 1m hits per month. STB would like the numbers to be significantly higher. Local partners in the destination handle those making enquiries directly to Singapore, whilst others are handled at the various overseas offices or by STB themselves. WorldRes handle about 100 hotel reservations per week from STB's site.

Data Management

STB maintain a product database that is used to publish general data to the various interfaces. Originally STB maintained this data through a postal request to members that was then keyed manually into the database. Since 1998, members have been able to maintain their own data via the trade extranet. Inventory is managed separately through links directly to WorldRes.

STB have taken a number of steps to assist the industry in their exploitation of ICT. They have organised seminars, held training events, worked with the Hotel Association to animate the members and encouraged technology suppliers to make presentations to raise the general awareness of the possibilities and provided grant funds for SMEs to purchase computers.

STB are not actively involved in customer relationship management at this time. WorldRes provide access to aggregated data on consumer bookings, but STB do not hold an integrated consumer database.

Distribution

Singapore tourism products are distributed through the various STB Web sites and other marketing activities. The accommodation products are promoted widely through the WorldRes distribution network, which runs to about 120 leading commercial organisations.

Financial

The building of STB's latest sites has been outsourced to various companies. STB spent about $2m on capital costs for the initial development and about $1m annually to maintain them. STB makes no additional charge to the 1% tourism tax to the tourism products or their partners for the infrastructure they provide, but of course the providers pay a commission to WorldRes on each booking made.

There are two staff members at STB responsible for the ICT developments and operations.

Specific Issues

STB have identified three key issues that will effect its future progress in the development of its DMS:

- Consumers are not yet ready to buy complex packaged products over the Web, they are happy with single, simple products, such as a bednight, but are not booking packages in significant numbers yet.
- The travel trade and the tourism providers tend to be late adopters of new technology and new business processes
- The new G3 mobile technology channels will be the key tools of the future

Future Development

STB have plans to develop functionality that will allow tourism providers to have mini Web sites made up from the Web pages on the main NewAsia – Singapore site. It is hoped that this functionality will be available in 2002.

STB recognise the importance of customer relationship marketing, but have no immediate plans to develop this type of functionality.

Conclusion

Singapore is clearly well placed in terms of its product to capitalise on the growth in travel and tourism, particularly as the trends in its key markets move in its favour. It has already invested in a number of integrated Web sites addressing each of its key audiences, but traffic is still relatively low and they have a strong need to raise awareness of the destination generally and of the Web sites specifically.

So far STB has not embraced customer relationship management, and this should be its next main focus to ensure that it can make the most of the trade it does have to generate more trade for the future.

3.4.5   Tirol Tourist Board / Tiscover

Destination Overview

The Tirol is one of nine provinces within Austria. It has over seven million visitors per year representing 38 million bed-nights. The province has a strong winter and summer trade and a large proportion of independent short-break travellers for whom pre-travel information is particularly important. Tirol is a key tourism area within Austria, accounting for approximately 40% of the Country's total tourism income.

Within the Tirol province there are 19 regional DMOs, and 159 local tourism offices (TICs). There are approximately 4,500 accommodation establishments promoted on the TISCover system (from farmhouse bed and breakfasts to 5 Star hotels), of which about 550 are bookable online.

DMO structure

Austria has a federal constitution and the nine provinces each have their own administration. The Austrian National Tourist Office's has the responsibility for international marketing and each of the provincial tourist boards have well-established roles in both domestic and cross-border marketing and information collection and management.

The Tirol Tourist Board was the originator of the TIScover system. At the time of embarking on the development of the TIS destination database in 1991, it decided to set up a separate company, constituted as a whole owned subsidiary of the Board.

Throughout the 1990s TIS GmbH has continued to invest in the development of the system and now the Web portal www.TIScover.at covers content for the whole of Austria in partnership with the Austrian National Tourist Office and 7 Public Private Partnerships with provincial tourism organisations. These organisations use TIScover software as their primary data management and online publishing tool.

The company, TIS GmbH, now operates on a commercial basis. It has a strong foothold in three German speaking markets, Austria, Germany and Switzerland, and is considering development in other destinations.

The overall objective of the Tirol's use of TIScover is: 'enabling all the service providers from the entire destination to participate directly in the electronic marketplace while providing a comprehensive and accurate information service to pre and post-arrival visitors.'

History of the DMO's DMS development

TIS GmbH, as subsidiary of the Tirol Tourist Board, was one of the early adopters of technology, commencing their investment in the early 90s and launching their first version of the proprietary TIS Destination Database in 1991.

TIScover has been developed on a continuous basis every since, with strong academic input from the university of Linz and Vienna. In 1995 TIScover became the first system of its kind to move to a Web-enabled platform. The latest version, launched in May 2001, is the seventh release of the software.

Current Status

The TIScover DMS is a Web-based Information and Booking System with comprehensive functionality (available in German and English languages). It currently offers the following features and functions:

- Tourism destination and product database maintained by regional or local tourism offices and accessed via an intranet (Content Management System)
- Reservation/Booking engine including an Electronic Payment System
- Data maintenance module allowing SMEs to maintain their own product data via an extranet, including simple PMS functionality for managing inventory
- Consumer database, enabling manual input and data capture from the full range of electronic processes
- Office suite enabling fulfilment of a wide range of office related activities, e.g. brochure requests
- Statistics and management information tools
- Translation tool
- Event publisher
- Advertising tool
- Currency converter tool
- One-to-one marketing tool
- CRM/address management tool

As well as the Web sites, TIScover recently launched a WAP service: wap.TIScover.com. This enables users to access destination-related interactive information, such as information on weather, avalanche hazards, snow conditions, accommodations, events and so on.

Performance

Key performance indicators are:

Total number of establishments promoted – 4,500
Total number of establishments bookable online – 550

Number of reservation-enquiries:

In the year 2000 TIScover generated more than 332,000 reservation enquiries and bookings. These have risen year on year and first quarter figures for 2001 were looking strong at 172,000. It should be noted that enquiries and reservations are currently counted together so it is not easy to understand what the real-time online bookings statistics are.

Website page views:

1998	4.3 m
1999	18.8 m
2000	134.1 m
2001 (January – April)	18.8 m

Visits:

1998	1.4 m
1999	4.6 m
2000	9.9 m
2001 (January – April)	6.6 m

Data Management

The ethos of the TIScover system is that local tourism organisation should have the responsibility for maintaining their own data to standards specified by TIScover. Individual suppliers can now maintain their own data, directly online, using a password-protected login. This was a particularly important enhancement as it has enabled providers to maintain their own inventory and thereby enable online reservations. TIS GmbH maintains the overall system and management modules on behalf of the Tirol Tourist Board.

Consumer data is owned by the individual provider and the local tourism organisation and held in the TIScover consumer database. Content is written to the database automatically whenever there is an electronic interaction.

Distribution

TIScover, the Austrian Travel Network, has become a well-established brand in its own right for visitor information regarding Austria. In addition to the direct promotion gained via the Internet, Austrian tourism products are also being promoted via TIScover on a number of commercial travel portals and distribution mechanisms, e.g. AOL, Expedia, Travelchannel, T-Online and START Amadeus, which provides links to the GDS system.

Financial

TIS GmbH received start up investment funding from the Austrian Government to build up the TIScover infrastructure. Incomes have, in the past, been derived from tourism operators paying to be featured on the system, and from local tourist boards and other organisations that use the system, paying a licence.

The level of these fees is reasonably modest with, for example, a small accommodation establishment with less than 10 rooms, paying about $30 per month for the most sophisticated level of participation and $10 per month for the simplest. Until 2001 no other fees have been charged to suppliers, but this funding model has been reviewed and it is anticipated that TIScover will change its business model to one that is a mix of commission charges and a low flat fee, as opposed to charging for a licence fee as previously.

TIScover now has considerable volumes of enquiries and transactions being handled through its system, so it believes that it has now achieved the critical mass required to change to a combined model. TIS GmbH has had a positive balance for the last three years and reinvests its profits in future technological developments.

TIS GmbH are committed to investing in the development of their product in the long-term, hence a budget of approximately $2m is set aside each year to ensure that the system continues to develop to meet the needs of its users and retain its place at the fore front of DMS technology.

In the German speaking markets Austria, Switzerland and Germany the systems are owned and run by TIS GmbH under it the TIScover brand. The company is now promoting the system to other destinations, but it expects not to be directly involved in these markets, except as a technical supplier.

TIS GmbH has approximately 45 staff based in Innsbruck as well as offices in Vienna and Carinthia, Austria.

Specific Issues

The Tirol Tourist Board has a major emphasis on training and skills development so as to ensure that data maintenance, back office functions, managing information on the Internet, designing Web sites and editing multimedia material are carried out effectively. Training courses are undertaken by a network of training partners and there is a TIScover Service Centre in each of the Austrian provinces that has as a main aim the development of centres of competence in electronic marketing consulting.

The development of the Web factory, a special unit set up to support the industry create effective additional image sites integrated in the main site, has also been a useful achievement.

Future Development

TIS GMBH plan a continuous programme of development. Specifically expected within the coming year are:
- A new design interface
- Tools for booking and call centres
- mCommerce
- Car Terminals
- Web TV
- Access Point (Public Terminals) Network
- E-Distribution – development of new world-wide distribution channels and markets
- Open TIScover – XML interface (e.g. PMS software for hotels)
- TIScover Club (special offers, discount for members)
- Full GIS Integration inclusive route planner, distance search (i.e. hotel with indoor swimming pool and golf course in 5 km distance)
- Near Search (i.e. near Date-search: the system offers alternative suggestions if there was nothing found in the specified period, i.e. a week later)
- Intelligent Search (builds up on previous search)
- User evaluation (User can evaluate destinations and accommodation)
- Follow – up actions (i.e. Mailings to customers)
- Shop system
- Customisation of home pages and loyalty tools

Conclusion

The Tirol Tourist Board has led the DMS development in Austria with great vision. Establishing TIS GmbH as a separate entity has allowed the company to invest in the continual development of the software, far more than the Tirol Tourist Board could have justified for its own purposes.

The Board has created a software development company that completely understands the operations of a DMO and has built the system upon that understanding. This has enabled the operation of the system within the Tirol a smooth process and that the Tirol has benefited from being part of the development process.

TIS GmbH recognised at an early stage that distribution was going to become the defining factor and has invested time and effort in establishing meaningful relationships with a number of high profile distributors that bring genuine added value to TIS's clients.

The following important factors have lead to the success of TIScover as a DMS:
- The start-up support of the Tirol Tourist Board and the PPP with NTOs and DMOs
- First mover advantage as founder of TIS Gmbh and the establishment of TIS GmbH as an independent operating unit
- The strong emphasis on information science
- The provision of services tailored to TIS main customer in the tourism industry including bookable and non bookable project
- The development of effective partner relationships with a wide range of public and private sector complementary organisations, especially the distributors.
- Distribution
- Traffic Management.

3.5   Case study summary table

A following summary table provides a quick reference chart to compare the five destinations.

Table 1 – DMS Summary Table

DMS functionalities					
	British Columbia	**Finland**	**Seychelles**	**Singapore**	**Tirol**
Destination overview					
Name	Tourism British Columbia	Finnish Tourist Board	Seychelles Tourism Marketing Authority	Singapore Tourist Board	Tirol Tourist Board /TIScover
Ownership status	Crown corporation Government	FTB + commercial subsidiary	Government department	Autonomous government agency	TIS GmbH commercial subsidiary of the board
Location	British Columbia (Canada)	Finland	Seychelles, Indian Ocean	Singapore	Tirol but also in used in Austria, Germany, Switzerland
Number of suppliers in the area	7,000 products, of which 2,800 are accommodation establishments	Room capacity: 63,400 (including 55,000 in hotels & serviced establishments	143 accom. providers	32,000 hotel rooms	4,500 accommodation establishments promoted on the TISCover system
Number of TICs / local / regional DMOs	120 local visitors centres	422 Finnish municipalities and counties	2 TICs	5 TICs	19 regional DMOs, and 159 local tourism offices (TICs)
Structure of the DMO					
Legal Framework	Government agency	Government agency	Government agency	Government agency	TIS commercial, TTB government agency
History of the DMO's DMS development					
Date of first launch	Not known (few years)	Operates a suite of tourism-related networked services since 1992	Planned for July 2001	First use of ICT (with a consumer facing site) in 1995	First investment in 1988 and first version of TIScover launched in 1991
Current Status					
General consumer site	Yes	Yes	Yes	Yes	Yes
Niche consumer site(s)	-	-	Yes	Yes*	-
Tourism industry site	-	Yes	-	Yes	Yes (extranet)
MICE site	-	-	-	Yes	-
Media site	Yes (sub-homepage)	-	Yes	-	-
Trade site	-	-	-	Yes	-
Product database	Yes	Yes	Yes	Yes	Yes
Consumer database	Yes	Yes	Yes	Yes	Yes
Content management tool	Yes	Yes	Yes	Yes	Yes
CRM tools	Yes (through traditional media)	-	Yes	-	Yes

Type of e-commerce facilities					
Real time on-line booking	Yes**	-	-	Yes – via WorldRes	Yes
On-line reservation request	-	Yes	-	-	-
Type of customers services					
TICs	Yes	Yes	Yes	Yes	Yes
Call Centre	Yes	-	Yes		Yes (mainly for industry professionals)
WAP	-	Yes	-	-	Yes
Kiosks	-	-	-	Yes	Yes
TV Channels	-	-	-	-	-
Data management					
Product database ownership	Tourism BC	FTB	STMA	STB	TIS
Method used for update	Collect at Provincial level by Tourism BC. Inventory collected manually by clerks at call centre	Content management tools via PROMIS server	Content management tools via password protected login	Content management tools via trade extranet. Inventory is managed separately via links directly to WorldRes	Content management tools, directly accessible online using a password protected login
Direct updating by suppliers	-	-	Yes***	Yes	Yes
Consumer database ownership	Tourism BC	FTB	STMA	STB	Owned by individual provider and local tourism organisations but is held centrally in the TIScover database
Distribution					
Where is the data content published	Tourism BC 's own site	FTB's own site + print	In STMA's own sites + print	In STB's own sites + marketing activities + through WorldRes	TIScover site, commercial travel portals and distribution mechanisms (AOL, Expedia, TraXXX Focus Online, T-Online and START Amadeus)

Note: '-' indicates that the function is not present

*   Events Websites.

**   Database non-available, could not go through the process.

***   Functions exist, animation in second phase.

4 Consumer Web sites

There are now thousands of destination Web sites on the World Wide Web. Some are commercially operated but many have been developed by DMOs. National tourism organisations promote whole countries, city and regional DMOs promote their designated area, and even small towns and villages often have an online presence.

Many DMOs have been slow to integrate their online activities within the framework of their overall marketing and visitor servicing strategies. Often Web sites have been developed by staff in the IT Department, rather than the marketing department, or worse still, some destination sites have been developed by people as a hobby. The picture is changing now as DMOs recognise the importance of e-marketing and begin to view their online activities as a key part of their overall business strategy and invest in it accordingly.

4.1 Step by step guide to development of a consumer facing destination Web site

Ideally consumer facing Web sites should form part of an integrated Destination Management System as outlined in the previous chapter. However, many DMOs have a limited remit or do not have the resources to build a sophisticated system. In these cases a simple stand-alone site can be effective, provided that the site is integrated with the overall marketing and visitor servicing efforts of all the organisations involved in managing and promoting the destination.

This section offers a Step-by-Step guide to help you plan and develop your Web site to meet the needs of your customers effectively.

Step 1 - Determine the role of your Web site within your overall marketing strategy

The first step is to consider the role of your Web site within your overall marketing strategy. This is particularly important if the destination is managed and promoted by several DMOs.

Start by setting your objectives and thinking about how a Web site might help you to achieve them. Examples may include:

To increase business for your destination and your suppliers, by:
- raising awareness of your destination
- providing information about things to do and places to stay
- providing virtual brochure and itinerary planning functionality
- locking in business by enabling customers to book accommodation or other products easily and securely online
- offering last minute deals and special offers, targeted to consumers with a high propensity to buy.

To generate revenue for your DMO, by:
- taking commission on sales
- selling products and services on line, such as travel insurance, local produce etc
- selling advertising (e.g. to suppliers to be featured on the site or through banner advertising)
- attracting sponsorship

To improve communications and relationships with consumers by:

- featuring news and special offers prominently
- providing 'call me' or 'text chat' functionality
- offering loyalty schemes to existing customers
- encouraging users to complete feedback forms
- encouraging users to participate in chat rooms and newsgroups
- providing opportunities for viral marketing, e.g. e-postcards, send this page to a friend options

To reduce costs by:
- directing enquiries to the Web site rather than by sending a printed brochure
- targeting potential customers more efficiently through relationship marketing and analysis of data on the use of the site
- tracking site usage to better understand consumers needs

To create good PR by providing:
- links to other useful sites and organisations
- corporate information on the site

You need to think carefully about your business case. Do you intend to drive bookings directly to your tourism businesses, or do you wish to become an intermediary and develop an e-commerce facility? What scope is there to partner a commercial company that could handle the e-commerce transactions for you?

If your destination is currently sold mainly through intermediaries then there is less need for you to handle online bookings. Instead, the need is to inspire customers to visit and drive them to existing mechanisms to purchase.

It is particularly important that you analyse your target market segments in terms of their propensity to use the Internet for researching travel information and booking. This will help you determine whether the Web will be an effective distribution channel for your destination and how much of your marketing budget should be transferred to online marketing.

Step 2 - Specifying the Web site functionality

Once you understand your objectives, it is worth spending some time looking at other destination sites to gather ideas on features and functionality. Use the case studies included on later in this Chapter and in the Appendix A as a starting point.

After you have gained a good idea of the sorts of features and functions that can be offered, you need to decide which you would like to include in your site and which weaknesses you want to avoid. Think carefully about what consumers in your priority market segments might require from the site.

Make sure you consider the following when drawing up your list:
- Visibility – make sure your site is easy to find by registering an obvious URL (Web site address) and registering it with the major search engines
- Speed – ensure the site operates quickly, with options to skip loading graphics for users with slow machines
- Design – make sure the site is attractive and easy to use, so that it holds the user's interest, and has intuitive navigation

- Content – provide content that is current, accurate, relevant, and sufficiently detailed. Use video, animation and images in a controlled way to enhance effectiveness, but without detracting seriously from performance
- Search tool – help users to find what they require easily with a search tool that allows them to select a number of criteria before launching a search or by navigating from maps or graphics
- Bookability – make it easy to check availability, book and/or pay for products and services on line, with assured security
- Links – provide links to other sites, reciprocated to allow easy return
- Customisation – recognise customers who have visited the site before and provide information to meet their known requirements
- Help – provide help to navigate the site and/or get help with queries about the content or booking, both online, through e-mail requests and/or by telephone
- Enquiry response – provide an efficient mechanism for handling booking enquiries, where on-line booking is not available
- Language – provide language options for your main markets, so the user can view the site in their own language.

By now, you should have a reasonable idea of what functionality you require on your own site, and you can start work on preparing a functional specification. This will form the basis of your tender document. In it you should describe your objectives, the features you require in your site and the way you expect it to work.

Step 3 - Preparation of a structure and design

Once you have drafted your functional specification, it is time to bring in technical skills. The structure and design of the site will depend on:

Business factors:
- the size of your destination and the number of individual products to be promoted
- the anticipated frequency of updating the information
- the order in which the products should be displayed, e.g. alphabetical, randomised, most recently updated, etc.
- whether secure on-line transactions are required
- the amount of customer data required.

Technical factors:
- the amount of multimedia material you envisage
- the relative importance of the search engines for users in finding the site
- the version of browsers predominant in the target markets – earlier generation browsers imposing considerably more constraints than later ones
- the level of screen resolution to be accommodated.
- whether to host your own Web server or buy the service from an Internet Service Provider.

If you anticipate promoting more than (say) fifty individual products and/or you wish to update the information on a regular basis, then you should build your Web Site so that it can be 'database driven'. This will involve using Active Server Pages, where each page is a template with data dynamically delivered into pre-programmed areas each time the page is activated.

The alternative, 'hard-coding' the information in static HTML pages, is viable for a very simple site, but would be too restrictive for sites where there are regular developments and changes to the data.

Make sure your technical and content people liaise at the early stages. They should work together to develop a navigation plan that shows the relationship between all the screens, and how one leads to another, together with the screen solutions that show the layout and graphic design of each page.

You need to strike a balance between a desire for full multimedia material to stimulate interest and promote the destination and the need to maintain a high standard of performance by the site. Users will not want to wait five minutes while a graphic downloads, no matter how good the quality. Simple and quick is much better than creative and slow.

In terms of your original objectives, if you need to raise awareness of your destination, then you will need more editorial information and less product information. You might want to include a context map, which sets your destination in the context of the world or an readily recognisable area, e.g. Europe. If your objective is to provide a booking mechanism for existing demand, the site needs to be quick and easy for the customer to identify what they want, and then move quickly to book it – for example, Travelocity's "Three clicks to book".

It is possible to create different URLs for different uses, so that you can bring users in at the appropriate point in the site. This is often achieved by putting an extension on the URL – for example, www.holland.com/book .

The design team will develop a look and feel for the site. This should reflect the corporate style of the destination if one exists and tie in with other marketing material and campaigns so that there is continuity for the consumer.

The following points should be considered:
- Keep the site simple and easy to use. Try to avoid a lot of clutter – potentially difficult if you are incorporating advertising
- Many search engines find framed based sites difficult to handle and may ignore them when returning search results. This is less of an issue with later browsers, but, in general, table based sites offer greater flexibility than frames based sites
- Try to design your pages so there is a limited need for scrolling. It is easier for the user if everything is in view on the page, but, if you have to scroll, be sure that core functions, like search and go buttons are located within the initial screen view
- Be careful with font types and sizes and the use of coloured text. Carry out some user trials to ensure all text is easy to read, and remember that you will need two colours for text representing links which will change when activated
- There is a growing convention for left-hand navigation, which you may or may not wish to adopt. Roll-overs and drop down menus are good ways of providing a large menu structure in an uncluttered way
- If you are providing links to other sites, ensure that they appear in a new window within your site, so that the customer will return to your site when he/she closes the others one. Alternatively ensure that your top navigation is carried across to the new site with a link back
- Tunnel and home pages need to incorporate the appropriate keywords high up on the page to ensure maximum visibility with the search engines.

Step 4 - Contracting an agency

It is likely that you will want to buy in some services from an agency. Depending on the capacity of your own team you can buy in services to:
- Work with you to develop the brand, look and feel of your destination
- Work with you to develop the functional specification of your site
- Develop the technical specification
- Build the site
- Organise the data collection and input of the products and editorial
- Host and maintain the site
- Project manage the implementation
- Register the site with the search engines and optimise the site's visibility over time
- Provide analysis of users and their usage of the site.

Guidance on how to contract an agency is given in Section 3.2.

Step 5 - Origination of product information in digital form

Moving towards originating product information in a digital format is a key aspect of cutting costs, improving quality and speeding up the business process. DMOs have traditionally sent out hard copy forms and asked suppliers to complete and return them, perhaps on an annual basis. This is clearly unsatisfactory in today's fast moving world but DMOs are not resourced to handle such a manual exercise much more frequently.

Many DMOs are tackling this problem by providing functionality that allows their suppliers to maintain their own product data in the DMO database, either through a link on their main Web site or through a dedicated password protected extranet. This approach enables suppliers to make changes whenever they occur at a time to suit them, whilst quality is driven up through constant usage and lack of transcription errors.

Usually, product data such as contact details, descriptions, directions and facilities do not change frequently. Inventory and price information is more of a challenge.
These data are really only of value to the consumer if they are completely up-to-date. If you cannot provide that, it is best to only publish a price range and provide alternative means of accessing availability information, such as a direct telephone number.

How your data is delivered to your site will influence the updating requirements:
- Pages built 'on the fly' (meaning that the site queries the database for the data it needs to build the page and then builds it 'in real time' while the user waits). This method means that the data will always have the most recent updates included.
- Period database regeneration (meaning that the data is changed during a period e.g. daily, weekly, either centrally or locally, and is then reconciled at the end of the period by a database regeneration when the records are compared and the changes made). This method means that data may be out-of-date until the next periodic update.
- Hard coded HTML pages. This method involves editing the HMTL code, so monthly changes may be as much as you can manage if you are a small organisation.

Editorial can be originated electronically and stored in a suitable format for retrieving or publishing later. If the resources are very large, you might consider indexing them with a key word search to enable easy access.

Multimedia and editorial resources also need to be managed digitally. You may already have a considerable number of transparencies, prints, video and slides, which can be processed into digital form relatively easily. Keeping such 'imageware' in digital form is a far more effective way of storing, cataloguing and retrieving it than if it were in a physical form. However, there will be a cost, so consider carefully what you may require realistically.

Several issues need to be considered when digitising existing resources:

- The required resolution of imageware (images used for small scale pictures on screen need only be scanned at 72dpi, whereas images to be output as print need a much higher resolution)
- The same image often needs to be scanned and then saved at several different sizes and resolutions
- Video for the Web needs to be compressed and reduced to 256 colours
- A nomenclature needs to be developed which is consistent and logical
- Care should be taken to ensure copyright and data protection rules are respected
- Text data, such as title, originator, keywords etc needs to be input against common terminology standards
- Text formatting should be kept to a minimum to enable it to be retrieved and used in many different applications.

Digital cameras have made the origination of product information in digital form a relatively easy job. However being able to operate a digital camera does not necessarily guarantee a good photograph. The skills of a professional are still required to direct a photo shoot and ensure that the composition of the picture is as good as the technical output.

Text based product information can be originated in several ways:

- Imported from legacy databases
- Manual input by keyboard and mouse
- Optical scanning of forms
- Touch tone telephony
- Voice recognition equipment

Once data has been entered, by whatever method, a rigorous validation exercise should be undertaken to ensure the quality of the data is of the highest standard.

Step 6 - Production of editorial and graphical material, taking account of the special characteristics of the Web medium

Most DMOs want to have an image and content rich Web site, but care needs to be taken to ensure that lengthy download times do not reduce the performance of the site. Video clips should be used sparingly as should plug-ins and animations. Use still pictures with fade and change animation effects to save space and time.

Digital cameras and modern software offer a vast array of features to help you take advantage of the multimedia nature of the Web. Panoramic 360° views, zooms and animations can all be accommodated, but take care that such features actually add value and do not distract your user from the main message.

The use of sound files with other features can sometimes cause difficulties. Video clips generally have sound files incorporated within them so are reasonably easy to accommodate. Separate sound files running together with silent video or change animations can sometimes be difficult to achieve without stilted pauses or the screen going momentarily black. Many users do not have sound cards, or have their sound disabled, so ensure that the site still works without sound.

Provide maps of the destination to help your users orientate themselves, having regard to copyright laws. Overlaying maps at different scales works well. If you need to show your tourism products located on a map graphic, this can be done dynamically from the database using map references, or through GIS technology, but this can be expensive, depending on the sophistication you require. Users do not enjoy reading large amounts of text on screen, so make sure your editorial is punchy, maintains interest and gets over the essential points without becoming too long.

Step 7 – Testing and validating your pilot site

Ensure that your Web development agency builds a beta version of your site, and has sufficient sample data to allow you to thoroughly test the system. Every combination of search criteria needs to be tested at least three times to ensure it returns the expected result.

First you must test and accept the software. You will need to:
- Draw up a software acceptance plan against which you will test the system and sign it off as acceptable
- Draw up a 'bug sheet' on which you will note any failures
- Test each function at least three times to ensure the system returns the expected result
- Regenerate the database and carry out the same tests to ensure they 'stick'
- Make some changes and test again
- Regenerate and test again
- Ensure the 'black box' data is being properly recorded
- Test that the processes for transferring files to the Web server work properly
- Once you have completed the acceptance plan, you will have a number of bug sheets detailing the failure points, these should be sent to the developer to put right
- Do not assume that all of these points will be corrected in one go. Carry out rigorous regression testing, to cater for the situation where the correcting of one fault leads to failures in functionality that was working properly previously.

Secondly you must validate the data. You will need to:
- Proof read all the data carefully for spelling mistakes and typographical errors
- Check the data for accuracy, include some form of validation check by the owner of the data
- Carry out some random checks to verify independently that the data you have been given is correct.

Thirdly you must validate the business processes, where relevant. You will need to:
- Carry out some sample transactions
- Ensure all the necessary response mechanisms are in place
- Put in a system for handling complaints.

Once these stages are complete, move on to a full testing, by revealing your site to business colleagues who understand tourism and have some experience of the Web. Ask them to evaluate the site, including transactions, and then provide you with comments on areas for improvement.

Ideally you should identify some independent users (perhaps students at a local University) and ask them to undertake the same process. It is more valuable if they are not experienced Web users, as this will reveal any weaknesses in your design structure.

Once these stages are complete, you can incorporate any changes into the site and revalidate the software.

Step 8 - Implementation, monitoring and evaluation

Once you have tested your site sufficiently and you are happy for it to be made available to the public, you should publish the URL and register it with the major search engines.

At first you will probably achieve high ratings on the search engines (assuming, of course, that you have paid careful attention to the design of the site). However, the way the systems work means that your position will soon start to slip and you will have to take positive steps to ensure you remain prominently. As the search engines are continuously changing their policies, you may wish to employ the services of a specialist agency to help you maintain your site's position as part of an ongoing maintenance contract.

Once your site is implemented you need to spend time analysing its performance, in terms of:

- the robustness of the site (i.e. monitoring down-time)
- its position in the search engines rankings
- the number of users of designated pages of the site
- the amount of business it is generating.

A key feature of the Internet is that users leave an electronic footprint that is a powerful aid to marketing. It is possible to obtain a wide range of information about users - where they are from, what time of day they visited, how long they stayed, what they looked at and what they brought, but the complexity of the data means that you must interpret it with care. A simple technique is to create different splash pages that are accessed by a URL unique to a particular campaign.

If time and resources permit, correspond with users who provide feedback to gain a deeper understanding about them and their needs, to supplement the statistical data.

There are several other ways of monitoring the performance of your site:

- To encourage users to register their details, provide incentives, such as a special offer, a quiz or a free-draw – for example: "Tell us the top 10 things you like about Holland for a chance to win a free weekend in Amsterdam".
- Set up a newsgroup or chat room
- Provide feedback forms
- Correspond by e-mail whenever possible
- Track the amount of business being generated.

Step 9 - Promoting the use of your Web site

There are three major ways to promote your Web site:

Promote the URL

This is often referred to as 'drive to Web'. It involves publicising your URL so potential customers can log straight onto your site. You can use different splash pages to help you track where the user found out about you, or bring customers into the site at the pages that specifically interest them.

You have many opportunities to publicise your URL and it should be promoted as widely as your telephone number. Print it on all your brochures, stationery, corporate material, promotional literature and in your advertising. Try to adopt a URL that reflects your destination name, something easy to remember like www.visitbritain.co.uk or www.australia.com

You may find that your ideal domain name has already been registered by someone else. This may be because another operator is using the domain name for a legitimate purpose, or it may be a cyber-squatter. If it is the later, you have the option to buy the name at the price asked, or sue for it to be released. The success of the latter action will depend upon the nature of your organisation.

There are now a wide range of 'top level domains' available. These are .com, .co.<country>, .org, .net etc. The recent addition of .info are particularly relevant to the travel industry. When registering your domain name, you might want to consider registering a number of 'top level domains' and have them all pointing to the your main site. You might also consider using a URL that carries your strapline, such as www.aspureasitgets.com, the URL adopted by the Seychelles.

Obtain links from other sites

Establish some links from other Web sites. These can often be arranged on a reciprocal basis at no cost; in other cases you will have to pay a fee. Links to sites of related companies or organisations (e.g. transport providers) tend to work well and can usually be set up on a reciprocal basis.

You may wish to purchase advertising on third party Web sites – for example, the search engines or the online travel agencies. Banner advertising is a traditional form of online advertising, but rates vary enormously depending on the amount of traffic that visits the site. You are usually charged a fee per 'click through'. It is just as important on the Web as it is on any other media to consider how you advert will sit on the screen and what it is surrounded by. The advent of 'banner washing' software (that removes banners as the site loads) means that banners are generally less popular now.

Many of the search engine providers and ISPs offer a registration facility so that you may register your site in particular categories of their directories. This is usually free and can provide a useful promotional platform, as these sites tend to have large volumes of traffic.

Search engines

If your destination is large or well known, you will probably be less reliant on the search engines, particularly if you have an appropriate URL, such as www.holland.com. In this case you stand a good chance of being found by users guessing your URL. Destinations that are less well known or have limited resources, may find the search engines particularly helpful. However, it requires continuing effort to keep your site at the top of the search engine listings. The search engines are constantly changing the criteria they use to rank sites. They have independent editors reviewing sites, but the sheer number of sites being added each day means that much of their work is done automatically.

You need to ensure your agency has a full understanding of the workings of the major search engines when they design your site. You must maximise the visibility of your site, so you need to carefully select a number of keyword s, and use meta-tags to help boost your ranking. Avoid spamming techniques to try and artificially boost your ranking, as many of the search engines are wise to these methods and impose penalties on offenders.

4.2   Critical success factors

The following factors are critical to the successful development and promotion of a consumer facing destination Web site:

- Ensure the message and content of your site is appropriate to your target audience
- Create a lively design, which maintains interest throughout the site, and reflects the nature of your destination and your DMO's corporate or promotional style
- Ensure your content is current and accurate and relevant to the target audience
- Ensure the navigation is intuitive with appropriate short cuts to key sections
- Ensure the functionality of your site meets your business objectives, such as awareness raising, information provision, transaction processing
- Develop partnerships with third parties (e.g. transport operators, mail order retailers) to help deliver content and/or provide a response/sales support mechanism
- Exploit multimedia features carefully, ensure they really add value and don't compromise performance
- Invest in the promotion of your URL and ensure you can be found easily by the major search engines
- Give people a reason to come back to your site and encourage them to do so
- Test the site thoroughly before launching it
- Monitor its performance, evaluate your results and make any amendments on a regular basis
- Employ all three main techniques to promote your site.

4.3   Case studies

In order to provide an overview of good practice by DMOs, thirty Web sites have been evaluated especially for this report. In order to carry out this research a wide range of sites were studied and a matrix of features and functions was prepared against which all sites were evaluated.

The sites were evaluated by tourism professionals, rather than consumers, so there is a risk that the emphasis on certain features has been too great or too little. It is hoped that before the next version of this publication, there will be reliable market research into the attitudes and requirements of consumers in respect of destination sites.

Methodology

Initially more than 100 sites were identified from popular destinations world-wide with an online presence. Many different sources were used to draw up an initial list. These included:

- Travel magazines e.g. Escape Routes, Condé Nast Traveller
- On-line destination guides e.g. Lonelyplanet, CityNet, Fodors, Travelocity, Infoseek, Expedia, Rough Guides, ITN's Travel Network, LeisurePlanet
- Search Engines e.g. metacrawler, Altavisita, Google, Yahoo, Looksmart.com
- Portals providing links to DMOs Web sites e.g. Travel & Tourism Intelligence site, IACVB site, Tourism Offices World-wide Directory.

The 100+ sites were initially reviewed and thirty were selected to be the subject of a more detailed analysis. To be among the thirty, the sites were reviewed against the following criteria. All thirty have at least the first three features:

- Links to regional/local DMOs
- Links to local private sector tourism business
- Interactive trip planner enabling search by category
- Booking facilities
- On-line registration of visitors.

A short summary of the main features of each site and a comparative analysis of the thirty sites are included in Appendix A.

Five sites were subsequently selected to provide the basis of a more detailed case study. They were selected to represent different types of DMO, from countries, cities and regions around the world. Each has an excellent range of functionality and demonstrates effective design principles. Some are long established, while others have only recently adopted e-business principles.

These five case study sites are analysed in some detail in the following sections.

4.3.1 Berlin

In 2000, Berlin, the capital city of Germany, enjoyed its best tourism year ever. The city received 5 million visitors, which represents a 20% increase on 1999. The number of overnight stays also increased by 20.4% reaching 11.4 million. Travel and tourism generate around US$3.5 billion a year to Berlin and support approximately 50,000 jobs.

Berlin Tourism Marketing GmbH (BTM) was established in 1993 with the mission to promote Berlin as a tourist destination world-wide. BTM acts as a service agency for single and group travellers and as an active information broker for the travel industry and the tourist. As well as providing tourist information on Berlin, BTM offers the following services:

- Reserve accommodation for single and group travellers
- Arrange event locations and restaurants for groups
- Arrange tickets for events, fairs, sports events
- Arrange railway tickets
- Arrange car rentals
- Arrange busses and transfers for groups
- Arrange tourist guides in current foreign languages and on special topics
- TICs
- Info Points

Since 1996, Berlin tourism related content on the Internet has been provided via an Internet domain own by the city of Berlin only. At that time the site was in German with only a small section in English. In 1997, in addition to this site, BTM launched its own site, containing only tourism related data in German and English. In 2001, a simple version of the site was introduced in French, Italian and Spanish. The site has been designed and developed in-house by BTM's 'Customer Services' department. The site receives approximately 25,000 unique visits and secures around 600 accommodation bookings per month.

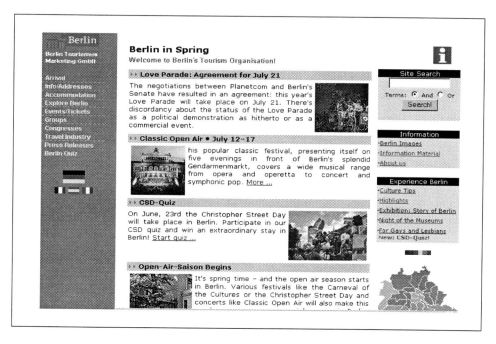

Berlin site homepage – http://www.berlin-tourism.de

The site was awarded first prize in the best Website in the hospitality industry's city category by the jury of the Internet competition 'Destination 2000'.

The site is mainly dedicated to leisure and groups travellers but also provides access to sections (sub-homepages) dedicated to the media, travel trade and MICE.

The site is very rich both in destination content and functionality. It provides special interest information for targeted groups such as young people, disabled, seniors, children and families, gay and lesbians and Jewish providing for each a list of relevant links and describing what the destination can offer this particular audience.

The site is attractive, well structured with a good balance between text and photographs of the destination. It is very easy to use, with a menu bar down the left side of the screen and available on each page of the site with lists of the sub-sections accordingly.

It provides visitors with various options to plan and book their travel arrangements.

- BTM call centre - Visitors can contact BTM via their call centre Monday to Friday (8am - 7pm) and Saturday and Sunday (9am - 6pm).

- On-line reservation request form - Visitors can complete an online reservation request form for a wide range of products including entertainment, sporting events and rail tickets (within Germany). Visitors are asked to provide their credit cards details, but the transaction is carried out offline and a confirmation is sent by e-mail or fax later once the reservation has been processed.

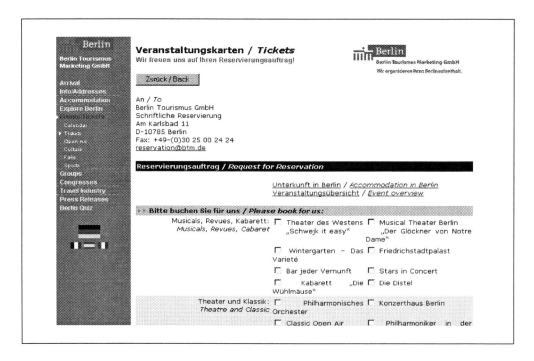

Site on-line reservation request form

- Online booking - Visitors can search the interactive accommodation database and use BTM online reservation service to book their rooms online via a secure server. BTM online accommodation database represents 90% of the total beds available in the city, from hotels, to boarding houses, apartment houses and youth hostels.

- The booking process is made easy with a user-friendly step-by-step procedure with comprehensive guidance available under the 'help' button.

Site step-by-step online booking procedure

There is a section dedicated to group travel that also has the facility for users to complete an online reservation request form.

If visitors choose to book accommodation or order other products online, they are asked to supply contact details, but no further profiling information is requested.

4.3.2   Caribbean Tourism Organisation

The Caribbean Tourism Organisation (CTO) is the international development agency and official body for the promotion and development of tourism throughout the Caribbean. Its members include destination countries and private tourism companies (airlines, hotels, cruise operators and travel agencies) involved in providing holidays and vacations in the region.

Its mission is 'to encourage sustainable tourism that is sensitive to the economic, social and cultural interests of the Caribbean people, preserves their natural environment and provides the highest quality of service to their visitors'.

The Do It Caribbean site has been developed by the CTO and its member countries to provide a Web gateway to all the Caribbean destinations.

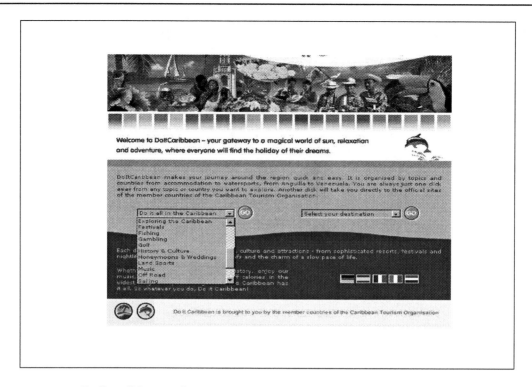

Doitcaribbean site homepage - http://www.doitcaribbean.com

The Do it Caribbean site is a consumer facing site acting as a portal to the Caribbean destinations. Not-surprisingly, acting as a gateway, the site contains very little destination content as its aim is to direct visitors to the sites of the individual Caribbean destinations' official sites. Nevertheless, Do It Caribbean is achieving this in a clever and effective manner, guiding the visitors towards those sites by using a sophisticated indexing method.

The site is visually attractive, very colourful and with pictures illustrating the destination. It is easy to use and well-structured. It has adopted an unusual, but effective, menu format, available in the homepage and consistently throughout the site. There are actually two different drop-down menus enabling to search the material contained within the site following different approaches, either:

- By destinations using the "Select your destination" menu with the list in alphabetical order of all the destinations/islands within the Caribbean.
- By special interest/or general topics, using the drop down menu "Do it all in the Caribbean" with themes such as accommodation, adventure, African American Caribbean, conferences, diving, eating out, ecotourism, exploring the Caribbean, festivals, fishing, gambling, golf, history and culture, honeymoons and weddings, land sports, music, off-road, sailing, special events, spectator sports, watersports.

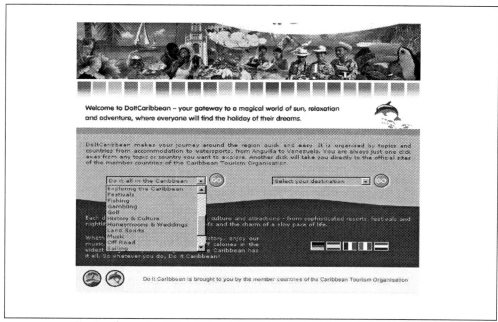

Illustration of all the themes covered in the DoItCaribbean site

Each destination has its own sub-homepage. They all follow the same format with:

- A link to the destination's official site
- A location map with a yellow arrow locating it within the Caribbean and its neighbouring countries
- Brief description of the destination
- "Did you know?" section including a short statement on main historical fact or unusual facts about the destination
- Internal link to the destination 'essential facts' page.

Example of destination "essential facts" page

Each theme also as its own sub-homepage with brief general comment on that theme/area of interest and a list of Caribbean destinations linking to pages on those destinations sites corresponding to the specific area of interest. This is a good indexing system. As an illustration, in the 'Eating out' sub-homepage, if the visitor click on Bahamas, this will link him directly to the Eating out/food page of the destination site and not the homepage, enabling visitors to go straight to the information they need.

"Eating out" theme sub-homepage

The site also provides an enhanced site key word search facility. This facility is accessible from the homepage as well as from every page of the site by clicking on the 'Search Do it Caribbean icon' (the blue dolphin icon) that leads to the 'Do it Caribbean Search page'. It is quite detailed as it allows visitors to select a few criteria (via a drop down menu) to narrow their search.

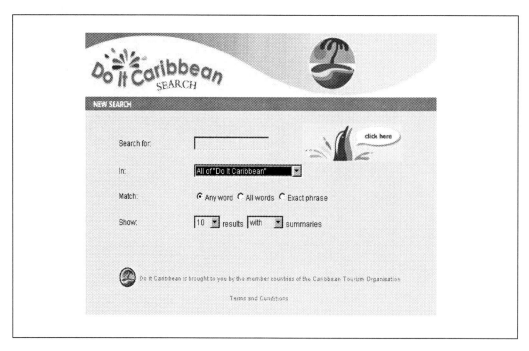

When visitors first enter the site they are encouraged to order the free Caribbean Vacation Planner by the appearance of a small window promoting the brochure. Visitors can also order the brochure at a later stage through their visit to the site as an 'order brochure' icon is available in the site. Visitors are asked to provide their contact details and answer some short questions.

4.3.3   New Zealand

International tourism contributes 4.7% to New Zealand's GDP. Despite strong growth over the last ten years, it remains a small destination in global terms with a market share of 0.45%. Nevertheless, Tourism New Zealand believes that the number of visitors could reach 2.5 million over the next five years and that the tourism industry could generate US$7.7 billion by that time. Visitor numbers topped 1.824 million in 2000.

As part of its global marketing campaign, Tourism New Zealand has identified the Internet as a key communication component and in July 1999, the first phase of the consumer Web site www.purenz.com was launched. The site had two main objectives:

- To encourage overseas visitors to come to New Zealand
- Connect potential visitors with the industry within New Zealand

The site was designed by a Wellington based company, Shift, and Tourism New Zealand staff continue to work closely with the team at Shift to incorporate the developments of the site.

The site is aimed at long-haul visitors from North America, Europe and Japan and short-haul visitors from Australia. The site is driven by a product database and to ensure the quality of the site content providers are encouraged to enter their own details into the database.

With a total marketing budget of US$ 22 million per annum, Tourism New Zealand can not afford to take the '100% Pure New Zealand' Campaign to all its 21 markets so the long term brand building focus on its 7 larger markets: Australia, UK, Germany, USA, Japan, Singapore and Taiwan. The site received 87,452 unique visitors in May 2001.

PureNZ.com is currently undergoing a significant revamp and will be re-launched in September 2001. Development will focus on improving:

- Site navigation
- Search functionality
- Visual content including the better use of images and maps.
- Site content in terms of depth and tone.

A content management system (CMS) will also be introduced in July and the operator database that holds the product listings showcased on PureNZ.com is also undergoing development.

New Zealand site homepage - http://www.purenz.com

The '100% Pure New Zealand' site is a tourism portal for New Zealand. Tourism New Zealand encourages visitors to make direct contact with the individual tourism operators featured within the online database and provides link to their own sites whenever it is possible. It does not provide a booking service, but does provide links to other DMO sites within New Zealand.

The site tries to focus on the visitor's experience, encouraging visitors to consider the destination for the type of experience it offers. This is done primarily through five themes or emotional realms e.g. wilderness, thrill zone, heartland, kiwi spirit and chill out and three functional realms e.g. Transport, accommodation and package Tours. Visitors can then find out about New Zealand not only by geographical location, but also based on their emotional needs as a traveller.

Each 'theme' has its own sub-homepage. Visitors can look at the entire listing by categories or choose to use the key word search facility of the theme restricting their search to within that theme. Visitors can also use the drop down menu facility to select a specific location and restrict their search to that.

Wilderness theme page

The site contains a general site search facility by key word enhanced by the option of using drop down menu to specify in which section the search should be undertaken.

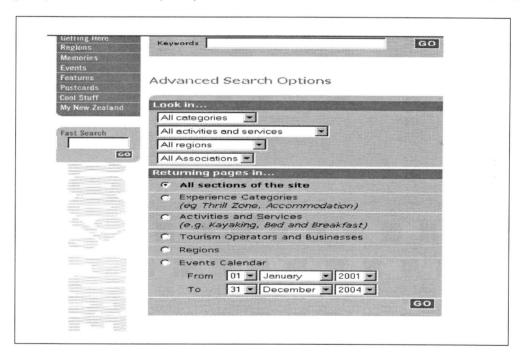

Advanced key word facility

The overall information contained within the site is divided into the following main areas:

- Themed sections: wilderness, thrill zone, heartland, kiwi spirit and chill out
- Service sections: accommodation, transports, events, etc
- Activities
- Individual Tourism Operators
- General information section e.g. about each region, how to get here

- Tools: discussion forum, e-postcards, Web testimonials about experiences in New Zealand, personal folder, screen savers, wall papers

The site is attractive with a consistent look and feel throughout, with the exception of two sub-homepages. These are 'Footprints' (travel journal/magazine) and 'Aussie Breakaway Holidays' (special offers) dedicated to Australian visitors with a link to a third party site for special offer booking.

The site is easy to use with the information and service menus on the left and the theme menu across the top. A range of colour ways is used to differentiate between sections.

'My New Zealand' (the site's personal folder/on-line brochure) is an excellent facility enabling visitors to save, print and e-mail their selected programme and also locate the different items on a map.

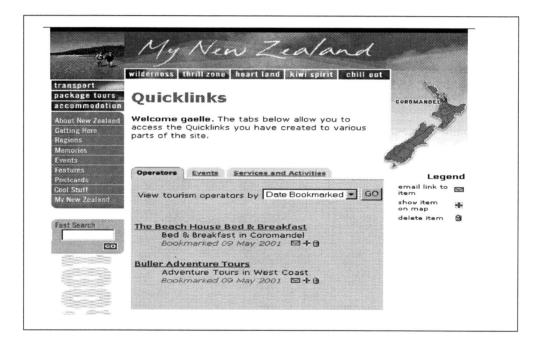

Site personal folder

Users are asked to register and specify a username and password in order to access and use their personal 'My New Zealand' folder. If they also wish to join the mailing list (with updates on special offers), they are asked to state their country of origin and e-mail address. Tourism New Zealand will then be able to provide them with offers directly relevant to their outbound country. On a random basis, when leaving the site, visitors are asked to participate in a survey, which is a good way of evaluating the site.

4.3.4 Singapore

Singapore is at the heart of Asia, receiving 7.6 million visitors per annum, 70% of which are from within Asia, with other primary markets being the US, Canada and northern European. Singapore is a premier destination for corporate meetings; it is an important economic and trading hub with a base of over 5,000 multinational companies. It has been the number one convention city within Asia consistently for the last 20 years. It has 32,000 hotel rooms, a staggering 50% of which are 5 star. Tourism accounts for 5% of GDP.

A fuller description of the destination and the Singapore Tourist Board is given in Section 4.3.4.

Singapore site homepage - http://www.newasia-singapore.com

The site is rich both in destination content and in its provision of visual information about the destination. This is a visually attractive site with photographs as wallpaper (on the homepage as illustrated above and each section sub-homepage). The site also provides an animated location map featuring flight routes and times which is good for setting the context for the user.

The site contains a main menu across the bottom with general tools and information and a main destination information menu on the right of the screen with products/services. The site is easy to navigate and a site map is also available.

The site is highly functional and uses some of the latest ICT tools to support its users, including a Text Chat service. This 'live chat' feature on the site enables users to link up with a Singapore specialist agent for assistance with enquiries and bookings using a text editor.

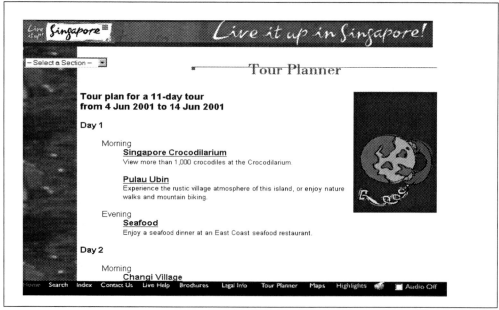

Illustration of the Text Chat Service

Users can search the product/service database either via listings (e.g. for attractions, shops, hotel/golf packages) or by specifying defined criteria (for accommodation, regional tours, festivals and events).

A particularly good tour planner enables visitors to create a customised itinerary based on their duration of stay and interests for tours up to 14 days. As mentioned, visitors are asked to enter their start and end dates and to select their areas of interest from a comprehensive list of topics. The search returns, for the appropriate dates, a tailor-made, day-by-day itinerary of tours detailed by morning, afternoon and evening activities. Visitors can learn more on each featured item by following the internal link to this particular product entry with details including description, contact details, location, opening hours, admission fee, touring time etc.

Illustration of the Tour Planner

Real-time online accommodation and packages booking, powered by WorldRes, is available via www.stayinsingapore.com. Visitors can search accommodation by specifying their check in dates, number of nights, property type, price range and amenities. They are then provided with a list of establishments with available rooms for their dates and matching their requirement.

They can then choose one of these establishments, select a room and complete the reservation by providing their personal contact details (including e-mail address) and credit card number (guaranteed by WorldRes's secure server). At the end of the reservation process, visitors are provided with a reservation confirmation number that together with their e-mail address will enable them at a later stage to view, change or cancel their reservation online. Alternatively, if they have registered as a Stay in Singapore member, they can use their username and password.

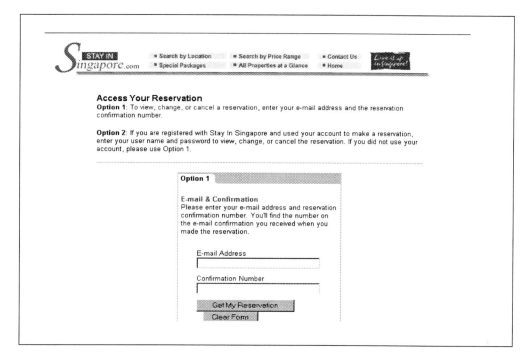

Stay In Singapore member log-in

STB is not actively involved in CRM at this stage. Nevertheless, personal information (contact details, gender, age, interest, occupation) is gathered when users are asked to register as a member of the STB mailing list to receive their newsletter. STB also gives users the opportunity to comment on their trip to Singapore (e.g. their general impression of the destination, preferred aspect, suggestions for improvements).

4.3.5   Tourism Vancouver

In 1999, Greater Vancouver received 8.3 million overnight visitors, of which nearly half were foreign visitors. It was estimated that Greater Vancouver would attract over 8.6 million visitors in 2000, generating US$2.5 billion in spending and supporting approximately 108,000 jobs.

Established in 1902, Tourism Vancouver is the Greater Vancouver marketing organisation (a non-profit business association). It is focused on increasing leisure travel, meeting and events business and encouraging visitors to stay longer and visit more often. Its mission is: 'to lead the co-operative effort of positioning Greater Vancouver as a preferred travel destination in all targeted markets world-wide, thereby creating opportunities for member and community sharing of the resulting economic, environmental, social and cultural benefits.'

Tourism Vancouver has over 1,150 members in the tourism industry and related fields.

Vancouver site homepage- http://www.tourismvancouver.com

Tourism Vancouver site is an excellent site and easy to use. It is mainly dedicated to leisure travellers but provides access to sub-homepages targeted at the travel trade, MICE, media and tourism industry.

The design is simple, with photographs (including a photo gallery and e-postcards) providing a good visual experience of the destination. The photograph situated as part as of the menu bar (in the homepage above, featuring a sea-kayak) changes as visitors browse through the site. The site uses different colours that help the user to navigate easily using a simple, but well-structured menu that is consistent throughout the site.

A complete range of products and services is accessible through an interactive database search facility: accommodation, airlines, events, attractions, activities, restaurants, tour operators, conference facilities, local services, shops and retail.

Visitors can search by specifying the main category and sub-category or they can narrow the search further by using the key word facility. They also have the option to view the results sorted alphabetically.

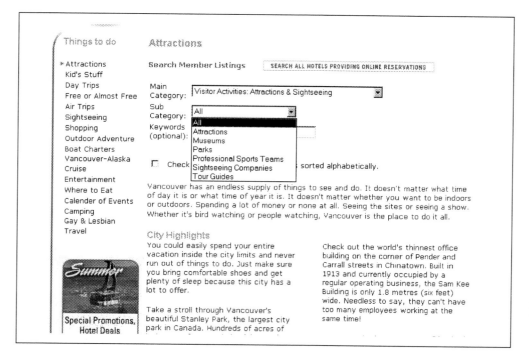

Illustration of Search facility by category

The results provide the minimum of information: short description and contact details (including links or URL of the provider site where it exists). More detailed information is available for accommodation establishments (rate, amenities, photographs etc) that can be booked online.

As in the case of Singapore, the online booking of some accommodation establishments and packages are powered by WorldRes, which provides secure online reservations with instant confirmation. In the case of Tourism Vancouver, the search of all hotels providing online booking is initiated via an interactive map enabling visitors to select the location where they wish to find accommodation.

Visitors are then provided with a list of establishments in the area they have selected, with brief description, rate and property type. They can select an establishment and view more detailed information including photographs and check availability for the dates of their choice. If the establishment has rooms available, they can choose the type of room they are interested in and can complete their booking. The booking process is similar to the one explained for Singapore and visitors also have the facility to view, change or cancel their reservation online at a later date.

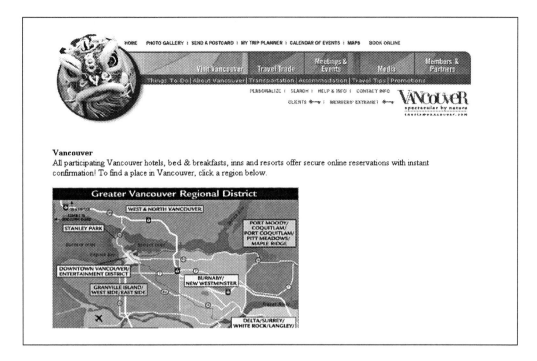

Illustration of the interactive map used to search for accommodation

Some packages can be book by telephoning the HelloBC call centre that is operated by the provincial DMOs, see the DMS Case Study for British Columbia in Section 3.4.1.

The site provides visitors the option of configuring the site's homepage to suit their personal preferences. This includes changing their personal profile (name, contact details, country, age, sex, type of visitors).

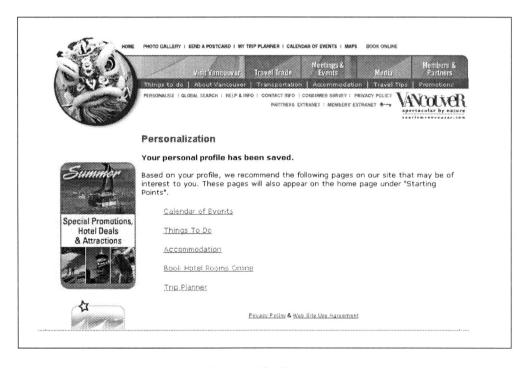

Personalization page

The site offers visitors the facility to use their 'trip planner'. This is a very standard facility enabling visitors to save and print (by using the print option from their browser's file menu) important addresses of product or service providers.

Tourism Vancouver has designed an online customer survey in order to gather information on their visitors' profiles, use of the Internet for travel information and planning and their opinions and suggestions on the site. This is not compulsory and there is no specific incentive to encourage them to participate.

4.3.6   Key features of a consumer Web site

From the analysis of the five DMO sites, a number of key features emerge as important. These are:

The homepage

The homepage is the entry point to the Web site. It should be attractive and enticing and clearly communicate the content of the site and help form a positive perception of the destination.

While being quite different in appearance and content, the homepages of the DMOs Websites have a number of characteristics in common. Generally they all imparted a substantial amount of information, but were clearly and simply laid out. They all provided a list of the contents of the site. Many provided a brief textual description of the destination, photographs, graphics and a logo or brand. The Singapore homepage is visually attractive with a special theme promoted (matching photograph and caption) that changes regularly. The homepage of the Canada site is well structured and also provides attractive photograph illustration of the destination.

The appearance of Web pages

The appearance of every page within a Web site is important. Looking at Web pages is a highly visual experience, thus, while transmitting information is the goal it is critical that the Web pages provide it in an innovative and interesting way, without clutter or confusion.

This can be done by using a variety of different methods: substantial blocks of text can appear unexciting, be difficult to read and require more mental effort from the user than alternative forms of information transmission. The use of different colours, pictures, graphics, maps, tables and symbols break up blocks of text and increase readability. The Canada site and Berlin site demonstrate good practice in that respect offering a good balance between the content itself and attractive photographs of the destination.

The use of multimedia can also be an effective way of maintaining consumer interest in a site. While forms of multimedia can take a long time to load, virtual tours and live cams are additional ways of making a site more interesting. The Singapore site provides a very rich visual experience of the destination with photographs snapshots and video. The Copenhagen site is also a good example, providing short video of Copenhagen and Denmark, 360 degree panoramic pictures, and photo galleries. The Trentino site provides a flash movie and Web cam.

General information contained within the site

The significance of the way information is transmitted increases if a destination has a particularly strong culture or customs, or special circumstances that should be known to prospective travellers. Additionally, information about how to get to a destination, its climate, geography, activities, events, history, telecommunications and public transport, will be very important for those individuals who do not have a base of knowledge about a destination.

Background information is often composed primarily of text. It is the kind of information that can increase clutter in a Web site. Thus the site should enable users to easily access the information, or skip it if they so desire. The Egypt, Malaysia, Mexico, Thailand and Singapore sites contain comprehensive information in this section as well as an FAQ section useful as a way of deflecting enquiries.

Interactivity – interactive trip planners and virtual brochures

The Internet enables consumers to take an active role in the marketing process. Users are more likely to stay interested in a site's information if they have an active role in selecting that information.

- *Interactive database search facility*

  Interactive functionalities such as database searches enable visitors to control which information to view and which to skip. Users can choose to search a type of tourism products and set specific criteria to refine the search result, e.g. location, price, availability and facilities.

  In that respect, the Ontario and Japan sites are good illustrations, enabling visitors to undertake detailed search for accommodation, events, attractions, packages, activities, tours. As a general guide DMO sites tend to focus on providing detailed search facilities for accommodation and events and use a more listing-type approach for other tourism products.

- *Interactive trip planner*

  The interactive trip planner generates an itinerary based on a number of criteria and specifications selected by the user. Particularly good tour planner facility is available in the Singapore site, which enables visitors to create a customised itinerary based on their duration of stay and personal interests. On the Irish site, a route planner is provided so that visitors can plot their destination(s) on a map and get detailed directions on how to get there.

- *Virtual brochure / personal folder*

  The virtual brochure allows users to save selected content to a clipboard, which they can save and/or print. In some cases, visitors have to register as a member to be able to use this functionality. This enables the DMO to capture further personal information from the user, which is used to enhance the DMOs customer database. The Switzerland is an example of good practice.

- *Online booking facilities*

  More and more DMO sites are now providing booking service for visitors: either by encouraging visitors to contact their call centres, by providing on-line reservation request or ultimately by providing real time on-line booking.

Most of the sites providing e-commerce functionality are only dealing in accommodation. The Berlin site is a good illustration of a DMO that has extended its portfolio to include on-line reservation facilities (request form) for musicals, theatre, museums, sport events and trains in addition to its accommodation. The London site is also an example.

- *Chat/Forum/Message Boards*

  Some sites, particularly Egypt, New Zealand and Switzerland, offer the facility for visitors to communicate with each other and discuss and share their experience of the destination

  Only two of the sites reviewed, the British Tourist Authority site and the Singapore Tourist Board site, have embraced the latest Text Chat technology that enables users to have a text based conversation with a DMO assistant. This service really adds value to the user experience and provide the 'human touch' that is often lost when businesses migrate many of their process online.

Site features

The following features contribute to a site's overall usability:

- *Link to the home page on every page*

  This is particularly important for large sites that contain numerous pages and internal links, where it is easy to get lost within the site. A home page link on every page will ensure that the user always has some kind of base to which they can return if they want to view a different category of information. This is now a basic navigation feature and adopted by almost all sites.

- *A list of the main contents on every page*

  This enables users to move between the main topic areas without necessarily going via the home page. The inclusion of this feature makes navigation very simple and intuitive. In that respect, the Edinburgh and Budapest sites are good illustrations.

- *A site map or index*

  This can be very useful to provide a quick overview of the site content. This is especially useful when there are a number of sections with sub menus. The Germany site uses different colours for the main headings and clear sub-headings with list of content all providing a direct link. The Ontario and New Zealand sites also provide guidelines on how to use the site in this section. Copenhagen contains an alphabetical site index covering all the major content areas.

- *Sub-menus*

  The use of rollover techniques on the main menu headings to expose the sub menus is very effective. The Ontario site uses this technique. In the Mexico site, the sub menus appear indented from the main heading that provides users with a simple site index at a high level.

- *Search results*

  Users get quickly frustrated when their searches are repeatedly unsuccessful. It is therefore essential for a Web site to be simple and easy to navigate, only offering the chance to refine the search when there is sufficient content in each section to ensure that the user is returned a reasonable list from which to choose.

- *Key word search*

  The presence of a search facility can save users a lot of time. However it can be very frustrating for the user if they type in a keyword and get a nil result. It is very helpful to have a short explanation of how the search tool is configured so that the user can understand its limitations. Results are often displayed as a percentage match, according to how closely related it is to the keyword entered. The Mexico site is a good example, and the Germany and Budapest sites provide an effective explanation of the search facility.

- *Languages*

  The Internet is being used by rapidly increasing numbers of people who do not speak English as their first language. In December 2000, research by Global Reach Background (www.glreach.com) identified that more than 52% of the world-wide on-line population do not have English as their native language. Thus it is becoming increasingly important to provide sites in different languages in order to be accessible for a wider audience. Increasing numbers of sites are providing their sites in more than one language: Singapore, Switzerland, Thailand, Britain and Wallonie/Bruxelles are good examples.

Some DMOs have decided to offer different gateways for their main target markets clearly dedicated to the country's main segment markets. Singapore Tourist Board and British Tourist Authority both show good practice in that respect allowing their Manager in the territory to create a unique look and feel for the site and create content relevant and appealing to the particular market and different segments within the market.

Language selection is usually made on the tunnel or home page. Once a language is selected it is important that all pages are refreshed in the chosen language for the duration of the session.

Special features can also contribute to enhance and complement the standard material contained within a site:

- *Context and location maps*

  It is very helpful for visitors if the site includes a map showing the destination in the context of the world or an easily recognisable area. Where the map is displayed on the site will depend on how well known the destination is in its target markets. Hence a relatively unknown destination like the Seychelles needs to show a context map as part of the opening sequence of the site. Somewhere better known, like Britain, could include it in a dedicated section that is easy for users to skip.

- *Directional maps*

  Maps to assist users to find their way to specific areas or tourism products are very useful. A number of commercial map suppliers exist but an integrated solution can be expensive. The Budapest, Canberra and Pennsylvania sites are good examples.

- *Currency converter*

  This can be very useful as usually prices/rates are only provided in the currency of the destination. The Germany and Spain sites provide good examples.

- *E-Postcards*

  Many sites provide the facility to e-mail postcards or greetings from the site. A user chooses an image from a gallery displayed within the site, and types a message to the recipient, leaving both e-mail addresses. Subject to the data protection provisions, these e-mails can be used for CRM campaigns. Seychelles provides an excellent example of this functionality.

- *Weather*

  Sites often provide short-range forecasts and current weather conditions for the destination; examples include the Germany, Switzerland and Trentino sites.

5   Networks for intermediaries

Most DMOs have well-established off-line relationships with intermediaries such as the travel trade, tour operators, meetings and incentive travel organisers and travel media. Because these groups are generally smaller in number and easier to contact than end consumers, it is relatively easy to migrate these relationships online through the creation of Web sites designed specifically for their use, push (e-mail) marketing and the application of the principles of customer relationship management, discussed in Section 1.4.

This section considers how you can work online with the three main target groups.

5.1   Travel trade intermediaries

If your destination has a significant amount of its businesses delivered through travel trade intermediaries such as tour operators and travel agencies, it is useful to provide a site (or a section of your main site) dedicated to their specific needs.

The most effective thing you can do to support intermediaries is to ensure that your destination is well marketed at a general level, so that awareness is high and customers ask for your destination when they contact a travel agency or tour operator. However this kind of general marketing is expensive and you need to use all your creativity to ensure that the intermediaries themselves can play their role in promoting your destination.

Travel trade intermediaries can support you in three ways:
- Include your destination and a selection of products as packages in their own brochures. This in itself will help to raise the profile of your destination
- Become specialists (or at least knowledgeable) in promoting your destination, which means they will have a strong product knowledge and be ambassadors for your destination in their area
- Partner with you to run special promotions in their outlets, or campaigns to their customer databases, with special offers, perhaps provided by some of your providers.

You should establish and maintain a relationship with as many intermediaries as you have the capacity to deal with. Use of CRM techniques will make this much easier, enabling you to deal with more companies more effectively. To do this you will need:
- A good contact management system, which will allow you to manage all your intermediary contacts, gather a range of information about them and record interactions between you and them
- CRM tools to filter the records and be able to target specific companies with particular messages
- Creative marketing personnel and a budget so new initiatives can be developed to engage companies in novel promotions and campaigns.

5.1.1 Features of a travel trade Web site

If you would like to produce a dedicated site or a section within your main site, to promote your destination to travel trade intermediaries, you might wish to consider including some or all of the following features:

- General destination material to help raise awareness of managers and staff. This will be broadly similar to that which will appear on your consumer site
- Detailed practical information to help staff answer queries from their customers, such as information about visas, currency, language, customs and religion, shop or bank opening hours, health, driving tips etc
- Information about travel options, e.g. the major carriers, airlines, ferries, rail and road links
- Details of the services provided by official tourist information centres, including a directory of them
- Access to the full product database, accommodation, attractions, restaurants, events etc, possibly including rates. (There may be a need to display varying levels of trade and retail rates, which would need to be done on a password protected basis to ensure that commercial confidentiality is maintained.)
- Online reservations for the full range of bookable product, or just accommodation, on the basis of either agreed net rates or additional commission
- Special promotions for intermediaries to offer their customers e.g. the Berlin Welcome Card or the London Pass
- Publications order form, so that companies can order hand-books or training manuals
- A directory of travel agents, searchable by services offered, affiliation or company name, including optional registration to help build up your contacts database
- Opportunities for tourism businesses to place advertisements to promote their services to travel trade intermediaries, who in turn will promote them to their customers
- Details of DMO personnel and information about the services and support they can offer the travel trade - e.g. familiarisation trips, destination product information/literature, special offers, VIP passes to major exhibitions
- Details of DMO's plans for attendance at forthcoming travel trade exhibitions and trade fairs
- Details of new products or initiatives that may be relevant to intermediaries, e.g. a new attraction opening
- Access to images and multimedia content in a digital format - a key benefit for tour operators, Destination Management Companies and journalists.

As for consumer Web sites, you may need to offer a number of languages, according to your key markets and the languages in which they are comfortable to do business.

5.1.2 Implementing a travel trade Web site

If you would like to develop a travel trade Web site, refer to the step-by-step guide for implementing a consumer Web site detailed in Section 4.1. The same broad steps will be required. Consider the list in 5.1.1 and decide which are the most relevant features and functionality for you and your travel trade contacts.

Be sure to involve the staff responsible for travel trade marketing when you are drawing up your user requirements and functional specifications. These tools will become increasingly important for them in their work, so their input is key.

101

5.1.3   Online travel intermediaries

DMOs must increasingly deal with the new breed of online travel agencies and reservation agencies such as Travelocity or Expedia, as well as traditional intermediaries like major travel companies such as Thomas Cook, TUI or Thompsons or Kuoni. Potentially, these companies may provide an effective way of extending the reach of your marketing and sales efforts. These new channels of distribution need to be evaluated in the same way that DMOs have assessed the value of traditional channels.

Not all product providers may wish to place allocation with the online intermediaries as it presents a challenge for inventory management that many are unable to face and margins are often perceived to be lower because of the commissions charged. For those that are well equipped to serve these channels, the opportunities are well worth test marketing.

Synchronisation of the database content needs to be very carefully monitored to ensure the data is current and accurate. Strict booking terms and conditions need to be in place to protect all parties involved in the transaction e.g. the supplier, the DMO, the intermediary and the consumer – all have a legal obligation to meet.

5.1.4   Examples of good practice

There are several sites that provide good practice examples.
- www.berlin-tourism.de
- www.tourismvancouver.com
- www.ste.com.sg

5.2   Meetings, incentives, conferences and exhibitions (MICE) organisers

If your destination has a strong MICE product you should develop a site (or a section of your main site) dedicated to the specific needs of MICE organisers and implement a programme of e-mail communication, applying the principles of CRM. This sector is highly appropriate for the use of these media, because both buyers and sellers have a high level of Internet usage for business.

To take advantage of the opportunities, you will need:
- A good contact management system, which allows you to manage all your MICE contacts, gather a range of information about them and record interactions between you and them
- CRM tools to filter the records and be able to target regular organisers with particular messages
- Creative marketing personnel and a budget to promote the destination to MICE organisers
- An effective response mechanism to be able to develop bids to win major events and respond appropriately to every day enquiries

5.2.1   Features

The features of a MICE site are very broadly similar to a Travel Trade site. Consider the list below and decide which are appropriate to you.

- General editorial material to help raise awareness of the destination. This will be broadly similar to that which will appear on your consumer site but with some additional content about its particular appeal to the MICE sector

- Detailed practical information, such as information about visas, currency, language, customs and religion, shop or bank opening hours, health, driving tips etc

- Information about travel options, e.g. the major carriers, airlines, ferries, rail and road links

- Details of the services provided by official tourist information centres, including a directory of them

- Full details of MICE product, venues, accommodation, catering, tours, gifts, PCO services, translators, transport, technical equipment, entertainment etc

- Access to the full leisure product database, accommodation, attractions, restaurants, events etc including conference or group rates

- Online reservations for the full range of bookable product or access to a special bed bank dedicated to a particular event

- Special promotions for MICE organisers to offer their clients e.g. the Berlin Welcome Card or the London Pass

- Details of DMO personnel and information about the services and support they can offer the MICE organiser e.g. familiarisation trips, destination product information/literature, special offers, etc.

- Optional registration to receive future information and offers about the destination e.g. new conference venues, function venues, etc. This feature helps to build up the database of MICE organisers.

5.2.2   Implementing a MICE Web site

If you would like to develop a MICE Web site, refer to the step-by-step guide for implementing a consumer Web site detailed in Section 4.1. The same broad steps will be required. Consider the features above and decide which of them will be appropriate to your circumstances.

Be sure to involve the staff responsible for MICE sector marketing when you are drawing up your user requirements and functional specifications. These tools will become increasingly important for them in their work, so their input is key.

5.2.3   Examples of good practice

The following sites offer good practice examples:
- www.berlin-tourism.de
- www.newasia-singapore.com
- www.tourismvancouver.com

5.3   Media site

To raise awareness of your destination it is helpful to work closely with journalists and other media personnel. Most destinations carry out some form of PR activity, and this role can be effectively extended through the development of a Web site (or a section of your main site) dedicated to the specific needs of the media.

Your media audience may include:
- Travel writers
- Feature editors
- Advertorial sales agents
- Photographers
- Film makers
- Travel programme makers
- News media, local and national.

It is important that you establish and maintain a relationship with your media contacts. As before, using CRM techniques makes this much easier, so you can now deal with a greater volume of contacts much more effectively. To do this you will need:
- A good contact management system, which allows you to manage all your media contacts, gather a range of information about them and their publications and record interactions between you and them
- CRM tools to filter the records and be able to target specific people or organisations with particular messages
- An effective mechanism for dealing with day-to-day enquiries
- A clippings service, or media archive, where all published articles, features and programmes can be stored, catalogued and retrieved.

5.3.1   Features

The features of a media site are detailed below. Many are similar in nature to a Travel Trade and MICE sites, but there are a number of specific features of relevance just to media representatives.   Again think about how many languages you need to support.
- General editorial material to help raise awareness of the destination. This will be broadly similar to that which will appear on your consumer site
- Detailed practical information, such as information about visas, currency, language, customs and religion, shop or bank opening hours, health, driving tips etc, again this is similar to your consumer sites
- Access to the full leisure product database, accommodation, attractions, restaurants, events, travel options and tourist information office services
- Online reservations for the full range of bookable product (if appropriate)
- Details of press conferences, current press releases or photo opportunities
- Story ideas, itineraries, event listings, interview contacts and useful links to encourage the journalists to produce articles
- Online forms to apply for press accreditation, filming permits or customs clearance

- A multimedia library to provide access to a wide range of digital images and film, with the ability to download or order online or through an e-mail order facility
- A press file or shopping basket function to allow users to gather a number of items into a single place before downloading or printing it
- Details of DMO personnel and information about the services and support they can offer media representatives e.g. familiarisation trips, product orientation collateral
- Optional registration to receive future information of interest. This feature helps to build the media contacts database.

5.3.2 Implementing a Media Web site

If you would like to develop a Media Web site, refer to the step-by-step guide for implementing a consumer Web site detailed in Section 4.1
The same broad steps will be required. Consider the features above and decide which of them will be appropriate to your circumstances.

Be sure to involve the staff responsible for travel media when you are drawing up your user requirements and functional specifications. These tools will become increasingly important for them in their work, so their input is key.

5.3.3 Examples of good practice

The following sites offer good practice examples:

- www.media.australia.com
- www.aspureasitgets.com/media *
- www.visitbritain.com/corporate/media_room.htm
- www.travelcanada.ca/travelcanada/eng/media
- www.berlin-tourism.de/english/presse/index.html

[* This site will be launched publicly in December 2001.]

6   Networks for the tourism industry

6.1   Getting SMEs wired and skilled

As a DMO you have a strong interest in helping members of your tourism industry become more competitive, and one of the ways you can do this is to create an online tourism industry network (technically, an extranet). Through this mechanism your stakeholders can access a wide range of functions and communicate with you, and each other, on a day-to-day basis.

It is important for you to establish how many of your tourism suppliers are online. With the increasing ubiquity of low cost computers and special connection deals from ISPs, more and more businesses now have access to the Internet for e-mail and use of the Web.

In many destination areas where Internet penetration is low, action has been taken to provide grants or incentives to encourage businesses to get wired and skilled. In some areas, public Internet points provide low cost access, e.g. at a library, post office, tele-working centres or Internet cafés. Other initiatives include support for those wishing to gain or update their computer skills or to get free or low cost consultancy from a business advisor on how to exploit the Web.

If you conclude, perhaps through a survey or a workshop, that a reasonable proportion of your tourism suppliers are able and willing to participate in an online community, then a tourism industry network could provide a key focus for your activities.

It is important for all your stakeholders, staff, trade etc, to see this online network as an organisational resource, part of their everyday activities and not as something special or extra to their existing workload. It should be their first port of call for information about tourism, and ideally be used as their browser home page.

To maximise use of the network, you need to ensure that a wide range of interesting and useful information and services is available and give users the reason to visit again and again. All players need to take responsibility for producing content for the site and maintaining it online.

By embracing the industry network concept, you can make savings through reductions in print and distribution costs on existing services and can often afford to provide services that were not previously viable. By proactively making information and resources available online, you can often make substantial savings in administration and staff time as well as in direct costs, for example responding to student enquiries or providing and tracking photographic images.

6.2   Features and functions

There is a wide range of features and functions that you can include in your industry network. Online networks allow you to be both proactive and reactive - to use 'push' and 'pull' tactics. In this way you can e-mail ('push') headlines, news and special links to users to encourage them to visit certain areas of the site, whilst users can visit the site to 'pull' information down as and when they have a need.

6.2.1 Publish corporate information

DMOs of all sizes have a general need to communicate corporate information. The type of content will vary according to the size and nature of your organisation, but the following are some examples:

- Background and history
- Organisational structure
- Strategy and high level business targets or operational plans
- Details of key stakeholders, funders and partners
- Personnel lists, including job responsibilities, contact information and potentially photographs
- Information about products and services, e.g. advertising, inspections, training courses, grant schemes, new initiatives
- Information about costs and benefits of membership (if appropriate)
- Information about departmental activities e.g. marketing, development, research
- Meeting minutes and reports
- Provide performance statistics.

You may well have much of the content readily available as you might already produce it for corporate brochures, annual reports, membership/activity rate cards, regular newsletters etc. Much of the information does not change frequently, so the cost of maintaining it is usually low.

You may produce content (such as your programme of marketing activities) that needs regular updating, as part of a reporting cycle or for printing in a regular newsletter, so this should not place any additional burden on staff.

By providing staff information and contact details on line, you enable quick and easy access for people wishing to get in touch, helping them to contact the right person, which relieves pressure on reception and switchboard staff.

Communicating information about your products and services is a key requirement, especially where you need to generate revenue from membership fees, participation charges and trading activities. New initiatives, campaigns and training opportunities also provide useful content.

You may sometimes act as host to VIP visits - politicians or visiting dignitaries. Publishing details of these visits helps to raise awareness and allows your stakeholders to support or lobby the visitor. You may publish a press release about it, or just a post-visit report for your own stakeholders.

Posting minutes of meetings and reports on the site as PDF files that can be downloaded by relevant users helps you to save on print and distribution costs and considerably speeds up delivery.

Your departmental performance statistics would probably be included in the departmental reports, but you could publish headline statistics in a separate section for quick and easy access. These could include membership numbers, brochure requests, reservations, enquiries, tourist information office visits, and Web site visits.

6.2.2   Publish intelligence and provide access to resources

DMOs are often responsible for producing or collating a wide variety of information and resources. You can organise these in different sections or groups depending on volume. The following list gives some examples:

- News
- Research reports and market intelligence
- Bench-marking studies/examples of good practice
- Business support information
- Information about industry events
- Training opportunities
- Training materials
- Employment opportunities
- Access to marketing materials
- Access to a multimedia library
- Press releases
- Details of press coverage
- Access to visitor information e.g. events listings, accommodation availability
- Security alerts
- Access to a directory of useful contacts
- URLs or useful Web sites with hyperlinks to them

The breadth and depth of the content will depend on the size and nature of your DMO. If you are a national or regional tourist board, you will want to provide a wide range of information and will therefore need a dedicated resource to source and maintain content on an on-going basis. If you are a local DMO, you will want to concentrate on information that can be easily maintained, potentially by linking to third parties, and focus on where it can provide added value for industry suppliers.

It is important to provide users with the reason to come back to the site. Resources therefore need to be updated regularly and fresh content needs to be sourced. News is an excellent way of making a site 'sticky', but, by its nature, it demands a significant resource to keep it fresh.

Tourist information offices, or you as the host DMO, can use the industry network to post details of forthcoming events or anticipated transport difficulties, which helps to spread the word quickly and raises awareness of local issues.

There are various resources and services for which users will be prepared to pay. Information that is in the form of reports or fact sheets can be produced as PDF files and made available for users to download. Most information can be offered free, but more valuable resources, such as copyrighted images, research reports or students' packs, could be made available for purchase via an online shop or through an e-mail order.

If you have a large resource library, it is useful to provide some sort of search mechanism. This can be simple keyword search through the site pages, or a more complex indexing of the whole site and potentially linked sites.

An industry network provides you with a quick and easy mechanism for raising security alerts, such as warnings about counterfeit money in circulation or a spate of thefts. Photographs can be posted quickly and particular groups of users can be filtered and targeted separately for maximum effectiveness.

6.2.3 Interactive services

An industry network provides a two-way communication mechanism between you and your users.

Product data maintenance

Through the restricted access of a username and password, individual business managers can gain access to details specific to their business that are held within your database. The most obvious example is product data – e.g. facilities, inventory and price information, but there is no reason why it should stop there; individuals could also maintain occupancy and business performance data online and view analysis of their own performance statistics, e.g. reservations and Web page or kiosk page views.

With the relevant authority, users could ask for third parties to have access to their product data and images held within your database; examples include guide producers, printers, Webmasters or inspecting authorities.

Tourist Information Offices

If you are responsible for one or more tourist information offices, the industry network could provide the mechanism for each tourist information office to maintain its key information online. This might include visitor numbers, retail sales, counter, telephone and written enquiries, bookings and brochure requests.

In a similar way to businesses, tourist information offices can use the data entry forms on the industry network to maintain the general destination information in its area. This might include information on towns and villages, walks, beaches, banks, hospitals etc. For those product providers that are not online or do not wish to maintain their own records, the tourist information office can offer an agency service and maintain the record on behalf of the provider.

Bulletin boards and discussion groups

You could encourage users to participate in discussion groups or post notices to a bulletin board. These types of functions can range from the very simple to the highly complex, but whatever level is chosen, it does provide a forum for interactivity between you and your users and the users with each other.

In a similar vein – you can use online response to canvas opinion, manage a formal vote or just provide a bit of fun for users.

E-commerce

Many DMOs are involved in e-commerce but some are not well placed to act as intermediaries or handle transactions. However, for those that do, there is scope to reduce costs and increase take-up by offering a wide range of products or services through an e-commerce or e-mail order function. Examples include:
- Membership subscriptions
- Advertising
- Training and training materials
- Exhibition applications

- Merchandise
- Books, maps and guides

6.2.4 Business to Business trading

Through your industry network, businesses can participate in a trading forum.
The extent to which you wish to get involved will depend on resources and need.
Examples include:

- You might offer preferred supplier status to particular companies, and enable them to supply information on their services to tourism businesses in your area and facilitate online purchasing of their products either through your own or their e-commerce facilities. The status of preferred supplier could be organised on a tender basis with payments to the DMO as a flat fee, or a commission on sales.
- You may provide opportunities for banner advertising or a classified section whereby relevant suppliers can advertise their products or services to members
- You may encourage your users to use the bulletin board to trade between themselves or to form buying consortia.

6.2.5 Users and Content

The nature and volume of content and functionality on the industry Web site will depend on the requirements of the users, and the particular combination of content will probably be unique to each DMO. Defining the content to include in an industry network should be a core part of your initial research and specification, as it must meet the aims and objectives of the site in relation to the target audience. Content should be current, accurate, relevant, concise and interesting.

There is a number of sources from which you can derive the content of your industry network site. Lists of tourism businesses from your central database can be published on a dynamic basis, providing a useful list of up-to-date contact details, organised by categories, for business-to-business communication and trading; research documents and other information resources can be saved as PDF files and posted online or managed directly in the content management system.

Most DMOs are concerned with how to manage the core content. This can be done using a dedicated content management system or through the use of a WYSIWYG editor such as Microsoft FrontPage or Dreamweaver.

You should have a very clear agreement with providers of third party content on the quality of their information, as any errors will reflect badly on you. Finding suitable providers and negotiating good deals is not difficult, but does need someone (probably not the technical project manager) with relevant business skills to do it.

Most industry networks have an archive element whereby items such as news, events, press releases etc remain live for a defined period and are then made available through an archive section.

Accuracy is important, as is relevance. The Web lends itself to short, concise copy, so use short paragraphs and bullet points rather than long sections of prose.

6.2.6   Costs and benefits

The development of an industry network is not an insignificant undertaking. You must be sure to provide sufficient resources to make the exercise worthwhile and useful to your organisation and its users.

An industry network is unlikely to be a net revenue generating activity, but there is some scope for offsetting costs by maximising income through, for example:

- Banner advertising
- Classified advertising
- E-commerce transactions – sale of DMO products and services online
- Sale of third party products to tourism businesses, with split commissions.

There is likely to be more scope for reducing net costs by using an industry network to deliver a wide range of functions and activities to users. Savings to users can also be expected, at least in terms of effort if not direct costs. Examples include:

- Product data collection and maintenance
- Performance data collection and maintenance
- Reduction in the need for a wide range of print, corporate brochures, newsletters, rate cards, fact sheets
- Ability to provide services online that are not viable offline
- Staff and administration time in servicing a wide range of enquiries.

6.3   Step by step guide

The following step-by-step guide will help you understand how to develop a tourism industry network for your organisation.

Step 1 – Specification of user requirements

In preparing a Specification of User Requirements (SUR), it is helpful to start by getting together with a group of colleagues to share ideas and have a brainstorming session. Identify all your target audiences and then prepare an initial structured list of likely requirements for each. You can use this as a framework for detailed discussions with potential users. For this purpose, organise a meeting with a small, but representative, group of each of the audiences.

Refer back to Section 3.2 for more information on creating a SUR.

Step 2 - Functional specification

Your Specification of User Requirements (SUR) provides the basis of your Functional Specification.

A Functional Specification is a site description. The scope of the document depends on the nature and complexity of the site and the extent to which you, as the client, have firm ideas about how the site should look and function.

Refer back to Section 3.2 for more information on how to produce a Functional Specification.

The Functional Specification often includes a draft Navigation Plan. This is a site map showing how all the sections link to each other, and giving a bird's eye view of the site content.

Open a more formal dialogue with potential software developers by sending them your Specification of User Requirements, your Functional Specification and Navigation Plan, and asking them to provide a firm quotation.

Step 3 - Securing finance

You may have sufficient money in your existing budget to meet the development costs, but if you have not, here are some tips on how to raise support, both financial and in kind.

- Produce a Business Case Report to help you persuade your organisation that it should allocate funding to this initiative, particularly by identifying potential costs savings from existing activities across all departments. Consider the following:
  - o Savings on product data collection and maintenance, including inventory and price information
  - o Savings on performance data collection and maintenance, e.g. tourist information office statistics, business performance survey data, occupancy data
  - o Reduction in the need for a wide range of print, corporate brochures, newsletters, rate cards, fact sheets
  - o Ability to provide online services not viable offline, e.g. student packs
  - o Savings of staff and administration time in servicing a wide range of enquiries
  - o Savings of staff and administration time in printing and distributing a wide range of information
  - o Savings through improved credit control by offering online credit card payments for a wide range of services, from subscriptions to advertising

- Identify your existing resources, both within your organisation and in those of your partners, for example:
  - o Do you have the skills and capacity to undertake the software development in house?
  - o Can the site be hosted by one of your partners, such as a Local Authority, to reduce charges?
  - o Do you have corporate identity branding guidelines that can be used as the basis for the site's 'look and feel'?
  - o How much of your existing staff resource and that of your partners, will be available to the project?
  - o How much of the required content exists already?
  - o Are there existing mechanisms through which you can promote the site and animate users, e.g. tourism forums, print newsletters, regular mailings?

- Consider income generating opportunities such as banner and classified advertising, e-commerce transactions with both your own products, e.g. merchandise and publications, and with third parties' products, e.g. insurance, merchant services. These are not likely to be sufficiently great to sustain the entire service, but could make a useful contribution to its costs.

- Investigate the potential for partnering with a commercial developer or linking with a commercial community site. These are often related to local or regional newspapers and are only too willing to enter partnerships for content provision.

- Investigate sources of external grant funding. Many Governments or their agencies have funds to support economic development and/or co-ordinate access to international support agencies that may be able to provide funds. Such organisations may well be keen to assist projects like this that help to improve the performance of small and medium size businesses.

Step 4 - Selecting a software developer

You may well already have a relationship with a software developer, perhaps your DMS supplier or the company that built your consumer site. If this is the case you may wish to work with them to develop your industry network site, otherwise you should approach several companies or invite open tenders. Much will depend on the complexity of your project and the size of the budget involved.

Refer back to Section 3.2 for full details of how to select a software developer.

Step 5 - Content management

You will probably already have a fairly good idea about the content that you wish to publish on your site. Much will depend on the requirements of your audiences, not just in terms of what the content is, but how it is presented.

Create a Content Management Plan document, give it a date and version number. Using your Specification of User Requirements (SUR) as a reference document, draw up a list of the content type you require for each audience group. Once you have a reasonable list, document it in your Content Management Plan. You will find that there are lots of over-lapping sections, so create a matrix that identifies the content type down the left-hand side and the audiences across the top.

Using this matrix, work with your colleagues to identify the sources of content. Be sure to involve all departments of your organisation. Ask everyone to identify what they can supply from existing sources; what other content they could provide and the amount of work involved in originating the material; and lastly, which third parties may be able to supply content.

The following check lists looks at content that may be available internally:
- Corporate brochures, annual reports, organisational accounts
- Business plans, strategies and action plans
- Sales literature, rate cards and prospectuses
- Holiday guides, leaflets and brochures
- Research reports, market intelligence documentation
- Survey results
- Tourist information office and call centre user statistics, enquiries and bookings
- Traffic statistics for consumer Web sites, call centres and kiosks
- Study sheets, training manuals, CDs or videos
- Image library
- Product database
- Membership database
- Reference lists

Consider the following external sources – some of which may provide content directly, or through a hyperlink to their own site:

- Your suppliers, in terms of maintaining their own data and inventory
- Tourist information offices in terms of maintaining public product details, like towns and villages
- Regional and national tourism organisations
- Economic Development Agencies, Government Departments
- Travel and transport operator sites
- Weather links, e.g. Yahoo
- Local directories, e.g. Yellow Pages
- Local community Web sites

Having identified the potential sources of content, you need to agree on an updating policy. Of course different types of content will require different frequencies of updating, but there is still scope for you to decide how much you can do within each section. News, for instance, could be updated everyday, or once a month, but the nature of the news needs to reflect the updating frequency.

Here are some general tips:

Product data

Information from your destination's product database may be of interest to tourism businesses, either as a source of information to give to their guests or for purposes of business to business trading. Your product database content may be maintained by your own staff, by an agent or, ideally, by your suppliers themselves – see Section 4.1, Step 5. However its done, you need to explain how current and accurate it is, reflecting your up-dating policy.

If you are introducing a business to business e-commerce element to your site, to help your tourism businesses to trade with each other, either you can provide links to your their e-commerce reservation facilities or you may wish your DMO to handle the transactions on your site, and perhaps raise income to help support the service that you are offering.

Inventory and temporary price changes

This data is really only of value to the consumer if it is completely up-to-date. If you cannot provide that, it is best not to publish anything.

General information

Much of the site content will be of a static nature. Here the issue is less likely to be updating it as keeping it fresh. It is important to maintain the user's interest, so publishing different items from within a section on the home page of that section can help to keep the site fresh.

Features

If you hope to attract users regularly then you really ought to be updating your site content each month or quarter. You can do this by publishing new features or articles and by up-dating activities or progress reports.

Event information

Any content that is date sensitive needs to be up-dated or 'churned' regularly. Past events should be marked so they don't show after the date of the event. If you are publishing an annual calendar, then you need to programme your calendar to jump to the relevant month according to the current date.

Performance information

Performance data of all types should be collected, processed and disseminated as quickly as possible. Try to organise survey results to appear soon after the survey has been completed, similarly with monthly occupancy statistics, publish them as soon as possible and show a graph of trends over the last year, or for the same period over several years.

News

When considering how you wish to publish news items you need to think about the frequency of updating required, as this will have a bearing on your choice of content provider. If you decide on something fairly simple, then it may be easier for you to gather the content and edit it in house before publishing it. If however, you want daily national news, then you will need to negotiate with a news provider to publish a live link. In a lot of cases content links are free, often supported by associated advertising, but in some cases you may need to make some form of payment.

Once you have organised all your sources, you must decide on a launch date and gather all your initial content and pass it to your developer. You will need to wait for current items until the week before you are due to launch, e.g. news, but in most cases the vast majority of the site can be sourced in advance. It is worth running the site live for a couple of weeks before launching it to your general audiences, to ensure a good testing period.

Step 6 – Test your site thoroughly

Once your site is released to you from your software developer you need to test it thoroughly. This will involve testing all functionality, ensuring user errors are handled satisfactorily and checking all content is correct and current.

Step 7 - Training

You need to ensure that all the people and organisations that are responsible for providing content are fully trained before the site goes live. They fall into two broad groups: your own staff and any third parties, particularly your tourism suppliers.

Training your own staff is normally relatively easy to organise, particularly if they are already competent computer users and are familiar with the Web. Training third parties however, may be a considerable undertaking.

It is well worth dividing your tourism suppliers into groups according to how experienced they are with computers and the Web, and then by level of impact within the destination. For instance, you might choose serviced accommodation suppliers that are confident Web users and train them first. Try to set up peer groups, so that your best suppliers can act as mentors to others in the their area.

You may need to provide some simple guidelines in a mailing and offer a telephone help service. In some cases it is useful to hold an advisory surgeries.

Step 8 - Promotion and animation

However good your site, it will have failed if your intended audiences do not use it. You need to develop a programme of promotion and animation to ensure everyone knows about your site, its benefits and how to use it.

Mailshots, e-mails, presentations and press articles are all ways of raising awareness. Just as with any commercial venture you need to stimulate people's curiosity. Run a competition on the site, or post a controversial topic on the bulletin board and ask your local radio station or newspaper to start the ball rolling. Get your politicians or industry leaders involved, anything that raises your profile.

Another tactic is to ask users to forward details of the site to a friend or colleague. This 'word of e-mail' referral can be very effective. Ask users to forward a specially prepared e-mail, and copy you for reference so you can reward them in some way.

When users log-in to your site, you can ask them to identify their preferences, so that in future they will be taken automatically to particular sections on the site. Alternatively, you can send users e-mails with Web page links embedded. When the user click on these links, they will be taken to the relevant sections of the site.

You should register your site with the major search engines, and have appropriate metatags and keywords in your site's code. Search engines are unlikely to provide you with major source of business for an industry network, but for those new to your area and audiences like students it could be a useful link. It is more important that you set up reciprocal links with organisations, such as local authorities, neighbouring areas, local community sites and colleges, in order to drive traffic to each other's sites.

6.4   Critical success factors

The following factors are critical to the success of the development and implementation of a tourism industry network:

- Engage with all your suppliers and other stakeholders and gain their support for the idea of creating an industry network
- Involve a wide range of industry representatives in the development of the specification to ensure that all users requirements have been taken into account
- Ensure your specification is realistic. Don't be tempted to include functionality you can't support or for which there is no real requirement
- Secure your finance up front and make sure you are not dependent on anticipated revenues, that may be at risk, e.g. from advertising or e-commerce transactions
- Select a software developer with experience, preferably one you have worked with before and who knows your organisation well
- Maintain control of project management. Designate a particular person to lead the project and create a project plan to manage the tasks
- Animate and train your users, especially in the first six months. Create reasons for them to use the site that will really add value and help them in their day-to-day responsibilities
- Rigorously test the site's functionality before releasing it to your wider user group. There will be no second chance to make a first impression

- Ensure your content is current, accurate and relevant and that you have a policy for updating dynamic content on a regular basis

- Ensure you have a arrangements in place for back ups, disaster recover and tracking (usually set up as part of your ISP's hosting and maintenance contract).

6.5 Case Studies

6.5.1 Canadian Tourism Exchange

Destination overview

Canada is a large country, mostly sparsely populated. It has a federal constitution with ten provinces and three territories. The Canadian Tourism Commission, established in 1996, is operated and financed on a public/private partnership basis. Each province and territory has its own tourism body, most of which have long been operating some form of DMS, always incorporating a call centre.

History

CTC's predecessor, Tourism Canada, had developed a tourism section within the Federal Government's Business Opportunities Sourcing System (BOSS). BOSS was originally a mainframe hosted online database developed in the early 1980s to hold data on Canadian businesses, especially in manufacturing.

BOSS – Tourism was first established in 1991 as a database of 'export-ready' tourism products. Entry into the database (membership) was free and by 1992, some 3,200 tourism businesses were registered; but the need to use a modem and dial-up to connect direct to its system, inhibited widespread use.

CTC took a policy decision in 1996 to focus on the development of 'better communication for the Canadian tourism industry' and the CTX pilot was initiated in mid-1997 to provide an online resource for the industry and an online community to facilitate the exchange of information and collaboration between members.

The preparatory work started in the beginning of 1998 and the site was officially launched in May 1999.

Current Status

By the end of the first month of operation, 4,000 users had registered. This figure was targeted to double by the end of 2000, but in fact there are now over 11,000 members registered.

There are four sections (or Exchanges) to CTX:
- Information exchange
- Promotions exchange
- Employment exchange
- Meetings exchange

Within the Information and Promotions Exchanges there is a focus on industry communication, both by CTC to the Canadian tourism industry and between its members. Users have to register to be members to gain a username and password to access the site. This is free, but there is a lengthy questionnaire to be completed which may be quite off-putting.

A contracted publication company manages CTX's press releases and press coverage material. They provide a daily press service from different media sources across Canada, approximately 10-15 articles a day and also check any press releases provided by members before they go online. CTC create some news articles internally and these are also published. Push technology is employed to notify members of news items that correspond with their specified preferences. There is a search function that covers both current and archived material.

There are twenty Discussion Fora on topics such as relationship marketing and ecotourism. The majority is accessible to any CTX member, though some are restricted to specific sub-groups.

Other opportunities for members to participate include inputting their personal product/service information that is then published to the consumer Web site, and posting press releases or new stories. The latter features are not particularly well used at the present time. Users are encouraged to suggest changes and improvements for the site in a feedback section.

Members can easily set up specific contact groups within CTX, enabling them for example to mail promotional offers to selected partner organisations. Additionally, links to individual members' corporate Web sites are incorporated when requested and there are powerful search facilities enabling users to identify potential partners or suppliers.

CTX is linked directly to the Canada specialist programme operated by CTC. This is a training and membership group open to travel agencies and other organisations who specialise in selling Canadian tourism products. The direct link between the Canada specialist Web site and CTX provides rapid but privileged access by users to a far wider range of product and contact information than was previously possible.

Other features of the site include CTC research data, publications, an events database, details of product developments and new niche products. The content is relevant to its audience, providing them with background intelligence information as well as opportunities to participate to development programmes.

Future enhancements are planned for the Promotions Exchange and full content in the Meetings and Employment Exchanges is expected in summer 2001.

Performance

There are 11,000 members registered, and approximately 7,000 receive news tailored to their interest sent to them via e-mail daily or weekly. This is passive participation, but nevertheless it is implies a reasonable amount of enthusiasm by users for the system. No detailed usage statistics are available.

Data Management

One full time Webmaster runs the site. He/she is responsible for chasing content and co-ordinating others to submit material. All parts of the organisation are responsible for managing their own inputs. For instance CTC's research department posts updated statistics to the site as soon as it is released.

Financial Aspects

Membership of CTX is free of charge and the development and operation of the site is fully funded by CTC. Over the two years of the project costs have been running at around C$ 2m per annum for development. The hosting and maintenance costs are C$600k per annum, but this includes the main consumer site as they are hosted together and share a common database.

Specific issues

Currently, some sections of the sites are not regularly used (e.g. discussion fora) and many members have complained that the navigation is difficult. Efforts are now being focused on improving these deficiencies and consolidating the existing functionality of the site rather than extending it further.

Members have recently been canvassed to gather their views and opinions on what works well within the site already and what new features and functionalities they would wish to see provided. CTC do not have the resources to train the large numbers of members involved, so the site's interface is in currently being re-designed to try to improve the navigation and draw more attention to those areas that are under-used.

CTX has a reasonably high awareness amongst the tourism industry generally, but it is recognised that persuading a large proportion of businesses to use it on a regular basis is a major challenge. CTX personnel recognise that many business managers do not have the capacity or the application to use the site its full potential and that animation of users is a clear priority.

CTC gathers a large amount of data about its tourism suppliers as part of the registration process on the site. There are clearly opportunities to exploit CRM and data mining techniques to develop a closer relationship with them and target their needs more specifically, but lack of resources has meant that little progress has been made in this area to date.

Push e-mail marketing will continue to be used to encourage members to update their product/services entry on a more regular basis.

Conclusions

CTC has taken a focussed approach to addressing the issues of cross-industry communication through the development of CTX, which clearly complements, rather than competes with existing DMO services provided at provincial level.

CTX's continued development will depend on a mix of inter-dependent factors including the extent to which it can provide added value to its members and their active involvement. CTX is a leader in its field and many other DMOs regard it as a model. It has clearly demonstrated the technical capabilities, but the challenge is now to encourage wider use.

6.5.2   Scot Exchange

Destination overview

Scotland is one of the four home nations within the United Kingdom. In 1998 tourism was worth £2,480m, £940m of which was generated from overseas visitors. Tourism employs 177,000 people, including some 17,000 self-employed.

Over the last 25 years, there has been a virtual disappearance of the main holiday market for UK residents and the rise of the short break. The growth in tourism in Scotland has come primarily from overseas markets.

Structure of the DMO

The Scottish Tourist Board (now operating under the name "visitscotland") is the lead agency for promoting tourism in Scotland. It employs around 225 full-time, permanent and temporary staff in its offices in Edinburgh and Inverness, and within the Scottish Travel Centre and Britain Visitor Centre in London.

The Board is headed up by the Chairman, who is appointed by the Scottish Executive for 3 years and the Chief Executive, appointed by the STB Board for a term of 3 years. Its prime responsibilities are:

- To market Scotland as a destination for leisure and business travel within the UK and overseas
- To market Scotland overseas in collaboration with the British Tourist Authority
- To work with the Local Enterprise Companies in developing tourism products
- To develop and promote visitor servicing and quality assurance schemes
- To support Area Tourist Boards in the provision of Tourist Information Centres, local marketing initiatives and in developing ICT
- To advise the industry on market trends.

History of the development

In 1998 the Scottish Executive carried out the largest and most inclusive consultation ever undertaken on tourism in Scotland. The main issues that emerged from the views of those who contributed were the need to:

- Understand customers and niches to market Scotland effectively
- Take advantage of new technology and methods of communication
- Develop and improve the marketing of Scotland
- Work together and raise the profile of tourism
- Improve quality and service
- Improve skills throughout the industry
- Tackle regionality and seasonality
- Support the tourism industry adequately   ·
- Make Scotland an accessible country
- Develop a sustainable industry that benefits all of Scotland.

As a result of this consultation a strategy was prepared to address the major issues based on the vision:

'To develop an industry that is modern, in touch with its customers, that embraces lifelong learning, that provides the quality of service its customers require.'

Among the actions to be taken to achieve this vision were 'Using knowledge effectively' and 'Knowing our customers' and to tackle this, it was proposed that:

"The Scottish Tourist Board, with Scottish Enterprise and Highlands and Islands Enterprise will establish a fully operational industry Website by June 2000. This will present relevant market research information in an accessible form, allowing tourism businesses to improve the nature and quality of the services they provide, and tailor their individual marketing plans to suit particular niche markets."

The main aim of the site was to provide 'relevant market research information in an accessible form, allowing tourism businesses to improve the nature and quality of the services they provide, and tailor their individual marketing plans to suit particular niche markets'.

Current Status

The site has been fully operational since June 2000. It is under continual development in accordance with a five-year business plan. Its main sections are:

- Tourism organisations - who does what and how they can help an individual business. It is a guide to the organisations involved in Scottish tourism at local, Scottish, national and European levels.
- Know your market - password-protected area exclusively for information for area tourist board members predominantly published by the Scottish Tourist Board
- Promote your business – exploring marketing opportunities and guidance on how to decide which is most appropriate.
- Business development - new ways of identifying, developing and introducing new thoughts, ideas and concepts.
- Media office - dedicated resource to assist the media in writing on Scotland or Scottish Tourism
- Events and conferences - an overview of up-and-coming trade and consumer exhibitions, together with conferences, seminars and workshops.

Performance

A traffic analysis programme 'Web Trends' operates behind the site and indicates a current average of 6,000 visitor sessions per month. It is not possible to identify all visitor origins or behaviour but the majority of regular users are involved in the ATB/STB network.

Data Management

The data is owned by the lead organisations, Scottish Tourist Board, Scottish Enterprise and the Highlands and Islands Enterprise. It is regularly updated by the in-house Web co-ordinator. The company that developed the site is responsible for major updates or developments to the structure.

Financial Aspects

A budget of $170,500 was used to finance the development of the site, split between the three partner organisations. The ongoing annual costs are divided in the same way.

Specific issues

The biggest challenge for this site, as with many industry networks, is raising awareness and increasing the usage levels. It is sometimes hard to convince people to change their habits at all, particularly when the perception of ICT developments is often that they create problems and the time needed for training has to be found in already busy schedules. After one year of operation, the statistics showed that 30% of the trade were aware of the site and it was being regularly used by 15%. These initial figures may be a little disappointing, but are expected to increase at a consistent rate as the site develops and awareness grows.

Future development

In accordance with a 5-year business plan, further features are to be added in partnership with the tourism trade. The first additions will be business networking via a discussion forum, and mailing lists (both of which are currently under development). The news section is also due to be restructured in order to widen the scope of the site and include articles from other countries, for instance, that might affect, or be of use to, Scottish tourism.

At the beginning of 2001 a tender process was underway, to identify a private partner to introduce a B2B e-commerce element to the site. Development of local and area trade sites is planned for 2001and 2002. These will be accessed through scotexchange.net and help to further enhance its role.

Conclusions

Awareness and animation of tourism businesses to use this resource is one of the biggest challenges. Despite extensive marketing and high profile exposure of the project, and bearing in mind that the original development was a result of consultation with SMEs, the usage statistics were still relatively low after the first year. Fully embracing the industry in this aspect of tourism e-business for Scotland is clearly a medium- to long-term proposition, requiring ongoing investment.

PART C – E-BUSINESS FOR SME'S IN TRAVEL AND TOURISM

"Information technology has created a new order. This is not the first time that scientific and technical advances have changed the face of tourism. Historically, lower air transport costs, made possible by the launch of the jet 'plane and later of the jumbo jet, the widespread use of the private motor car, the introduction of business computing and office automation and the advent of global distribution systems have each, in turn, contributed to the globalisation of the travel industry, allowed new consumers access to tourism and paved the way for new alliances between operators."

"But the phase we are entering will obviously be even more decisive than the previous ones. Information and communication technologies, owing to the incomparable wealth of information they convey and the tremendous freedom they give the individual consumer by providing direct access to services, are creating a new order. New kinds of enterprises are emerging, such as "virtual travel agencies", whose turnover is skyrocketing; other more traditional companies are having to specialize or form alliances, and still others are having to adapt or go out of business, whereas, for their part, the airlines are selling a growing share of their supply of seats direct over the Internet."

Mr. Francesco Frangialli
Secretary- General
World Tourism Organization
(WTO)[1]

Introduction to Part C

Through its Business Council, the WTO is the only intergovernmental organisation open to the operating sector. The WTO Business Council membership is open to organisations from all tourism-related sectors. It offers an ideal opportunity for exchanging views and networking, with both public and private sector representatives. The WTO Business Council includes airlines and other transportation companies, hotels and restaurants, travel agencies, tour operators, visitor attractions, educational institutions, industry associations, and other tourism industry interests in 70 countries.

This report on "E-Business for Tourism", which builds on the success of "Marketing Tourism Destinations Online" in 1999, reflects the great diversity of the WTO Business Council. In particular, Part C sheds light on the needs and priorities of its most promising group of members, the Small and Medium-Sized Enterprises (SMEs), in such diverse tourism sectors as hospitality services, travel agencies, tour operators, and visitor attractions.

The unprecedented opportunities and challenges opened by e-commerce, which have been addressed mostly from the perspective of large organisations, are equally important for SMEs that operate in various segments of the tourism value chain, represented by the various stages in the production and delivery of travel and tourism services. Indeed, companies of all sizes are using the Internet to attract more tourists, streamline their processes, create more valuable services, and become agile competitors.

However, SMEs are facing more stringent impediments to the adoption of e-business [2]. Part of the problem relates to the scale and affordability of some information technologies, as well as the facility to implement them in the context of rapidly growing and changing organisations [3]. In addition, new solutions configured for large, stable, and globally oriented firms have little strategic fit with small, dynamic, and locally based operations [4]. For these reasons, the needs of SMEs must be addressed according to several factors, such as their position throughout the industry, growth potential, long-term priorities, etc. As well, these factors evolve according to the entrepreneurial life cycle particular to each firm.

Despite these challenges, the opportunities brought by e-commerce (trading products and services on the Internet) and the benefits offered by e-business (reengineering business processes through the Internet) are more than sufficient to encourage SMEs to formulate new strategies, adopt new management practices, and invest in new IT solutions. Therefore, this is why Part C of this report will review the best practices that are most relevant to SMEs, and provide some guidelines as to where these organisations should focus their e-commerce efforts.

In Section 7, we will first provide a brief overview or "map" of e-commerce and e-business applications and indicate which ones are most relevant to SMEs in each segments of the tourism industry (see Table 4). Then, throughout Chapters 8-11, we will review the strategies, best practices, and solutions that apply specifically to each broad segment of the tourism value chain: Hospitality Services, Travel Agencies, Tour Operators, and Visitor Attractions.

7 Industry overview

The emergence of e-commerce anc
Sized Enterprises (SMEs) perplexed.
unanswered, such as:

- Will current travel and tourism SME
  business customers?

- How can SMEs effectively sustain
  firms?

- Is there a clear path for SMEs in \
  business?

These questions are forcing SME Exe
the way they have been using ne'
e-business strategy. Indeed, the In
a much faster pace than they hc
survive these changes, or to perf
selling services and doing business.

World Tourism Organization Business C

travel sites and the airline
travel agencies [5].

More than 66% of w
2001 to buy trave
tourism service
addition, more
This contact
disloyal tr

Curren
spe
H

However, forging a new e-business strategy is a major challenge, as the impac..
SMEs are complex, given the many players and their particular needs. There are
obviously great differences in setting up an e-business strategy for a small hotel, a
small travel agency, a small tour operator, or a small visitor attraction. A great
diversity of IT applications is used throughout the tourism value chain, which makes
the "mapping" of the impacts on SMEs even more difficult than some other sectors.
In addition, the majority of the tourism IT infrastructure still operates on legacy systems,
software, and hardware, and few companies are investing properly to transform
these applications for e-business and e-commerce.

In order for SMEs to play a more active role in this transformation, it is important to
address three issues. First, small firms must understand where the growth of tourism e-
business is heading, as the trends point out to dramatic changes throughout the
whole industry. Second, small firms at all stages of the tourism value chain must
understand the strategic importance of practicing e-commerce and e-business, and
learn how to value and capture new opportunities, offered by e-Tourism. Third, small
firms must stop investing in inferior solutions, and target their efforts at more strategic
e-commerce technologies.

7.1 Growth of tourism e-business and impacts on SMEs throughout the industry

The sale of travel and tourism services online have become by far the leading
Business-to-Consumer (B2C) sector on the Internet, representing more than 25% of all
consumer purchases online, even higher than stocks trading services, books sales,
and computer software and hardware.

Several studies reveal that changes are dramatic and fast-paced, influencing not
only the travel distribution channels, but also which tourism service provider can
effectively capture customers through this channel, and effectively relate to them.
For example:

- About 16 million people have booked travel arrangements online in 2000 (out of
  33 million lookers). Of those who have booked, 47% purchased only from airline-
  run sites. Another 35% percent have purchased from both independent online

, while 18% have developed a loyalty towards online

eb travel buyers used an online discount throughout 2000-
online, indicating the necessity for both travel distributors and
roviders to adjust their pricing mechanisms very rapidly. In
than half of all Web travellers request customer service assistance.
is a travel marketer's best opportunity to build brand loyalty among
avellers [6].

tly, only 6% of online corporate travel, or US$4.4 billion, is booked through
cial Web travel portal-like systems that follow pre-set corporate policies.
owever, studies predict that figure will grow to $12 billion, or 9% of the total by
2002 [7].

- In the United States, the volume of online travel sales is expected to reach US$40 billion in 2003, which will represent 17% of total sales of travel throughout the industry, compared to only 7% in 2000 [8, 9].

- Within only 6 months (from November 2000 to April 2001), the number of Europeans visiting travel Web sites has increased by nearly 4 million, with clear seasonal trends: in Britain and Germany, the peaks in usage occur in July, January and February; in France, the peaks are seen in July and March. During the peak periods, Web surfers from these countries spent more time on travel sites than other popular categories, including retail and news and information sites [10].

- In 2001, nearly 3 million or 18% of Canadian adults said they have used the Internet to book an element of their travel plans, including air travel, hotel stays, or car rentals. As well, 92% of Canadians who have booked part of their travel online said they are now using travel agents less because of the Internet [11].

Given such a dynamic online demand, and the rapidly changing consumer behaviour, the Internet is creating a totally new competitive environment. Indeed, the relative market share of various travel products will evolve rapidly in the United States, with airline tickets decreasing rapidly from 68% of market share in 1999 to 60% in 2003, with other products taking more room (see Table 2) [8, 9].

Table 2 - Online travel sales forecast by segment in the United States

(In Billion of US$)	1999		2000		2001		2002		2003	
Airline tickets	$4.7	68%	$9.0	62%	$14.2	62%	$19.2	61%	$24.0	60%
Hotel	$1.1	16%	$2.6	18%	$4.1	18%	$5.3	17%	$6.7	17%
Car rental	$0.5	7%	$1.3	9%	$2.3	10%	$3.1	10%	$4.1	10%
Vacation, cruise	$0.2	3%	$0.4	3%	$0.8	3%	$1.4	4%	$2.4	6%
International sales	$0.5	7%	$1.2	8%	$1.7	7%	$2.4	8%	$3.0	7%
Total	$6.9	100%	$14.5	100%	$23.0	100%	$31.4	100%	$40.1	100%

Source: [8, 9]

As well, specialised travel sites will make a dent of about 10% points in the dominant position held by online travel agencies (e.g., Travelocity, Lastminute, etc.) and airlines portals (e.g., Orbitz, etc.), giving some hope to those willing to enter various segments dedicated to niche services, such as the sale of targeted and customised vacation packages (see Table 3).

Consequently, it is clear that the competitive dynamics created by the Internet will lead to dramatic shifts in the strategic position of each player throughout the tourism industry. The questions posed in the beginning of this section will need to be answered taking in account the changing role of each product, distribution channel, and pricing mechanism. As well, SME Executives will need to be much more attentive than in the past to defending their relative position against large firms dominating either distribution or some service sectors.

Table 3 - Online travel sales forecast by type of site in the United States

(In Billion of US$)	1999		2000		2001		2002		2003	
Online travel agency sites	$3.3	48%	$7.1	49%	$10.9	47%	$14.8	47%	$19.0	47%
Airline sites	$2.6	38%	$5.0	34%	$8.1	35%	$11.0	35%	$13.8	34%
Hotel sites	$0.6	9%	$1.4	10%	$2.2	10%	$2.9	9%	$3.6	9%
Car rental sites	$0.3	4%	$0.8	6%	$1.3	6%	$1.8	6%	$2.3	6%
Vacation and cruise sites	$0.1	1%	$0.3	2%	$0.6	3%	$0.9	3%	$1.5	4%
Total	$6.9	100%	$14.5	100%	$23.0	100%	$31.4	100%	$40.1	100%

Source: [8, 9]

7.2 Strategic importance of e-commerce and e-business for SMEs

Whilst the rapid growth online travel is forcing most SMEs to reconsider how they can benefit from e-commerce, it is not clear how each sector will respond and how e-business strategies will differ among firms. Indeed, the tourism industry in practice is very fragmented, and represented by, on the one hand, a large number of small enterprises and on the other, a small but powerful number of global and national operators.

For example, small firms are key aspects of economic development and employment growth within European and local economies, and policies to support and enhance SMEs are evident at European (EU) and national levels [12]. However whilst occupying the largest number (93 % of all firms in the EU), SMEs represent a tiny proportion of total turnover and have below-average "value added per employee", when compared with medium and larger firms and despite their growth potential, small entrepreneurs are seldom regarded as serious partners in community development through tourism. Small firms may traditionally lack both capital and research and development resources and capability and the scale of operation required to justify investment in IT. Over 85 % of European accommodation suppliers are not listed on airline Computerised Reservation Systems (CRSs) that serve travel agents world-wide.

Both large and small tourism businesses are working on all sides of the Internet at the same time, trying to transform their industry into one of the most technologically advanced of the service sector [13]. The goal is to attract and hold more customers while lowering operating and procurement costs by making their supply chains more efficient. Airlines, hotels, travel agencies and others are using the Internet to layer efficient, feel good services for customers; open new sales channels; and drive suppliers to offer lower costs and speed product delivery with online procurement.

Activities range from allowing travellers to download flight information over wireless devices, to creating B2B e-marketplaces for the airline, hospitality and cruise industries.

Within this context, the survival of existing tourism SMEs, and the development of new ones, will depend greatly on their adequate use of innovative e-business applications. The effective use of these new approaches will depend on overcoming the barriers to the implementation of e-business [14]. Indeed, whereas advanced, IT-savvy SMEs eagerly embrace cutting-edge technologies; the more traditional, delivery-focused counterparts are more leery of adopting groundbreaking business practices based on new technologies. A variety of internal and external roadblocks are preventing many companies from keeping up with the pace of e-business. The key to success in the emerging New Economy requires identifying the organisational barriers to e-business and turning them into strengths.

This will require small firms to develop a more strategic approach to IT investments. So far, only large corporations have made significant efforts to go beyond the basic use of Web Sites and reengineer their processes to perform e-commerce. The greatest challenge for SMEs is to go beyond their vision of such new capabilities as merely "luxuries" and focus all their attention on finding solutions appropriate to their size and competitive position [15].

In that perspective, Chapters 8-11 of this report will analyse the various strategies, practices, and solutions available for SMEs in tourism to build their e-commerce capabilities. In order to do so, and before going on with each industry segment, we need to identify a number of opportunities available to each category of SMEs, according to their functional priorities.

7.3 Mapping e-commerce and e-business applications

Various segments of the tourism value chain use e-commerce in different ways (see Table 4). The "architecture" of each application, which includes process, information, and technology structures, is not the same, given the diversity of firms, markets, and products. However, we can map these applications according to their common functionality, or the generic operational purposes for which they have been designed.

To facilitate our discussion, we identify 2 broad categories that are Front Office and Back Office, where each category includes roughly 5 major applications. While each one is important for and practised in each segment of the tourism industry, this report will discuss only those that are the most strategic and current to each type of SMEs.

So far, the tourism industry has made several efforts to integrate Front-Office applications within its business processes. However, most of these IT solutions use legacy platforms (i.e., pre-Internet), which for the most part have not yet been connected to the Web. Based on the lessons learned from large firms that have been experimenting with e-business, we identify several opportunities that SMEs should consider in order to plan their e-business Strategy:

1. **Marketing and advertising**: This is where Web Sites have been used the most, whether a firm is delivering tourism services or acting as an intermediary. However, very few companies have exploited the diversity of solutions available to advertise their services and attract new customers online. We will look here at those solutions that complement existing SMEs efforts, such as the

services offered by Destination Management Systems (DMSs) and the great variety of advertising solutions offered by small IT suppliers.

2. **Distribution channels**: This issue has not yet been resolved for most firms. Only large airlines have recently attempted to bypass travel agencies, but for the major part the value chain remains unchanged as most firms do not want to jeopardise their existing channels merely to fuel momentum to their online offerings. We will review these recent events and describe certain alternatives available to SMEs.

3. **Reservation and payment**: This is one of the most advanced and well established area, where leading solution providers have made significant efforts to offer new e-commerce services to SMEs. We will address some of these initiatives and attempt to gauge their potential for small firms in tourism.

4. **Customer Relationship Management (CRM)**: This is the most strategic but least understood e-commerce application. For SMEs in tourism, the problem remains one of defining a strategy to exploit the quality-value-loyalty chain on the Internet. We will explore the most recent strategies, practices, and solutions that SMEs must adopt.

5. **Loyalty programs**: This type of application is well established but lacks strategic integration with new e-commerce solutions such as CRM. Therefore, we will look at this issue and discuss the possibilities for SMEs to better use existing loyalty programs.

As for Back Office applications, it is only recently that tourism firms have made some efforts to reengineer their processes and implement new Internet solutions. Indeed, the majority of industry players (at all stages in the value chain) have concentrated on managing quality and productivity. However, the rapid pace and global scale of competition is forcing all firms to consider better "information management" practices in their Back Office operations as well. Although the lessons in this area are only emerging, we can find some highly interesting options that SMEs in tourism will need to exploit in order to gain sustainable competitive advantages:

6. **Supply Chain Management (SCM)**: This is one of the most important areas to help reduce the unit cost of a firm's service offering. However, new supply chain solutions, such as e-Procurement, are facing significant obstacles due to the insecurity felt by most firms throughout the tourism industry. We will discuss these issues and attempt to map the possibilities for SMEs to gain from a rapid transformation of the value chain.

7. **Enterprise Resource Planning (ERP)**: This is one of the most traditional areas, where SMEs in tourism have made significant efforts to invest in customised accounting and financial management systems. However, the importance of integrating online transactions with legacy systems has created tremendous insecurity as to where companies should invest their new IT efforts. We will review some cases in this area and find out which trends matter the most for small firms.

8. **Human resources**: This area of the back-office is rarely automated in SMEs. However, there is a great diversity of HR recruitment, management, and development solutions available for e-business. We will look at some of them and attempt to identify some new strategic opportunities for SMEs where HR functions are most crucial for both quality and productivity performance.

9. **Operational control**: This is a type of application that has often lacked integration with other ones. As new customised ERP's will come to embrace both legacy and online technologies, we will witness the transformation of operational control systems into more integrated applications, along with SCM and ERP's. We will address such a challenge and outline what it will offer to SMEs.

10. **Product development**: This is the least exploited area of e-Tourism, where tremendous opportunities are offered to improve existing operations through cutting-edge technologies, reposition traditional services on new markets, and even conceiving innovative business concepts. We will explore the innovative possibilities the Internet has opened for SMEs, indicating which avenues are the most promising in e-Tourism, especially through the use of data mining and business intelligence applications.

With such a diversity of applications, it is understandable that not all firms will use all of the emerging e-commerce solutions. Therefore, each segment of the tourism industry requires a customised e-business Strategy, which we will address for each sector in Chapters 8-11.

Table 4 – e-commerce applications by segment of the tourism industry

	Hospitality Services	Travel Agencies	Tour Operators	Visitor Attractions
Front-Office				
1. **Marketing & Advertising**	• Individual Web Site • Destination Management Systems	• Catalogue Referencing • Affiliates Programs	• Package Lists on Travelmarts • Package Customisation	• Catalogue Referencing • Online Previews
2. **Distribution Channels**	• Inclusion in Packages	• Network-Based Portals	• Direct Access for Agencies	• Inclusion in Packages
3. **Reservation & Payment**	• Online Accounts	• Reservation Systems	• Payment Processing	• Online Ticketing
4. **Customer Relationship Management**	• Front Desk Automation	• Client Profiles	• Call Centres	• Automated Guidance
5. **Loyalty Programs**	• Frequent Client Points	• Customised Deals	• Over-Commissions	• Frequent Client Points
Back-Office				
6. **Supply Chain Management**	• E-Procurement	• Reservation Systems	• Inventory Management	• E-Procurement
7. **Enterprise Resource Planning**	• Customised Accounting Systems	• Customised Accounting Systems	• Customised Accounting Systems	• Customised Accounting Systems
8. **Human Resources**	• Online Recruitment • IT Training Services	• IT Training Services	• IT Training Services	• Online Recruitment • IT Training Services
9. **Operational Control**	• Property Management Systems	• Agency Management Systems	• Tour Operator Systems	• Attraction Management Systems
10. **Product Development**	• Room Technology	• Package Assembly	• Package Assembly	• Content Production

7.4 Structure and content of each sector analysis

As SMEs in tourism discover all the diversity of IT applications that are transformed by the Internet, and the great business opportunities made available through them, they also encounter a tremendous difficulty: the need for a finely customised e-business strategy.

Indeed, it has been demonstrated countless times that SMEs in various sectors fail to develop further merely for the absence of a clear game plan for growth. Unfortunately, small organisations have a tendency for getting caught within the hectic rhythm of daily business operations, thereby drowning their managers into endless details and decisions. Under such circumstances, rare are the managers who find the time necessary to formulating a coherent e-business strategy, often overlooking completely the impacts of the Internet.

Therefore, Part C of this report will serve you as a guide to initiate your learning process, and that of your whole management team and organisation. Although most managers will often read primarily the information pertinent to their own sector, we strongly advise you to read all of the report, and especially all of the sector analyses, whether they are Hospitality Services, Travel Agencies, Tour Operators, or Visitor Attractions. You will benefit greatly in understanding the challenges faced by your colleagues across the tourism value chain, which may have feedback effects on your sector. To help you formulate, implement, and control your e-business strategy, each sector analysis provides you with the followings:

- **Targeting your e-business strategy**: First and foremost, before jumping to conclusions as to what new technologies you need, take a look closely at the various trends that are transforming the tourism industry in general, and more specifically those of your sector. We hope that the e-business strategy you have in mind properly responds to these trends, but if not you may wish to target it differently so as to use these trends to your advantage.

- **E-Business applications and functionality**: Although a smart executive will find it easy to devise a coherent e-business strategy, many of them will often stall as they assess the various technologies they should adopt. Although the number of applications, systems, and solutions is too wide to be covered in this report, we indicate what technologies are strategic in your sector, explain their innovativeness, and point out what to learn further.

- **Step-by-step guide to implementing your e-business strategy**: Once you have chosen a clear direction for your strategy, and have started learning about e-business applications, you can confidently draw an implementation plan for your strategy. For each sector, we have mapped the typical sequence of changes lived by an SME that is relatively new to e-commerce and e-business. These steps will help you focus your learning and planning.

- **Critical success factors for your e-business strategy**: Even if you have experience in managing Internet technologies, it does not guarantee at all that your e-business strategy will be successful. We indicate here the most important lessons in managing e-business projects, and talk about the issues to watch out in particular for SMEs in your sector.

- **Case studies of innovative e-business solutions**: Since the step-by-step guide will often focus on what to do and why it is important to do it, you will want to find some starting points to evaluate various technologies that could prove highly useful for your strategy.

- **Future of e-commerce and e-business**: As you will read through the analysis of your sector you may find the diversity of issues too large. After digging deep into the particularities of your e-business strategy, it is always good to step back and think through what future may offer you. This will help to create some feedback loops to revise your emerging ideas.

8   Hospitality services

8.1   Introduction

To small hotels and associated foodservices, e-tourism sounds like a liberation from many constraints they have seen for several years as the primary threats to their occupancy rates and profit margins. So far, at the top of their e-commerce (selling services electronically) and e-business (operating processes electronically) priorities is "direct marketing", where small hotels have tried to go beyond their listings in regional hospitality catalogues, and reach out to new potential markets through their own Web sites and e-marketing [16]. In addition, many hope to diversify their distribution channels, escaping the bulk sale of rooms to consolidators by concluding transactions directly, thereby performing price discrimination in the same way tour operators achieve it with various packages. Finally, many small hotels and foodservices hope the Internet could serve as a platform to integrate the legacy systems they have been using for years.

These are only a few of the many strategic opportunities opened by e-tourism, and merely mimic the traditional benefits of Information Technologies (IT). However, as we identify and analyse the various applications available for e-business, small hotels can rapidly discover new ways to conceive their business and to achieve higher objectives, exploiting the true power of the Net.

8.2   Targeting your e-business strategy

The Internet allows small hotels and their foodservices to pursue totally new business objectives, allowing them to reach higher capacity, grow stronger in front of local competition, and play a more important role in the future of their destination internationally. In so doing, they must take in consideration a number of opportunities and challenges that affect large and small firms equally, and some others that affect SMEs more stringently. However, the firms that will succeed in managing these trends will be better prepared than others to create distinctive advantages through e-business, instead of constantly lagging in a "me-too" position.

Among many others, three trends affect small hotels most dramatically. First, the Internet offers a renewed opportunity to attract international visitors. Second, the greater flexibility in booking systems allows visitors to customise their tours around specific hotels. Third, the tremendous advantages offered by customer loyalty are now available to small hospitality services that manage their long-term relationships with clients, on a one-to-one basis, instead of the traditional mass marketing approach.

8.2.1   Attracting international visitors

The rapid globalisation of both business and entertainment has led a greater number of international visitors in new and alternative destinations. However, since international travellers are always insecure about service quality and reliability, they tend to prefer large hotel chains, leaving them with little budget flexibility and stricter plans to discover destinations.

But with the help of new technologies, these travel consumers should represent one of the most promising markets. Capturing the attention of these international visitors, earning their confidence, and making them discover the hidden charms of a destination, are among the most interesting challenges for small hotels, inns, and Bed & Breakfasts (B&B).

The Internet can prove a powerful tool to achieve such objectives given the increasing importance of the e-tourism market. According to the Travel Industry Association (TIA), among the 59 million American travellers who used the Internet to search for tourism information in 2000, 25 million bought travel services online [17]. In April 2001 alone, travel consumers made US$512 million in hotel reservations on the Internet, representing a 64% monthly growth rate [18].

Small hotels should not be afraid of attempting to capture some of this new business. Instead of merely serving to sell "excess capacity", the Internet should be primarily a way to transform a service by attracting a completely new breed of clients, one that should be more loyal and profitable for small hotels.

As a small hotel manager, you must think through carefully how your e-business initiative may help you attract international visitors. To do so, you must:

- Revise your traditional approaches in evaluating and keeping international relationships,
- Identify the areas and concepts that remain uncovered by your local competitors,
- Analyse the key factors that determine the trust behaviour of your international clients,
- Conceive a distinctively international character and a Web design that demonstrates it,
- Advertise in specialised portals and at very strategic periods in foreign markets,
- Ensure your information and reservation sections are useful for international travellers, and
- Build a strategic database of international clients who may serve as referrals.

8.2.2   Offering customised packages

Another trend brought by e-business, and that follows the previous one, is the facility for travellers to choose their room's features, and to make it the centre of a complete trip package, hence allowing full customisation of tourism services.

Indeed, the Internet has empowered tourists by giving them greater selection, and especially the opportunity to check for themselves which services they want to purchase. In addition, as several e-tourism portals have discovered, the hotel portal is the best place to plan a trip, since most activities are location-specific and sensitive to distance from hotels.

Large hotel chains have only recently started to allow the full customisation of services [19]. When a consumer visits a hotel's Web site to evaluate lodging options, they have the ability to also check flight and car rental availability and prices, and even book their entire trip. The capability provides complete travel planning to visitors, strengthening customer relationship. As such, by providing complete travel assistance at the suppliers' Web sites makes customisation more feasible for all industry partners, while giving a strong and memorable impression that the hotel is really the one responsible for this service to consumers.

Consequently, full service customisation should become one of the most effective ways to distinguish your small hotel and give it a clear position in your destination. To properly target your e-business strategy around this innovative approach, you should make sure the following steps are respected throughout your strategy formulation process:

- Survey what your present and future client would want to in their customised package,

- Analyse how clients would like to use this information and visualise it on their account,

- Search for destination-specific and out-of-town partners to include supplier information,

- Connect to other search engines that may offer comparative prices for local services,

- Make customisation an easy task for customers by helping them with sample packages,

- Make total billing and expense reports easy to obtain for all transactions on your site, and

- Transform your hotel into a centre of attraction with a systematically expanding network.

8.2.3 Maintaining long-term relationships

The massive arrival of international travellers and the importance of customisation are combining with a more dramatic trend in the hospitality sector: the death of "brand loyalty" and shift to "price loyalty" [20].

The implicit message to the hotel industry is that large properties will not experience the success enjoyed during the mid-1990's, as factors such as the Internet and high hotel rates will play a future role in low occupancy rates.

The new generation of affluent travellers is taking advantage of the wealth of information on the Internet to find better prices and value for a vacation. Customers will be driven by price and become disenfranchised with current brand names, as the Internet becomes more popular as a search tool.

Consequently, this will lead to a radical restructuring and fragmentation of tourism markets, one that could help fill the gap between large and small hotels. Given the latter's undeniable value/cost advantage and facilities to customise offerings locally, they are best prepared to compete on e-markets and to build loyalty on price.

Furthermore, a valuable vacation to a traveller will be determined by convenience, which means a full itinerary created on the Internet before a departure. For this reason, hotels will have to work harder at convincing travellers that brand name hotels are still convenient and predictable. It remains unclear whether such retrenchment will be a profitable strategy.

Therefore, small hotels should exploit these trends in order to establish and maintain long-term relationships with more visitors, beyond the traditions of "staying in touch" with the few worldly tourists that each hotel has the privilege to attract over several years.

Such relationships will no longer take so much time to build, neither run the risk of being abandoned by lack of communications, nor be limited in the possibility of offering special rewards to loyal customers. By better structuring and planning information exchanges with their guests, and by building habits through well-targeted special offers, smart managers will be able to exploit the true power of e-commerce, that is one-to-one relations on a mass basis.

These are only some of the many benefits offered by Customer Relationship Management (CRM) applications (for a brief introduction to CRM, see Section 2.3 in Part B of this report). With the possibility to capture large amounts of information on their visitors, small hotels will finally have ample opportunities to demonstrate their human touch and distinct customer service by optimising their guests' experience. In addition, such tools will help managers forecast "just in time" the needs of their visitors, to the point of detecting the right moment for price discrimination or service quality improvement.

As such, CRM represents the most powerful application for your small hotel, the one that will demonstrate your ability to equate the sophisticated management of large hotels, while preserving and enhancing the character that has made your mark. In order to achieve properly this equilibrium between such strategic characteristics, you must:

- Re-assess to what extent you are effectively exploiting your value/cost advantage,
- Revising all your Internet communications so as to put the right spin on all messages,
- Discover what is most important for each client and ensure the staff is aware of it,
- Keep future special offers aligned with the specific needs and behaviour of each client,
- Build automated offer generation mechanisms to please customers with online surprises,
- Ensure that the relationship is kept over several years, asking for regular updates,
- Demonstrate your world-class scope by offering high-level news about your destination.

8.3   E-Business applications and functionality

As small hotels and their foodservices are formulating their e-business strategy, they are discovering a wide range of new Internet-based Information Technologies. Indeed, achieving the objectives outlined previously requires a certain degree of IT investment. Interestingly, the variety of applications, their functionality, and their affordability, makes e-business much more accessible to SMEs than the previous generation of technologies.

Most small hotels may believe that investing in new tools and infrastructures is a very risky move. However, one must understand the relationship of each application with the ones that have existed so far in the hospitality industry. As well, we must distinguish how these assets are now acquired by SMEs, which makes investing in them much more flexible than in the past. Among the many tools that must be considered by managers, we find:

- Main Web site:
Naturally, Web sites technologies evolve so rapidly that few hotels are been able to keep up with the pace. However, one must understand here that the real challenge lays elsewhere: a design that builds confidence is more beneficial than a handful of high tech features. Fortunately, investing in a Web site is much more affordable than it was just a few years ago, and small hotels can now easily renovate this important client-facing asset, while integrating it with their back office applications.

- Internet Booking Engines (IBEs)

One of the most important aspects of any Web site is the choice of transactional features. Adding online reservations integrated directly with an inventory of rooms is an important prerequisite for practising e-commerce. Interestingly, such transactional Web sites are now readily available through various vendors, who often re-configure the pre-formatted Web sites that come included in popular packages sold by major software makers. Consequently, managers can focus on properly designing their reservation processes, and help vendors deliver a highly functional solution at low cost. In addition, and most importantly, several of these vendors (sometimes the same who sell online Application Service Provider or ASP and Enterprise Resource Planning or ERP solutions) have integrated these Web sites with industry-leading Central Reservation Systems or CRSs, making their solution extremely attractive to small hotels that can rarely capture all the benefits of being present on such systems.

- Web site promotion

This is one of the most forgotten tasks in e-commerce. Too often, managers view their Web site as a stand-alone piece, making little efforts to bring their clientele to use it. Fortunately, a variety of options are opened to small hotels, from joining a Destination Management System or DMS that will enlist their site in a fully integrated catalogue on their destination, to planning a systematic advertising campaign to make a small hotel known to specific market segments in some specific period of the year. The choice of the right e-marketing solution depends greatly on the resources at the disposal of managers, and since these are generally very limited, the preferred option is most often one of enlisting in a DMS.

- **Customer Relationship Management (CRM)**

Smart managers who plan their e-business investments well can use their remaining resources to exploit the full potential of the Internet. By developing an integrated IT infrastructure, they can gather large amounts of data on their clients, which they can then systematically search to detect behavioural patterns or build profiles that help employees better satisfy the needs of each client on an individual basis. As such, CRM solutions can be implemented (often integrated as part of the other systems described here), which allow small hotels to build stronger relationships over the long term, and develop a push marketing approach similar to that of large hotel chains.

- Property Management Systems (PMSs)

A variety of simple PMS software packages have been sold to small hotels by regional vendors. Very few of these vendors have offered their clients an "Internet" upgrade. A more interesting trend is emerging where new vendors are offering entirely Internet-based systems. Instead of being sold and housed at the owner's property, these are now hosted on the vendor's servers and delivered on a subscription or per access basis. As such, Application Service Providers or ASPs are among the most powerful tools in the e-business strategy of small hotels and foodservices.

- Accounting and financial management

Most small hotels and foodservices manage their money in very traditional ways, creating sometimes a cumbersome process of conciliating books and controlling productivity. However, the rise of ASP-style Enterprise Resource Planning or ERP software allows SMEs to modernise their accounting practices, and to benefit from a close integration between their PMS and ERP applications, which are now equally affordable and may come from the same vendor.

- E-Procurement

Although small properties are renowned for their unbeatable value/cost advantage, few managers take the time to control costs in buying their supplies. With the rapid development of e-markets where large and small buyers can easily purchase goods and services online, E-Procurement is becoming a very effective new tool for SMEs willing to control their costs. The beauty of such systems is that they may function separately from the larger enterprise systems, or can be integrated at affordable costs.

8.4 Step-by-step guide to implementing your e-business strategy

By clearly targeting their strategy and using the right applications, small hotels and their food services have the opportunity to be active players in the field of e-commerce and e-business. They must respond properly to the key trends in their market segment, in order to create distinctive advantages that will strengthen their position relative to large hotels.

However, large firms have already taken several actions and used a great diversity of best practices, which has not been the case with small hotels. Therefore, a priority for the smart manager is to implement the practices of their market leaders, but achieving similar results with much smaller capital inflows. To do so will help small hotels match the capabilities of large ones and better compete on e-markets.

As any other investment, e-business should be viewed as a "journey", one with several steps that build upon one another. Throughout these steps, which we describe here, one should be constantly aware of a key lesson: the benefits of IT do not come immediately after implementation, but most often in subsequent steps, as the building blocks are put together. As we shall see now, synergy in e-business is 80% of the equation, and an SME willing to benefit from such investments must make sure to complete its evolution.

By studying the recent experiences of large hotels, small ones can easily detect a number of important steps that must be followed in order for them to achieve similar advantages. Although the evolutionary path varies, most small hotels should follow five phases:

- **Phase 1 – Developing your Web site**: Without a front-end, there is no e-commerce (sales online), and little possibility to become an e-business (various processes online). Two steps in that phase are (1) Building a Fully Transactional Web Site, and (2) Adding Features to Facilitate Customisation.

- **Phase 2 – Positioning your Web site**: Once your Web site is developed, a number of important steps must be taken so it gets known and attracts clients: (3) Advertising Your Competitive Advantage, (4) Joining a Destination Management System (DMS), and (5) Putting Rooms in e-Travel Portals.

- **Phase 3 – Reengineering your reservation process**: As your e-commerce activity grows, your processes evolve and become more articulated, to the point of: (6) Streamlining the Reservation Process, (7) Integrating Front and Back Office Functions, (8) Connecting to Central Reservation Systems (CRSs), and (9) Offering M-Commerce to Last-Minute and Busy Travellers.

- **Phase 4 – Building your Back Office**: Although Back and Front Office applications are most often developed in the same time, many firms prefer to invest in Front End solutions first since these are the ones driving the hotel business. But as the volume of business to manage increases substantially, the need for a more sophisticated Back Office emerges very quickly, which can be enhanced by: (10) Outsourcing Internet Solutions, (11) Performing E-Procurement, (12) Integrating E-Procurement and ERP, and (13) Gathering Business Intelligence.

- **Phase 5 – Re-configuring your property**: Finally, in later stages in your firm's evolution, you will want to invest more heavily in new infrastructures, and even in more diversified services, especially by: (14) Connecting Rooms to the Internet, (15) Building a High Tech Property, and (16) Developing Innovative e-commerce Services.

8.4.1   Phase 1 – Developing your Web site

Step 1 – Building a fully transactional Web site

To properly complement the services they offer, and to effectively attract and capture new e-tourism clients, small hotel managers should create a highly functional Web site to simplify travel planning and build confidence (for an introduction to e-marketing and Web site structures, refer to Section 2.3 in Part B of this report). Unfortunately, most SMEs in the hospitality sector see Web sites as a mere reproduction of their glossy brochures, with the possibility to change prices and add general information at will. These practices are far too limited, and have not had any measurable effect on occupancy rates [16].

Currently, the trend is to make Web sites more functional by adding new transactional features such as room customisation, credit card verification and room reservation, reservation of neighbouring activities and products, etc. To do so, small hotels must attempt to mimic some of the efforts of larger hotel chains, which have been able to capture the attention of travel consumers, even to the point of driving as much traffic as the dominant portals [21].

In order to build confidence, they have applied some tools that consistently catch the eye of travel consumers and serves as a seal of quality, such as the ability to view a room virtually, a technology that is becoming more affordable [22]. These solutions allow managers to create dynamic video tours of hotels and resorts, combined with extensive distribution of marketing data on some of the Internet's most popular travel sites.   In addition, they provide the complete applications for Internet-based advertising including: digitising, storage, and streaming of the video productions as well as tracking the effectiveness.

Step 2 – Adding features to facilitate customisation

Although technology has been slow to follow through many promises, some breakthroughs in the area of customisation should fuel key trends further in the years to come, and will make these tools available to SMEs [23].

Using software that allow for customised service reservation, hotels can sell their rooms, but also offer information on, as well as possibly even sell, a great diversity of complementary services, such as theatre tickets for example.   Most of the time, travellers get a travel itinerary, but they would like to have some content so they would know what's happening in the destination they are visiting, what the weather is like, where to go to eat.

But one must be cautioned against travel service providers selling more than their core products online. Hotels should stick to selling hotel rooms. SMEs need not to spend their budgets putting together complicated or, at best, mediocre partnerships.

Customisation-oriented Web sites are very effective to convert online visitors to online buyers by providing choices and more comprehensive information for would-be travellers. Current e-commerce applications have not been designed to let online travel providers market or sell products other than their own. New applications that allow customisation can automatically search for offerings based on a customer's profile and then present those offerings to the user.

The application lets users create dynamic customer profiles, import data from existing customer-loyalty programs, and deliver personalised travel alerts, information and promotional offers.

Small hotels will soon be hit by this trend, which should be viewed not so much as a threat but rather as a great opportunity to distinguish themselves even better than large hotels do. While branded hotels will tend to focus on the standard visitor's itinerary, B&B's and Inns can easily leverage their local contacts to build-up a great diversity of trajectories for their guests to choose from. As such, this technology, which will rapidly become affordable and diffuse to small hotels, will become a powerful tool to really exploit their strategic strengths.

8.4.2 Phase 2 – Positioning your Web site

Step 3 – Advertising your competitive advantage

When advertising their services and Web sites online, small hotels must learn how to play on their strengths. One of them is their unparalleled value/cost advantage, especially for hard-to-access destinations. Indeed, small hotels (in particular those in vacation destinations) have had a tendency to sell their rooms in bulk to consolidators. While finding such financial security is tempting in a context of low occupancy rates, the smart hotel manager will want to resist this tradition, to advertise and sell their rooms by themselves.

Their best asset, a very attractive value/cost ratio, is an excellent mechanism to catch the attention of the budget-conscious international traveller. However, it must be complemented with a world-class (confidence-building) image, and a Web site that allows the user to browse and reserve the activities that clearly demonstrate the human touch of small hotels. Finally, it must be advertised strategically, going beyond regional listings of B&B's and Inns, and attempting to associate to special events. In essence, advertising must be viewed not merely as a fixed cost of doing business, but as a way to help customers save time, which in turn is factored into the value of the services offered by hospitality SMEs [24].

Step 4 – Putting rooms in e-travel portals

Other options will be opened to SMEs, such as putting rooms in a variety of e-travel portals, so that guests can easily set up their own personalised tours, or select from several typical tours along their tastes. The smart hotel manager will properly weigh the relative costs of selecting either a proprietary solution, or joining a portal, or both, depending on the type of traveller it wishes to attract and the breadth of the offering it intends to deliver [25].

In particular, e-travel portals can benefit small hotels with distinctive advantages (whether it is convenient location, proximity to attractions, traditional ambience, special quality/cost ratio, etc.). Most e-travel portals offer customised search capabilities around specific criteria that can help small hotels to stand out more clearly from the pack. Such popular features as a "Value Index" or even a "Clientele Preference" rating can serve to this end. It can help travellers to list hotels based upon relative value, so as to get the most for their travel budgets. After the user determines their lodging criteria, from amenities to travelling with children or pets, the Value Index ranks the available hotel choices. Consequently, e-travel portals allow travellers to properly customise their orders, while allowing hotels the opportunity to better satisfy their customers.

Step 5 – Joining a Destination Management System (DMS)

Among the many best practices useful in streamlining the reservation process of small hotels, local partnerships happen to be among the best mechanisms to access technology [26]. Indeed, Destination Management Systems or DMSs represent an important and flexible entry point to e-commerce for SMEs (for an introduction to this topic, see Chapter 3 in Part B of this report). These solutions are most often offered free to small tourism service providers, with only a base fee for connectivity, training, and a small fee per transaction. Such e-tourism markets are rapidly becoming an excellent reference for the advised traveller willing to optimise any destination-specific trip, as well as an essential tool for the SME willing to complement its e-strategy.

As we can see, small hotels can proceed with individual solutions, so as to integrate their systems one by one to the Internet, thereby changing their practices incrementally [27]. However, other approaches exist at the community level, such as DMSs, which can lead with time to the same results as an ASP, but at much cheaper costs [28]. The result is a dramatically more functional platform, one that is maintained by and for the community, with greater probability to build innovative solutions and functionality, since industry players are actively involved in its development, especially as it may help less developed ones to position their destination more effectively on global markets [29].

8.4.3   Phase 3 – Reengineering your reservation process

Step 6 – Streamlining the reservation process

Some players in the hospitality industry have been building a world-class online reservation process, fully integrated with back-end operations and accounting systems. However, Internet Booking Engines or IBEs are still perceived as a major challenge by most hotels. Yet, one needs only to look at a few success stories to discover the great potential of e-commerce for both large and small hotels, as well as the profitability of such an investment in technology.

The challenge is to make a "transactional" Web site one that converts lookers into bookers. Two forces have been stunting the growth of IBEs for the hotel industry. One of those factors is the difficulty with which a hotel chain can "commodities" and "digitise" its offerings. Unlike selling commodities such as books online, a hotel room brings with it such variables as: smoking or non-smoking; double occupancy or single occupancy; time availability; and hotel amenities. A second force is the problem of intermediation: a hotel room is something often bought by a traveller's corporate travel office or in conjunction with other travel services such as rental cars and airfare. Selling a room on the Internet therefore, has not been a quick and simple proposition for hotels of all sizes, even for large chains [30].

Contrary to the perception that technology is expensive to install and operate, various cost/benefit analyses demonstrate that the cost of IBEs is competitive and perhaps less than conventional reservation processes [31]. More importantly, it becomes evident that the cost of introducing and operating e-commerce in small hotels is easy to control, as part of the basic infrastructure for the operation of the enterprise. Consequently, the smart manager will want to match their competitors' advantages mostly by exploiting the latest, more flexible solutions, which allow better possibilities to control cost [32].

Step 7 – Integrating front and back office functions

While ensuring high profitability and usage of this major asset, IBEs must also become the centre of a small hotel's information management strategy. This requires a systematic reorganisation or reengineering of several front and back office applications, so as to ensure e-commerce yields its full potential. Although very few hotels have implemented such efforts, a great variety of all-in-one, integrated applications have been developed specifically for the hospitality industry.

The priority for small hotels is to ensure that such reengineering comes at low cost, most often as part of their outsourced ASP. Before selecting an IBE, managers should make sure it can effectively connect to back office software, or at least be integrated with the ERP functions offered by the ASP. In addition, one should make sure that the transactional functions are properly augmented with proper features, such as: allow clients to obtain demographic information, review maps, check on world-wide hotel availability, and reserve rooms with the value-added capacity to continuously modify their selections through personalised accounts. All the features should be directly integrated with the back office activities of all third-party service suppliers [33].

Step 8 – Connecting to Central Reservation Systems (CRSs)

Interestingly, IBEs are a way for the hospitality industry to integrate, complement, and then go beyond traditional infrastructures, such as the traditional Central Reservation Systems or CRSs, operated by various companies world-wide and used by travel agencies. Naturally, a small hotel that already appears in such systems may wonder why it should join a new IBE. The answer is fairly simple in the sense that they are interdependent, thus both necessary. Indeed, CRSs have been connected through the Internet, and are directly accessible through IBEs of various solution developers. However, CRSs alone will not be capable to drive all of the potential traffic to a hotel, since IBEs capture most of the Internet e-tourism.

Therefore, hotels that have the greatest chance of maximising reservation power incorporate the Internet into a strategy that also realises the important roles of global distribution systems, and the roles that travel agents still play [34]. This in turn is well justified by the tremendous growth of CRSs and the importance of the Net for their sustained performance. Indeed, Hotel bookings made through the major GDSs - Amadeus, Galileo, Sabre, and Worldspan - increased by 11.4 per cent to almost 50 million bookings last year. Net hotel reservation delivered by CRSs totalled 48,787,000 bookings in 2000, an increase of over 5,000,000 bookings in comparison with the 1999 total of 43,781,000 net reservations. Based on an average daily rate of US$130 and an average length of stay of 2.2 days, 2000 CRS hotel bookings produced over US$13.95 billion in revenue for hotels world-wide. Since 1993, CRS bookings have grown in average at 200% per year [35].

Some advanced technologies have been developed to facilitate a cost-effective implementation of an integrated IBE/CRS strategy [36]. First, a few solutions help to connect CRSs to both front and back offices, allowing a seamless integration of these legacy infrastructures to any e-commerce initiative [37]. The benefits are tremendous, as the access allows an instant management of a hotel's resources and reservations, thereby allowing a better control through Enterprise Resource Planning or ERP management systems. Second, the increased importance of M-Commerce has brought new solutions that help firms to connect their operations to mobile transactions [38]. Third, some solutions have been offered to integrate existing reservation systems with late room reservation portals, allowing hotels to capture new market shares and sell excess capacity more easily [39]. As such, these infrastructure allow SMEs to exploit the full synergy between IBEs and CRSs, overcoming the space-time limitations that both have been sharing until recently.

Step 9 – Offering m-commerce to last-minute and busy travellers

Customisation is increasingly becoming an opportunity with last minute travellers. Although the various applications discussed so far will become dominant for planned guests arrivals and for those willing to lend their loyalty to small hotels, the growth of busy travellers and the premium opportunities they offer should not be overlooked. According to a recent study by Cap Gemini America Ernst & Young, it is projected the number of U.S. Internet users using cell phones for wireless data applications will increase from 3% in 2001 to 78% by the end of 2002 [40].

Interestingly, the needs of last minute travellers will be even easier to satisfy than in the past, thanks to customisation features. However, one key dimension to satisfy this segment must be considered: mobile commerce or M-Commerce, which is the facility offered to busy travellers to access reservation systems through their mobile units (e.g., cellulars, PDA's, etc.).

These are comprehensive, device independent wireless solutions targeted for the Hotel Industry. With one-touch functionality, consumers can securely, conveniently, and remotely make reservations regardless of locality. They allow customers to view available accommodations, check pricing, and make reservations in real-time. By offering M-Commerce, hotels can benefit from automated accommodations booking, reduced operational expenses, and increased channels of business.

Although such solutions appear farfetched for small hotels, several distribution channels are currently being built that will make this technology accessible and affordable for SMEs.

8.4.4 Phase 4 – Building your back office

Step 10 – Outsourcing Internet solutions

The trend towards outsourcing IT has been very intense throughout the service sector, as well as in some manufacturing industries. However, hospitality services have been relatively slower at adopting this practice. The primary reason for this situation may have to do with the nature of IT in hotels: it is primarily small scale and local, concerning only part of the staff based in offices and front desks, focused mostly on putting information in order instead of automating simple tasks, and mostly dependent on the evolution of large industry-wide systems. It occurs that since the latter have not evolved very fast, hotel managers have not seen any good business case for changing IT infrastructures.

The advent of e-commerce is forcing the industry, especially small hotels, to reconsider their approach in managing IT [41-44]. Transferring all Front and Back Office applications to an integrated Application Service Provider or ASP is an attractive option for SMEs to gain access to systems with similar functionality as that of large hotels, especially by partnering with services at the local level [45]. In addition to offering more versatile solutions than proprietary packages, an ASP remains the owner of the application and must ensure its continuous development, providing its client base with the latest technology. Finally, an ASP relieves small hotels from all the typical headaches associated with managing IT, since it performs all maintenance and operational functions through the Internet seamlessly and securely, allowing employees to access data through their browser.

Step 11 – Performing e-procurement

Although streamlining the reservation process is one of the most important challenges touching the whole hospitality industry, it is only recently that hotels have started improving another strategic process, the one by which they purchase goods and services online, or commonly called E-Procurement.

This application is highly strategic since hotels and foodservice companies are among the largest buyers of maintenance, repair, and operational/overhaul or MRO products and services. Most of these supplies are managed through contracts, and hotels rarely enjoy more than a handful of sourcing channels or distributors for each product and service categories. In addition, the need for MRO supplies are often unpredictable, and can become a major irritant for managers in terms of unit cost, service quality, inventory turnover, and procurement cycle time.

These are exactly the problems that Supply Chain Management or SCM applications are designed to resolve, with the hope to radically improve the performance of hotels. However, they require some degree of reengineering of procurement and purchasing processes, as well as new strategies in sourcing MRO supplies.

To facilitate this transition at all levels and for all actors in the value chain, large hotel chains have decided to consolidate their buying power, give up their reliance on large distributors, and connect directly to suppliers in order to reduce unit costs. Such initiatives have led to the creation of more robust and versatile applications specifically designed for linking various suppliers together with their buyers, and to automate the whole procurement process.

Therefore, SCM holds many promises that need to be properly weighed by small hotels too. Clearly, the increased efficiency of purchasing alliances could save industry partners millions of dollars each year, as purchasing managers gain better control over their supplies and also cut down on off-contract purchases, which remains a costly problem for the hospitality sector [46]. For small hotels, new alliance-based SCM applications can solve many of traditional problems since they offer:
- A more simple and predictable process in getting and responding to bids,
- Easier accessibility to a wider choice of suppliers, since Web-based e-procurement applications only require a standard Internet browser for participation,
- Avoidance of manual catalogue searches, with easy uploading of keyword-searchable catalogue information,
- Accurate market-clearing mechanisms such as reverse auctions, which can reduce the prices paid for goods and services by as much as 20%,
- Better product support, which is now only a mouse click away.

Step 12 – Integrating e-procurement and Enterprise Resource Planning (ERP)

However, small hotels face a more stringent limitation that may prevent them from properly participating in such marketplaces. Since few of them have access to an ERP, it will be difficult to integrate e-procurement functions with back-end accounting and inventory. Consequently, the functionality and business model of various SCM solutions must be compared, so as to detect those that fit best with small hotels' needs.

Each solution is distinct and can serve a variety of needs. E-hubs take digital marketplaces a step further by integrating their client or anchor companies' ERP and accounting systems to produce total end-to-end solutions and, in doing so add significant additional value to the business model. For those companies still struggling with ERP installations and legacy systems, however, integrating these into an e-Hub solution may be a challenge over the short term. For the industry at large, it would be helpful to have a standard platform for e-procurement solutions, although any such standard may be too much to expect given the industry's record with IT in the past, and the competition already established in this arena.

We are witnessing the emergence of entirely Web-enabled enterprise and property management solutions, provided by Application Service Providers or ASPs that host and manage complementary SCM software from a central facility. Hoteltools.com is an example of this model where property management, reservations and supply chain integration are aggregated into a single online Enterprise Information Portal or EIP [47].

For smaller companies and independent properties, the ASP model represents an opportunity to access technology and systems that would otherwise be either too expensive or too complicated to consider. Clearly, the completely networked world of hospitality is not too far away. Industry portals are forming to provide industry specific content and resources, e-procurement in some cases, auctions, employment listings and links to third parties. Among the revenue sources these businesses are relying on are commissions, subscriptions, advertising and the like.

To fully realise the benefits of E- Procurement, small hotels will need to answer several questions particular to their case [48]. Among others, they should ask:

- What systems are still necessary, and how should we continue to use legacy platforms?
- What skill sets do we need to acquire, and will it be easy to operate new systems?
- How will our traditional "requisition-to-pay" process be affected?
- Are there any up-front costs to join in with an ASP for smallscale buying?
- Will the ASP partner assume responsibility for managing the application?
- Will the ASP services free resources to be focused on other areas deemed more critical to your core business?

As smart managers will find appropriate answers and strategies, it is highly probable that small hotels will progressively find value in using the Internet for procurement, and that they will develop key strengths allowing them to grow faster and expand their supply base as needed. As they will acquire e-purchasing skills, their staff will become accustomed to SCM applications, to the point of making small hotels active members of hospitality e-purchasing communities. Some examples are found with VerticalNet's e-hospitality.com, hglobe.com, and hospitalitynet.org, which bundle targeted content, career services, and discussion forums along with procurement services. Consequently, small hotel staff using such e-communities can cause a "contagion" effect on the rest of the organisation, demonstrating that E-Procurement applications, coupled with richer contents and ASP functionality, can prove a valuable approach to managing supplier relations as well as the complete information management needs of small hotels [49].

Step 13 – Gathering business intelligence

We regularly find periods of intense and sometimes hostile competition between small and large hotels at local levels. The same competition occurs between dominant vs. alternative destinations at a regional level. Some travellers can benefit from market instability, mostly through lower room prices and more affordable destinations overall. However, this is evidently not the right strategy to follow in attracting the bulk of tourism demand.

Interestingly, the rise of e-commerce and the implementation of more integrated Front and Back Office technology, can lead hospitality SMEs to use information more efficiently so as adjust their competitive strategy according to the needs of the market. Instead of constantly "reacting" to competitor attacks to steal their clientele, small hotels can become more pro-active by studying their existing and potential customers, determining behavioural patterns, and targeting them with customised offers that beat the competition before it even moves.

Achieving such agility requires some business intelligence tools, an area that represents one of the most advanced applications in e-commerce. New technologies can help uncover client behavioural patterns by searching and analysing transaction data, Web site visitor logs, advertising click-through, destination information usage, database queries and downloads, etc. The accumulation and online analysis of such large amounts of data is becoming more feasible, thanks to the use of better workflow management solutions, which allow hotel managers to control their operations in real time, and gather and analyse the right data at the right place at the right time, whether on the Internet or internally [50]. Consequently, business intelligence has become feasible for SMEs capable to exploit their data sources, learn from them, and make appropriate decisions.

Once managers can know what clients want, they can offer them exactly what they want, at the price they want it, and at the moment they want it. They can effectively achieve superior "price discrimination" or matching the price the client is really prepared to pay. The output of intelligence software can then be passed on to a CRM application that in turn monitors all online transactions so as to execute the decision rules that apply to each guest. These may be to add free features to a room, change room prices to a special rate, offer another day at rebate, give a reduction on complementary services, etc. In addition, offers can be customised whether the transaction is made through CRSs, e-travel portals, hotel Web sites, or even mobile portals [51]. In effect, business intelligence software are made to exploit all data sources, from simple transactions to complex loyalty-cards profiles, whether online or offline.

Internet-based intelligence does not serve only to perform CRM functions, but also to assess business performance in real time. For example, data may be gathered on the effectiveness of online advertising through the integrated functionality of IBEs [52]. By discovering certain effective reactions on the part of customers, the advertising may be redirected to pages where they can lead to best results in concluding reservations. As well, managers can also assess the effectiveness of various online initiatives, measuring the "conversion rates" of visitors into new clients, and then detecting what customisation strategies work best.

Although intelligence capabilities have been added most often to Front Office applications, other business functions are now being touched equally by this wave. For example, Property Management Systems (PMSs) can be enhanced with business intelligence applications, in order to perform yield management functions [53, 54]. By closely monitoring online transactions, e-yield software can advise in real time about the relative value of various transactions, one visitor at a time, and optimise room prices to their real value. The information remains constantly up to date by seamlessly consulting inventories, transactions, and complementary services, and providing each client with the optimal service mix that matches their needs and readiness to pay. The information can then be passed to a PMS that will ensure room and guest decisions are passed on to managers who will ensure operations are executed as the order specifies it. In essence, once business intelligence can be fully integrated with existing e-business applications, it can serve to automate several decision-making tasks that would hardly be optimal if processed only by hand.

Therefore, as managers learn how to exploit the power of business intelligence, they discover a new way to manage not only their Front but also their Back Office more efficiently. Most often the issue is to detect, throughout the digital work and data flow of a firm, the patterns of optimal vs. sub-optimal management. This may range from employee time control to highly detailed inventory management techniques. Consequently, intelligence software can make Back Office applications more useful for decision-making, going beyond their mere function of "putting information in order". The objective is obviously to make hospitality operations less chaotic and reach a level of performance that could hardly be imaginable (let alone observable) if it was not for integrated e-business systems.

To conclude, there is a certain evolution in how small hotels will be able to adopt business intelligence. Once managers have learned how to automate Front Office and then Back Office decisions, they will progressively be able to automate environmental scanning and strategic positioning decisions. Given the emergent solutions to integrate such applications with both Internet and internal systems, repetitive decisions will increasingly be taken by software, while leaving the more subtle and soft decisions taken by management. With e-business, small hotels will therefore be called to concentrate on their inner strengths, that is people.

8.4.5   Phase 5 – Re-configuring your property

Step 14 – Connecting rooms to the Internet

The commitment of small hotels to implementing e-commerce best practices must be viewed within the broader context of property infrastructure development. While new systems and solutions are becoming increasingly affordable, complementary assets and services, such as room connectivity, must be considered as necessary tools to accelerate the impact of e-commerce on the enterprise. Consequently, any strategy to grow a small hotel into a more robust and world-class may require some basic investments to make properties more high-tech.

As a clear indicator of its importance, hotel Internet access details are included in The 2001 Corporate Rate Hotel Directory, which is the first major travel directory to do so. The decision to include hotels with Internet access was made following a survey, which found that 44% of business travellers consider it very or extremely necessary to have Internet connections at their hotels [55].

Several hotels are rushing to meet these new needs, offering a high-speed Internet service in every room, and even in other parts of their hotel. Such service gives guests high-speed Internet and e-mail access, on-demand fax services, high-quality printing and workgroup connectivity. All services are accessed from the guest or meeting room by simply plugging a laptop computer into the in-room port [56].

The future of room connectivity may not determine the progress of e-business for small hotels, but may play an interesting role over the longer term, as managers try to develop new services that exploit such infrastructure. Indeed, technology investment is merely one step in the direction towards more profound changes in the way the hotel functions.

Step 15 – Building a high tech property

Evidently, making small hotels more high tech requires managers to realise that technology and their Internet presence should not be stand-alone initiatives, but rather advocate restructuring of all its assets, whether they are tangible (i.e., property fixed assets) or intangible (i.e., systems, staff, culture, etc.).

Hence, reengineering strategic and operational processes must be complemented by a more systematic development of managerial skills and staff professionalism. Training on marketing and management as well as on the use of IT will enable SMEs to appreciate the new developments and take full advantage of the emerging e-commerce tools. Consequently, marketing and management should drive technological development, rather than the opposite, which is the essential message of making small hotels more high tech [31].

We can therefore envision the emergence of small hotels that properly focus their investments in IT, not so much to make them "look" but especially "function" like high tech hotels. This will have to be achieved at lower operating costs and with much smaller capital inflows than those hotels member of international branded chains.

Naturally, the relative feasibility of such initiatives for small hotel will depend on what they want to achieve with their new infrastructures. As we have seen so far, best practices focus on integrating Front and Back Office systems to make information more manageable. However, these initiatives can be directly connected to new systems and networks that will allow employees to perform such front-end processes as check-in/check-out more efficiently [57]. As well, new IT infrastructures and their complete integration should lead to more fluid communications, with the possibility to develop the "paperless" hotel, even allowing guests to retrieve data on their account after they left the hotel, so they can process their travel claims more easily with their employers [58]. The objectives in such cases are to build a habit of e-business on the parts of both the employees and customers, in order to get them used to functioning virtually while preserving confidence in service quality and reliability.

The fusion of high tech properties and e-commerce will inevitably lead to a more transparent and efficient hospitality sector. Small hotels can greatly benefit from such investments as it can allow them to grow a group of more loyal guests, who find greater value with small hotels since they combine a distinct human touch with the efficiency of high tech operations. By integrating the best of both worlds, small hotels will be better able to position themselves online as well as offline, providing them greater coherence in their image, and the possibility of creating a highly valuable brand name associated with technology. Essentially, small hotels should view e-commerce and IT as a unique opportunity to transform themselves, grow faster, and reach a more lucrative stage in their organisational life cycle.

Step 16 – Developing innovative e-commerce services

The decision to outsource all e-commerce, Front, and Back Office applications may provide significant improvements in the short term, but can also prove an excellent opportunity for small hotels to diversify their activities in the long term. This may be the case for some hotels that accept to develop new technological advantages and play a more active role in e-commerce by partnering with local IT experts and developers.

Small hotels can participate as "lead users" in the development of innovative new services and Web site functionality specific to their needs, such as guidance about a destination, selection of complementary services, build visitors profiles, loyalty point systems, etc. These innovative solutions, once developed in partnership with an IT-based firm, can become opportunities for smart managers to diversify activities by earning a revenue in diffusing the solution, and perhaps investing in joint ventures with e-commerce service providers, helping to further develop and mass market innovative e-tourism solutions.

Although this vision may seem far remote for most hospitality entrepreneurs, it takes a more real and immediate meaning as we look into some interesting cases where small hotels in various destinations have succeeded to become innovators in partnership with technology developers, especially by providing industry knowledge to help develop new e-services.

An interesting case of e-commerce product innovation can be found through a hotel's relationship with CRSs, especially those that constantly invest in new Internet functionality [59]. New Web sites developed for hotels represent an ideal "test bed" for technology firms to develop functions that allow hospitality firms to compete through their distinct advantages, whether it is a superior value/cost ratio, a special location in a destination, unique loyalty program features, or simply unbeatable complementary activities [60]. By playing a role of early adopter, the smart manager can effectively position its firm not simply as a technology user, but also as a key beneficiary of its progressive diffusion. As such, these innovative functions can help hotels develop new e-commerce best practices, and especially become world-class references for their industry segment.

Small hotels can also become innovators through their relationship with local e-commerce service providers. These technology-based SMEs are constantly looking for partners to play a leadership role in developing, testing, and marketing innovative solutions. These are often related to new Web services that go beyond the needs of a single hotel and require access to the knowledge base of the whole hospitality industry. For example, consider the creation of new "comparative shopping" functions, or also new functions that help reserve local complementary services [25]. Such cases can be an excellent opportunity for hospitality entrepreneurs to play a leadership role in their community, gathering momentum from local actors around the new solution, and helping them to learn how to exploit its power. This leadership position can pay a lot over the long term, as smart managers can lead their industry to change and become clever in its use of e-commerce.

Once a small hotel starts playing a leadership role in its community, it may have a deep impact in the transformation of its destination. It can act as the core of various touring packages, which can be compiled and proposed to travellers through destination-based portals, even helping to build special travel clubs for their destination [61]. Once these customisable offerings gain popularity, the small hotel that initiated them can earn a reputation of innovator and creative tour designer.

The property at the core of these efforts can gain more value and brand name recognition, with relatively little cost.

However, hospitality SMEs can go beyond their industry segment and become external or even full partners in new e-commerce ventures. Various opportunities exist to diversify and invest in the marketing of new Internet solutions that become a complementary activity for the entrepreneur [62]. This type of involvement requires much more than just providing information on how the new e-service should be structured, implemented, and operated. It means that a small hotel becomes the partner-promoter of a new application that potentially become big business, many times bigger than its core hospitality activity.

Clearly, small hotels can play an increasingly active and diversified role in e-commerce. Starting as simple lead users of new Web solutions, smart managers can decide to play a local leadership role in perfecting and diffusing innovative solution. They can also gather momentum in the community to build innovative travel products based on new Internet solutions thereby profiting more directly from new technologies they contribute in developing. Finally, hospitality entrepreneurs can diversify further their activities by taking part in e-commerce ventures, and even playing a supplier role to Internet firms requiring industry-based participants that can provide the knowledge base to deliver online services.

Naturally, becoming an innovative small hotel is a long evolutionary process. One must expect that such highly advanced activities will grow in importance, as several hospitality entrepreneurs, in various destinations, will become "first movers" to practice e-commerce in their community. Evidently, before innovating a firm must have reengineered its organisation and learned how to use the latest applications. Once smart managers accept to transform their SMEs, to build new competitive advantages, and use them strategically, the benefits of the Internet to small hotels and associated foodservices will be certainly greater than even our most optimistic expectations.

8.5 Critical success factors of your e-business strategy

Responding to e-commerce strategic trends and implementing new best practices requires a simultaneous effort to strengthen technological capabilities by adopting innovative solutions. As we have seen so far, Front and Back Office applications must be reengineered, reconfigured, and reintegrated together to ensure a seamless electronic operation before, during, and after hospitality services are delivered. We have also seen several reasons why such technologies are becoming increasingly affordable and easy to implement for SMEs.

However, there are a variety of ways to acquire such infrastructures and systems, as well as several alternatives in managing/operating the applications. As the e-business "journey" unfolds and new difficulties arise, many small hotels and foodservices may be tempted to abandon or merely scale back their initiatives.

In order to avoid such situations, we must pay close attention to the critical success factors for implementing an e-business strategy in the hospitality sector.

- Targeting your strategy on the right objectives is by far the most important factor. Too many small hotels and food services have built a Web site merely to establish their online presence, giving little thought to the full potential offered by the Internet. The objectives outlined earlier can serve as a beacon for smart managers in search of convincing ideas to build their business case, and steer their e-business initiative in the direction they see fit.

- Taking calculated risks is also an important factor to avoid exhaustion throughout such a long e-business journey. Obviously, no one can predict for sure if your Web site will effectively attract the clientele you are targeting. Neither can any technology guarantee you a definite advantage on your local and regional competitors. However, such risks can be calculated fairly accurately, and with a relatively sharp timeline, by the smart managers who understand their destination and market trends. These are the very lessons that must direct technology investment, resisting the tendency of other stakeholders to corrupt the strategic thinking of e-business initiatives.

- Selecting an all-in-one vendor can become a key survival decision, as many Internet-based solutions are emerging, but few have been properly tested and integrated with existing systems. Consequently, smart managers will want to play a more active leadership role by being first to partner with local vendors to share the risks of some new technologies. In order for an e-business initiative to work, managers must be prepared to steer their IT partners and inspire them about the great business opportunities offered by the functionality you want to develop. Indeed, the most successful hotels and foodservices will be the ones that take the initiative of asking vendors to study their case in details, specify new solutions that meet these needs, test these systems with existing ones, and then market the resulting application in other regions. Such an approach can provide small hotels with a definite advantage over their competitor at the local level.

- Finally, viewing your e-business initiative as a way to grow is a message that must remain constant throughout your efforts. Instead of viewing such investments as a continuation of past strategies, one must see the Internet as an opportunity to break free of the barriers that prevent small hotels from becoming medium-sized and large-independent hotels in their destination. The practice of e-business, and the potential markets that can be captured, can effectively accelerate the graduation from small to large hotel.

8.6   Case studies of innovative e-business solutions

Among the many Internet-based technologies used, we find several interesting case studies that may lead small hotels and foodservices to formulate and implement a high-impact e-business strategy. We review here some cases of leading edge technologies in 4 areas of great potential for the hospitality sector:
- Application Service Providers
- E-Procurement Partnerships
- Property Management Systems
- Competitive Intelligence

8.6.1   Application service providers

It is clear that e-commerce technologies are much more accessible and affordable than they appear at first glance. Small hotels can confidently build their business case and start adopting such solutions, at the pace they want to and proportionately to their capability for change. Consequently, building technological advantages will lead hospitality SMEs to better protect their market base, capture e-tourism consumers, and deliver their services with greater agility and reliability, all with a very reasonable IT investment.

HotelTools

HotelTools Inc. has successfully begun implementation of its next-generation enterprise management platform. The rollout marks the launch of HotelTools' industry leading ASP solution, providing hotel owners and operators with the tools to manage multiple properties, rates and relationships in real time. HotelTools has developed agreements with multiple chains and will deploy its next-generation technology to both new and existing customers throughout 2001 [42].

Newtrade

Newtrade Technologies Inc. delivers advanced e-business solutions that enable hospitality companies to improve online operations and sales performances. Newtrade's innovative platform, TravelSpaces, provides automation, end-to-end connectivity and e-channel distribution management solutions through various distribution channels, including Global Distribution Systems (GDS), reducing costs and maximising visibility and revenues [44].

SynXis

SynXis Corporation, a provider of reservation management and distribution services for the hospitality industry, announced that Morristown, NJ-based Headquarters Plaza Hotel has migrated to the SynXis Agent reservation management system. The 256-room Headquarters Plaza Hotel is a well-known business hotel serving the local corporate and social community for 18 years.

SynXis was selected as the exclusive provider of reservations technology and electronic distribution to Headquarters Plaza. SynXis Agent, a JAVA-based Internet solution, provides Headquarters Plaza with seamless connectivity to the 500,000+ travel agents using the four major Global Distribution Systems (GDSs) to book hotel reservations world-wide. SynXis also enables the property to be booked through major Internet travel portals such as Travelocity, Expedia, Yahoo and PlacesToStay.com. Using SynXis' online booking engine, Book-A-Rez, Headquarters Plaza's Web site (www.hqplazahotel.com) now supports on-line reservations with instant confirmations to guests using the Internet to make hotel reservations.

"We chose SynXis not only for the significant cost savings we will experience with the system, but also for the new level of control we will have over our room inventory," said Bob McIntosh, Director of Sales and Marketing for Headquarters Plaza. "SynXis gives me the power to make automatic rate and availability updates right from my PC – across all channels or to each channel individually. So I can get immediate results to the adjustments in our marketing strategy, and that translates into a better bottom line."

"Headquarters Plaza is a strong, well-known independent hotel that is committed to growing its leisure and corporate business in a cost-effective, hands-on way," said Elmer Coppoolse, Vice President of SynXis. "SynXis technology is a perfect fit for Headquarters Plaza, providing extensive GDS and Internet distribution plus real-time control that helps maximise occupancy and rate."

SynXis is the exclusive provider of JAVA-based technology that allows hotels to centrally manage room inventory across all booking sources, for one or multiple properties. Using the SynXis Agent™ Control Centre, a hotel inventory dashboard, reservations from all sources are consolidated against a centralised inventory. Hotels can easily control rates and availability across all channels from one easy-to-use interface. This flexibility and control can be accessed anytime, from any location with Internet access [43].

Zoho

Zoho Corporation, the premier online marketplace for the hospitality industry, announced its new budget tracking and inventory management applications. The addition of these functions enables Zoho marketplace members to more completely manage the entire purchasing lifecycle online - from tracking and managing operational budgets to monitoring and maintaining inventory levels to instantly purchasing operational goods and services.

Designed for the unique requirements of the hospitality industry, Zoho's new budget tracking feature will allow members to create monthly and yearly operational budgets, monitor and control spending at the expense account level, and report on departmental budget variances. Zoho members will also have access to real-time accounting of both actual and committed monthly spend levels and detailed analytics for purchases to date and related spending patterns. By utilising the budget capability, Zoho members can gain insight into the impact of planned purchases on monthly forecasted spend, enabling them to efficiently control and allocate funds. In addition, using projected occupancy and other standard metrics, Zoho's budget tracking will allow financial managers to easily adjust or recalculate budgets at any time, adding flexibility and improving purchasing decisions.

Zoho's new inventory management capability provides members with a virtual warehouse, enabling department managers to review and evaluate product usage and monitor current inventory and availability from their desktops. The inventory management function will empower property managers to make informed purchasing decisions based on up-to-date and accurate inventory levels, eliminating the costs and inefficiencies of placing small, last-minute orders for operational supplies or likewise eliminating excess inventory spend and managing costly storage requirements for over-purchases [41].

8.6.2   E-Procurement partnerships

A great diversity of SCM integrated with ASP solutions is being proposed to the hospitality industry. Several names in the news include GoCo-op.com (working on P-Co with Marriott and Hyatt), Zoho.com (with Starwood as a shareholder), PurchasePro.com (with Hilton), and others such as ifao.net or hsupply.com working with a variety of hospitality companies and independently owned properties [63, 64].

Alliances to create digital marketplaces furnishing diverse products and services are breaking down trade barriers and offering access to hospitality companies of all sizes. Deutsche Bank currently estimates a $60 billion domestic and $100 billion international market for hospitality e-Procurement, including furniture, fixtures and equipment (FF&E), renovation and construction, service contracts, operating supplies and food and beverage (F&B). Cost savings from more efficient supply chain transactions are currently estimated to be at $3.5 billion to $4 billion in the United States alone, and $7 billion globally. Hospitality procurement of more than $20 billion domestically and $10 billion internationally is forecast to be online in the next 12 to 18 months [48].

Consequently, both large and small hotels can effectively benefit from such E-Procurement partnerships, so as to reduce the unit cost of their supplies and build competitive advantage.

Avendra

Five major hotel chains (Marriott, Hyatt, Bass, ClubCorp, and Fairmont) have formed Avendra, a venture that will leverage the $80 billion a year in hospitality supply, and streamline purchasing by jointly forming an online procurement network.

The venture has the potential to provide tremendous value to hotels, their owners and the operations of other industry participants, according to Hyatt's president, Scott Miller. Marriott chairman, J.W. Marriott Jr., said the partnership is an example of the way his company and others are embracing the new economy by finding faster, more efficient ways to serve their customers. GoCo-op will provide the core e-commerce technology and work with hotels and other technology vendors and service providers to integrate the front and back-office systems needed to make the proposed procurement strategy work.

Avendra now manages the centralised procurement business for all five of its founders. Through these companies' owned, managed, and franchised properties, Avendra has immediate access to serve more than 4,000 hotels (650,000 hotel rooms) and 250 clubs in North America, which together purchase over $10 billion annually in goods and services. In addition, Avendra currently serves almost 500 franchised properties not affiliated with the founders' brands, and plans to significantly expand this business. Finally, Avendra's programs are supported by nearly 500 suppliers and represent more than 700,000 items [63, 64].

8.6.3 Property management systems

Property Management Systems (PMSs) can be enhanced with business intelligence applications, in order to perform yield management functions [53, 54]. By closely monitoring online transactions, e-yield software can advise in real time about the relative value of various transactions, one visitor at a time, and optimise room prices to their real value. The information remains constantly up to date by seamlessly consulting inventories, transactions, and complementary services, and providing each client with the optimal service mix that matches their needs and readiness to pay. The information can then be passed to a PMS that will ensure room and guest decisions are passed on to managers who will ensure operations are executed as the order specifies it. In essence, once business intelligence can be fully integrated with existing e-business applications, it can serve to automate several decision-making tasks that would hardly be optimal if processed only by hand.

E-Yield by IDeaS

IDeaS has developed an e-yield Revenue Management Solution enables hotels, chains and resorts to maximise total revenue and increase revenue per available room (RevPAR) by automating decisions that accept the most profitable business mix.

The e-yield application suite is designed for seamless integration with core hotel technology systems, including property management, central reservation and sales & catering. The e-yield solution is available in property-based, centralised or ASP-based configurations. A Web-based user interface allows clients to remotely access e-yield from any browser. The only completely automated decision solution in the industry, e-yield is also the only solution to forecast both group and transient demand, and the only solution to calculate the value of each type of demand [65].

Fidelio Exchange by MICROS

MICROS Systems has created MICROS-Fidelio Exchange, a new two-way interface that integrates MICROS's CRS and Customer Information System with any hotel Property Management System (PMS). The new interface facilitates full synchronisation of reservations, including shares, multiple rooms, wait list, no shows, cancellations, allotments, rate definitions, package definitions, and guest profiles, as we as a central lookup for customer profiles. The MICROS-Fidelio Exchange provides full support for centralised yield management and the ability for economical and fast deployment of OPUS 2's TopLine PROPHET Enterprise Management System, a yield management application developed by MICROS subsidiary OPUS 2 [66].

Bevinco by The Consortium

A group of six hospitality businesses in Dallas, Orlando and Nashville have announced the formation of a unique business model, called "The Consortium." "As an allied group of business-to-business operators with vast hospitality experience, we can offer insider industry knowledge and field-tested capabilities to assist owners and operators with operational challenges.

Their innovative computerised inventory system is based on weight, not volume, and works with incredible accuracy to eliminate pilferage and inventory shrinkage. Bevinco determines beverage cost potentials for businesses by performing an analysis of sales and bar practices, then institutes its unique inventory control system if the initial audit identifies potential for increased profits [67].

8.6.4   Competitive intelligence

Finally, small hotels are among the first to benefit from intelligence applications dedicated to competitive monitoring. Indeed, managers are constantly wary of what other hotels are doing or how they are reacting to some strategic moves or other initiatives [68, 69]. Unfortunately, answer these concerns requires a market information gathering power that only large hotel chains can purchase. However, with the progressive interfacing of various e-business applications in various hotels, and the compilation of such data through third party information analysts, competitive intelligence applications can be operated at much smaller scales and more affordably than in the past.

HotelNet

Tracking the fluctuations and special online offers of competitive hotels is currently a time consuming and difficult task. With numerous travel sites available, a revenue manager can spend hours checking competitive listings on these various sites. Now, Newport Beach-based Hotel Net Marketing introduces Check-Rate, the first known Web-based product designed to save time and provide competitive rate listings in an easy-to-read online report. Check-Rate quickly searches up to ten travel sites and five competitor hotel listings to simplify online yield management. With Check-Rate, a subscribing hotel's revenue manager has continuous access to an easy-to-read online report, which posts "real-time" rate information for their chosen competitive set on the travel sites they select [68].

IntelligentView

IntelligentView.com has introduced the industry's first dedicated source of aggregated data for comparing and measuring key elements of Web site performance. IntelligentView WebData Series provides customised reports that enable hoteliers to measure and improve site performance, in real time and in relation to local and industry competitors. This unique ability to compare and monitor Web site performance against a competitive set is particularly important since the medium is constantly changing. The product was officially launched at ITB in Berlin and has been in beta test for several months, resulting in many subscription applications [69].

8.7   Future of e-commerce and e-business

What about the future of e-commerce and e-business for hospitality services? For one thing, it is clear that the hospitality industry has been relatively stable over the past decades, with a fairly constant duality between small and large hotels, as well as a constant squeezing between hotel operators and their distribution channels, primarily with Tour Operators. But with the new type of competition emerging, the future is probably going to be different.

Indeed, given the need for evolving towards a more dynamic approach to marketing your small hotel and operating part of your processes online, a number of conclusions must be clearly kept in mind, which point to some key future directions:

- With the rapid change in traveller and tourist lifestyles, tastes, and consumption habits, the structure of the industry will inevitably shift in favour of the companies best able to satisfy the new customers, in all the diversity of their needs.

- So far, e-commerce has not had yet the full-fledged impact that we forecasted. However, unlike other service industries touched by the Internet, current statistics about e-tourism (which represents 25% of online sales to consumers) are among the most solid and serious predictions we can rely on. Indeed, the size and profitability of opportunities offered by e-commerce in travel and tourism services can hardly be overlooked.

- As well, it can be dreadful to disregard the threat of volume displacement or substitution effect, where a company could easily loose a major share of its markets, simply for failing to adopt the right e-commerce best practices.

Therefore, small hotels and associated foodservices find themselves at the crossroads, and must chose wisely before jumping on the Internet bandwagon:

- On one hand, they can choose not to change their approach too dramatically, and pursue business as usual, with the expectation that growth will be slow, but with the satisfaction of keeping operations running with very small capital inflows.

- On the other hand, they can commit to pursuing growth, especially by investing in e-commerce and e-business technologies and infrastructures, proportionately to the kinds, volumes, and shares of markets they want to capture through online transactions.

Judging by the sudden and frenetic awakening of large hotels to e-business imperatives, it appears clear that the second path offers the biggest and most profitable opportunities. Yet, small hotels must still weigh properly what e-commerce holds for them, and how important a player they can become in this area.

As we have discussed throughout this section, three dimensions must be addressed, so as to ensure that your initiatives are coherent.

- First, small hotels will need to choose very carefully how they want to respond to leading Strategic Trends, especially by deciding how they want to differentiate themselves online.

- Second, they will have to implement new Best Practices, especially related to the reservation process, so that they can match the strengths of industry leaders.

- Third, these initiatives will have to be supported by an active investment in Innovative Solutions, thereby exploiting a number of new, more flexible, and more affordable applications available through partnerships with small e-commerce solution providers.

Consequently, the future of e-commerce and e-business for the hospitality industry, and for small hotels in particular, holds more opportunities than threats. As such, formulating an a totally new e-business strategy may be done with the following in mind:

- Smart managers can be confident that their objectives in entering new Internet markets can be met with success. As long as key success factors are respected and the scale of initiatives are reasonable, the odds are in favour of the small hotels that will try to enter early and fast.

- Strong market growth, easier entry into distribution channels, and access to cheaper technologies that integrate seamlessly with legacy platforms, are just a few of the excellent conditions to justify a business case for e-commerce in small hotels.

- The task is now one of strategic planning, especially by envisioning a new company that commits to growth and evolves at another stage in its lifecycle, at the pace of the Internet and its e-tourism consumers [70].

9   Travel Agencies

9.1   Introduction

The rise of e-commerce and e-business has left most travel agents worrying about their future. Some believe in apocalyptic scenarios, where the Internet would reduce their business to merely serving a small (even micro) niche of traditional customers who resist online transactions. Others remain more passive, as they view the Internet as a marvellous tool to search for their client's information, but expect that e-commerce will remain a small activity that will not go beyond the offline business volume. Finally, we find the general opinion shared by an increasing number of travel agents, where e-business is viewed merely as a further extension of the systems and applications they had been using so far, and that will become pervasive but will still require a high degree of interaction with travel agents.

Despite the diversity of opinions, it remains that adapting to new information technology is a top priority on the agenda for the travel agency industry. The importance of the Internet in the tourism industry cannot be ignored anymore. Consumers are turning to the Internet in ever-increasing numbers, both to obtain travel information and to buy travel products. According to the Travel Industry Association (TIA), more than 59 million Americans used the Internet in 2000 to get information on destinations or to check prices and schedules, growing almost 400 per cent over the previous three years. Of that group, TIA said 25 million actually purchased travel products or services in 2000, representing a 382 per cent jump over the figure for 1997[17].

As the business of travel agents moves online, they must decide whether they want to be part of this movement and how to invest in new technologies that will allow them to compete on the Internet. However, before a travel agency decides to commit to e-business, it should ensure its strategy is well targeted on the key trends driving the industry.

9.2   Targeting your e-business strategy

As the head of a small travel agency, there are at least three important strategic decisions that will determine greatly the type, scope, and performance of any e-business initiative. First, you must demystify Internet booking and its impact on travel agencies, which will lead you to decide whether to commit to e-commerce, and if so what direction to take. Second, you must shield your business from the inevitable changes occuring in the industry, mainly by adopting an alternative revenue structure, and by charging service fees in order to be less dependent on commissions paid by airlines or sell alternative travel products. Third, you must move beyond the ticketing business, which is rapidly becoming a "commodity service" readily available through the Internet, and get into new value-added services that will ensure your differenciation and long term growth.

9.2.1   Getting realistic about e-commerce and e-business

Too many travel agents view e-commerce as a very complex activity, requiring technologies that are not accessible to the common agency. As well, many look at the overall offering of E-Travel agents and portals as a service that will become, with time, unbeatable in diversity, price, quality, flexibility, etc. These perceptions fail to recognise two realities:

- E-Commerce and e-business technologies are becoming more affordable and therefore more accessible to all SMEs in the tourism business, including travel agencies.

- Internet booking is not the panacea for all the tourism industry, and a lot of improvements remain to be introduced, which could be done by offline travel agencies (see Table 5).

Table 5 – Myths and realities regarding booking travel on the Internet

Myth	Reality
The cheapest airline fares can be found on the Internet.	No single Internet supplier offers the cheapest fares. And with fares changing constantly, comparison-shopping is essential. Because they have the complete fare picture, travel agents can find the best fares and can suggest cost-saving options such as alternative airports or Saturday stay-over.
Shopping for travel on the Internet gives you instant information.	Yes, but the information may be incomplete. Also, many sites – notably those of some airline-ticket consolidators – are not much more than billboards: "Call us for current prices" is the best you get. Also consider the time it takes to find and access the sites that interest you. It's all too easy to begin a small investigation and suddenly realise you've been online for two or more hours.
The Internet allows you to inquire without disclosing any personal information.	Often you can. But some sites require that you give your name, address and E-mail address before you can access any information. And beware of any site that requires your credit card number before you book your tickets.
The Internet can do anything a conventional travel agency can do.	There's no question the Internet can sell you just about anything these days – including travel. But selling is only a part of a travel agent's job. The rest is personal service. If you buy a ticket over the Internet, whom do you call to make last minute changes in travel plans? To re-book or make a change in your hotel reservation?
The Internet is driving travel agents out of business.	In fact, several travel agencies operate on the Internet. It's simply another tool that your full-service travel agencies use to serve their customers in this e-commerce age.

Source: [71]

As a travel agency discovers the feasibility of entering into e-commerce, it must also learn the important steps to follow in order to become an efficient and reliable e-business. Indeed, whether your objective is to build a more agile back office with little or no electronic relationship with clients, or to complement an existing offline agency with an online offering, or even to develop an entirely new E-Travel portal, all these options require the creation of a solid e-business architecture. As we will explore further, the IT infrastructure of travel agencies is evolving rapidly, and is affecting both offline and online agencies.

However, the window of opportunity for building an e-business strategy may be rather short. As a small travel agency, you must be very careful not to plan your Internet initiative as a long shot, to avoid getting caught in the middle of the road by other trends. In order to build a coherent and realistic strategy, you should make sure to:

- Challenge the misconceptions of the Internet around you and create a true debate

- Commit to an e-business initiative and lead the whole firm to get onboard altogether
- Analyse how the Internet may offer innovative functionalities for your existing operations
- Re-conceive your services by complementing your offline capability with online delivery
- Make online booking as a driver of other services, so as to diversify your Internet offering
- Learn from online interactions and gather the right data to discover client behaviour
- Ensure the human touch of your services can effectively be reproduced online
- Benchmark your innovativeness and renovate your booking applications regularly.

9.2.2   Moving beyond ticketing

As discussed, with the emergence of e-commerce and e-business, the role of the travel agent has changed. It used to be one of gatekeeping, where agents were responsible for most travel sales in the whole industry. However, now more than ever, the travel agent job is becoming centreed on "shopping", as agents specialize and are constantly looking out for the consumer's best interest by helping them find the lowest possible fare. In fact, the travel agent business is slowly (but surely) becoming one of "brokering" and "consulting", instead of merely "ticketing".

These trends come at a time where the tourism value chain (or the interlocking relationships linking travel consumers to service suppliers) is under dramatic shifts, which had been presaged for some years. For example, several airlines believe they no longer need an intermediary to sell their product. Their sales on the Internet are cutting into travel agents' business. Airlines and other travel suppliers are squeezing the travel agent as they cut commissions and sell directly to customers. In the first six months of 1999, about 1,800 American travel agencies went out of business, according to the Airline Reporting Corp [72].

Despite these trends, airline ticketing remains one of the leading e-commerce segment due to several converging factors. The· ease of substituting one remote channel for another and the lack of physical fulfillment have made the traditional visit to a travel agency or to an airline ticket office obsolete for the purchase of airline tickets. Today, the phone call has given way to the Internet as the next step in this evolution. Many airlines are battling non-airline-affiliated travel agencies for total domination of online distribution such as Travelocity and Expedia, the two larger online travel agencies.

Therefore, it is clear that the adoption of the Internet for booking airline tickets will continue regardless of how this channel war plays out, but the possible lack of competition will not be positive for customers. In order for your travel agency to position itself amidst such market turbulence, you should carefully prepare your e-business strategy, make sure to:

- Look at ticketing as merely an attraction factor, an opportunity to get price-loyal clients,
- Develop new services that will distinguish you and position you as the hassle-free agency,
- Build a Web presence that consistently reflect these characteristics and leverage them,

- Create a virtual network of specialised tourism consultants operating on your Web,

- Exploit location-specific opportunities, such as getting personal advice on demand, etc.,

- Advertise aggressively on price and sell packages to get complementary margins, and

- Teach customers to move upscale away from basic and towards higher value packages.

9.2.3 Adopting an alternative revenue base structure

In the same time as they commit to e-business, both online and offline travel agencies should prepare for a future without commissions, if they have not yet done so. They must also continue to increase airline ticket sales or they will risk losing complementary sales of hotel rooms, car rentals, and more profitable travel packages and cruises [73].

For instance, Rosenbluth International gets credit, though sometimes very grudgingly, for having anticipated several of the economic trends that have shaken that industry recently. In the early 1990's -- years before the airlines enraged travel agents and even drove some out of business by slashing commissions on tickets sold -- Rosenbluth began sharply reducing its dependence on commissions and instead started charging corporate clients fees for providing travel-management services [74]

Six years after the airlines first introduced a series of commission cuts that would forever change the shape of the travel agency industry, the American Society of Travel Agents (ASTA) has found that today the clear majority of travel agencies are charging services fees with no adverse effects. The results of this survey send a message loud and clear, that travellers value the services of their travel agent and are willing to pay a fee for the expertise and experience they bring to the table.

Results of the 2001 Service Fees study show that 88 percent of all ASTA member agencies charge service fees for all or some of their services, and in spite of initial scepticism, agencies have encountered little to no resistance from clients. Some travel agency staff found it very hard to ask for a service fee, especially with friends and longstanding clients. But when they are explained the logic that they are professionals and deserve to be treated like professionals, hesitation fades away. Rather than losing clients, agents have found that the implementation of service fees has made very little difference in the size of their client base.

On average, the survey found, ASTA agencies have retained 91 percent of their customers. Prior to 1995, on average, only 20 percent of ASTA agencies were charging service fees. Today, of those agencies that have gone to a service fee schedule, 84 percent of them have been instituted since the commission cuts in 1997. Of those agencies that are charging fees, agents have found that clients are more willing to pay for some services over others. Among the services clients are least willing to pay a fee for are hotel-only reservations (18%) and car-only reservations (15%).

Although a clear majority of travel agencies are now charging fees, the services agencies charge fees for and the amounts they charge vary. The price for issuing airline tickets — the most common service for which fees are assessed — ranges from $5 to $25 per ticket, with a $13.21 average. The vast majority of agencies that charge fees have a standard fee for all airline tickets issued. Compared to 1998, the average service fee for issuing airline tickets has gone up about $3 [75].

Travel agents, faced with dwindling commission rates on ticket sales and declining use of their services, have turned to selling tours, cruises, and travel insurance to make a profit [76]. One other potentially lucrative niche is meetings. The companies that will survive the coming shakeout will offer high touch, not just high tech. Meeting planners need service - just automating the booking process is not the answer [77].

Overall, this trend should lead you as a travel agent to draw some defensive strategies, in order not to get caught off-guard as you will want to focus on implementing your e-business strategy. Indeed, the choice of travel niche must be made in accordance to the kind of tourism e-business your agency may want to enter, and especially whether it will be sufficiently lucrative to help sustain e-business investments. Therefore, your analysis should take in consideration the following steps:

- Analyse what, when, how much your clients are ready to pay, whether offline or online
- Target for fees the products and services where "price elasticity" or sensitivity is lowest
- Teach clients the basic rules of value-for-money by making their online shopping easier
- Build integrated Web-based account statements that transparently display fees or taxes
- Use internal Activity-Based Costing (ABC) to identify clearly price/cost advantages
- Change pricing policies and ensure that clients see that you make them benefit
- Give Internet prices that reflect low operational costs and give service quality measures.

9.3   E-business applications and functionality

Once a small travel agency has properly targeted its e-business strategy, and has put in place the right shielding mechanisms to ensure its sustained financing through offline sales, it must select the type of e-business applications it will invest in.

Fortunately, the diverse application of Information Technology (IT) has lead developers to offer travel agencies a wide array of Internet-based solutions. These must be analysed according to the type and scope of e-business strategy an agency may select, whether it is to renovate Front or Back Office infrastructures (or both), or to develop a new E-Travel portal that will leverage the speciality and brand of an offline agency, or even to merely set up a Web presence for the agency to perform its more traditional ticketing role.

The following e-business applications must be considered, as they offer new and sometime complementary functionalities, in comparison with existing systems and solutions:

- **Internet connectivity:** The Internet is a pervasive technology medium that travel agencies can, and must, leverage and exploit. Use the Internet as an alternative to a leased telecommunication line to connect with customers and suppliers - to connect to the world. Use it to communicate with customers via e-mail and use it to connect with customers from home. For single workstation or small volume producers, the Internet can be used to connect to the CRS to conduct reservation business. Depending on the proximity of the agency to the Internet Service Provider, and to local-call charge policy of the phone company, network costs can be reduced fairly substantially. Agencies using, for example, Galileo's

FocalpointNet product to connect directly to our Apollo host system via the Internet are saving around 25 to 40 per cent compared to a leased line [78]. Travel agents should use the Internet to obtain information, and perhaps fares not available elsewhere, to make their services more available to their customers. A wealth of information is available on the Net, and CRSs are now enabling access to Internet information directly form desktop products via Web portals. Competing successfully will, in large part, be determined by the agent's ability to add value to the travel transaction for the customer. They can tap into that value with Web travel and destination content. Information about destination weather, visa requirements, local attractions, maps, travel books and more are all available on the Web.

- **Main Web site:** Few travel agencies have taken the time to develop an online presence, contrary to many others in the tourism industry. Yet, agencies benefit from the fact that the primary purpose of their Web Site is not transaction but information. Indeed, contrary to other service providers (e.g., hotels, attractions, etc.) who must care more for property accounting, travel agencies must find a way to help their clients make informed choices. Fortunately, with the development of new Destination Management Systems (DMSs) and other integrated solutions as Application Service Providers (ASPs), agencies will find their Web Site very affordable, as mainly a challenge of designing its content and promotion.

- **Global or Central Reservation Systems (CRSs):** Although these are the traditional tools of travel agents, they must also become more integrated with an agency's Web Site, since they represent the primary e-business function facing clients directly. Fortunately, most CRSs have been connected to the Internet, and are very often part of a complete package for ASPs operating their own integrated Internet Booking Engines (IBEs) for various tourism service providers, including destination specialists and travel agencies. CRSs now provide a variety of solutions allowing the Internet to be used to actually conduct business with customers and to have a Web site through which travel and valuable services are sold. There are off-the-shelf products that can be branded with the agency logo and there is the ability to build flexible and scalable sites that font-end to the CRS core using structured data.

- **Customer Relationship Management (CRM):** Of all the actors throughout the tourism value chain, travel agencies are the ones who entertain with each customer the most frequent and repetitive relations. In addition, they are also the ones who have the most impact on their choices, and therefore who can happen to learn the most from them. As a travel agency grows, and becomes virtual as a result of its e-commerce activities, it must find ways to manage the high volume of client data, needs, tastes, and behavioural patterns, so as to optimise the shopping offers made to each client. Solutions like CRM, integrated with high technology Call Centres, are essential tools in that case. The name of the game is multiple channels of distribution and points of presence. Travel agents want to position themselves to sell travel however their customers want to buy it - over the counter, over the Web or over the phone.

- **Supply Chain Management (SCM):** Of all the systems that remain the least integrated with Front and Back Office applications, we find the relationship with suppliers such as consolidators and tour operators. These systems, even when connected to the Internet, are not properly integrated with the internal systems of agencies. Yet, they are often the source of major headaches for agency managers, as they are the systems that distinguish travel agencies from the common online booker, and are the primary tool to meet consumers' value/cost expectations. Consequently, any e-business initiative must take into account the possibility of partnering with various suppliers to develop customised connectors between internal agency systems and supplier systems, in order to build a seamless SCM system, and a high degree of agility to respond to client demands quickly and on target.

- **Agency Management Systems (AMS's):** Small travel agencies rarely computerise their internal operations and accounting. Yet, operating jointly an offline and online agency, channelling clients to the right travel expert, empowering employees in making important decisions with various channels, and especially learning to operate in a virtual fashion, all require a close look at workflow management. In addition, with the multiplication and decentralisation of decision-making, AMS's must be closely integrated with Enterprise Resource Planning (ERP) solutions, whether they are used for basic control (e.g., strictly for the purpose of managerial reporting) or more diffused across partner organisations (e.g., used by various agencies in a collaborative alliance of specialised travel agents).

9.4 Step-by-step guide to implementing your e-business strategy

Once a small travel agency commits to e-commerce and e-business, there must be a careful implementation of the strategy so as to prevent the least disruptions of ongoing operations. Each agency will have its own evolution depending on the pressures felt in its market segment (e.g. generalist vs. specialist; vacation vs. corporate; branded franchisee vs. independent agent, etc.). However, small agencies that have had little experience with the Internet (which includes the majority of agents) will most likely evolve through three phases:

- **Phase 1 – Scaling your strategy and resources**: Small agencies must first solidify e-business initiatives by: (1) integrating online and offline activities, (2) sharing IT through alliances.

- **Phase 2 – Building infrastructure and competencies**: Then they must build their key assets: (3) integrated Front and Back Office applications, and (4) competent human resources.

- **Phase 3 – Focusing applications on service excellence**: Finally, systems must be exploited to: (5) build customer loyalty, (6) gather market intelligence, (7) provide customised products based on intelligence, and (8) identify high growth niches in which to specialise.

9.4.1 Phase 1 – Scaling your strategy and resources

Step 1 – Transforming into a "click & mortar" travel agency

Nowadays, a great number of traditional travel agencies, or so-called "brick and mortar" agencies are pursuing an online strategy, and are changing themselves to become "click and mortar" agencies. There are combining two types of business: offline and online.
As discount brockage chief Charles Schwab said, "Future business success will hinge not on pitting brick-and-mortar companies against online-only efforts, but in successfully integrating the two". [78]

Combined "Brick & Click" model now allows consumers to choose how to access travel products and services based on their individual preferences (e.g., Uniglobe, which has made the most efforts to integrate its bricks and clicks) [79]. Consumers have access on the Web to a comprehensive array of innovative travel plans and tools, technology and customer services. There are on the market some booking engines that simultaneously search for the lowest airfares and travel dates while also displaying alternate available dates in a single screen. New Web sites were launched offering several innovative features including a package channel and a tours channel [80].

Therefore, to become a click and mortar agency, at least 2 major efforts must be accomplished [81]:

- **Get connected to the Internet:** The following is a review of a number of options that would allow an agency to get connected to the Internet. These include modems, mini-routers and a server connected with a router. On modems, this is the way many small organisations started because the cost is low. The downside is that while you get an Internet connection, there is no "professional" e-mail, no network security and no Web publishing. The mini-routers solution offers Internet connectivity for the whole office at a low cost, but again, no "professional" e-mail, no network security and no Web publishing. The third option is a server connected with a router, but that this can be an expensive option that would be out of the rearch of many small agencies and would require a technical specialist to connect it. To fill in the gap, some application service providers have developed an all-in-one solution designed for small businesses with between five and 50 users. It is a hardware solution that provides "professional" e-mail, network security, Web publishing and Internet access.

- **Get found on the Internet**: While many agencies simply put up their Web sites and hope for the best, it is simply not good enough as getting found on the Net can be a "complex" game. The following are four key issues that agencies should look at when putting up a Web site: Making sure it serves "real" travellers; Making sure you get found; Getting it on the screen fast; Making sure it works technically and in all browsers. In order to get people onto your site it helps if you besome a specialist. For agencies, there are specialities, such as scuba diving, cruises, golf, tennis, etc. that can be used to attract travellers to the site. On getting found on the Net, travel agencies have to be warned against making the assumption that many do that the site has to have fancy graphics and special effects. In many cases this could be a negative factor. Agencies should optimize their site's content and layout for all search engines. And it is with search engines that things get a little tricky, even complicated. Sites have to be registered with the search engines and then regularly updated. The goal is to get your site into the top ten that appear in a search for your particular area of expertise. People are busy today and that means your site needs to get on screen fast, so travel agencies are advised to cut the clutter. Travel agencies must make sure that the site works technically and in all browsers. It has to be emphasized that it is wise for a travel agency no to get ahead of the market and the technology that is actually in use.

Step 2 – Joining alliances

Worried travel agents are just one sign that although on-line travel still has a long way to go in many countries, it is already starting to shake up established relationships in the industry.

In the new world of travel sales, historically low-tech travel agencies are realising that change is the key to survival. Internet companies, as well as airlines and other travel suppliers that offer online booking services, are pushing them out of the market. In 1999 alone, corporate travellers dropped more than $7 billion on travel expenses online. The online travel market will reach $20 billion by 2001. The two-pronged menace of dwindling commissions from airlines and the proliferation of Internet competition have forced travel agencies to ask themselves if they have outlived their usefulness. Travel agencies are responding to the threat of dis-intermediation with solutions such as embracing IT or providing speciality services [82].

Airlines, hotels and cruise lines are looking to deal directly with their customers via e-commerce, while Internet start-ups are trying to capture a chunk of the travel budget. For the scores of traditional travel agents who sell the vast majority of tickets, tours and packages, adapting today is essential to protect business tomorrow.

It is not only travel agents that are changing. The industry as a whole is grappling with how to handle this new way of distributing its products. Anyone familiar with the current reservation systems, ticketing procedures and fare formulas that are the tools of the travel business would say a change is welcome. The first to feel the shift are the traditional middlemen [83].

The travel agency business, reputed for its high degree of fragmentation, now has the opportunity to consolidate around e-commerce initiatives. Alternatives range from alliances, franchising, or even independent networks. But all options are seen as winning strategies, especially in the face of mounting pressures from both clients and suppliers. Small and independent travel agencies cannot afford to pay alone the high costs of IT solutions development. Joining a large group or being part of a travel agencies network in order to have access to the latest travel technologies appears to be an interesting solution.

Around the world, there are numerous travel agency consortia groups in operations, which put an emphasis on the use of IT. Some are nationwide network of many hundred of, even thousand of travel agencies featuring agents dedicated to providing consumers with the finest in vacation packages, cruises, tours and all types of leisure travel services. They use the group's Web site to promote their brand and services. The typical features that can be seen on their Web site are the followings (for example, consider the group "XYZ-Travel.com"):

- Enjoy The Convenience Of The Web: Shop for all your travelling needs at home, from the office, on the road virtually anywhere.

- Relish The Personal Attention Of A Qualified Agent: It all just starts on the Web. One-to-one service is important to XYZ-Travel.com. You'll be contacted by a certified XYZ- Travel.com member agent, who will offer you personal attention, security and confidentiality.

- Delight In Valued-Added Vacations: XYZ-Travel.com member agencies offer some of the best travel values "out there." Pick a destination, and let your XYZ-Tavel.com agent find the perfect vacation for you.

- Finding AXYZ-Travel.com Agency: Simply input your address in our Agency Finder to locate the member agencies closest to your geographic location [84].

Having a strong brand is key for any travel groups to succeed online. Branding competition is fierce among the large travel groups. Forrester Research expects this online booking to grow six-fold over the next two years. How are the existing players going to compete? The broad strategies are to e-enable existing brands, launch new online businesses and to capitalise on the control of product. A e-business strategy for travel agencies alliances should include the two following elements: Firstly, to make sure all their existing brands have an online sales capability. Secondly, to launch a super-brand, one single distribution entity at which I could throw huge chunks of marketing budget to create an online travel business which would achieve high consumer recognition. There is a need to do this because if marketing effort is spent across too many brand entities, none would achieve recognition and they would all remain lacklustre businesses [85].

9.4.2   Phase 2 – Building infrastructure and competencies

Step 3 – Creating a high-tech operation

In the current travel business context, both Front and Back Office automation are a must to gain efficiency and profitability, and to meet customers' expectations.

There are applications that enable agents to market products and services to appropriate customers by sending tailored emails from within this new technology. The agent's role is changing from being merely a single point of sale on the high street. With these new functionalities, independent agents can compete against the Internet and TV. For a monthly fee, and at the nod from a customer, agents are able to turn to their online customer database put on that technology, and email out the promotions and product news their clients opt to hear about. The service can be used either as a one-off, when the customer comes in to the agency to see what's currently available, or it can be set up to send out daily emails detailing the various appropriate holidays on offer, up until a specified date. Brochure facility permits agents to attach pages from brochures to emails.

Other features can offer an Expert Finder service. This logs up to five areas of personal expertise for each agent, meaning that when customers call with specific enquiries about a certain country or activity, they are quickly directed to an agent well qualified to advise them. All this has been specifically developed from feedback from agents. It's all about enhancing the customer service experience: promoting the right product to the right customer at the right time. Agents are no longer just a point of sale. They are a whole selling system. [86]

A leading business-to-business travel distribution company has developed a technology to help travel agents more quickly and accurately complete the ticketing process. The company's system checks agent-created request records for accuracy, then automatically issues passenger tickets - all in a matter of seconds. This technology provider offers a unique value proposition to travel agencies and corporate travel departments by aggregating the complete inventories of the world's four major Global Distribution Systems (GDSs) - Amadeus, Apollo, Sabre and Worldspan - into a simple-to-use Internet-based platform. Its customers also have access to hotel inventory providers Pegasus and Hotel Quest [63].

Travel agency consortias have now access to an application that enable them to connect with customers and sponsored tour agencies, and to streamline processes associated with its tour planning and organising functions. They can conduct online order processing, catalogue management, ticket reservation, hotel booking, and CRM [87].

Customers of a major online travel agency in Europe have been given more choice and control when booking their travel following the introduction of a new technology platform, Expert Searching and Pricing (ESP). The enhancements to the site will offer customers the followings: an immediate wider selection of flights and fares to choose from, including new Flexfare, saving on the need to scroll through pages of fares; improved user interface with more control over searching criteria giving the customer what they want to see instantly; and new European city to city driving instructions, eliminating the need to buy road maps when hiring cars or taking a driving holiday [88].

Step 4 – Training staff with new technologies

In the service sector such as travel and tourism, the quality of a company's human resources is often the factor that makes the difference between competitors. Nowadays, to succeed in the travel business, staff's needs to be trained on a regular basis to the use on new technologies in their field.

The single-most important factor affecting training today is technology - and, in particular, the Internet. Tremendous advances and changes to technology within the retail travel community have created an environment in which people at all levels must become knowledgeable with respect to technological applications and their own job. There are a few essential factors at each level that should be considered when contemplating your technological future [89].

Owners: Although not always a "hand-on" person, owners need to ensure that their agency is moving forward with technological changes and not just maintaining pace. Owners should be:

- Using the Internet as a distribution channel for their agency, contemplating the development of their own Web site, providing the necessary tools to facilitate bookings and gathering information.

- Increasing supplier leverage and global presence by becoming part of a larger buying group (e.g. consortium, chain or franchise). Agency owners need to have greater clout in their negotiating power. As a whole, the retail industry must be able to strike deals for compensation for the services provided. Alignment with larger groups is required to accomplish this goal and having a market share of 25 per cent or more will earn the respect of suppliers and ensure that travel agencies are a force to be recognised.

Managers: They have one of the toughest areas to cover. Not only do they need to set and lead by example, but they must also provide the training climate to ensure that staff is keeping up do date. Managers should be focusing on the following areas of their business:

- Upgrading their counsellor skills to ensure that they are competent to use the search engines wisely and source material in a timely fashion.
- Investing in human resource programs to retain their current workforce.
- Hiring people who embrace technology and are willing and able to share information.
- Obtaining management skills necessary to run a profitable business.
- Practising Web/e-mail marketing.
- Supporting change-management within their offices to move counsellors from the "bricks and mortar" stage to the "clicks and mortar" stage.
- Targeting market segments. It is no longer enough to be a general merchant. In today's marketplace, it is possible for even a small agency outlet to appeal to a much broader client base. If an agency has a speciality or knows how to service a niche market, it doesn't matter where their storefront is located. Remember, potential clients can reach them through the Internet.

Counsellors: These actors are required to be skilled in searching out information from the Internet in order to provide better customer service to their clients. Counsellors should be:

- Using the Internet as an additional information channel. Hard-copy reference materials are the traditional ways of researching destination information, etc. for clients, but they can be quite expensive and often required the purchase of updated texts on a yearly basis. Examining the content of existing Web sites is an excellent way for counsellors to ensure that the information they are passing along to clients is never out of date.

- Using the Internet as a secondary transaction-processing (reservations and ticketing) channel. With a proliferation of consolidators, low-cost airlines and tour operators that can be only booked online, the Computer Reservations System (CRS) is no longer the only source.

- Using booking engines found on the Internet to expedite reservations for corporate clients who are very comfortable with technology.

- Reading the daily news and enhancement pages of your CRS for new ways to deliver products and services to your clients.

Educators: Traditional ways of technology training by retail travel programs need to be updated to produce graduates who are qualified to perform in the technology-based world of online bookings and Internet research, Travel programs and instructors should be:

- Allowing for distance learning and testing via the Internet.

- Providing "real-time" tools (live CRS, Internet etc.) to learn technology-based administrative systems.

- Including industry veterans in their advisory committees to maintain school programs that are relevant.

- Creating measures of achievement that are based on student employment within the industry rather than how many students graduate from the program.

- Listening and responding to comments from owners/managers regarding the ability of placement students to work on live systems without having been trained on simulated ones. Textbooks and simulated systems are not enough to provide technology-savvy, entry-level counsellors into the marketplace.

Most of the travel agents associations around the world recognised the importance of training staff to the use of new technologies. They put the emphasis on education with diverse new offerings. Travel agents repeatedly hear that the key to success in today's market is to specialise, and skills and expertise are always in high demand [90].

There are several examples of typical theme and topics covered in IT seminars for travel agents. For example, consider the one entitled "Isn't it time to join the e-commerce revolution and be "enormously profitable?", which covers the following typical topics [91]:

- Optimising Your PC.

- Email Tips and Tricks.

- Cyber Travel Specialist.

- Web Page Design. How to Build a More Meaningful Workplace. Learn how to create or enhance your present site to increase your profit and sales, track your number of hits for demographic studies, or eliminate huge postage bills just by utilising the Internet.

- E- Business/Commerce: Learn how to negotiate net prices and still make money.

- Surfing the Internet. Building International Partners for Inbound and Outbound Tourism Opportunities Launching a group business from your agency may seem overwhelming and time consuming, but, with a little guidance and training, the job will be easier and the rewards priceless.
- Building a network of international partners offers an unlimited opportunity to expand your client base and see your profits soar.
- What agents can do to keep thriving in the electronic age, and provide a peek at some new opportunities created by technology and the Internet.

Many other kinds of training programmes are offered to travel agents. Another interesting example is that of Cruise Lines International Association (CLIA), where travel agents who don't have time for on-site training programs can log on to its online training site to train at home and in the office at times that are convenient for them. Numerous CLIA-affiliated travel agents have signed up for CLIA's cyber training program, studying three core courses for the Cruise Counsellor Certification Program - "Cruise Vacations: An Introduction", "Principles of Professional Selling" and "Power Selling Techniques" - online at their own pace. Agents can log onto the www.theacademy.com Web site or link to the site from the Travel Agency Resource Centre on CLIA's www.cruising.org Web site. Once in the program, they hit the "continue" button, do the interactive demos and study the materials" [92].

9.4.3   Phase 3 – Focusing applications on service excellence

Step 5 – Developing customer loyalty

Internet purchasing of travel has its limitations, and nothing can replace good, attentive service from a travel agent. Hence those agents who give good service will survive. Use of technology though can help to develop a loyalty programme, which will contribute to maintain agency's profitability.

Building customer loyalty, doing proactive marketing, or one-to-one marketing. All these business concepts have to be implemented in order to have success in a highly competitive industry such as the travel industry. For instance, American Express has a long tradition in developing innovative loyalty programmes or initiatives. It has been testing recently a free Internet service for cardholders. The service, called American Express Online, provides free unlimited Web access, with 24/7 customer service, a Web-based e-mail account with the AmexOL.net domain name, and single-click access to American Express card account information and promotional offers [93].

Independent travel agencies or travel agency consortia groups could benefit in using Customer Relations Management (CRM) tools and solutions available on the market. Such new Internet-based CRM tools are designed to help travel agencies build customer loyalty and make the transition from order taking to proactive marketing. They enable travel agents to better service and sell these products to their travel clients by providing Web-enabled client registration, customer self-service, agent-assisted service, and permission-based email marketing.

The technology can help to increase look-to-book and loyalty. The technology eliminates the complexity by delivering professional travel expertise in a personal, reliable way - real-time, every time. With the integrated expertise behind such advice tools, technology can deliver quality, on-target recommendations that no single expert, no matter how experienced, can match.

Another technology provider has created advice tools, which custom-fit leisure and booking resources to the individual lifestyle of each traveller. It is built on the notion that every person's tastes are unique, like a fingerprint. In contrast to primitive checkbox profiling, which treats every leisure interest as having the same value, these new technology capture not only the likes and dislikes of every person, but also the relative degree of each person's leisure preferences. Such technology profiling has the power to hold billions of unique profiles, truly representing every person on the planet [94].

Step 6 – Gathering market intelligence

One key rule of the success for big online travel agencies such as Travelocity and Expedia relies on the extensive use of databases and data-mining management. Travelocity uses an NCR data warehouse with consumer information it gleans through Web transactions. It utilises this data to personalise communication with return visitors to the site, who must register to use Travelocity's services. The travel firm's marketing staff uses Cognos online reporting software to target visitors with appropriate offers, yielding a healthy "looker-to-booker" ratio of almost 9 percent. The company is majority-owned by travel distributor and technology firm Sabre Holdings, and relies on its parent's computer reservations mainframe, which it said has proved scalable and reliable. Travelocity has added proprietary search tools and other Web applications to handle tasks not suitable for a mainframe.

Microsoft spin-off Expedia, meanwhile, has built a transaction engine called Expert Searching and Pricing that imports published airfares and hotel prices from travel partners via XML to a central database. ESP's PC server architecture yields results faster and in greater quantity than a mainframe would. Expedia went with the diffuse server approach so it could scale not just with its user base, with the types of products it sells, which now include packages combining air and hotel fares, cruises and specially negotiated fares. The company stores customer information in a database server farm for scalability as well.

Another travel site is Priceline, which has implemented its own specialised technology for its unique name-your-own-price business strategy. The company struck cut-rate partnerships with airlines, rental car companies and hotels, which use a computer interface to enter special fares into a secure "partition" server operated by Priceline. The travel firm then takes consumer price requests for certain air routes, for example, and crunches the partition data to find a match. Priceline uses 100 percent proprietary technology. Whether Priceline's business model will ever work is still in question, and the challenges facing both Travelocity and Expedia are still quite large. Among them is the growing online presence of the airlines themselves, which are developing applications for managing frequent-flier miles and for airport check-in that the travel sites may not be able to replicate [95].

Small travel agencies cannot afford the same databases solutions than these large online companies. However, they have the option to buy from a technology solutions provider specialised in the travel business, a solution that suits their needs, and which they can afford financially.

Step 7 – Creating custom-made travel products

Whether setting up dinner reservations for an important business deal, booking a flight on the road with a cell phone or using e-marketplaces to expand sales channels and cut costs, companies in the travel and hospitality industry clearly are being transformed by the Internet.

Travel agents who want to use the Internet to put together attraction lists for their clients may find their job is a lot easier as a result of the development of Web tools such a new one, arrived on the market recently, that automates the process of grabbing data and printing it in an integrated travel agenda. The application allow user to incorporate any of the many thousand places featured in the supplier's Travel Encyclopaedia into an itinerary or agenda. The information can be "dragged and dropped" onto specific days and in any order required on a personal travel calendar. As well, the software allows the addition of personal appointments, meetings, flights, hotels or family visits. If an attraction is closed on a specific day, the software will give users warning of that fact. It takes national holidays and differing seasons into account, as well as day of the week. The document can be printed as a personal destination guide that provides a day-by-day outline for the traveller [96].

A new application provides travellers with an easy and convenient way to access customised travel information anytime, anywhere, while also enabling the travel professionals to offer more effective customer service and more efficient travel planning. In addition to containing all components of a traveller's itinerary (air, car, hotel, cruise, rail, tour), this application provides full-feature graphical displays of destination-specific data, thus empowering travellers to see everything from: Airline seating charts; Weather updates; Hotel maps and driving directions; Currency exchange; Bed and breakfast information; Destination & restaurant information; Real-time flight-tracking data including the latest arrival and departure information; Links to over 500 airports' Web sites world-wide; Metrics conversion tool; Interactive world-time clock.

Interestingly, such an online itinerary tools can also being made available to customers world-wide via localised Websites designed to suit their specific needs. The application also lets users print travel plans; offers a customised e-mail option that notifies friends and family or business associates of the latest changes in itinerary. Once a trip is booked through one of the thousands of travel professionals or online booking sites connected to the system, an e-mail containing the trip details along with the URL link to the Web site is immediately sent to the traveller by their agent. The traveller reviews their e-mail trip details or simply clicks the link to launch their personalised travel itinerary. If the traveller does not have access to e-mail, it is possible to obtain travel plan details at anytime by logging onto the Web site [97].

A technology service provider offers to travel agents an application that provide retailers with the ability to regularly post "packaged" travel product on the supplier Web site. This service provides travel agents with a new vehicle through which they can promote and sell their products to consumers using the Internet. Consumers using the supplier Web site will have the ability to search for posted product using a variety of categories - destination, type of vacation, family, hotel, airline, car rental, etc. – and when they click a button for further information, they will ultimately end up at the agency's own Web site. Independent retailers, squeezed by decreasing revenue streams, generally can't afford to spend many thousands of dollars developing an e-commerce system for their agency. The supplier provides agents with an opportunity to better target their promotional and selling activities on the Internet [98].

A technology provider has developed a series of software programs that will allow him to unite the travel agent and the travel supplier in a cost effective model that will allow them to increase their distribution and their profitability. The company has indexed and catalogued thousands of Web sites. Staffers are now checking those URLs to ensure that the sites catalogued are legitimate travel suppliers sites. Along with this inventory, the company will also be going out to suppliers to convince them to store their product information in the supplier's XML database. By doing this, agents will have access to that information in a form that will allow them to electronically publish it and send it on to their clients. The key applications in the software package include a Customer Relations Management (CRM) component, which allows agents to target market to their clients. This is a major plus for agents because it allows them to grow their business by having a better marketing machine than their competition.

Just as important, is the systems search capability, which reduces the amount of time the retailer will spend looking for the product they want. Once the information is found, agents will use the system's trip builder component to put together an offer document that outlines what was requested and offers one or more options. That's sent to the client and the client can then respond - using a collaboration engine that's also part of the package - accepting, making additional suggestions or requests or tailoring the elements until they get what they want. There's also a media module that provides agents with articles on a destination, hotel, etc., weather information, and other standard features [99].

Step 8 – Specialising in a growing market niche

Travel counsellors possess a depth of travel alternative knowledge and know how to match that knowledge to satisfy the needs and desires of their customers. No matter what their speciality, travel agents know how to ask the right questions to get to the heart of the matter. For instance: Does planning golf vacations tee you off? What's more important to you: that the course is highly rated or the hotel? Perhaps you play and your spouse doesn't. What about sightseeing? How much are greens fees? How about lessons? Let your travel agent find the answer for you. Fancy a spa vacation? Are you looking for resort and or a retreat? Are you seeking unique types of treatments, or perhaps you'd like to mix your spa stay with a soft adventure experience? Do you prefer an all-inclusive resort where one price covers everything? Your travel agent spa specialist will find the right combination for you.

To ensure the consumer is well-served, the American Society of Travel Agents (ASTA) has developed a special interest certification program where members learn the different aspects of special interest travel, including family travel, soft and hard adventure travel, eco-tourism and travel for a mature clientele. The results have been satisfying for both travel agents and their clients. Among the more popular specialities for ASTA member travel agents are cruises, tours, luxury travel, family travel, adventure travel, beach vacations, customised travel, travellers with disabilities and golf vacations. More unusual, among ASTA members' 90 different catalogued specialities we find: genealogy travel, dive vacations, educational travel, sports tours or travel for women or singles [100-103].

9.5   Critical success factors of your e-business strategy

The transformation from a traditional (purely offline) travel agency to a modern, high tech, and mostly hybrid (both offline and online) agency is a long and risky process. Several factors can come to play a part in the relative success of any e-business initiative. In the case of a small travel agency, the following should be considered carefully at each step:

- Above all, making a decision is crucial. Of all the actors in the tourism industry, travel agencies have been among the slowest (and sometime the most resistant) in reacting to the emergence of e-commerce and e-business. This may have to do with the fact that most small agencies are run in a collegial fashion, which may diffuse and slow down the decision-making process, and also prevent any effort to effectively delegate and accurately control the task of building and running an E-business initiative. Jumpstarting a project of that sort requires sustained commitment, and small travel agencies must be aware that their organisational profile puts them at risk in managing such technologies.

- Not being afraid to share resources and knowledge with other agencies. Chances are that your e-business initiative will never see the light if you rely strictly on your own capital. Forging alliances is crucial, but unfortunately is not a natural tendency of small travel agencies, since they are notoriously fierce competitors based mostly on location. Yet, one must understand that the competitive landscape and space is definitely not the same in e-commerce. Customers are not attracted merely by local proximity (although it has a certain importance), but primarily by breadth of service, expertise, and best value/cost guarantees. This is only achievable by allying with partners who, most often, will develop a different specialisation than your own. Consequently, the fear of alliances and networks should be easily overcome by adopting a realistic vision of e-commerce.

- Specialising wisely and sticking to ones' guns. Unfortunately, an E-Travel agency may soon be flooded by a wider diversity of demands coming from online channels, as opposed to its traditional street-level demands. This can easily create disruption of ongoing operations, and lead an e-business initiative to be much less profitable than offline activities. The best way in such a case is to specialise in those segments the agency is most likely to reach a reasonable level of profitability, minimising the time it requires to customise orders and relate to a limited but easily accessible base of suppliers.

- Finally, probably the most important lessons of all is to never loose your human touch. Small travel agencies are renown for their quality of service. However, as we see with large agencies, the rapid shift to Call Centres and intensive Web relationships can kill the bond that an agent most often develops with her/his clients. Consequently, e-business initiatives should be aggressively disciplined around the principle of staying close to the client, even if in this case it may mean a slightly less profitable e-business initiative. Too much optimisation in this case can lead to dire (and unforeseeable) consequences over the long run. The best is to make sure that your e-commerce and e-business initiatives are at least as profitable as your offline activities, and then start improving from there.

9.6   Case studies of innovative e-business solutions

Unfortunately, there are very few case studies of how existing travel agencies have succeeded to move online, since most of the industry has paid more attention to new entrants such as Travelocity, Expedia, and Lastminute.

However, there are a few examples worth mentioning, which should inspire small agencies in formulating their e-business strategy.   We want to address here the following issues:

- Finding Opportunities For Segmentation And Specialisation

- Growing a Small Online Travel Agency On The Side

- Joining an Online Referral Service

- Becoming A Click And Mortar Agency

- Applying e-business Technologies To Improve Service

9.6.1   Finding opportunities for segmentation and specialisation

According to a survey conducted by research companies 16.9 million trips, representing 6.4% of trips abroad by Europeans, are initiated on the Internet, with almost a quarter booked and paid for online [104]. With such growing numbers, it has become clear that the Internet has created opportunities for travel agents that are increasingly unavoidable.   In addition, given the traditional segmentation of European markets, it is even more interesting for travel agents who can properly serve a segment that falls in their competencies.

The online travel market splits broadly into two sectors: start-ups, and established, "bricks and mortar" businesses. For some of the start-ups, their target market is a close fit for the profile of the typical Web user. Youngtravellers.com, for example, launched in September 2000, allows advertisers and marketers to target what the company describes as a notoriously fragmented audience, travellers before they leave their home country.   The site offers recruitment, accommodation, insurance and travel, and also enjoys a strong offline presence via a strategic partnership with the 1st Contact Group.   This has 180 staff throughout London, advising travellers on everything from visas and shipping services to the local pubs.

The specialist online travel business, IfYouTravel, targets four market sectors through dedicated   Web   sites: IfYouSki.com,   IfYouGolf.com,   IfYouDive.com   and IfYouExplore.com.   The company was formed in May 2000 by the merger of three leading winter sports travel sites, which at the peak of the 1999-2000 season were serving up to five million pages a month to over 750,000 users, generating gross sales in excess of £1.2 million (6.0 million euros). Senior management cites several reasons that can explain such performance: the consumer is adventurous and confident, so will not be afraid of booking online, and is hungry for content on both the activity itself, which is available all year-round and the holiday being booked.

9.6.2   Growing a small online travel agency on the side

With mounting competition from large travel portals that offer everything the brick-and-mortar agency used to do, small travel agents must find new niches to specialise, with the hope of making better margins than past activities. Here are two interesting cases that should inspire would-be-entrepreneurs throughout the tourism industry to build their own small travel agency online [105].

Castaway

Castaway began life as a sideline for a backpackers' hostel. Four years later it is now a full-time online operation for two people, turning over approximately US$500,000 per annum. This is expected to double in 2001. Over time, the client base has changed to include North American business people and expatriate Britons from South East Asia. Castaway now has four Web sites mirrored across the planet to speed access. One challenge has been making suppliers aware that it is an e-mail based operation and encouraging those suppliers to operate online.

A few conclusions may be drawn from Castaway's experience:

- Move quickly to get online. Castaway estimates that the lead-time is now 12-18 months and growing due to the number of businesses coming online.

- If you don't have the technical skills to create a site, develop a relationship with someone who will design and continually upgrade your site.

- People often overestimate the business and expect too much to happen too quickly. From a business perspective, slow and steady growth that you can cope with and continually adjust to is preferable.

- Companies often fall into the trap of not advertising and promoting their Web sites. There is no point in having the best product and customer service system if nobody knows the electronic address.

- One of the questions they are most frequently asked is 'Are you real?'. Clients have been put off by computer links and recorded messages — keep your site "human" and use it to promote your company's credentials (e.g. membership with respected bodies, etc.).

In summary, Castaway has found that being online is a much cheaper way of doing business than having a shop front. It is fast and efficient, sells well to the market and gives the principals some personal flexibility to conduct business when it suits them.

Boyz-Brick-Road

Boyz-Brick-Road has created a business that specialises in arranging travel for members of the gay community using the Internet. The business has been operating for two years and has grown steadily over that period. Current turnover is about US$200,000 per annum with this expected to double in 2001, with the profit being ploughed back into the business.

It caters to a niche market, which works well because gay people tend to be heavy users of the Internet: 50 per cent of the annual turnover is linked to the Sydney Mardi Gras. Currently the business cannot make airline bookings online but it is looking to establish hot-links to airline reservation systems.

Although the site is relatively young, there are some lessons learned from Boyz-Brick-Road that all online travel agents should consider:

- The tourism industry as a whole needs to change its thinking. Sometimes Internet businesses are not recognised as buyers of tourism product, because they do not have shop fronts, even though they may sell more product than businesses that operate from offices.

- Clients assume that if a supplier has e-mail capability it will have a Web site, but many do not. Businesses must maintain their sites by continuously changing and improving them, if they are to remain fresh and current and attract revisits. This maintenance can be expensive and appear to be a distraction from the day-to-day business, but is important to the value of the site in the long term.

- As the doorway to the business, the site needs to be promoted to the particular target audience. In designing the Web site it is very important to give serious consideration to how clients will navigate their way around the site. It must be simple, obvious and user friendly while promoting other aspects of the site.

9.6.3   Joining an online referral service

In the uncertain world of e-commerce, one thing is clear: More people are researching travel on the Web than buying. The latest Travel Industry Association of America (TIAA) research shows that 25 million travellers booked on line in 2000, but another 34 million looked but did not book. Trend-watchers say most people prefer to talk to a live person for complex travel plans, and many still fret over credit card security. This sets the stage for a new kind of partnership - one between travel agents and a new breed of Web companies offering referrals to those agents.

The lead-generation companies claim to have what agents want: clients who are screened and proven ready to buy a trip. And agents have what the traveller wants and what the Web companies would like to deliver: personal service and expertise. The scramble to snare agent-experts as participants in the untested referral plans started only recently, and results should emerge soon.

Key players include the likes of eGulliver, Ez2plan.com and Webeenthere.com - all looking to attract a coterie of traditional retail agents, promote them as travel experts or specialists and offer their services to consumers who are looking for travel on the Internet.

The thinking is that by giving consumers the option of e-mailing an agent who specialises in the activity or destination they are looking for, Internet lookers can be turned into bookers in an off-line environment that is more personal and hence more comfortable to them. As the tipster, the referring Web business would earn a fee of some kind from the agencies.

Another group of referral sites, among them Respond.com and Netgenshopper.com (which has an agreement with the Institute of Certified Travel Agents), offers referrals for a number of professions, not just travel.

In addition, traditional agencies and consortia, such as American Express, Carlson Wagonlit, Travelbyus, Vacation.com and Virtuoso, have Web site features, based on ZIP code, speciality or both, that are meant to bring consumers to their members or affiliates. While it is too soon to say who will come out the winners, some early attempts at a clicks-and-bricks strategy have fallen short of expectations.

In 2000, Travelocity and Virtuoso, the luxury agency network, signed a deal in which the on-line mega-agency offered its users the option of connecting to a high-end travel specialist.

Travelocity charged consumers a $25 fee to contact a Virtuoso agent; this was meant to ensure that the consumers were serious about buying travel (the fee was taken off the price of a trip, if booked). But Virtuoso officials conceded the fee didn't work, and the program is in limbo. Management concedes the fee is no problem once the consumer has a relationship with the travel agent, but paying a fee without knowing that person is trickier. Virtuoso is now talking with Travelocity about a new referral system, without the fee [106].

9.6.4 Becoming a click and mortar agency

Several small travel agencies may need to join larger alliances in order to access the technologies required to operate on the Internet. Several market leaders have made this effort, an example that SMEs can also follow (with smaller proportions) or perhaps appropriate by joining such groups.

Uniglobe

While most of the big pre-Internet-era travel agencies have hesitated, Vancouver-based Uniglobe Travel International - the largest single-brand travel agency in the world, with 1,100 branches in 20 countries - is pursuing a promising online strategy. Uniglobe is aiming to carve out a lucrative online niche by combining a high-tech site with one of the strengths of old-fashioned travel agencies: the human touch.

Uniglobe's online subsidiary, Uniglobe.com, is focusing on one of the old company's strengths. In addition to regular plane, hotel, car, and other reservations, it can offer several specialised products with more advantageous revenues, such as cruises, which typically generate 15% to 20% commissions, compared with the 5% to 6% common with air, car, and hotel bookings. Moreover, selecting a cruise involves a broader range of considerations than, say, picking a flight, which many people choose solely on the basis of price. That makes cruises a natural for an old-line travel agency.

Most important, Uniglobe has a technical capability that few of its competitors have, one that plays to its strengths: an online chat function. For example, if a customer can't find the answer to a cruise question, a few keystrokes open a window that allows a chat in real time with one of 75 "cruise travel specialists. Within seconds, they can answer questions that would normally have you combing fruitlessly through "Frequently Asked Questions" lists on most Websites. You can also email questions to Uniglobe; a response is promised in 20 minutes. If you're more traditional and think all this online chat is useless, the company also has a 24-hour help-line.

Uniglobe has been aggressively pursuing partnerships to build its visibility in the U.S. Visa, for example, promotes Uniglobe on its site and is in turn promoted on Uniglobe.com. And How2.com has given over its travel area to Uniglobe. Most important, Uniglobe persuaded market leader Expedia to give it a special cruise section within the Expedia site. That, naturally, leads customers to Uniglobe.com. Uniglobe pays Expedia an unspecified fee for each booking that comes through that channel [79].

As well, Uniglobe.com has also launched a new "Travel Shop", and announced ten affiliate partners, to provide travel products and services to leisure and business travellers. The service includes dinner and theatre reservations, ground transport links and local information. Uniglobe will receive a commission or a fee from each of the new partners signed up to back the Travel Shop as products and services are purchased [107].

Finally, travellers looking for airfare bargains can also find of them directly on Uniglobe.com. Through an alliance with Hotwire, it allows the agency to offer unpublished fares if a customer can be flexible in their choice of itineraries, and the ability to access these fares through its site should ensure an enhanced revenue stream for Uniglobe.com [108].

Thomas Cook

For established travel agencies, as for the start-ups, the Web presents opportunities, but also a threat. One of the first "bricks and mortar" groups to go online was Thomas Cook in 1996. At the time, with the growth of the Web and the fact that travel as a sector in terms of e-commerce was up there in the top three, it realised that if it didn't get into it and become a serious player in this area, it could potentially have problems with its business in ten years' time.

Today, the site offers 2.5 million holidays and flights from 400 airlines. According to figures from Internet research company NetValue, in numbers of unique visitors and reach, the site was second only to Lastminute.com in August 2000.

But the online operation is attracting new customers rather than cannibalising the company's existing retail business. Almost 50 % of visitors to the site have never booked with Thomas Cook in the past. It's a completely new market, as it is now talking to a group of people that its retail distribution arm had never talked to.

Senior management admits that the Web is influencing the company's approach to its retail outlets. The company is aiming to provide Internet access for customers in some of its branches at least, to reduce queuing time and to give customers the choice of doing their research online, rather than talking to an agent. The way the market is going, and the fact that travel is quite an intuitive thing to buy interactively will change the way that the retail business looks [104].

9.6.5 Applying e-business technologies for service excellence

Whether large or small, travel agencies can find a wide diversity of e-business applications that will help them perform better. Here are a few examples from market leaders [109].

McCord Travel Management

Until recently, Chicago-based McCord Travel Management oversaw travel policies for its 2,000 corporate clients from a network of call centres. Business travellers who needed to know if their plans complied with their company's policy had to submit requests by fax, and agents wouldn't respond for 24 to 48 hours. Clients found this waiting period annoying and they pleaded for improvement.

Today, to the delight of its customers, McCord's policy analysis process takes mere minutes. By combining third-party and proprietary technologies, the company has launched a Web application that queries a client's travel policy as the traveller is booking a trip. If the proposed itinerary adheres to the policy, the traveller can go ahead and book a ticket; if an itinerary is no good, the application will suggest alternatives that work and then wait for a reply. With the help of a data-mining tool, corporate travel managers can also use the application to generate reports about travel expenses for individual employees, departments or the whole company.

American Express Travel Related Services

In late 1997, New York City-based American Express Travel Related Services replaced its phone-based reservation system for corporate clients and launched Corporate Travel Online, customisable mining software that queries different databases, finds the cheapest rates available, then lists them on the Web. Agents in any of the company's 1,700 offices world-wide can access the system, as can individual corporate travellers. Since then, the system has quadrupled the number of bookings agents can take in a day. And because the site presents clients with a list of the cheapest travel options, they can save an average of 20 percent.

Corporate travel comprises only half of American Express's travel business. In 1998, the company revamped the technology that drives the other half: leisure travel. This new system, called the American Express Travel and Entertainment Hub, offers online booking to a more general audience. Travellers can use it to book flights, reserve hotel rooms, check out vacation packages and buy tickets to sporting or cultural events. In contrast, the services one might find at the company's storefront locations seem...well, old-fashioned.

Rosenbluth International

Philadelphia-based Rosenbluth International is taking a similar approach. On the leisure side, the company recently purchased Biztravel.com, a Web-based travel agency geared toward small businesses, independent businesspeople, and frequent travellers. Among other features, Biztravel.com keeps track of customers' frequent flyer miles and calls or pages them when their flights are behind schedule.

The whole process used to involve meetings and phone calls, and generally took weeks and months. Now, travel managers can set up a corporate account and feel confident they're getting the best deal in a matter of hours. This technology has revolutionised the way their clients do business. Rosenbluth's statistics support this claim, since overall sales have nearly tripled in the past two years.

Carlson Wagonlit Travel

At Minneapolis-based Carlson Wagonlit Travel, the new slogan for leisure travel at subsidiary is "Click, Walk and Talk," which means customers will get the same level of service whether they book online, at an agency or by phone. To show employees they should send this message to customers, Carlson invested in a password-protected Extranet that offers agents marketing information, Web-based training, travel brochures and the latest company news, which they use to get customers the best and cheapest deals. Carlson encourages its 1,200 agencies to log on every day and provides monetary incentives to those who log on most consistently. The Extranet also has eliminated the need for paper communication among the company's offices.

The company also plans to roll out a new proprietary customer relationship management (CRM) system to make the booking experience more personal. Based on previous travel choices collected and stored in an Oracle database, the system will offer discounts, special deals and other services to repeat customers. When they log on, the offers will pop up on their computer screen. When they call or stop by, a flashing message will notify agents of any special promotions.

9.7 Future of e-commerce and e-business

What about the future of e-commerce and e-business in the travel agencies sector? Here is a selection of comments and opinions from travel industry experts and analysts, which summarise the key trends and issues for the next few years [110-113]:

Online bookings:

- Online bookings will expand as more travel agencies move to the Web. As travel agencies develop more of a Web presence, the number of Internet bookings will grow.

- Business travellers are now paying more attention to Internet booking because companies large and small are increasingly wiring their travel departments to provide internal online booking engines affiliated with their existing travel agencies.

- Online business should reach 17 percent of total sales within the next four years.

Strategic Uses of the Internet:

- Travel and hospitality companies are working both sides of the Internet at the same time. The goal is to attract and hold more customers while lowering operating and procurement costs by making their supply chains more efficient.

- Online sites that offer both - the high-tech of the Internet coupled with the high- touch of online, i.e. real-time assistance - will attract the most new customers.

- Airlines, hotels, travel agencies and others are using the Internet to layer efficient, "feel good" services for customers; open new sales channels; and drive suppliers to offer lower costs and speed product delivery with online procurement. Activities range from allowing travellers to download flight information over wireless devices, to creating B2B e-marketplaces for the airline, hospitality and cruise industries. Although Internet use by the travel and hospitality industry is widespread, e-commerce use is just starting to gather steam.

Brick-and-Mortar Agencies:

- The rate of decline brick-and-mortar agencies will slow because leading technology providers are developing systems to capture the knowledge and skill-base of hundreds of agencies and combining them into a virtual powerhouse of travel knowledge.

- Soon we may see acquisitions of brick and mortar companies by Global Distribution Systems (GDSs) to assure segment loyalty in the long run and capitalise on the true industry strength, the individual travel agent supported by phenomenal technology.

Home-Based Travel Agents:

- The number of home-based travel agents, either working independently or as employees of a travel agency, will grow exponentially.

- Much of the travel agency skill-base has left the industry. The home-based agent concept will allow the industry to recapture that talent.

Consumer Behaviour:

- Industry statistics show vacation shoppers use the Internet to gather information, but most still call suppliers directly or use a travel agent.

- Consumer will use flight-only auction sites less frequently in the future and only when the lowest price is the primary consideration. The numerous restrictions, lousy flight connections and poor service have made these sites lose their appeal.

Consumer Power:

- There will be continued consolidation of online leisure travel sites wherein the consumer will be the big winner: true travel portals for complete leisure travel services.

- At one time, part of a travel agent's job was to direct customers to the vendor offering the highest bonus. Now, the Internet has helped shift the balance of power to the consumer. Virtually every supplier - airlines, hotels, car-rental companies, trains, cruise lines, even national limousine services - has its own Web site, and many offer bonus frequent-flier points to those who shop direct.

Loyalty:

- Travel sites that can build brand loyalty and concentrate on old-fashioned customer service will emerge as the winners in this crowded field.

Branding:

- The future belongs to a relative handful of Internet companies that can establish themselves as major brands, with easy-to-use technology to provide the best service within well-defined travel niches.

- "The big get bigger, the smaller get focused, and the middle dies,"

10 Tour operators

10.1 Introduction

The business of Tour Operators is by far the one that remains the most misunderstood and least transparent in the eye of the general public. Unfortunately, this situation is not improving, especially considering that this sector is dramatically underrepresented on the Internet. Indeed, only a few large consolidators, package developers, and tour operators are offering basic information on their Web pages, with even fewer offering integrated transactional functions to their travel agents (let alone directly to their customers).

With the emergence of e-tourism, Tour Operators must rethink the way they conceive their role as both product developers and intermediaries. The industry has not yet addressed all the issues that matter. But with the rapid re-configuration of offline vs. online demand, as well as new tourism products being developed through partnerships between both traditional and Internet firms, tour operators should prepare to play a part in this transformation.

10.2 Targeting your e-business strategy

Entering into e-business and e-commerce may entail a number of unforeseen changes for the small tour operator. As large firms are entering the Web and reengineering their applications, the SMEs of this sector are increasingly squeezed on both sides of the market.

On one hand (supply side), the small TOs traditional competitive advantages (i.e., unique products and customisation) are being superseded by the power of Internet Booking Engines (IBEs), and the greater breadth of TOs operating online. On the other hand (demand side), e-tourism customers are increasingly educated, and are loyal only to the TOs that offer unfailing quality, trustable transparency, and lowest prices, all in one package.

Clearly, SMEs in the TO business must take these trends seriously, and must be prepared to use them as opportunities for growth. Therefore, small Tour Operators will have to be extremely careful in setting up their e-business strategy, more so than in any other sectors of the tourism industry, since they are the latest entrants on the Internet. For that reason, they must be aware of, and align with, the key trends brought by the Internet, and that are transforming their industry.

There are at least three major trends, which have been further accelerated by e-commerce and E-business. First, the industry is rapidly consolidating, reaching greater concentration levels than never before, but in the same time witnessing a great fragmentation of market demand into numerous niches. Second, the relationship with travel agencies is changing rapidly, with the possibility of exacerbating the pressures on this crucial distribution channel. Third, new online entrants are becoming increasingly difficult to compete with.

10.2.1 Concentration and niche market structures

It is estimated that, in average, 20 % of tour operators account for 80 % of tour operator revenues. The trend toward a small number of large operators and a large number of small niche tour operators is well entrenched in many countries in the world. It is expected that in the future there will have a fewer but bigger vertically integrated tour operators, which is likely to bring a greater stability in the tour operations business. It is expected also that niche operators will replace small, non-aligned tour operators [27].

As well, in a near future, tours may be packaged and sold differently. Possibly (although depending on trends) there may be fewer choices in the number of companies, but product lines may actually increase. Independent tour operators will need to be creative and set themselves apart in order to compete. Smaller tour operators will survive, but they may have to evolve. Personalised service will always be important in the travel industry. Smaller, independent tour operators must concentrate on their niche - some product that they do better than anyone else - and capitalise on it to keep their business strong. Smaller tour operators are also more adaptable to change. They will have lower operating costs and can change quickly to adapt to consumer needs [114].

These two seemingly contradictory trends (i.e., supplier consolidation and demand fragmentation) must be dealt with in a coherent fashion. Therefore, your small Tour Operation business should make sure it follows clear steps to build its new e-business strategy:

* Weigh the impact of these trends on your speciality and what options remain opened,

* Define the key competencies of your firm (e.g., product development? marketing?),

* Decide whether to merge horizontally with other TOs or vertically in service/distribution,

* Analyse the possibility of achieving a new competitive position through the Internet,

* Target a number of areas where your organisation should innovate to survive online,

* Identify the various applications that will be required for this type of innovation, and

* Build a business case for investing in the new IT and e-business solutions required to do it.

10.2.2 Changing relationship with travel agencies

There is an underlying trend to increase direct distribution that e-commerce is only serving to accelerate. Operators that already deal directly with the customer are planning to move a significant proportion of their business to e-channels. Companies with mixed distribution are moving in the same direction, but more slowly. Tour operators that own their own agent networks are apparently no less enthusiastic about the potential benefits of e-commerce than those that rely on third parties. A recent survey points to a reduction in volumes of business through agents of all kinds of around 15% within three years. The survey shows that while most operators are keen to use e-commerce to push the direct distribution model, they fear it will not be easy. Pre-eminence of existing distribution channels seems to be the most serious obstacle [115].

The main challenge for tour operators is to embrace the technology and put it to work. Other challenges concern the ease or otherwise with which tour operators are able to manage the transition from third-party to direct distribution. The biggest threat is that posed by new market entrants – companies coming to the market with skills the tour operators don't have, and able to move faster because they are unencumbered by agent networks and outmoded business models [115]

By moving booking systems out of agents premises in favour of Web-based on-line systems of their own, tour operators stand to reduce their overheads, eliminate commissions and cut marketing and fulfilment costs. Recent findings suggest that these savings could amount to a three- or even four-fold improvement in gross margins. The survey also shows that for most tour operators these benefits remain theoretical. Most are struggling with a number of issues surrounding the choice and deployment of suitable technology, as well as initial investment required. Among the thorniest is how to integrate Web-based selling systems with back-office systems handling everything from airline reservations to order processing.

Clearly, giving up on travel agencies is a big opportunity, but also a very big challenge, one that may break the back of small Tour Operators that proceed too quickly without a strategy. Consequently, the decision to make this move should analysed carefully:

- Identify priorities, whether low cost, innovation, responsiveness, capturing clients, etc.,

- Focus your products around your key priorities, keeping your margins in mind,

- Define how e-commerce and e-business functions will play a role in your new products,

- Study some innovative Internet functionalities, such as time-based price discrimination,

- Decide to what extent you want to be close to your customers, whether loyalty will pay,

- Target your initiatives proportionately to the scale of your resources and competencies,

- Find external partners if necessary, e.g. a small group of travel agencies moving online,

- Assess carefully the possibility of achieving larger volumes online than offline,

- Weigh the temporary losses due to transition from agency-based to direct distribution,

- Schedule the launch of your new e-distribution initiative in a growth period in your niche,

- Develop an aggressive advertising campaign, different from your traditional ones, and

- Keep control of supplier costs, as price pressures on Internet are tougher than offline.

10.2.3 Competing with new entrants

Tour operators do not know where to turn for technological solutions, they lack the expertise to deploy e-commerce systems, and they do not know how much they will need to invest in technology to join the game. Although flights and holidays are now widely advertised on the Internet, very few sites can take real-time bookings or process transactions, and nothing is available to match the range and depth of services offered by travel agents. This situation must change, if TO SMEs want to survive. The question is not whether e-commerce will come to the travel industry but who will get there first, and with the right products and services.

What established tour operators fear most are new entrants: it may be easier for technology suppliers to move into travel than for travel firms to move into the technology business. The early signs are that these fears are grounded: it is significant that the most prominent players in the emerging on-line travel business are not established players but start-ups online operators (i.e., discount operators). These companies have joined the market with no legacy systems to worry about and no intellectual baggage about the way the industry works.

Behind the first wave of new market entrants there is a second, potentially far more threatening force: companies with industrial-strength technology, deep pockets and considerable expertise in the design and deployment of e-commerce systems. Asked to identify the company leading the way in travel industry e-commerce, half the respondents named Expedia, the Microsoft-owned travel company that operates exclusively on the Web. Established tour operators know that companies like Expedia will be the competitors of the future. They also know that if they fail to address themselves squarely to the e-commerce question their own companies could soon be booked on a one-way ticket to nowhere [116].

Although entering into e-commerce may present a major technological challenge for some Tour Operators, it is clear that they are most often better equipped than technology leaders to develop more innovative products and services for online sales and delivery. Therefore, new entrants should not be viewed as enemies but rather as possible allies, those that may indeed provide the key assets that are lacking to most SMEs to launch their e-business initiatives.

Consequently, all managers watching the existing competition in their niche must do so through a realistic assessment of these threats, as well as the development of clear strategies to palliate to the lack of online technologies and capabilities. Therefore, your organisation should be prepared to:

- Scan the online and offline environments very carefully before jumping to conclusions,

- Learn what are the winning factors in your niche online, and which ones you control,

- Analyse the key mistakes of new online entrants in your niche, as a kind of free lessons,

- Redefine your technological needs and the possibility to go at it alone vs. with partners,

- Identify your core competencies or "negotiation chips" useful to forge new alliances,

- Ensure your organisation listens to technology partners so as to stimulate innovation,

- Manage projects in a multifunctional form instead of traditional development silos, and

- Focus on fully exploiting e-business functionalities that are most affordable and proven.

10.3 E-business applications and functionality

Setting up an e-business strategy for a small Tour Operator may lead you to believe that the Internet is a land of pure opportunities. However, the need to use the right technological resources is un-escapable, and you should analyse carefully which applications are required, what functionality they provide to your organisation, and to what extent they would serve the purpose of your strategy.

Fortunately, since IT is regularly used by many small TOs, studying new Internet technologies will not appear so difficult or foreign to most managers. The challenge will be primarily in understanding what is innovative about each new solution, and how it integrates with legacy or existing systems. The following applications must be taken in consideration within the core of your e-business strategy:

- **Online presence:** As indicated earlier, this is where most TOs are found lacking. The type of information that is presented on corporate Websites resembles too much those of their glossy package brochures. Yet, online customers are expecting much more than static contents, and even dynamic audio-video contents may not be sufficient. What is the most strategic in this client-facing application is to reach a high level of flexibility in providing the information requested by customers, and to create a high level of interactivity with both databases and back office processes and staff.

- **Customer Relationship Management (CRM):** This application presents totally new opportunities that Tour Operators may never have envisioned on a massive basis. Although all TOs maintain a call centre to help travel agents in need of information, and although CRM is most often connected to such service centres, using CRM with a massive base of online consumers is a totally different challenge, both quantitatively and qualitatively. Therefore, small TOs must be careful in setting up their strategy, primarily by identifying which parts of CRM are most relevant to their overall initiative, and how innovative will be its use throughout e-business processes. The priority in most cases will be to ensure that CRM does not represent a bottleneck for your operations, but rather enhances workflow and makes it more seamless and effortless to perform customisation.

- **Supply Chain Management (SCM):** Although most TOs have their ways to relating with their travel and tourism service suppliers, it is important to reconsider how these processes can be integrated online as well. Most systems in this area are rather isolated, sometimes with various departments of the same TO not even working together. In addition, SCM may prove a key success factor in fast growth, as once Front Office applications succeed in attracting and capturing demand, SCM applications may be the ones saving the day for the small TO that want to satisfy all this demand, and must access suppliers quickly and effectively.

- **Integrated product development:** As a small tour operator, it is unlikely that you will abandon new product development and package design functions in the first years of your e-business initiative. Indeed, as e-tourism may soon reflect the same seasonality as offline tourism does, this function may prove to be one of the most useful in difficult times, in order to avoid losses, and therefore solidifying your overall e-commerce business model. This requires package design tasks to be integrated through a fluid workflow, where staff can effectively leverage the diverse knowledge base, supplier base, and client base to discover the most innovative products that the market may sustain, and to target their design and launch with the highest levels of accuracy possible. Consequently, far from being a mere complementary support system, integrated product development may represent a key tool for long-term survival, especially as product innovation will become the name of the game in Internet competition for TOs.

10.4 Step-by-step guide to implementing your e-business strategy

As a small Tour Operator that has been capable to formulate a clear and concise e-business strategy, you must now plan your implementation in such a way that maximises your success.

Unfortunately, since TOs are among the latest to enter into tourism e-business, chances are your firm will have to evolve through the whole implementation process, from start to finish. Clearly, the evolution of SMEs like yours will require a good dose of courage, as the passage from a purely offline to a hybrid offline/online, or even a pure online, Tour Operator can be a long journey, one which may require strong backing and patience.

Consequently, in order to be prepared for hitting the road, and with the hope to better expect and control the factors of your firm's evolution, you must make sure all your team understand the value of each phase as follows:

- **Phase 1 – Moving towards e-marketing:** Since Tour Operators are primarily product developers and marketers, they must first learn how to better relate to their distribution chain, primarily by: (1) Balancing Marketing and Technology Priorities, (2) Moving From Brochures to Interactive Marketing, and (3) Managing Digital Contents.

- **Phase 2 – Adapting technological infrastructures:** Once marketing functions have been adjusted, a major adaptation must be made to Front and Back Office applications, mostly by: (4) Overcoming Technological Barriers, (5) Outsourcing Technology Solutions, (6) Connecting to Major Reservation Systems, and Streamlining Your Supply Chain Management (SCM).

- **Phase 3 – Making product development more flexible:** As small Tour Operators learn how to "domesticate" their e-business solutions, they must progressively build some innovative New Product Development best practices, mostly by: (8) Customising Offers in Real-Time, (9) Adopting a B2B2C Model, and (10) Implementing Customer Service Solutions.

10.4.1 Phase 1 – Moving towards e-marketing

Step 1 – Balancing marketing and technology priorities

Tour operators nearly all agree that e-commerce is critical to their survival, but are struggling to resolve technology and business problems that threaten to stop their e-commerce plan from taking off. For instance, a recent research found Britain's biggest tour operators preparing to use e-commerce to move from agent-based to direct distribution via the Internet. The need to cut costs, and commissions paid to agents make that group an obvious target. The survey points to an expected reduction in business conducted through agents of at least 15% over the next three years.

At the same time, tour operators plan to expand the range of services offered directly to customers via the Internet to include everything from travel information, online bookings and payment, sale of value-added services such as insurance and car hire. Today, with one or two exceptions, they offer nothing more than marketing information, flight details and general tourist information on their Web sites. Three quarters of the 36 companies in the survey, who account for more than three-quarters of the £8 billion (13.18 billion euros) UK travel market, identified "technical barriers" as the biggest obstacle they face [117].

Step 2 – Moving from brochures to interactive marketing

How would travel agents react if tour operators stopped printing brochures? Some experts wrote about fluid pricing and the possibility that it will not be too long before prices are no longer printed in brochures but just available online. This could have a profound effect on travel agents, but would agents be even more troubled if tour operators no longer printed brochures at all?

A few tour operators have stopped already producing brochures - concentrating solely on producing a nice Website. Of course, there are still delighted to take bookings from agents but are not worried about having its brochures racked. What if other operators follow the same lead? There could be good reason to do so. Brochure costs are a massive financial burden on operators, one that they are continually seeking to reduce. The brochure will not die out. People inherently like to browse paper-based information. However, if there are such large savings to be made, how can technology help?

How about the virtual brochure? A customer walking into an agent to find a holiday in a 4 start hotel in a foreign destination could walk out with a 20 page brochure specific to his/her requirements rather than five 100 page brochures with a whole raft of holidays that are of absolutely no interest. This would entail agents being able to download brochure content. (Holding that much electronic brochure information locally would not be feasible.) They would need broadband network access (dial-up modems would not be good enough) and high-speed colour printers to quickly produce a brochure for a customer whilst he or she is waiting. But this is beginning to sound expensive. The total cost of PC's, printers, and fast ADSL connections. Who is going to pay - the agents? After all, this is a service they are going to be offering to attract customers; also they are operating the equipment on their premises. But it is just impossible to imagine agents paying for this.

How about the tour operators? They would be the ones making the huge savings in print costs. But, of course, that is the idea, making savings rather than re-spending the money. Also, if operators subsidised the equipment, how would they feel about competitors' material being printed out on machinery they have paid for? Unless you know otherwise, it does not sound as though it would happen.

Some experts predict that as consumers get used to searching for travel on the Internet and digital TV, operators will divert funds from brochure production to these channels [118].

Within five years, some experts predict the travel brochure will be playing second fiddle to the virtual tour. A tour operator has developed a solution that Instead of flicking through a resort brochure, the consumer will pull up a Web site, click on the virtual tour button and within seconds be offered a tour of hotel bed-rooms, restaurants, foyers, swimming pools and so on. This TO offers a wide viewing frame, high quality graphics, a navigational aid and a download time of seconds rather than minutes. The images span up to 360 degrees to give a clear impression of the venue [117].

Step 3 – Managing digital contents

As tour operators commit to e-business, they will have to change the way they manage the informational contents about their offerings.

For now, the industry is geared up to producing printed brochures. Typically, brochure content will come from many sources. Images might be slides or prints held by a repro house, and hotel and resort description may be written on a word processor, probably within the Marketing Department. Prices will be held in spreadsheets by the Product Planning team. This all comes together in brochure production.

However, this process is great for brochure, but unfortunately lousy for anything else. A few enlightened travel companies have realised that this is a real issue and are changing the way they work. Bigger tour operators and travel companies are investing in content management systems. These are basically depositories of information that is held within a database (which should content allotments, prices, commissions, availability etc.) such that it can be fed out to any delivery channel, be it a Web site, brochure production, Wireless Access Protocol (WAP) site or CD ROM. This one sentence description belies the technical and organisational complexity of getting content management properly set-up. It is worth the effort though. The payback is ongoing savings in time and effort throughout the publishing process and improved control of data.

What tour operators say on their Web site should now agree with what they print in their brochure. Lead times are reduced and accuracy increased. One may think that content management is only applicable to the big a T.O., but this is not the case. Whilst it may not be worthwhile for smaller companies to invest in expensive content management systems, there is much that can be done with a PC and some common sense [119].

Despite some of the current limitations of on-line media, e-commerce may lead to improvements to the quality of brochures. In the medium term, on-line brochures can be expected to include high-quality images and sophisticated search facilities to reduce the time taken to match the consumer's requirements. Probably the most significant improvement, though, will be in the ability to change brochure content immediately to reflect price changes or special offers. The ideal on-line medium for electronic brochures may well not be the Web at all but digital TV. Digital TV has the bandwidth for high-quality images and multimedia. Just as importantly, TV is a group activity where the Web is solitary one. It is easier to imagine the family choosing the annual holiday gathered round the television set than crowded around a home computer [116].

The travel industry is using new channels to market such as the Web and interactive digital television, but taking full advantage of these opportunities requires a single integrated solution to support both traditional print media and the new technologies. Therefore, TOs should turn to those firms that offer such innovations, and allow them to achieve their goals with the least investment and fastest pace. Many options are available, for example:

- A technology provider has used its experience in developing customised e-commerce applications to produce a media-independent publishing solution for the travel industry. The problem that currently arises for many travel companies is that they use different publishing systems for the traditional and new media channels - one to handle the printed brochure, and one to create a Web version. This may be further exacerbated in the future with additional publishing applications for interactive digital television (idTV) and wireless devices. Maintaining dual systems is very resource intensive and inefficient, particularly since brochures contain a wide mixture of content including text, images and pricing data [120].

- Another technology provider has developed a system that allows a tour operator to create a single brochure database that can be published to any type of media. The system stores all types of content in a relational database, which can be transformed and output as required, either to a format ready for printing, or to a format such as HTML, XML or WML for display on a Web page, interactive digital television (idTV) screen or mobile phone. Systems such as this one offer a flexible solution that will integrate all aspects of a company's publishing operations across different channels. Companies that can grasp the opportunities provided by these new routes to market, and which can quickly personalise their proposition for individual customers will gain a significant advantage over their competitors. The Internet now operates with diverse client devices, and content management solutions will be required to enable organisations to publish to these devices from a single source [120].

10.4.2 Phase 2 – Adapting your technological base

Step 4 – Overcoming technological barriers

A survey has revealed a wide gap between the potential and the reality of e-commerce in travel. Most companies today have a Web site, the majority of which offer little more than a company profile, some marketing information and on-line brochures. These sites are technically undemanding to build and draw on readily available skills in HTML and Web server administration. Full-service e-commerce systems capable of handling real-time reservations and end-to-end transactions are at the pre-planning stage. One reason is that the skills required are an order of magnitude higher than for a simple marketing-oriented Web site. They include TCP/IP and other networking, database administration, transaction processing, security, user interface design, and system integration skills.

The capability to get legacy systems to work with the Internet protocol is particularly important, because the only viable e-commerce systems are those in which the front end is fully integrated with the back end, and all the back end systems are interconnected. Tour operators use a variety of different and incompatible systems that were never designed to communicate with one another. The opportunities to rationalise these systems are limited. To complicate things further, many of the systems involved in a typical booking don't belong to the tour operator but to a third party – an insurance company or airline, for instance – but new interfaces are currently developed to meet the needs of specific TOs (i.e.: Sabre) [115].

Step 5 – Outsourcing technology solutions

Some tour operators chose to outsource their technology solutions. Reasons for doing so are numerous. They switch to a technology expert provider because it is the right technology partner for the next stage of their development. Their technology partner allow them to concentrate on what they do best - selling holidays – confident in the knowledge that their technology is secured for the future.

By outsourcing to an expert provider's managed services operation, they are securing a scalable infrastructure to support their expansion plans. They can benefit from advanced hardware, software upgrades, year-round maintenance and help desk support without a major upfront capital investment. Solutions provided by their technology partner enable them to cope with issues such as reduced margins and rapidly changing technology and distribution opportunities. In short, outsourcing is a strategy by which tours operators may secure the best technology on the most convenient terms.

Several options are available to TO SMEs, and it they must be carefully weighed against one another. Here are a few examples that should be considered:

- An advanced technology company has develop a product designed to fulfil the need for a practical, reliable, consistent, affordable, user-friendly, PC based program that fully automates a wholesale tour operation. It consists of a core product line that is supported by customised modules. These customised modules allow tour operators to modify the software to adapt to their business, whatever their requirements may be [121].

- An application service provider, specialised in software solutions for German-speaking mid-sized tour operators, has developed a software that connects tour operators with travel agencies that generate the majority of their orders. Tour operators can now offer 30 000 travel agents throughout Europe a quick and easy way to evaluate and book tour packages through the Internet. The average time required to book a tour has been reduced 92%, from 25 minutes to 2 minutes. The system is a comprehensive booking system that allows tour operators to manage everything from order processing to maintaining customer records to accounting [122].

- Another ASP has developed an online booking engine that provides cost-efficiencies along the entire travel distribution chain in the Hawaiian travel market, from supplier to end-customer. Leveraging the Web as a delivery mechanism for the software service will provide this company's customers, such as travel resellers, with access to an unprecedented real-time inventory of hotel rooms, flights, car rentals, and attractions, as well as automated customer service features. For travel suppliers, this application will provide a much-needed, low-cost distribution channel combined with access to a broader target market [123].

Step 6 – Connecting to major reservation systems

Clearly, operating in an outsourcing mode can also open the door to integrating traditional Global Distribution Systems (GDSs). Indeed, few TOs take this opportunity seriously, preferring to operate their own reservation infrastructure in may instances.

Many options are opened, especially into an integrated fashion, along the trend of outsourcing. For example:

- A solution has been developed jointly by a GDS and an application service provider (ASP) that will see the ASP provide connection services that will link vacation providers directly with its new browser-based distribution application. The agreement sees the GDS integrating the ASPs connectivity technology, which enables a single cost-effective connection and interface between tour operators and GDSs. The result is that the GDS users will have real-time access to reservations, availability and pricing, plus access to the rapidly expanding e-market-place of vacation products linked by the ASP technology [124].

- A global provider of destination content, technology and distribution services to the travel industry, has developed a solution which enables a live feed of inventory to a Web-based distribution system that, in turn, directly connects to global travel distributors. This distribution system contains pertinent booking information about tours, attractions, events and related destination products. The company's list of online and brick-and-mortar travel distribution partners includes Expedia.com, OneTravel, Biztravel.com, Travelution, Sabre and Worldspan. This means that suppliers who sell everything from bear watching tours in Canada to scuba diving excursions in Fiji to Broadway theatre tickets can bring their products in real time to the computer screens of distributors across the globe. Qualified suppliers who want to take advantage of this unique capability simply provide their up-to-date business and pricing details for inclusion in the database [125].

- Another provider is using new Web and network technologies to enable travel vendors to distribute their services electronically to travel agents in a more advanced way than current systems, and at a lower cost per booking. Today travel vendors pay $2 to $3 for each booking made by travel agents through Global Distribution Systems (GDSs) or Computer Reservations Systems (CRSs). Telephone reservations cost the vendor in excess of $10 per booking to handle. This supplier uses Web technology across private communications networks (Intranets) to reduce the booking fees charged to travel vendors by at least 75%. This supplier's solution converts the vendors own existing in-house system output into dynamic Web pages/booking screens, enabling agencies to make real-time reservations through a password protected, travel trade only Intranet Web site. Several large European travel agency chains are upgrading their networks to the IP (Internet Protocol) standard, which enables access to Web sites. Several CRSs are also planning to enable their agency customers to access Web sites, and many agencies have already subscribed to their own standard leased or dial-up connections to the Web. These new communications options at last present travel vendors (tour operators, ferry, rail, travel insurance companies etc.) with the opportunity to reduce their dependence on today's expensive distribution systems and on telephone bookings [126].

- In reference with an Intranet Web site, Pickup lists a number of direct and indirect business benefits arising from the implementation of intranets. Direct business benefits include: savings in paper; savings in print production and distribution of newsletters, policy documents and telephone directories; increased efficiency of staff; increased turn-around for sales quotations; savings in replacing legacy systems. Indirect business benefits include: knowledge management; improved motivation; shared common visions; communication and change; keeping in step with new technology; competing with external media; aiding communication in disparate organisations; modern working practices; synergy of the work force; free market research; innovation from everyone; relief from information overload; breaking down the "silo" mentality [127].

- Finally, an ASP, in conjunction with the U.S. Tour Operators Association, has produced new software, on CD, that works in conjunction with an Internet site and will allow for continuously updated information. One of their software's components searches through thousands of vacation options by destination and type of vacation. It will compare products from several tour operators at once. The Electronic Brochure gives users access to all the operator's tour and vacation options, eliminating the need to call the reservations department. It will show availability of departure dates; price the tour selected based on gateway, dates and pre- and post-options, and allow electronic reservations [128].

Step 7 – Streamlining your Supply Chain Management (SCM)

While Front Office applications may have been well integrated and may operate properly, they can cause a small TO to actually get drawn under an ocean of demands it may have difficulty to meet. This situation may well make this SME regret having entered the Internet and having invested in e-commerce and e-business technologies that only creates hassles.

Unfortunately, the Tour Operation business requires an extremely complex Supply Chain Management (SCM) application, since a great diversity of service suppliers (i.e., hospitality, foodservices, transportation, accompaniment, attractions, entertainment, etc.) must be readily available once tourists book with the travel agency or the tour operator. Consequently, the priority to properly integrate, harmonise, and especially synchronise the flow of demands to suppliers is crucial for the success of e-business in the TO sector.

Fortunately, several options are opened for SMEs to reach such levels of synchronisation. For example, most technology solution providers have developed systems that are highly suitable for a wide variety of tour operators and travel organisers, and include a number of unique features that help to streamline the SCM application and make it effortless for TO staff to operate. The most popular features most often include [129]:

- Accommodation driven search screen that gives graphical availability displays for requested dates, with strong search facilities by features, resort and country,

- A quote feature that allows multiple changes to client quotations until booking is confirmed,

- A facility to allocate passengers to flights, accommodation, and extra fees for accessing visitor attractions (e.g., golf course, ski passes, etc.),

- An automated e-mail facility that allows resort reports to reach resort representatives quickly and cost effectively.

As well, some other solutions may be available in separate packages, responding to the needs of various TOs, who may have diverse and sometimes more specialised needs, according to their product specialisation (e.g., TOs that book hotels for summer vacations, etc.). A number of interesting solutions can be found in various segments, for example:

- A company focused on providing reservation solutions for the tour operator market, and a leading provider of hotel industry transaction processing and electronic commerce services have developed a solution that automates the reservation process related to booking hotels for tour operator packages. This solution provides tour operators with an electronic method of delivering hotel room reservations directly to the central reservation systems (CRS) of the hotels with which they have negotiated room allotments. As a result, the traditional tour operator method of transmitting room reservations to a hotel by email or fax will transform into real-time electronic transmission of reservation data directly into the hotel's CRS. This automated process will result in a reduction of operating costs for the hotel and the tour operator, as well as a potential increase in revenue yields. Other benefits of this product include greater efficiencies in contracting and managing negotiated tour package room rates and allotments [130].

- A leading provider of information management and electronic distribution solutions for the travel industry, has designed a robust, state-of-the art, inventory management and reservation system for tour operators. The system has partnered with the world's leading developer and distributor of database technology, Oracle. Oracle is a solution in use by over 80% of Fortune 500 companies. This relationship with Oracle means that this system will run on any platform, enabling companies to continue using software such as Microsoft and Adobe. Since this system uses Microsoft Windows, the learning curve for employees is flat. All staff will be familiar with the format, so they'll quickly learn to perform tasks such as product loading, packaging, inventory management and reservations. Designed for high volume processing and distribution, this system is the ideal in-house tour management and reservation system for outbound tour operators (or a combination of outbound/inbound) dealing primarily with travel agencies. Main features include the synchronisation of multiple databases (accounts payable, accounts receivable, client documentation, etc.), reservations and inventory control (air, motor coaches, multiple island resort holidays, cruise, car, rail, etc.) [131].

10.4.3 Phase 3 – Making product development more flexible

Step 8 – Customising offers in real-time

Time is a critical factor when it comes to servicing customers and getting the information needed to provide the ultimate travel planning experience. Tour operators must recognise this trend, especially since the Internet allows them to perform customisation in real time, using leading edge e-business technologies to make use of information more efficiently.

In order to customise offers and reach higher levels of customer satisfaction and loyalty, it is important to equip your staff with the most effect Customer Relationship Management (CRM) tools. In addition, some advanced technologies may be needed in order to properly exploit the mountains of data generated through CRM applications, and that must then be analysed in order to identify the best new business opportunities. For example:

- Managers can now use sophisticated data warehouse solutions to create competitive tour packages and to illustrate presentations. Both marketers and customers have instant access to a reservation system through the Internet and through the introduction of self-service kiosks. With around-the-clock access any gaps between the company and customers are closed. Data warehouse solutions are be built for rapid query response, detailed customer profiling, in-depth marketing, and advertising analysis. The solution also allows for competitive analysis of pricing and package customisation. The technology can allow agents and customers to easily retrieve, manipulate, and store complex sound, text and graphic files for pictures and detailed descriptions of featured accommodations. In addition, the technology can be used for Web design, presentation tools, and print-on-demand capabilities [132].

- A technology provider has developed a data warehouse solution for tour operators that give users almost instantaneous access to the best offerings that meet their needs. Because they encounter no access problems, managers can quickly evaluate packages and promotions, and customise or alter them to fit localised markets or trends. Agents and customers receive responses in less than one second, system downtime is virtually eliminated, and access is amplified.

- A leading provider of travel reservation platforms and online consumer travel services has acquired a leading provider of call centre software to the hospitality industry, which enhances its existing reservations technology solution. The rationalised product offering will focus on a total solution for the call centres of travel intermediaries and tour operators, as well as a direct online solution for travel destinations and outfitters. This new technology seamlessly integrates and automates many aspects of central reservations, allowing reservation agents to easily assemble complex travel packages in real-time. The online solution will offer the same capabilities for travel service providers, in effect creating a 24-hour online agent for their reservation needs [133].

Step 9 – Adopting a B2B2C model

The fact that small Tour Operators must do business on both sides of the equation (B2B and B2C) is forcing them to rethink the way they structure their "development" and "brokering" functions. Indeed, some TOs may be tempted to abandon product innovation and package development tasks, and focus almost entirely on leveraging their consolidation capabilities to perform strictly "brokering" functions, similar to market makers for bulk supply and buying.

This may take a variety of forms, and several options are opened to small TOs. For example, an ASP has launched a solution that enables operators to build a dynamic exchange for the buying and selling of products and services. This solution provides its own unique value proposition to both buyers and sellers. In this application, a single request allows buyers to interact with multiple sellers and consequently receive offers from all of them in complete privacy. Sellers bid for the buyer's business, which creates a much closer relationship than that of the reverse auction model, where only buyers see only the best bid and have no opportunity to interact with all sellers.

To facilitate this, the application provides sellers with the ability to specify the types of requests they are interested in and are able to service. Sellers can see the request details and decide which to focus on and which to ignore. Sellers can further add value by creating the best package for the buyer: Aside from offering the products that the seller carries, the application has the ability to facilitate a seller who wishes to buy products and services from another seller. This allows a seller to bundle or package the best deal that meets the buyer's request, and buyers get a better deal. Sellers get to do a deal which they may not be able to offer otherwise. Through this feature, this new application is able to extend the existing notions of B2C and B2B to become a B2B2C model [134].

Step 10 – Implementing customer service solutions

Tour operators can gain competitive advantage by adopting technology that provides better responses to online enquiries. Efficient customer service is fundamental to any successful business, and is especially so on the Internet, where customers have little patience and less incentives for loyalty. Hence, it is critical for businesses to have prompt and accurate response management solutions that are not only efficient and manageable, but also easy to implement as well.

To streamline its online customer service support, a TO must begin looking for a system that could offer accessibility, user-friendliness, multi-lingual support, and an open architecture supporting industry standard Internet protocols. Few solutions can meet all these conditions especially designed for tour operators.

For example, one leading Asian online travel marketplace has adopted an ASPs customer service solutions for the Internet. With this solutions installed, the TO can provide real-time, more personalised and accurate responses to online enquiries. This ASP provides customer service software for online businesses, including self-service, live online assistance and email-based communications.

These solutions form a critical part of any e-Service model and offer multi-channel interaction management across the customer cycle. The ASP solutions cover an extensive area of customer contact points and can be integrated with Customer Relationship Management (CRM) applications. It allows this TO to give their customers an interactive e-travel experience, which is fundamental to retaining customers as well as converting online enquiries to actual bookings [135].

10.5 Critical success factors of your e-business strategy

Given their late entry, small Tour Operators are most likely to face a great deal of challenges, more than any other actors along the tourism value chain. Consequently, several factors should be under close control by the managers responsible for implementing e-business strategy. Among others, the most important critical success factors should be to:

- Weigh new e-commerce opportunities carefully, and avoid chasing too many initiatives at the same time. Going beyond your specialisation too quickly may derail all your efforts and render your strategy ineffective, and perhaps fail.

- Do not hesitate in partnering, especially when you don't have the necessary technology at hand. One of the reasons why Tour Operators have been slow in adapting to the Internet is their traditional reliance on internal IT resources to set up and run their applications. Consequently, there has been a tendency to overlook e-commerce, since it rarely fell in any body's internal IT budgets, and was hardly doable on a fast track basis.

- Go beyond existing systems when redesigning your processes. Too often small TOs are not making money offline because of traditional and ineffective business methods, especially in their relationship with suppliers, and in helping travel agents with reservations. Carrying these practices into your Internet initiatives would literally ruin all the potential benefits offered by e-business.

- Stimulate innovation in both products and services. Contrary to your traditional functions offline, your organisation will have to differentiate itself not simply through its packages, but also in the way it sells them, as well as how it can help its online customers effectively rely and depend on your firm for all kinds of travel and tourism services.

- Test your applications and solutions under variable levels of operating volumes. Since the Tour Operator business can be a highly variable and seasonal one, it is crucial to make sure your e-business strategy, practices, and solutions are all aligned, and perform consistently whatever the time of the year, and however heavy the volume may become.

- Prepare to launch new and diverse business lines after your first success, with potentially separate online brands. Indeed, small Tour Operators, when they market offline, are always integrating all their products under one brand for the sake of quality recognition and specificity. However, since online consumers are becoming increasingly fragmented, and are attentive almost exclusively to the information and advertising that concerns strictly their own particular needs within a very narrow time frame, it is often better to avoid tying all your e-business innovations together. Chances are that, after launching successfully an initiative in your traditional business line, your TO company will want to launch various other Web portals where other niches will be exploited under different online brand names, but always within the firm. The other initiatives can later become opportunities to perform spin offs, thereby becoming bargaining chips to partner with other players for later projects.

10.6 Case studies of innovative e-business solutions

New e-business opportunities for Tour Operators can be captured for firms of all size. However, case studies about market leaders indicate a number of best practices, as well as innovative solutions, that may require some homework to build the right infrastructure. However, the major part of success depends on the creativity of its business leaders.

These points are demonstrated as we address 3 issues that Tour Operators (especially small ones) should consider very carefully in formulating their e-business strategy:

- Developing New Concepts for Online Tour Operators

- Integrating e-business Applications for Growing Tour Operators

- Becoming a Click-and-Mortar Consolidator

10.6.1 Developing new concepts for online tour operators

The creation of Tour Operators offering niche products should become one of the most important trends in the industry. This will depend in great part on the entrepreneurial behaviour of tourism SMEs, which will require a radical change in order to act swiftly and join the e-business fray. Here are a few examples of new online Tour Operators who have taken the lead in their own niche.

Reservations Africa

Reservations Africa online is a small tour operator specialising in southern Africa, and created by a long time Canadian travel agent who wanted a career change. In July 1996, this firm was among the first of its kind to build a complete Web site. Since then, the company has racked up US$1.5 million in sales in 1999, and US$2 million in 2000. The owner and staff rarely meet more than a few customers face to face. About 10 per cent of the company's business comes from retail. The rest are direct bookings over the Internet.

Customers view the tours on the Web site, which lists complete tour information and prices. Clients then fax or email bookings directly to the manager. The Internet's biggest advantage is that it's the cheapest, and yet most effective, form of product distribution and marketing. Even a high-speed cable connection is cheaper than a Yellow Pages ad.

The Web site also helps screen out the frivolous enquiries that can gobble up agent's time without leading to sales. When the agent receives an email enquiry, it is clear that the customers already know the product, the price, and are more likely to be "bookers" than "lookers".

With email, a phone line, fax machine and Fed-Ex, this small company can give customers a level of service that is equal or better than traditional "counter top" sales. With Web-based sales and service, it matters little that the firm is based in Victoria, BC on Vancouver Island.

Clearly, managers recognise that a Web page will not produce profits on its own. Like all successful travel agents, success is still based in thorough knowledge of the product and excellent customer service. The manager travels to Africa frequently, keeping tabs on new properties, services, and other developments in the destination.

While the Web will boost customer enquiries, it will also raise the workload. Having a global presence on the World Wide Web means customers may call or email at 6 am or 10 pm. Agents will be working seven days a week, since it is always 9 to 5 somewhere in the world [136].

Amethyst Travel

Amethyst Travel provides a bespoke Web service for travel enthusiasts looking to explore the scenic delights of Scotland and Ireland, and also for golfers wishing to play some of the most famous and historic courses in the world. Offering tailor-made, carefully planned vacations, the sites are attracting visitors from North America and across Europe.

A former airline employee with 15 years of experience founded the site. Having experienced life with some of the travel industry's major corporate players, the employee-turned-entrepreneur reckoned there was scope for a Web site specialising in Scottish excursions. In 2001, Amethyst Travel's Web sites have expanded into Ireland and are attracting tourists from all over the world to Celtic shores.

The various Web sites developed since then are aimed at selling the appeal of some of the world's most majestic landscapes, as opposed to promoting hotels and guesthouses in a consortium of adverts. Their tone and style are very much in line with the unspoiled nature of the countries they serve. Rather than automated online booking and payment, the sites act as a first point of contact for arranging the finer points of your trip by e-mail and over the phone with your personal tour operator.

The sites have recently expanded to cater for Irish holidays due to an enormous amount of public demand, and include testimonials from many previous delighted Amethyst customers.
With spectacular photography, the travel sites describe some of Scotland and Ireland's most scenic tourist attractions. A separate, dedicated golf site caters for this niche market of clients with a more sporting agenda in mind.

Amethyst's carefully selected accommodation ranges from 5-star hotels to family-owned guest houses, all of which have been visited personally by managers during intense research periods prior to going online.

The research that goes into the running of this Web service is crucial to its success. The Web site offers a platform on which Amethyst can announce the fruitful results of its "taste and try" tourism method to the rest of the world.

The impact of the Web site on tourism has been as significant as on any industry, and the fact that Amethyst's content is translated into German, French and Swedish means that its potential audience is even larger than that of most Web sites.

Although only in its second year of operation, Amethyst Travel's Web sites are showing massive growth potential. The number of bookings for the summer 2001 season has doubled from last year and, with the introduction of the Irish service, the outlook is extremely bright [137].

10.6.2 Integrating e-business applications for growing tour operators

The integration of legacy systems with the Web is most often the key roadblock that Tour Operators face when entering in e-business. The importance of keeping existing systems running, and relying on rich existing databases, must be emphasised in such strategies. Here are a few cases that explain clearly how partnering with leading Information Technology service providers can offer the best options to Tour Operators of all sizes.

Alpitour with IBM

Every year, the Alpitour Group, Italy's largest tour operator with annual sales of over US$1 billion, organises holidays for 1.2 million customers. The group operates through 4,000 independent agents located throughout Italy. Alpitour has relied on Information Technology for over a decade to manage transactions with its agency partners.

Since the mid-1980s, the group's agents have been able to check availability and make bookings through Alpitour's EASYBOOK system. Though this mainframe based application is accessed by 3,300 of the groups agents, in 1997, Alpitour felt there would be significant advantages in making the system available on the Internet, mostly for cutting costs.

There were substantial opportunities for savings - use of the proprietary networks linking the agencies costs several hundred thousand dollars a year - a cost that was entirely paid for by Alpitour. An Internet solution could reduce these costs considerably since agencies would access the system through their own Internet link.

At the same time, the group wanted to find a solution that required only a PC and Web browser without additional software or hardware requirements. It already experimented with a client-server version of EASYBOOK using dedicated software and we discovered that installing and maintaining applications on several thousand independent client platforms all over the country was logistically impractical.

Alpitour turned to IBM to create an Internet interface to meet its new needs. Keeping the previous mainframe system, and making its data transacted on the Internet, kept the whole processes of the Tour Operator kept properly in place. The solution represented a protection of Alpitour's original investment. The existing application involved several years of effort and investment - by upgrading it to the Web environment, Alpitour extended its value and given it a new lease on life. This new solution combined the strengths of the existing system with the flexibility of the Internet.

Alpitour plans to take full advantage of the new possibilities the Web offers with regards to graphics and details on holiday destinations. On-line holiday brochures have a long way to go and the examples found in the industry so far are not very impressive. On-line publishing requires a special approach and the firm needs to find a way of informing visitors about what we have to offer in an enjoyable, practical way. The Internet is going to radically transform the travel business and it intends to be ready for the enormous opportunities it represents [138].

Travel Planners, Inc. with Proxicom/Microsoft

Travel Planners, Inc., sells customised packages (including the housing and travel arrangements) for events, trade shows, conventions, and meetings nationwide. The growth of the Internet was a critical factor in the decision by Travel Planners, Inc., to develop a new reservation system. The company has built a new call centre reservation application that would replace the existing system, incorporate all its functionality, and extend a real time, self-help version of the system to online customers. The new Travel Planners reservation system is capable of handling all the housing needs for the company's clients over the Internet, and its call centre staff is poised to provide services even better than before.

Before that, the company had a simple Web site that allowed users to fill-out e-mail-based reservation requests, but the Web site was not integrated with the existing call centre reservation system. While Travel Planners' toll-free 1-800 numbers and the latest in call management technology had insured the fastest possible handling of reservation calls, and its integrated fax system provided customers with hotel confirmation within 24 hours, the company could not provide real-time reservation booking online.

What Travel Planners needed was a next generation call centre, or contact centre, that would provide both phone and Web-based services. The new contact centre would provide better customer satisfaction and improved operating efficiency as well as opportunities for cost reduction and revenue growth. Proxicom, a Microsoft partner, was called upon to develop the solution.

The new hotel reservation system provides significant capability to support customer transactions across the Internet. The system, which contains an enterprise database used for reservation processing, accounting, contact management, and report tracking, was designed and built to scale as business needs grow, to interoperate and integrate with other reservation systems, and to be easy to maintain.

Online customers now have real-time access to details that were formerly only available to the call centre staff such as information about events and about the host city. Key solution features include a hotel inventory management application developed specifically for event tracking and management; a call centre application used by Travel Planners employees to manage reservations; and an extranet Web site for use by customers who prefer to manage their reservations without assistance [139].

10.6.3 Becoming a click-and-mortar consolidator

Three brick-and-mortar consolidators have made important efforts to offer a better service to their customers.

Hotel Reservations Network (HRN)

Hotel Reservations Network (HRN) is as a hotel consolidator, selling discounted hotel rooms from call centres. HRN is majority-owned by USA Networks, is a 10-year-old, profitable company that has successfully focused on an under-served, highly fragmented market.

The Web also gave HRN a new revenue stream — selling through affiliated Web sites. It now has 1600, including Preview Travel, Cheap Tickets, Orlando.com, Vegas.com — the list goes on. These affiliates make $15 a pop per booking on HRN's turnkey solution.

Meanwhile, HRN still makes money on its original model as a retailer. It has long-term relationships with hoteliers, purchasing large blocks of hotel rooms essentially at cost and selling to consumers at a mark-up. It also helps hotels sell distressed inventory during slow cycles.

Although HRN's sales have more than doubled — and it had to double its call centre staff as well — selling over the Internet (now representing 80% of its revenues) is a more efficient process, which costs roughly 40% less than selling exclusively through a call centre, according to the company [140].

TRX

TRX, originally a division of WorldTravel Partners that became an independent company in 1997, is focused on fulfilment and customer service — call centres and the like — and hardcore back office work such as quality control, ticketing, document distribution, transaction accounting and management reporting.

TRX's Web strategy is B2B, and one that bets on online travel retailers' and travel suppliers' needing to build customer loyalty through personalised service. TRX is beefing up its original mandates — customer service and fulfilment, quality control, document distribution — to allow online retailers and suppliers to provide the best of those features in a consistent way across a variety of media [140].

Skylink

Skylink is a consolidator that consolidates the tenders of some sixty carriers for travel agencies. In so doing, it is able to present customers with the best offers available on the market. It is a service much appreciated by the agencies, but that requires a phenomenal capacity for managing information. The company has grown rapidly, just like the entire industry, and the carriers' offers have not escaped this trend. Their success is based first on an exceptional capacity to manage information. It works with a map offering flights to all destinations in the world, representing from 175,00 to 200,000 different rates. The computerisation of the search and reservation process has done a lot to simplify the task.

Skylink acknowledges that technological investment was paramount to its progress, knowing that these tools are deciding factors in maintaining a competitive edge over the competition. However, behind the machine are consultants that must know how to master all this information. Senior management wanted to strengthen the strong points that had helped create the consolidator's reputation. It focused particular attention on making the relationship between consultants and customers closer. To do this, no expense was spared in training, so the company could become the best in their market [141].

10.7 Future of e-commerce and e-business

What about the future of e-commerce and e-business in the tour operators sector? Here is a selection of comments and opinions from travel industry experts and analysts, which summarise the key trends and issues for the next few years [115, 120]:

E-Business costs

- E-Business is expected to reduce costs in most areas. In one area, though, they are likely to rise. This is, not surprisingly, the need for investment in IT networking and infrastructure.

- Travel agents currently share the costs of running the networks that deliver booking information and reservations. With travel agents out of the picture, tour operators will need to shoulder these costs for themselves.

- The networks underpinning e-commerce systems will almost certainly be more cost-effective to run than today's over-priced travel industry networks. But that remains to be seen.

- Most tour operators expect network costs to be higher in the short term with e-commerce. There is much less certainty about the cost of building e-commerce systems. Some of the assumptions tour operators are making about the long-term benefits of e-commerce will turn out to be wrong.

E-business systems as a competitive advantage tool

- As competition moves on-line and intensifies, cost savings will have to be handed straight back to the consumer in the form of discounted holidays and more competitively priced value-added services. Or they will need to be invested in better e-business systems for the sake of competitive differentiation. Also, while self-service applications will ultimately be cheaper for the tour operator, they also make the consumer more independent.

- The Internet makes it easier to shop around to get the best deal on each component of the holiday package. Shopping around is something conventional travel agents are there to prevent. Despite their firm belief that e-commerce will lower the cost of doing business in some areas, it is not at all clear that tour operators can realise these savings in improved profit margins.

- As with other sectors of industry, the question arises: what happens when everyone is doing it? As e-commerce systems mature, not only will the playing field be levelled, it also looks likely to be more crowded. The winner will be the consumer. A recent survey of tour operators has been conducted. Asked who would benefit most from e-commerce in the travel industry, 63% said consumers and only 31% said tour operators. Only 6% of respondents identified agents as the main beneficiaries.

- Tour operators are embarking on a perilous journey with little idea what sort of industry they will be working in when they arrive. However uncertain the route and the destination, internal or shareholder pressure to improve margins and external pressure from new players means that staying put is simply not an option.

Holiday Brochures

- Holiday brochures are big business, and the tour operators have seen the Web not only as a natural extension of the printed media, but also as an opportunity to sell holidays direct to their customers, offering increased margins, greater brand loyalty and personalised marketing.

Strategic uses of new technology

- The spread of the Internet to a wider range of devices and the advent of new digital services are also creating new opportunities for the travel industry.

- The fast-developing interactive digital television (idTV) market is seen as a natural route for the tour operators to peddle their wares, particularly because it will increase the penetration of these services into homes that do not currently have a PC.

- Wireless and handheld devices present another interesting opening, with the potential to offer late availability holidays directly to the customer, and further down the line to integrate location-specific services as well. By combining information from an electronic brochure with a customer database, this type of marketing can be very accurately targeted.

11 Visitor Attractions

11.1 Introduction

Visitor attractions are numerous and very diversified, and the emergence of e-commerce and e-business means different things to each segment of this industry.

But so far, it has been surprising to see the uniformity of reactions throughout this sector. Overwhelmingly, attraction managers look to the Internet as merely an interesting tool to advertise their services to tourists everywhere, overcoming the inherent limitations of localised attractions. Unfortunately, this view of e-marketing lacks dynamism, as it takes mostly a mass communications perspective, and evacuates most of the benefits offered by e-commerce.

However, a growing number envision e-business as a unique opportunity to build a closer relationship with visitors, and even a way to make their attractions more flexible, integrating IT seamlessly throughout their operations, before, during, and after each client visit.

Clearly, managers of small attractions must learn to appreciate the opportunity for growth and profitability offered by e-business. They must overcome false appearances that the Internet is a tool only for large firms, and must identify the various changes they can effect in their organisation to capture the benefits of e-commerce. In particular, they must formulate an e-business strategy that meets the requirements of their business segment, put a business case foreward to get their companies to invest in e-business, and lead their firms to the forefront through the innovative use of IT.

11.2 Targeting your e-business strategy

Attractions, entertainment, and recreation firms constitute an important sector of the travel industry. Most leisure travellers are interested in participating in some level of entertainment or education offered by such firms. This varied sector includes, for example, themes parks, national parks, museums and exhibitions, zoos, aquariums, theatre and cultural events, sports events, and skiing. With a more synthetic classification in its "Tourism 2020 – Market Segments" publication, the World Tourism Organisation (WTO) has selected the following ten tourism products as representing the most important and/or dynamic currently:

1. *Sun and beach tourism,*
2. *Sports tourism,*
3. *Adventure tourism,*
4. *Nature-based tourism,*
5. *Cultural tourism,*
6. *Urban tourism,*
7. *Rural tourism,*
8. *Cruises tourism,*

9. *Theme parks tourism, and*

10. *Meetings and conference tourism.*

Some of the firms which run these attractions are large, such as theme parks and ski resorts and have high needs for IT to control their operations. Smaller operators, including small museums, zoos and cultural events may also use new technologies but to a lesser degree.

However, the arrival of the Internet as a (if not the) dominant channel to reach tourists means a number of changes for visitor attractions operators. Indeed, some time in the future - and probably sooner than later – attraction SMEs will have to revise their technological needs and reposition their enterprises around e-commerce and e-business.

Although each firm will make use of the Internet in various degrees, all will have to cope with a number of new strategic realities, and attempt to [142]:

• Send an almost limitless amount of information straight into the homes of their customers,

• Satisfy their clients' needs to research holidays and entertainment in a flexible way,

• Offer a "virtual tour" of the attraction they are interested to visit,

• Allow clients to perform transactions for various services,

• Stay in touch with all customers, whether past, present, or potential ones, and

• Remain open to let customers wow or boo, even without leaving their living-room.

Traditional visitor attractions SMEs that fail to adapt and take advantage of these new opportunities will face significant competitive disadvantages and may jeopardise their future prospects. Strategic actions are required to improve their competitiveness in order to survive the intensive competition emerging in the global marketplace [143].

Among others, we find three areas to target actions around a coherent e-business strategy. First, visitor attractions must learn to manage their information strategically, especially in the case of customer-facing processes. Second, attraction managers must use IT to create more flexible operations, which will be capable to satisfy a more diverse set of needs, and lead their business to attract more profitable visitors. Third, small firms must go beyond the tradition of "self-reliance", and learn to cooperate with other organisations at all levels, so as to share resources for developing their e-commerce and e-business capabilities.

11.2.1 Managing attraction information strategically

The tourism product is a unique type of product. Some of the characteristics that differentiate it from other products, and make it so information intensive, are its heterogeneity, its intangibility, and its perishability. The international scope of the industry, and the fact that tourism is a service industry, also contribute to its "information intensity" [144].

Tourism information, in addition to being very voluminous, is very diverse in nature. Examples of typical tourism information needed by all consumers include:

- Destinations,
- Facilities,
- Availabilities,
- Prices,
- Border controls,
- Geography/climate, etc.

Travellers in different times and different places need Pre-Trip, In-Trip, and Post-Trip information. Pre-trip information in the planning phase of a trip is required in the traveller's home or the prior destination. It tends to be more static and is required in the earlier stages of the trip decision-making process. The later stages of the trip decision-making process and once the traveller embarks on the trip tend to require more dynamic information. The type of information (pre-trip versus in-trip) required at different times depends on the type of tourist. For example, adventurous travellers or impulsive travellers will need little or no pre-trip information, whereas risk-averse travellers and those with long planning times will need pre-trip information to be both static and dynamic. In general, travellers are leaving more of their decisions until they are at the destination. This need for more in-trip information is spawning new applications of IT. Finally, post-trip information can become an important dimension of a visitor's experience, as tourism is notoriously a word-of-mouth business, where transparent quality assessment and referrals are a priority.

Destinations are developing creative information systems to make visitor information easily accessible in the destination. Information kiosks and TV-based systems in various forms are common.

Along with this trend, however, the need for pre-trip information is not necessarily diminishing.
Static, pre-trip information is usually distributed with brochures, guidebooks, and CD-ROM, whereas static, in-trip information is typically distributed using kiosks, guidebooks and brochures.

Dynamic pre-trip, in-trip, and post-trip information require online connectivity through various means, whether fax, email, computer reservation systems, interactive TV, the Internet, and Destination Information Systems (DIS's). Although there is significant progress in organising this information and digitising it, a lot remains to be done to make use of this information strategically.

Therefore, as a small visitor attraction, you must focus attention on this priority and try to:

- Review the various stocks and repertoires of information about your attraction,
- Identify which use have been made of them and through which channels,
- Perform some market segmentation based on information use and behavioural patterns,
- Point out the types of information having the most impact on customer satisfaction,
- Harmonise the medium and the message so as to optimise the impact on markets,

- Integrate the various channels through which this information is being communicated,

- Formulate a e-commerce strategy to move from information to transactions, and

- Complement this information strategy with coherent e-business initiatives.

11.2.2 Creating more flexible operations

Most of the problems visitor attractions face today when designing and implementing online strategies stem from the fact that they try to fit everything into existing structures and models. On the Web, however, we need to change the way we think about doing business. Change initiatives require considerable management effort, especially to adopt a visionary stance in face of a rapidly evolving tourism industry [144].

Therefore, attraction managers need to redefine the nature of their business and the underlying models and processes. This requires fundamental organisational changes that have to be managed carefully.

Since the Web is ever evolving and new challenges occur at the speed of thought, these changes should be directed towards increasing the organisational flexibility and openness to change. Becoming a learning organisation is vital for establishing competitive advantages in the new economy. Learning is not restricted to areas within organisational boundaries. Therefore, profound change also involves a rethinking of who the partners and competitors are and how networks with other organisations could increase the organisational capacity to learn.

Organisational goals that were suitable in the past become increasingly outdated. Change implies questioning old goals and functions and establishing new organisational frameworks. Whatever the type of sector, all visitor attractions basically face the same organisational barriers, thus, the first ones to overcome these obstacles will be the winners on the Web.

Consequently, in order to prepare the ground for implementing e-commerce and e-business initiatives, you should make sure that your management team is ready to:

- Visualize your attraction as human experiencing and information processing systems,

- Identify the parts of this system that are most essential to create/deliver value for visitors,

- Benchmark the attraction to measure how innovative it has been and why/why not,

- Define new components and functions that can distinguish this attraction from others,

- Focus change initiatives on making the attraction more flexible both offline and online,

- Put up a team to analyse operations in order to find ways to accommodate innovations,

- Build consensus around the need for change and the value of this business case, and

- Ensure that change can proceed as quickly as possible, given the speed of competition.

11.2.3 Exploiting the power of alliances

Competition blurs on the Web. Since everything changes so fast and entry-barriers are basically non-existent, competitive advantages can become irrelevant shortly after they have been realised. Only boundary-less organisations that are able to form networks with others quickly in order to pool resources and leverage competencies can take advantage of this dynamic nature of the Web. However, most visitor attractions are struggling with the issue of cooperation and knowledge sharing [144].

Collaboration is especially important in the tourism industry where the products/services and the information about them are extremely dispersed. Horizontal and vertical integration, but in a less formal way than traditionally, make it easier to overcome the lack of expertise and resources most SMEs face. Managers should consider internal and external markets, i.e., organisational departments, suppliers, customers, current competitors and research organisations as potential partners. Collaboration is so difficult today because we are still stuck in a mind-set that is shaped by competition and power structures. Giving up knowledge hoarding and understanding that the value of knowledge increases when it is shared is essential for collaboration efforts.

As such, once your small attraction have accepted this premise, your team will be able to formulate a highly effective and profitable e-business strategy, as long as you can:

- Locate the various competencies required to implement your e-business strategy,

- Review your existing partnerships and assess how they stimulate vs. hinder change,

- Weigh the value of collaboration and the factors that will bind new partners in alliances,

- Scale e-business initiatives to the resources of the partners network sharing efforts, and

- Structure bi-lateral and team relationships to make learning and knowledge sharing fluid.

11.3 E-business applications and functionality

Although the challenge of strategy formulation is surmountable, most small attractions tend to give up at the moment of assessing their technological needs. As they realise how obsolete their organisation has become, managers are tempted to dismiss e-commerce and e-business altogether, betting that most firms in their business segment will do the same.

This reaction is understandable, considering that very few operators are using IT to efficiently track their markets and operations, and to control access and quality throughout their facilities [144]. Naturally, we must recognise that many attractions have been quick to embrace the Internet, and to design their own homepages on the Web, so as to market themselves electronically in numerous ways, in order to complement local destination offices and Global Distribution Systems (GDSs). However, very few have made the step towards more integrated and coherent approaches, thinking it would neither bring in more visitors, nor allow them to achieve higher profitability.

But as a visionary attraction manager, once you have formulated a clear e-business strategy, it is possible to properly weigh the value of this new Internet business case. Indeed, you must be cautious not become overwhelmed by new technological needs, and try to think of this as an evolution instead of a revolution. As such, you must consider a number of basic applications, which offer most of the functionality required to implement a typical e-business strategy, especially in the case of small attractions with a poor track record in IT:

- **Web sites**: The evolution of Internet technologies has made it easier for small firms to build Web content that is more dynamic, and that can be updated more frequently at low cost. In addition, audio-video effects have become fairly widespread, and as your customers' bandwidth is now much cheaper, there should be no hesitation in focusing on upgrading the media that deliver your message to customers.

- **Reservation systems**: Interestingly, there has been an important trend in this area for a couple of years, as traditionally closed systems have been connected altogether on the Web, and made available directly to customers. In addition, the fact that attractions can be readily booked side-by-side with hospitality and transportation is a remarkable progress in reservation mechanisms. As a small attraction, you should be attentive to the new integrated solutions marketed by Application Service Providers (ASPs), who have integrated reservation systems into complete packages that allow your attraction's Front and Back Office applications to be integrated and managed online.

- **Customer Relationship Management (CRM):** Web information usage and transactions generate mountains of data about each of your past, present, and potential clients. It is essential to ensure that your staff can make use of this data effectively, so as to treat each customer on a one-to-one basis, from greetings to goodbyes. However, this application is the one that challenges most small attractions, since it offers a level of functionality that they are not capable to absorb and properly exploit. Therefore, all the benefits of CRM must be properly weighed, so as to identify innovative uses of IT that are not readily recognised by your management team.

- **Attraction IT infrastructures**: You should make sure not to invest solely on Front Office applications and find a balanced approach with Back Office as well as operational systems. IT can effectively be used to monitor and control the usage and activity of the attraction. This takes the form of electronic ticketing and entrance control systems used by parks, theatres, sporting events and others. New technologies can also help to create or enhance the experience of the attraction. As successive generations have come to expect dynamic, multimedia entertainment, the attractions industry has responded with a similar level of technological sophistication, particularly in the area of entertainment.

11.4 Step-by-step guide to implementing your e-business strategy

Once your strategic priorities have been set to the context of your business segment, and as your team learns about new e-business applications and discovers innovative functions they can perform, you can progressively enter into the process of customising such solutions to your firm's special needs.

The implementation of your e-business strategy will naturally depend on your firm's experience in using IT and the Internet. However, the majority of small visitor attractions are still configured around an offline business model, which prevents them from properly exploiting the opportunities offered by e-commerce. Therefore, however important is IT in your business segment, or whether or not you have experience with the Internet, chances are that like all SMEs, your firm will go through a typical implementation process:

- **Phase 1 – Creating and diffusing more attractive informational contents**: Along the strategic priorities identified earlier, you must first build new applications that will effectively respond to the pressing need to use information more strategically, primarily by: (1) developing an internet presence, (2) advertising your attraction online, and (3) harmonizing your various e-marketing channels.

- **Phase 2 – Creating seamless e-business processes**: Then you must build key applications around the most strategic value-creating processes within your attraction, and make sure they are seamless or require little effort from your staff to deliver value, which can be achieved by: (4) Streamlining Your Reservation Process, and (5) Modernising Attraction Facilities.

- **Phase 3 – Becoming an agile and innovative attraction**: Finally, all your organisation must be geared to exploiting e-business and IT, so as to increase customer satisfaction, in particular by responding to some important technological trends: (6) Enhancing Your Visitors' Experience, and (7) Implementing Virtual Reality.

11.4.1 Phase 1 – Creating and diffusing more attractive informational contents

Step 1 – Developing an Internet presence

Researchers have demonstrated that investment on electronic presence and distribution through the Internet represents good value for money, as lookers are progressively converted into bookers, and e-business starts to materialise for innovative operators [143].

Over the last ten years, the preferences and behaviour of tourists have shifted away from standardised packages, designed by tour operators, to individualised products, specifically selected and arranged to meet customer's requirements and interests. This change leads to a higher involvement of customers directly in the trip planning [145]. This provides visitor attractions businesses with an opportunity to develop their own space in the e-marketplace for marketing their products directly to potential customers.

Developing an online presence requires different skills and new approaches because of the distinctive characteristics of its medium, the Web. The Web not only combines the characteristics of traditional media but also offers unprecedented richness and reach, a platform for new forms of communication, and an enormous growth potential at a cost that cannot be matched by any other type of advertising media.

Traditional advertising strategies alone cannot capture the possibilities the Web offers, but are still necessary to create awareness and bring a user to a particular Web site. Consequently, as a small attraction, you must be aware of the basic rules of business on the Web [146]:

- **Consumer focus is crucial on the Web**: Understanding the online consumer and understanding the essence of a good Web site is crucial for successful online advertising. Internet users are far from being a captive audience. They can easily go to another site if one site does not meet their needs and expectations. They have developed their own culture of what is acceptable in terms of advertising on the Web. Their attitudes differ from those of off-line consumers. They expect advertisers to know what they want. The providers of tourism and travel information are numerous and the logic behind their sites is usually based on real-world organisational structures instead of focus on the costumer. That makes it extremely difficult for them to attract attention.

- **Interactivity and experience matter**: In reference to user attitudes and the importance of choice and the intangibility of tourism products and services, the significance of interactivity and experience for online advertising efforts must be stressed. Online consumers do not only want information, they seek entertainment when they go onto the Web. They are more active than in the case of TV advertising or ads in print media. If their attention cannot be retained, by offering them an enjoyable experience on the Web site, they will quickly switch to a more exciting site. A variety of innovative technologies are already available for incorporating interactivity and experience into the Web site design.

- **Customisation builds on online research**: Understanding the Web and understanding the characteristics and needs of the individual customer is a prerequisite for successful one-to-one marketing. The Web offers a variety of opportunities to collect data from online consumers that can be used for personalised advertising messages. The cost of customisation on the Web is negligible but it is not free. Internet users become more and more reluctant in giving away personal information. They are only willing to do it if it comes with a clear benefit for them.

- **Measurement is a challenge**: It can be difficult to justify the move toward Web-based advertising. Resources are usually only allocated to initiatives that have the potential to be successful. But, measuring effectiveness and impact of advertising strategies on the Web is a challenge because traditional measures cannot capture the various dimensions of online advertising. They are based on off-line concepts (like circulation statistics) and are likely to undervalue the effectiveness of a site. Especially in tourism where, for the most part, advertising success cannot be directly translated into sales volume or other monetary measures, it is very difficult to evaluate online advertising campaigns and Web sites in general.

The design of a Web page needs to reflect the selected strategies, such as personalization and interactive marketing. Seeing the Web site through the eye of the consumer helps in determining what content and design should be used. More has to be learned about consumer information processing and decision-making on the Web in order to be able to achieve the necessary customer focus. A continuous dialogue between Web designers and advertising experts is essential for achieving consumer-focused sites instead of technology-driven Web pages. Web sites have to offer choice and personalization. The Web is a pull medium, which means that consumers do not want to get swamped with boring mass emails they cannot relate to. Interactive online advertising renders it possible to tailor the site content and outlay to the needs of the individual consumer. It supports a personal identification with the information provided on the site. Chat rooms, testimonials, etc. help create communities on the Web that are necessary for communicating experiences.

It is not enough to collect data through log files, profiles or online questionnaires. The data needs to be carefully analysed, cross-referenced with offline studies (including census data), and compared with existing consumer typologies. The next logical step is to create databases in order to make the data available for future reference or for other organisational units, to facilitate the comparison of different datasets, and to transform data into knowledge. These databases need to be compatible so that they can be integrated in existing systems and data can be exchanged easily. Consumers want incentives for giving away their personal data. Such incentives are user profiles that allow a customisation of the Web site, opportunities to enter contests, special offers or coupons, etc.

SMEs cannot rely on traditional advertising measures when trying to assess Web site effectiveness. Evaluating the navigational ease of a site can serve as an indicator for how likely a site is to successfully communicate the information it offers. Providing feedback tools on the site is another form of measuring how effective a Web site is. Caller data and visitor surveys can also be a rich source of information in terms of analysing the impact created through online advertising. Getting the support of those who control important resources is critical. It will be very hard to justify the move towards Web-based strategies with monetary arguments. Since measures for the effectiveness of online advertising have yet to be developed, it is probably better to emphasise the strategic importance of Web-based advertising instead of establishing goals that cannot be met because they cannot be operationalised and measured.

Step 2 – Advertising your attraction online

Beyond the mere development of an online presence through a Web site for one single attraction, e-marketing is rapidly evolving and portends incredible changes to the tourism industry itself. Tourism SMEs should be aware of a number of issues, which provide a solid foundation for developing strategies, effectively exploiting the strengths of the emerging technology. Several implications must be taken in consideration[146].

A combination of online and offline advertising strategies seems to be the best way to fully use the capacities of the Web. A Web site is not a stand-alone advertising tool. Banners and cross advertising are necessary to control Web traffic. Portals are the most important entry point for users in search of tourism information, thus listing your Web sites with them is crucial. A consistent advertising message distributed through different media leads to synergies between online and offline strategies. Since the Web differs from other media, the focus has to be on doing things differently – not just doing old things cheaper and faster. Marketing strategies that respond to the nature of the Web are strategies that are based on personalization, experience, involvement and permission - in contrast to traditional marketing that builds on mass communication, tangible products, one-time selling instead of forming relationships, and unsolicited interruption.

The variety of existing Web-based technologies is great and their possible applications are numerous. The technology itself, however, does not lead to

[6] The following is based in large parts on the Abstracts from the White Paper on Advertising Strategy and Information Technology in Tourism, edited by National Laboratory for Tourism and eCommerce, University of Illinois in Urbana-Champaign, March 2000.

advertising success. An integration of Web technologies and advertising strategies is essential. A successful integration requires a favourable organisational environment and innovative approaches [146]:

- **Organisational barriers hinder technology implementation**: Limited resources, lack of proper management, insufficient knowledge, lack of communication, legal regulations and restrictions, and ownership issues are the most frequently mentioned barriers to technology implementation and adoption. In particular, smaller attractions are usually overwhelmed by the amount and complexity of barriers they encounter when trying to establish online advertising strategies.

- **Online advertising requires innovative approaches and organisational reconfiguration**: There is a need for new approaches to be able to capture the benefits of the Web and to cope with the threats it poses. The most successful players on the Web are those who have either applied old advertising strategies in an innovative way or have introduced completely new concepts. Continuous innovativeness, however, cannot be achieved with 18th century organisational structures and concepts. Organisations have to rethink their structure, culture, strategies, and business processes. As mentioned above, online advertising is a knowledge-based strategy. Yet, traditional bureaucratic structures restrict knowledge transfer and learning across all organisational levels.

Web strategies that utilise innovative technologies are important, but still have to fit into the overall advertising strategy. The characteristics of the target audience and the product or service offered determine to a great extent the technology that can/should be used. Tourists and tourism professionals, for example, differ considerably in terms of information needs and information processing.

In addition, the technology level of the target group should be kept in mind when integrating features like videos into the Web site design. Integration also means that advertising strategies have to be adapted to the Web. Reading Web based content, for example, can be very strenuous for human eyes. Thus, simply copying content from existing brochures onto the Web will not create the desired online advertising impact. Online advertising requires a holistic approach that comprises consumers, technologies, strategies, and business processes. Advertising on the Web is based on building relationships, not on merely selling products and services.

Effective communication between all individuals and organisational units involved in the design and implementation of online strategies can greatly facilitate the process and enhance the outcome. Expertise should, if possible, be acquired in-house to have more control over the outcome and to be able to increase the intellectual capital of an organisation, which is necessary for developing innovative approaches. If an external agency is charged with the design and/or implementation, goals and expectations have to be clearly communicated.

Online advertising is not just another sales effort. It involves the creation of a business on its own and, therefore requires proper management and sufficient resources. Creativity is an imperative. However, being creative and trying new things comes with a risk. SMEs need an organisational culture that encourages innovations and risk-taking and sees failures as opportunities to learn. Organisational structures should be as flat as possible so that information can be passed on easily and ideas be shared extensively. Learning has to occur on the individual as well as organisational level. Knowledge creation is useless if the knowledge is not processed and transferred, so that active learning can occur and become incorporated into the online advertising concept.

Step 3 – Harmonizing your various e-marketing channels

Several options, beyond an attraction's Web site and advertising banners, can be harmonised with an e-marketing strategy [142]:

- **Home shopping**: The arrival of technology that allows video, sound and pictures to be piped down telephone lines straight on to television screens means that, in the future, viewers will be able to enter virtual stores and examine goods or, in the case of holidays, walk around hotels, resorts, and attractions.

- **Booking kiosks**: In order to test people's likely response to home booking and to determine what services they are most likely to buy from their armchairs, either on the Internet or on an interactive television channel, companies have started selling a range of products on electronic kiosks located in shopping malls, banks, hotel lobbies and even on street corners. Consumer's Catalogue Showroom stores in the USA pioneered computers that allowed customers to see pictures of items on sale, watch advertisements for products, and if they wished, examine competing items. In the U.K., Thomas Cook began selling a limited range of products, including city-breaks and beach holidays, on touch-screen kiosks as long ago as 1994.

- **Use of CD-ROM's**: At the moment, not all telecommunication lines have a high enough bandwidth to allow video to be transferred from one to the other. Trying to send this down existing cables would be like trying to pour the contents of a reservoir through a straw, but where fibre-optic cable replaces copper lines this becomes possible. The technology is progressing at a faster rate but fails to meet total demand. Yet, it will not be today's consumers but rather those who have learned how to use the Internet, from electronic encyclopaedias to computer-literate youngsters of the next generation, who will be travelling in cyberspace.

Although these solutions can be relatively technology-intensive, small attractions can benefit from options available on the Web, but differing somewhat from traditional e-marketing. Some interesting examples exist, and your attraction should take a close look at each alternative:

- **Online magazines**: Whether you are looking for a classy hotel, a deserted island or a luxury spa, such travel sites as Condé Nast Traveller magazine is a good place to start. From the Top 50 ski resorts in the world, to the best golf resorts, the site will recommend how, where and when to travel in style. Consequently, it attractions willing to capture the attention of the international traveller must get access to key magazines [147].

- **Recommendation software**: Rand McNally has released two new Attraction Pack collections for its TripMaker software program. These add-ins provide travellers with specialised information ranging from such recreational activities as camping and hiking to trips to ski resorts and golf courses. Collection one includes a database listing selected sites for camping, fishing, boating, hiking, and other outdoor recreational activities. Another database lists state and national parks, forests and recreation areas, while a third contains hundreds of beaches all over North America where the user can plan a quick trip on a sunny day or a beachside vacation, and various spots where you can go white-water rafting, mountain climbing, and other more rigorous forms of relaxation. Collection number two's databases list hundreds of winter ski areas, including rope-tow beginner hills and posh alpine resorts. You can also learn where you can play golf and tennis on public and semi-private courses and courts. If the sedentary life mixed with an element of chance is your idea of a good time, you can peruse a listing of major horse and dog tracks, selected casinos, and gambling destinations in the United States [148].

- **Online videos:** Travelago Web site offers more than 1,800 streaming videos for more than 850 destinations. Attractions have the opportunity to provide Travelago site users with streaming video about their business, place links to Web sites and reservation systems, post property pictures and information, run a banner ad on the Travelago network and have their listing appear among "highlighted" properties for a destination. Their listing can also be placed on the Yahoo! Travel portal through Travelago's distribution partner program. Visitors to Travelago or its partner Web sites can watch videos, gather comprehensive information on hotels, restaurants, and attractions in each destination, and make their reservations online using one of Travelago's many booking engine partners. Travelago lets people feel confident about booking travel on the Web by allowing them to "see where they're going before they go." "Travelago is the world's largest streaming travel video content provider". It provides the most comprehensive travel library on the Internet - at the highest quality, using state-of-the-art technology. With 10 percent of all world-wide Internet page views dedicated to travel and destination research, Travelago is uniquely positioned as a quality business and leisure travel-planning tool. Once a traveller watches a Travelago destination video that features a particular hotel, restaurant, attraction or activity, that person is 70 percent more likely to book a video-related activity over something that just has a simple text listing. Videos turn lookers into bookers [149].

Unfortunately, the e-advertising solutions we have outlined so far are extremely rigid, that is they are delivered in a time-space dimension that requires a lot of planning, and can not easily attract visitors at the last minute. However, other options are available for small attractions that operate in zones that are difficult to access, or in segments that are very much time-dependent (i.e., those visitors consume on an impulsive basis). Interestingly, these solutions can be integrated with previous options, sometimes making them more flexible through the use of Mobile e-commerce or M-Commerce:

- **Interactive maps and photographs**: GlobeXplorer's comprehensive library of world-wide aerial and satellite photography is available through several sites. MapQuest is the first brand to feature this new technology. Through GlobeXplorer's delivery technology, consumers enjoy interactive aerial photography of many metropolitan and suburban areas, top travel destinations and some of the world's most well known locations. Integrating aerial photography with digital mapping provides travellers with an easy and convenient way to orient themselves to new places. For example, AOL members and MapQuest users who are planning a trip can plot a journey, see a map, and view the corresponding travel area in an aerial image. Using the navigation features provided by MapQuest and GlobeXplorer, the traveller may zoom in or out, and pan left or right, to visually find roads, rivers or other points of interest [150].

- **Wireless location services**: Libertel, a European telephone company, is launching a mobile location-based service using the Wireless Application Protocol (WAP), which is made available to its more than 3 million subscribers in the Netherlands. Such solutions help subscribers discover information about local resources such as shopping, entertainment and services while also providing another route to market for businesses. A similar service, which went live in the Sass Fee skiing resort in the first quarter of this year, allows Swiss GSM users to access localized information on weather forecasts, slopes, and ski-lift availability, along with details of avalanche threats and road conditions. Other services available on the Swiss location-based service include details of taxis and bus services, restaurants, shops, sports activities and emergency contact numbers. The information services are available in English, French, German and Italian [151-153].

11.4.2 Phase 2 – Creating seamless e-business processes

Step 4 – Streamlining your reservation process

The reservation process of small attractions is often targetted as one of the primary cause for lack of customer satisfaction. This is natural as it remains the most important customer-facing process of any attraction. Your whole organisation should become more aware of the priority to reengineer and streamline this process, so as to make transactions as seamless and effortless as possible, thereby increasing efficiency, speed, quality, and responsiveness.

Several solutions must be explored to reorganize your reservation process [144]:

- Most paid attractions and entertainment facilities can benefit from automated ticketing and entrance control, and in some cases systems, which also monitor usage. Computerised ticketing systems store information on the attraction or event, generate tickets and process payments. The database contains information on events, times and prices (of which there may be many), and reservations including group bookings. It must also be able to generate tickets immediately for customers arriving at the event and to handle commissions.

- Ticketing systems for theatre, concert halls and other attractions with numbered, designated seating need more detailed reservation systems. Seating plans showing occupied and unoccupied seats need to be viewable on screen, and tickets must, of course, show the seat numbers. Attractions and events often use centralised ticketing agencies, which manage ticketing for multiple events. These agencies have huge databases of many events.

- Other examples go as far as a "Virtual Box Office Ticketing". New solutions are developed regularly, such as those of Ticketingsolutions.com, an online ticketing system built by Community Internet PLC, an e-commerce specialist, which has been involved in large-scale ticketing for organisations ranging from global entertainment companies to the Badminton Horse Trials. By registering on ticketingsolutions.com every travel business can sell tickets via their Web site. Organisations can utilise the optional "e-commerce module," a cross-selling tool that targets visitors with offers specific to the service they are purchasing, e.g., an airline could sell branded merchandise alongside tickets. An optional "mail module" enables travel businesses to inform visitors about forthcoming special offers that may appeal to them. This helps an organisation to build up a database of visitors. Customers visit the virtual box office via the organisers' own site and purchase tickets online. As soon as an order is placed, the customer is automatically sent an email with full details about the booking. Systems can handle more than ten billion ticket sales per year, and customers can pay via the approved secure credit card system [117].

Step 5 – Modernising attraction facilities

Some attractions such as national parks, museums, sporting events, theatres and some theme parks require only one general entrance fee, which is paid upon arrival. Others, particularly theme parks, many require payment for individual rides, events or experiences once inside the park creating needs for more complex systems. Various solutions exist to meet the needs of such attractions [144]:

- Smart cards and tickets with magnetic strip cards are particularly helpful to monitor entrance into an entertainment facility with multiple experiences since they store payment information. They remove the need for payment at each point and the inconvenience thus created for visitors.

- Turnstiles requiring the insertion of a smart card or ticket can control entry into many types of events and attractions such as sporting events and outdoor concerts. Portable ticket collection stations are another option for use when access to the facility's power and cabling is not possible. These are particularly useful in large outdoor national parks, zoos or other natural attractions.

- Admission tickets can also be bar-coded allowing the information from the ticket to be sent to a computer system running ticket collection software. This software automatically cancels used tickets, notifies ticket collection operators of counterfeit tickets, prevents admission fraud by employees and provides other revenue control functions.

- Some attractions such as museums and parks may use IT for signage to guide visitors around the attraction for the best experience and to provide information on exhibits. The signage may be in the form of audio-visual electronic media, which can easily be changed as necessary.

- Kiosks or information pillars with CD-ROM players inside have a significant contribution to make to help guide visitors around the attraction. They are also used to give the visitor multimedia information on exhibits.

11.4.3 Phase 3 – Becoming an agile and innovative attraction

Step 6 – Enhancing your visitors' experience

The attractions and entertainment industry is changing rapidly to provide visitors with ever more enjoyable, thrilling, educational and diverse experiences. Whilst technology is not leading the way, it is providing more options for the development of entertainment and educational experiences.

Visitors to theme parks expect to experience some form of altered reality, either in a purely entertainment mode or in an educational or "edu-tainment" mode [144]. This can be accomplished mechanically as, for example, in the various rides and roller coasters of amusement parks. It is also possible to create an altered experience for a visitor using both mechanics and electronics together. But the electronic creation of more sophisticated altered experiences is now common. An advantage of electronically created experiences is that they can be more easily changed than mechanical or electro-mechanical experiences. Equipment to electronically create the experiences comes in a variety of forms varying from high quality audio and visual equipment all the way to virtual reality "pods". There is a whole industry of companies selling such technology to theme parks and attractions, competing in their ability to produce the most stimulating visitor experiences.

Museums, aquariums and zoos also use information technologies to give visitors simulated experiences at the border between entertainment and education. Science museums were the first museums to use technology to bring their exhibits to life. Since they are curators of "concepts and ideas" in addition to "things" (as aquariums, natural history museums and zoos are) they have had to be more creative in bringing their museums to life. To successfully give the visitor an experience of a "concept", electronic and interactive exhibits have been used extensively. Themed "walk-through" of exhibits that are enlivened by movies, sound and direct interactive experience are common today in museum exhibits of all types.

Step 7 – Implementing virtual reality

Virtual reality technologies are likely to increase and become more and more refined so that visitors can experience changes in time and place at will.

Virtual tours must be approached from both technological and personal factors, and defined as an experience of tele-presence in a virtually created environment using multimedia technology. The World Wide Web (WWW), as the most evolved network media, offers great potential as a marketing tool for the following reasons [154]:

- WWW has great diversity in both terms of richness and interactivity. It delivers a variety of data ranging from text to streaming multimedia, and the degree of interactivity is defined by the user.
- WWW could be impersonal mass media or very personal media enabling the tourist to have his/her own virtual experience.

Therefore, through virtual tour users can gain experiential information that has been available only through actual experience. However, research suggests that virtual tours may impact a number of aspects related to travel behaviour. The primary effects of the virtual tour are hypothesised as the followings [154]:

- Information research behaviour will be changed because tourists can get great benefit will less cost.
- Tourists can enhance the memory of destination and create a personal story of the destination. Then they form more vivid and clear destination image.
- Tourists could be in a better position to choose destination because the uncertainly from experiential information will be removed.

One of the most interesting contributions of the virtual tour for the tourism industry is its ability to affect the implementation of sustainable tourism. The virtual may enable tourism marketers to avoid unnecessary development of environmentally or culturally important resources. Sustainable tourism is typical type of experience-oriented tourism and the destination usually provides very unique and exotic experiences; thus it is especially difficult for tourists to form an accurate destination image. Virtual tours can help potential tourists to develop expectations about what they can experience at the destination. Importantly, tourists can learn about the uniqueness of destination and appropriate behaviour through virtual tour in a natural way.

11.5 Critical success factors of your e-business strategy

Although small visitor attractions have been quick to use the Web for e-marketing, it does not guarantee at all the success of their e-business initiatives.

However experienced your team may be with the Internet, the following success factors should be monitored very closely throughout the implementation process:

- Get out of your traditional work environment and develop a new vision of your attraction. As manager, you are the one responsible to challenge the views of your colleagues, staff, and even competitors.

- Watch-out for technological changes and your competitors' moves. A small visitor attraction can easily be superseded by the fact that other firms, who have waited a bit longer before launching e-business initiatives, have been able to integrate within their project the latest, more effective, and sometimes more affordable technology. Timing your project right also means timing relative to competition and technology.

- Share the task of learning about new e-business applications and discovering innovative uses of them. Idea generation is much faster and effective when the whole team takes ownership of the new solutions.

- Leverage the intelligence of your local industry partners. Talking with local hospitality firms, travel agencies, and tour operators, may help you to identify totally new types of customers with whom you can effectively relate online.

- Challenge your team to come up with something innovative. If your project proposal offers little else than some update of what you already have in place, it will be difficult to extract more value from e-business. Therefore, make sure you indeed focus on e-business, and not simply on implementing some "fancier" or the latest IT infrastructure.

- Put up a realistic business case that tackles the most important sources of value for your visitors. Unfortunately, those in charge of an e-business initiative often loose sight of what is needed, which may be sometime little more than a basic transactional function.

- Stay close to the visitor's experience throughout the attraction. Too often we notice that new e-business solutions do not necessarily enhance this experience, but remain focused primarily on efficiency. Striking a balance between quality and cost is crucial.

- Test your new solutions with a small sample of your real customers. Although this appears obvious, most e-business project (which always unfold under time pressures) tend to assume we can skip this step, or that it will cost too much time and money for what it's worth. Testing is not a simplistic "validation" process, since too often teams take it as just one way to get management to accept the thing. Testing is primarily a check on the "performance" of the new e-business solution, to see if it can survive in real-life operations.

- Harmonise your infrastructure throughout the attraction site. Too often operational problems occur because Internet-based systems have not been installed so as to connect 100% with legacy applications, leaving a brilliant idea under-utilised at 50%.

11.6 Case studies of innovative e-business solutions

Given the wide diversity of market segments in the visitor attractions business, some case studies have been identified for those segments with most likely to require an e-business and e-commerce strategy.

1. *Cultural Tourism*
2. *Nature-Based Tourism*
3. *Sports Tourism*
4. *Urban Tourism*
5. *Rural Tourism*

11.6.1 Cultural tourism

This segment has often been viewed as the most interesting test-bed for applying IT. Most often, cultural tourism implies museums, historical sites, major exhibitions, theatre, real-life immersions, etc. Since these attractions are visited by a variety of small and medium-sized groups, the challenge of managing operations seamlessly before, during, and after visits is tremendous.

To achieve superior performance in managing cultural attractions, it is crucial to understand the way the demand of cultural tourism is composed, and therefore to adjust the value chain and the service chain to address them more specifically to Internet uses enhancing the advantages offered by the Internet.

A recent survey has revealed how Internet users consider the demand of cultural tourism as a form of general tourism, which comprises different forms of tourism [155]. For example, the majority of the respondents established their wish within the framework of a special cultural offer, which goes beyond the simple visit of museums and historic sights. Instead, it comprises consuming cultural offers such as gardens and parks, craft industry and traditional evenings.

Furthermore, the need to comprise and view cultural tourism as a wider form of tourism, and therefore the need to reengineer the traditional value chain, has become evident. Beside information on dates of events, concerts, festivals and guided tours, the majority of the respondents have considered general information (history, chronicle and background information) and tourism information of the destination and on the accommodation more important than other specific types of information to be included on an attraction's Web site.

The results of this survey demonstrate the changing tourist behaviour and provide suggestions for a competitive offer of cultural tourism online. The Internet, as a malleable form of brochure enables simple and attractive ways at all stages of the services chain (from the simple gathering of information, to booking and reservation and customer relationship) to answer the developing needs and new behaviour of tourists. Cultural tourism has to be integrated in the general form of tourism, while the specific offer of cultural tourism has to be completed by other forms of tourism.

However, most cultural attractions experience sudden highs and lows in demand volumes. Therefore, beyond the mere function of informational Web sites, it is crucial to ensure that their e-business solutions are aligned with broader goals. Indeed, their applications must allow them to capture all that demand, at the moment it presents itself, and to deliver the best quality service to preserve their reputation, as well as to match what is visible online.

As discussed earlier in this report, there is a wide diversity of e-business applications that come in handy as several tasks can be put online:

- Attracting visitors through e-marketing

- Allowing them to preview the attraction contents

- Offering rebates for group sizes and frequency of visits

- Managing reservations and payment

- Selling attraction-related products and souvenirs

- Coordinating groups on site during visits

- Enhancing the visitors' experience

- Building a personalised Web page with news on topics of choice

To perform each task, various Web solutions and sites have been developed, where cultural attractions can effectively bypass the hassles of managing their e-business applications themselves, and rely rather on various options available on the Internet. Here are a few examples of solutions and best practices for small visitor attractions:

- **Building an online presence:** The fastest growing area of applied technology in cultural attractions lies in the display and dissemination of images. Indeed, the World Wide Web is now an important way to advertise exhibitions and provide visitors with information. An example of leadership in this area is the network of Montreal cultural institutions, which are reputed for their agility in using the Internet to attract residents and visitors form Canada and abroad. The Greater Montreal Tourism and Convention Bureau lists most of the surveyed institutions on its Website and a significant number of them have also developed their own sites [156].

- **Online reservations:** To sell tickets to arts consumers, CultureFinder has been recognised as the reference to know what is on the agenda of museums, orchestras, theatre groups, and other organisations throughout the U.S. and Canada [157]. Customers can buy their tickets online, or simply browse the listings to see what is happening during that week in over 1,500 North American cities. If consumers live in or frequently visit one of 65 major U.S. cities, they can even sign up for the site's email newsletter. It will give them advance notice of the latest hot-ticket events before they are posted to the site.

- **Complementary information:** Because of their stature and massive presence amid destinations, museums can be excellent centres of attention for a whole variety of tourism SMEs. As such, such cultural attractions must rely on their popularity to build Web sites in partnership with local organisations, so as to make the envy of other destinations. For example, the Louvre has become one the most interesting places to help visitors plan their trip throughout Paris [158].

- **Interactivity on museum Web sites**: Another approach to attracting visitors is to offer a virtual sample of the cultural contents available. Several methods of organising a virtual visit to a museum are possible. The main point is to transform a lonely experience, as virtual visits are today, into a more engaging experience, where several people can be involved together. Some examples in that vein can be found at the Museum of Science and Technology in Milan, where virtual visits have been a factor in its success [159]. Similar efforts are found at the Smithsonian Institution, which not only allows surfers to take an online tour of current exhibits, but also do research in the museums' archives and participate in educational programs [160].

- **Back Office applications for virtual tours:** The challenge of setting up a complete online touring application may require complex partnerships, which are often available only in experimental environments, such as universities. One interesting example in this sector is the Drexel Digital Fashion Project, a joint initiative between the College of Information Science & Technology and the College of Design Arts at Drexel University [161]. It represents the first of several planned projects that will be combined to form the Drexel Digital Museum. The impetus for the project has been the need to provide access to Drexel University's rich collections of art, textiles, clothing, ceramics, and artefacts from around the world. Creating a searchable database of digitised images and supporting documentation for each piece offers a means by which the collection may be accessed by students, scholars, designers, and other interested individuals around the world. An analysis of potential users and resources was undertaken to provide a user-centred framework for designing the database and to identify low cost methods for delivering the database.

In addition to using e-business and e-commerce, cultural attractions must also consider the important impact of new technologies on the nature of their products. Several applications can be used, in particular many of them that can be connected directly with other applications oriented towards e-business:

- **Guiding visitors:** Alternative advances are being used to make the museum experience more accessible to the general public. As such, several of museums use videos or computers to enhance exhibits. But there are factors limiting the immediate integration of new technology. Some administrators noted that the costs of adding new technologies can be prohibitive. For example, some Canadian institutions have had to pay as much as $50,000 in rental fees for an infrared audio guide to complement tours, which could only be justified with substantial attendance. In one case, a museum that evaluated the potential of an infrared audio guide decided against its use and hired seven summer student guides for the same cost. Some commentators also argue that such technologies can reduce visitor interaction with the artefacts and other attendees [156].

- **Delivering content:** Cultural attractions can also be the theatre of some technological prowess. For example, New York's Hayden Planetarium, which is housed in the Rose Centre for Earth and Space, a recently opened wing of the American Museum of Natural History. The planetarium is a unique combination of various advanced projection systems. It should soon be replicated in other revamped or new space theatres around the world. What makes the Hayden a technological leap forward is its combination of analogue and digital technology, allowing clients to view complex special effects communicating astronomical knowledge more vividly [162].

- **Enhancing experience:** The New York Zoological Society manages 5 parks and conducts international education programs as well as more than 300 conservation projects in 53 countries. This non-profit attraction is working on incorporating more technology into its exhibits, such as: interactive kiosks and interactive theatres, touch screens allowing voting functions, high-quality cameras to do video distribution from the exhibit to the Web, and a special database, the animal collection system, to automate tracking of how many animals by species we have, sort of like an inventory management system [163].

- **Stimulating creativity:** Artistic expression and technology can also merge in innovative ways. One example is from a major art exhibition at New York City's Guggenheim Museum. The exhibit combined for the first time the artist's interpretation of physical and mental space with the power of DVD. The exhibition, entitled "Invested Spaces in Visual Arts, Architecture & Design from France, 1958-1998", maximised every aspect of DVD's potential. Zuma Digital, a specialised DVD-only studio, developed the 45-display museum installation [164].

11.6.2 Nature-based tourism

Evidently, small beaches, adventure, and nature-based attractions do not need much technology to operate, as their products and services are mostly centred on letting the visitor experience peaceful, clean, pure, original, and exotic environmental habitats. However, one key issue in that sector is e-marketing.

For example, since beaches are relatively isolated in most cases, and since they depend on visitors "living nearby" or at least "passing by" at the right moment, they must make sure to develop a unique character that will make their advertising highly attractive. In addition, competition in this sector is based primarily on quality of the site itself, which can be confirmed only by word-of-mouth mechanisms, a marketing tool that remains slow and narrow in scope.

To palliate to this, various Web sites have been created for beaches to advertise and even get listed under some quality evaluation system, taking the form of a referral service. For example, an outdoor athletics site, GORP.com, has created a section for classifying US beaches [152]. Among others, beach operators can advertise and get classified according to their true value. The categories are:

1. Best Sand Playground
2. Best Water Playground
3. Best Camping
4. Best Swimming
5. Best Solitude
6. Best Biking
7. Best Wildlife Spotting
8. Best Hiking
9. Best Sunrise
10. Best Sunset

This site is among the largest and most trafficked Web site dedicated to outdoor recreation, nature-based, and adventure travel [165]. With nearly 250,000 pages of content, the GORP.com site offers a complete package of authoritative, award-winning content; a large, active community of outdoor enthusiasts; and a full-range of e-commerce offerings drawing nearly 30 million page views per month. Started in 1995, GORP offers a full-service active travel-booking feature with thousands of trips, accessible via the Web or telephone.

11.6.3 Sports tourism

Over the past 20 years, sports tourism has boomed. Entire cities and counties in various countries can capitalise on sports in two ways: attracting existing events and/or creating their own events [166]. Sports activities and events (either participative or observer) constitute a significant portion of the attractions and entertainment industry. Several examples demonstrate that IT and e-business can become integral parts of sports tourism:

- Major sporting events (e.g., Olympic Games, summer and winter), various team games such as football, baseball, hockey and basketball, and individual sports such as marathons, skiing, tennis and golf are all enjoyed by tourists. Computer systems are used throughout these activities to control entry to the events. IT is also used to track details of the play on the form of electronic scorecards. The ticketing and marketing of these events also relies heavily on the use of computer databases. One of these sports in particular, skiing, is using information technology in interesting and specialised ways [144].

- Companies have started to build Web services into some of their applications, although not into mission-critical programs yet. One such company is Intrawest, a Vancouver, British Columbia-based resort and golf course operator that accepts online reservations for lodging, ski rentals, lift tickets, and lessons [167]. Intrawest added Internet services to its collection so that customers can book more activities online, including restaurant reservations and non-resort-related functions such as snowmobile rentals. The Web-services architecture allowed Intrawest to combine online and physical operations systems. The surprising part of it is that using the Web is much better business than in the past.

- For those clients interested in learning about the wonderful world of scuba diving and snorkelling, the Cayman Islands Department of Tourism has developed a Web site, which provides a one-stop shop for those who want information on diving in general and opportunities for diving in the Cayman Islands specifically. Visitors to the site can search more than 250 dive sites in the Caymans and get information on minimum and maximum site depth, Global Positioning Satellite (GPS) co-ordinates, shore reference point, type of dive (wall, wreck, reef, etc.), suitability for snorkelling, as well as a comprehensive site description of which, in many cases, there is a digital image of the dive site. Information on and hyperlinks to dive operations are also included and users can keep up-to-date on dive news in the islands by registering to receive an e-mail newsletter [168].

11.6.4 Urban tourism

As several authors have commented, urban tourism is almost certainly among the most misunderstood and underestimated of all tourist types [169]. Whilst increasing attention has been given to city and urban tourism, local areas within larger cities or urban areas also present difficulties in terms of the measurement of tourism activity and the separation (and inter-relationship) of such activity from local and other trade and movement. It is at this level however, that local tourism development occurs through local government, local trade associations and town centre revitalisation strategies. It is crucial to understand the role of the Internet in linking the local with the global.

Very often, urban tourism revolves special leisure outings complemented with common activities in a special setting. A typical visit profile encompasses leisure shopping (street and crafts/antiques markets), exhibition and sports attendance during the day time and weekends, and a night-time economy based on late-night shopping and arts and entertainment - from cinema, performing arts and a host of fringe venues such as pub theatres, music and comedy clubs. Cultural tourism and speciality shopping are therefore high attractions to both tourists and locals alike.

Given the complex and fragmented nature of urban tourism, its promotion and management is often in the hands of either a major Destination Management Organisation (DMO). However, a growing number of specialised organisations are taking the leadership of some destinations, building Web sites around their own attractions, while partnering with local tourism service providers to develop complex Web strategies. The Internet can become an important element in attracting more visitors to an urban destinations, and to manage customer relationships in an integrated fashion. The visitor attractions taking such leadership position must think about a number of issues that go beyond its regular concerns as a singular attraction, and try to focus on the particular nature of urban tourism. For example:

- An important focus in urban tourism is "experience-oriented tourism", which emphasises activities, events, and fantastic or exotic experiences. However, it is hard for tourists to form a clear destination image without direct experiences. With the development of Internet, tourists have become able to access interactive multimedia easily [154]. Interactivity and multimedia are key factors to create virtual environment and provide virtual experiences. With experiential information, a virtual tourist creates his/her own unique memory and personal story which in turn enables him/her to form a more vivid and clear destination image and to reduce the uncertainly about destination.

- It is a top priority to properly target advertising to capture the attention of the most interested and interesting visitors. Tourism e-business portals can help in achieving that by offering complementary services to their regular online banners function to urban attraction operators. For example, Travelocity.com and TravelCLICK have entered into a long-term Relationship in which TravelCLICK will provide Travelocity with advertising and value-added promotional messages from local travel, hospitality, and destination advertisers around the world. Under the agreement, geo-targeted promotional messages from TravelCLICK's local advertisers are shown on Travelocity Web pages when a consumer indicates a desire to travel to a specific market. These geo-targeted promotional messages give Travelocity's 25 million members access to customised hotel offers and discounts at their destination city [170].

- As well, it is increasingly important to make destination activity booking more flexible, going beyond individual attraction systems, and joining industry-wide solutions. Another example from Travelocity is a partnership with Viator, which will enable online customers to not only view the most popular activities at their selected destination, but also make reservations directly on the Travelocity site through Viator's technology, along with flights, lodging and/or ground transportation. The approach Viator has taken with Travelocity is to pre-select the most popular tours and attractions in destination cities, and to make these easy to look at and book right on the site. In its initial stages, Viator destination information will be delivered to Travelocity customers through the personalised reservation confirmation email known as "Bon Voyage". Travelocity will be adopting a page on its site where those booking trips to the world's most popular cities will also be able to make reservations for the top activities and attractions in those locations [171].

11.6.5 Rural tourism

Compared to other forms of visitor attractions, rural tourism is one with the most promising opportunities, while remaining the least explored by most offline and online tourism operators. As such, rural destinations need to understand the commitment required to develop viable and equitable tourism, and the nature and extent of the associated costs and benefits. It is as important for the destination and the community to attract the "right" sort of tourist as it is for tourist to access the "right" product.

A key issue is to understand the precise role of different types of information within the rural tourism product, and how e-business and e-commerce may play a central role in managing such information and transactions [172]. This ultimately means that for certain situations, knowledge has to be delivered at different times and in different ways by both human and technological processes. In the same way that prior warning will spoil a surprise, inappropriate information delivery can have adverse effects upon a tourism experience. As reach and capability become more advanced, there is a need to re-examine how rural attraction operators can effectively manage both online and offline relationships in a seamless fashion. When a true market oriented approach is adopted, then the tourism comes first, with benefits accruing from satisfying needs. This, in the context of rural tourism, may invoke high short term costs but with long term benefits, economically, culturally and environmentally.

Since the rural tourism industry is still in its infancy, another area where IT may play a part is in product development. Analysing e-tourism market data, building a picture of the rural tourist, and conceiving new concepts that could be effectively sold online, are all tasks that can be facilitated by computer-based packages which encompass new thinking, state of the art databanks, and scenario building, coupled with technical (soft and hardware) and procedural (marketing expertise) helplines. However, the development and implementation of an on-line product development template package, or indeed communication networks and training packages, is subject to a number of constraints at the local level. One is the incentive to become involved, and another is funding for pumping ongoing development and training efforts.

However, there is no doubt that rural tourism can effectively benefit from e-business, to the point perhaps of entering the mainstream of visitor attractions. This would benefit the whole tourism industry, through diversification and higher satisfaction of e-tourism consumers, who are notoriously innovative in their tastes, and in the way they plan their visits.

11.7 Future of e-commerce and e-business

What about the future of e-commerce and e-business in the visitor attractions sector? Most analysts agree the changes will be tremendous, and that the impact will be felt at all points in the attraction value chain, from front-end to back-end, throughout all operations and management.

However, no one can tell if small attractions will be capable of focusing properly on the right strategy, and of investing in the right technologies. So far, tourism and travel experts agree on at least a few conclusions [172]:

- Even with a fuzzy picture at the global level, there is a great diversity of actions being taken at lower levels that will lead small attractions to evolve quickly.

- Innovative entrepreneurs who reengineer their business processes and take advantage of the emerging opportunities will gain major benefits and enhance their profitability and viability in the global marketplace.

- Information Technology has much to offer future tourism activities; it is envisaged that benefits to the industry and the tourist will accrue from the refinement of the "big picture" - the front office, and form added applications to the back office, particularly those involving the public sector and community involvement in planning.

How to get users to move from simply looking at a site to booking the product available on the site? A recent study revealed that - in terms of travel - the top five reasons for which customers remain reluctant to use the Internet to book their activities include:

- Concerns about credit card security,

- Reluctance to share personal information,

- Fear of having a problem,

- Wanting to have a travel agent to call in case of emergency,

- Having a preference to use an off-line travel agency.

Since keeping online customers loyal is still a major hurdle on the Internet, how can we expect the evolution and performance of e-commerce in the years to come, especially for small visitor attractions, for which investing on new Internet technologies appears extremely risky?

- On the issue of security, R. Broadhead, president of Intervex Consulting, says simply: "The Internet is inherently secure. It is human error that causes problems." In fact, he points out that a group of experts recently broke the highest level of code for credit card security. However, it took seven months to accomplish it and involved the use of 292 computers at 11 locations.

- Another problem is that many sites simply don't encourage users to come back. The simplest way to do this is ask the user if you can send them an email. It is an inexpensive and powerful way to capture these potential customers. Companies send e-mail newsletters to site users because it is viewed as providing valuable information.

- Mass customisation in not only a trend, it is popular with the consumer. The travel industry is urged to make the online transaction process easy for the consumer. "There aren't too many sites that allow one-click ordering." Many of the travel sites don't help their users by capturing and retaining personal information, which means every time that person returns to the site they have to re-input their personal details. Successful sites, like Expedia and Travelocity, do and they even greet their users by name.

12 Conclusion

"The overall aim of the WTO New Information Technologies Section is to provide leadership in the field of Information Technology (IT) and Tourism and guide members through the new developments, to help bridge the "digital divide" between WTO Members. The followings are the associated objectives: 1) Develop and expand the Information Technology (IT) in tourism knowledge base, disseminate existing knowledge to country members and industry members, and provide them with tangible tools; 2) Facilitate standardisation of procedures and dissemination of good practices for all Members; 3) Encourage partnerships in IT between the private and public sectors; 4) Assist and support stakeholders that tend to lag behind in IT resources and expertise, such as developing countries, peripheral destinations or small and medium-sized operators."

Abstract of the WTO 2002-2003
Programme of Activities

Part C of this report was written keeping in mind the overall aim and the associated objectives of the WTO New Information Technologies Section. As we conclude, we need to emphasise again the importance of taking actions. The emergence of e-commerce and e-business is transforming the whole tourism industry, but is affecting each sector differently. As we have demonstrated in Part C of this report, it is important to properly map the dominant trends, and delineate specifically how Small and Medium-Sized Enterprises (SMEs) must evolve in each segment, so as to be successful as they enter the foray of Internet competition. The need for drawing a coherent strategy is more important than ever, especially as most firms enter the Internet in the middle of its lifecycle.

Too often, we find a lack of responsiveness to technological change in the tourism sector. Several reasons (or false perceptions) can explain why the vast majority of Brick-and-Mortar SMEs in the tourism industry have yet to fulfil their e-business ambitions:

- Fear of the unknown, belief that technology is too complex, that it is not affordable.
- No focus on growth, search for status quo, lack of resources to invest in new initiatives.
- Too late to enter anyway, all good spots are seen as taken, incapable to compete.

These views summarise in themselves about 80% of the perception problem of tourism executives. Consequently, the importance to take an active stance, and to draw out strategies that will be effectively implemented, must be re-emphasised constantly.

Since this problem is present in all sectors of the tourism industry, there is a need for synthesising the lessons drawn from the sections of each sector. As a manager willing to unlock the potential of an SME, you should try to remember the following principles:

- **Targeting your e-business strategy**: Never loose sight of the broader trends driving the tourism industry, and especially those driving your own sector. Before reading this report, most managers will have had a preliminary idea of what they would like to do on the Internet. Yet, most often it will have been based on partial knowledge, or very quick observations. Clearly, targeting your e-business strategy on the most important drivers of competition in your sector will contribute to your success.

- **E-business applications and functionality**: As soon as you thought you had the final and most optimal architecture for your e-business infrastructures, you discover some innovative applications have just come out on the market. If staying abreast of technology is really an important differentiating factor for your firm, then you may want to outsource altogether the tasks of identifying, exploring, comparing, testing, costing, and selecting the right applications. However, most of these tasks can often be performed at low cost within your firm, since keeping up with the latest technology is crucial for only a small minority of SMEs in the tourism industry. It is not technology that will make your e-business strategy cleverer than your competitors' one, but primarily the way you have reconceived your products and services, and the business model and processes that support them.

- **Step-by-step guide to implementing your e-business strategy**: Too often, implementing an e-business strategy is viewed merely as a following a "recipe". This could not be furthest from reality, since strategy implementation rarely follows in a linear fashion. Therefore, once you have become aware of the typical step-by-step evolution of SMEs towards e-business, you must rethink your overall strategy and ask which ones of these steps you can effectively accomplish, what resources will be required, whether they will produce the value your existing and future customers are expecting, etc. Clearly, if one lesson must emerge from this report, it is that e-business strategy is a journey, a tedious iterative learning effort, not an end in itself but merely an evolutionary process, towards a more fluid and more dynamic way of managing your existing and future business.

- **Critical success factors for your e-business strategy**: Another important lesson stemming from this report is the importance of staying on-guard to avoid mistakes. Indeed, countless successes and failures have been encountered with e-business strategies in other sectors. However, SMEs in the tourism industry, because of the fragmented and turbulent nature of their competitive environment, must be even more careful than other firms in the management of their e-business initiatives.

- **Case studies of innovative e-business solutions**: Although lessons learned from other firms may be useful, it is always necessary to weigh the contextual factors that have helped some solution to work or not in some places. Chances are that some technologies that look perfectly affordable and a good fit with your strategy, may finally be a nightmare when comes the time to implement it. Fortunately, smart SME managers will developed the flair for these problems (much more so than in large firms) as they will often rely on their double capability to attend closely to "operation" and "strategy" in an integrated fashion.

- **Future of e-commerce and e-business**: In the end, whatever your strategy may be, there are extremely few SMEs who will have a significant impact on their own sector, let alone on the whole tourism industry as a whole. Therefore, it will always be necessary to think about the future, to visualise what technology may look like 5 years from now, and to find new topics to enlist in your learning agenda. As such, e-business strategy formulation never ends, and continues as long (and as fast) as your desire to remain a leader in your sector.

Overall, the analysis of each travel and tourism sector has offered a balanced perspective as to what should be done, why it is strategic, where managers should learn about it, and how certain companies have done it. These lessons should serve to stimulate the creativity of your management team, and create a vocabulary around which you will be able to communicate e-business initiatives throughout the organisation, as well as among partners within your industry.

Above all, you can count on the numerous players throughout the travel and tourism industry, who are ready to join your efforts in upgrading your firm's e-business capabilities. Technology is increasingly more accessible, and it is only a matter of knowing what you want to achieve, and then communicating it properly to a team of committed business leaders.

Chances are that, by following the lessons identified in this report, you may well become one of these leaders in your own sector and market niche. We sincerely hope that once this occurs, you can be part of the next edition of the WTO Business Council report, and come to share your experience with the whole tourism industry.

Appendix A – Review of consumer Websites

Introduction & methodology

The selection of consumer Websites was undertaken in two stages:

Stage 1

Initially more than 100 sites were identified from popular destinations world-wide with an online presence. Many different sources were used to draw up an initial list. These included:

- Travel magazines e.g. Escaperoutes, Conde Nast Traveler
- On-line destination guides e.g. Lonelyplanet, CityNet, Fodors, Travelocity, Infoseek, Expedia, Rough Guides, ITN's Travel Network, LeisurePlanet
- Search Engines e.g. metacrawler, altavisita, google.com, Yahoo, Looksmart.com
- Portals providing links to DMOs Web sites e.g. Travel & Tourism Intelligence site, IACVB site, Tourism Offices Worldwide Directory

Stage 2

The 100+ sites were initially reviewed and 30 were selected to be the subject of a more detailed analysis. To be among the 30, the sites were reviewed against the following criteria. All 30 have at least the first three features:

- Links to regional/local DMOs
- Links to local private sector tourism business
- Interactive trip planner enabling search by category
- Booking facilities
- On-line registration of visitors

This Annexe contains a short summary of the main features of each site (except for the 5 selected site selected for the case studies) and a comparative analysis of the 30 sites.

The 30 selected DMOS are as follow:

National DMOs Websites

COUNTRY	12 NATIONAL DMOs	URL
Canada	Canadian Tourism Commission	www.travelcanada.ca
Caribbean	Caribbean Tourism Organisation	www.doitcaribbean.com
Germany	German National Tourist Board	www.germany-tourism.de
Egypt	Egyptian Tourist Authority	www.touregypt.net
Japan	Japan National Tourist Organisation	www.jnto.go.jp
Malaysia	Tourism Malaysia	tourism.gov.my
Mexico	Mexico Ministry of Tourism	www.mexico-travel.com
New Zealand	Tourism New Zealand	www.purenz.com
Spain	Turespaña	www.tourspain.es

Switzerland	Switzerland Tourism	www.myswitzerland.com
Thailand	Tourism Authority of Thailand	www.tourismthailand.org
UK	British Tourist Authority – US gateway	www.visitbritain.com

Regional DMOs Websites

REGION	7 REGIONAL DMOs	URL
Andalucia (Spain)	Turismo Andaluz	www.andalucia.org
Edinburgh (UK)	Edinburgh & Lothians Tourist Board	www.edinburgh.org
New York (US)	New York State Division of Tourism	www.iloveny.com
Ontario (Canada)	Ontario Travel - TraveLinx	www.travelinx.com
Pennsylvania (US)	Commonwealth of Pennsylvania, '100% Pure Pennsylvania Experience'	www.experiencepa.com
Trentino (Italy)	Azienda per la Promozione Turistica del Trentino	www.trentino.to
Wallonie Bruxelles (Belgium)	Wallonie Bruxelles Office de Promotion du Tourisme (OPT)	www.belgium-tourism.net

Local DMOs Websites

CITY / COUNTRY	11 Local DMOs	URL
Barcelona (Spain)	Turisme de Barcelona	www.barcelonaturisme.com
Berlin (Germany)	Berlin Tourismus Marketing GmbH	www.berlin-tourism.de
Budapest (Hungary)	Budapest Tourism Office	www.budapestinfo.hu
Canberra (Australia)	Canberra Tourism & Events Corporation	www.canberratourism.com.au
Copenhagen (Denmark)	Wonderful Copenhagen	www.visitcopenhagen.dk
London (UK)	London Tourist Board	www.londontown.com
Paris (France)	Paris Convention & Visitor Bureau	www.paris-touristoffice.com
Singapore (Singapore)	Singapore Tourist Board	www.newasia-singapore.com
Vancouver (Canada)	Tourism Vancouver	www.tourismvancouver.com
Vienna (Austria)	Vienna Tourist Board	info.wien.at
Zurich (Switzerland)	Zurich Tourism	www.zurichtourism.ch

Aggregate analysis of the functions and services offered by the 30 DMO Web sites evaluated

FUNCTIONS & SERVICES OFFERED BY THE SITE (first page)	
Generics	
Flash introduction	2
Location context (where are we?)	14
Logging procedure (select country of origin, click on icon...)	11
Language selection	24
Logo/brand	30
Menu	30
Travel Information	
Culture/History info	16
Climate info	23
Travel essentials info (money, customs, clothing, shopping...)	21
Transport info	29
Itineraries/tours info	25
Travel insurance info	3
Image gallery	14
Maps	26
Tips/FAQ	14
Links to regional/local/national DMOs	23
General Information	
Company/organisation information	22
Contact details	26
Employment opportunities	3
Privacy statement/disclaimer/terms & conditions/copyright	18
Information on the design of the site (browser compatibility, Webmaster, site host...)	8
On-line security transactions info	9
Warranty & return policy	4
Research data/customer survey	15
Links to other corporate sites	10
External links to related sites	30
Special features	
Visitors comments/testimonials	8
Weather report/forecast	7
News/report/magazine	10
Newsletter (with news, offers...)	15
Chat/newsgroup	6
Postcards	12
Design & functionality	
Top menu	30
Sub menus	10
List of content on every page	26
Link to homepage on every page	27
Site map	13
Use of Internet protocols consistently	29
Use of flash	12
Use of java applets	9
Use of animated gifs	22
Multimedia	30
Textual description of destination	29
News (headlines, brief summary...)	16
Special/last minute offers	14
Exchange rates (converter)	5
Job status tracking & amendments facility	4
Search facility – by key words	22
Search facility – by category	28
FUNCTIONS & SERVICES OFFERED BY THE SITE (second page)	
Search explanation/guide	13

Contest/prize	3
Registration (join club, newsletter)	21
On-line brochure/personal folder	10
Links to advertisers / banners	10
Links to partners (eg. Government)	23
Local time	4
Date	5
List of awards given to the site	1
Online customer service/consulting	2
E-mail form for enquiry	29
Request form for brochure	13
Products Search/list	
Accommodation	28
Flight	12
Car Rental	14
Packages	11
Attractions	23
Activities	20
Events	29
Restaurants	12
Tours	27
Tours operators / travel agents	11
Conference facilities	6
Local services & businesses	5
Shop & retail	15
Product Information end points	
Contact details	29
Multimedia	18
Availability	10
Rates	23
Textual description	27
Facilities	23
Quality accreditation from governing body	15
Booking facilities	
Completion of e-mail/fax form (reservation enquiry)	9
Real-time on-line booking and confirmation	10
Link to 1/3 party site(s) for booking	12
Call Centre	15
Contacting provider direct	28
On-line registration	
During booking procedure	7
To enter competition/draw	2
To create personal brochure	5
To shop	1
To access chat/forum	2
To subscribe to newsletter	14
To Join club	0
On-line Shop	
Clothes	1
Souvenirs	1
Books	2
Maps	3
Minimum total order value	0
Other Web sites	
Site dedicated to the Tourism industry	8
Site dedicated to MICE	15
Site dedicated to media	10
Site dedicated to travel trade	9

Summary of consumer Websites

Canadian Tourism Commission (CTC) – http://www.travelcanada.ca

The site is very much built as a portal to the official destinations sites within Canada. Nevertheless, the site contains well-presented content and an efficient search facility enabling the user to search directories of all products and services by category and location.

It is an attractive site, with high quality pictures of the destinations, well balanced with the content itself. E-postcards and a virtual tour are also available so visitors may have a more in-depth visual experience of the destination. The menu headings are kept very simple and shortcuts to all the different part of the site are available in each page making the navigation through the site easy.

The site uses search facilities to enable visitors to find the product they are looking for. But they encourage people either to click through to the service providers own site or to the DMO's site of the specific area within Canada they wish to travel to, in order to finalise their holiday plans. There are no booking or reservation facilities on the site, this is left to the province or local DMO.

CTC takes the opportunity to gather consumer data, such as contact details, demographics and travel preferences from users at key stages in the site, eg as part of the registration process to subscribe to their newsletter, or to send an e-mail feedback form.

This site provides a good example of a country portal that makes the most of its relationship with the regional and local partners.

German National Tourist Board (GNTB) – http://www.germany-tourism.de

This site provides an excellent portal to Germany. It uses an interactive map of Germany to facilitate searches at all levels, country, regional and city and has a wide range of general information about the country as a whole. There are sub-homepages for the various regions, with links to related sites, including those of DMOs.

The homepage suffers from a bit of information overload, but the site remains attractive. Multimedia is used extensively throughout the site, there is a unusual cartoon-like virtual tour on the theme of aliens going on holiday to Germany, which is used to give the location context. There is a number of Java applets and animated gifs, as well as an interactive picture book (where you can zoom in and out). Unfortunately, the later is a little bit slow and only 2 pictures are available at the moment.

The navigation through the site is straightforward, the main menu is very simple and site map is available. The site contains a good event search facility but does not offer the chance to search for any other type of product. The site does not provide booking facilities but offers links to 1/3 party sites (such as hotel groups) for accommodation booking. Germany does have an on-line booking site www.booking-germany.com, which is only accessible to tour operators & travel agents, but they have decided not to integrate this with their main country portal.

Visitors can subscribe to an online event newsletter. During the subscription process, GNTB takes the opportunity to learn more about the preferences of their visitors regarding the area within Germany they are the most interested in, as well as the type of events. This enables them to provide each subscriber with a newsletter tailor-made to their own interest.

The best feature of the site is the excellent interactive map through which the user can search for destination content (country, region, city level).

Egyptian Tourist Authority – http://www.touregypt.net

The site is very rich in content with good destination guides on the main cities, which have sub-homepage and a detailed main menu. The site resembles a search engine or directory site with a wide range of type categories listed on the homepage, which makes it a bit confusing for the user. The page design is not consistent on all pages that adds to the users difficulties.

Once past the initial confusion of the homepage the navigation is fairly easy. There is a link back to the homepage from each subsequent page and the main menu is omnipresent.

The site provides good access to its comprehensive directory with all sorts of resources (from hotel to cinemas, restaurants etc), but only accommodation has a search facility, all the other products and services are provided as a list. Hotels can be searched by location, grade and key words. Booking is available by contacting providers direct (often through a link to their site) or through a 1/3rd party site.

Users can register to receive a newsletter and participate in a chat group, which involves submitting an e-mail address. No further customer data is collected.

This site is very rich in content, but the information may not be presented in the most user-friendly format.

Japan National Tourist Organisation (JNTO) – http://www.jnto.go.jp

This site has good content with general destination information complemented by more in-depth practical guides for local destinations. There is an in-depth interactive directory, searchable by category, as well as a travel and transportation section from which visitors can view timetables for domestic flights and railroads.

The site is attractive with a user-friendly menu in the homepage similar to that used by Expedia. There is a menu with icons for each category type (accommodation, transportation, events etc).

The navigation is relatively easy, although it could benefit from a menu on every page to allow users to browse through the site from one subject to the other, without having to go back to the homepage.

Search facilities are available for all the main products: accommodation, shops, restaurants, attractions, events etc). Each category can be generally search by type, time/date, geographical area, rate, retrieval rate, retrieval rate, retrieval rate, retrieval format. Visitors can check availability for accommodation and use the on-line booking facilities to book some of the establishments online. Interactive maps are also used throughout the site in parallel with destination information. An interactive map section is also available (country level, regional level, sub-regional level), from which visitors can zoom in and out and locate facilities such as: activities, accommodations, restaurants etc.

JNTO does not seem to gather information on its visitors' preferences and profiles at any stage through the site. The only time visitors are asked personal information is during the booking process where they are asked to register and provide their contact details.

Tourism Malaysia – http://tourism.gov.my

This site has a lot of good content. Malaysia Tourism is currently improving its site functionality, with enhanced multimedia features and new technologies, such as Text Chat (a text based conversation with a professional tourist assistants) and personalized travel planning facilities now under construction.

Parts of the site are slow to download. The repetition of different menus within the homepage tends to be confusing, although in general terms the site is easy to use. Some pages do not contain a list of content nor a link back to the homepage, constraining the user to use the 'back button' on his browser toolbar.

Tourism Malaysia's Hotel Directory can be search interactively but the site does not provide on-line booking and only gives address, telephone and fax numbers of the establishments, so that visitors have to book direct with the establishment.

Tourism Malaysia does not gather any personal details from users. It uses Outlook Express News Group software for enquiries and feedback and allows people to post and view questions and answers.

Parts of the site are slow to download and some sections are still under construction. The Text Chat facility with an online travel adviser is a good feature, as is the currency converter and the personalised travel planner.

Mexico Ministry of Tourism – http://www.mexico-travel.com

This site is very rich in content, providing global and local information through the provision of sub-homepages for each region, which act as mini-sites within the main site. Search facilities are available within the mini-sites but do not allow cross regional searches. As a consequence, a countrywide search by category is difficult and has to be undertaken using a key word facility.

The site is attractive with a similar look and feel for all destination sub-homepages, reproducing the same format, menu, functionality and features. Many java applets and animated gifs are used, which has some impact on the slow download speeds. Navigation is easy with the main menu displayed on the left hand side of the screen, on every page. Unfortunately the link to 'home' leads to the tunnel page and not the homepage.

An interactive map of the country acts as the starting point to the destination search. Selecting a region takes the user to that region's homepage with a map showing the main cities, for which mini-sites seem to be under construction. The key word search is enhanced by the ability to specify the section of the site in which you wish to search. As visitors browse through the site they can save and print details of products and services within a 'travel organizer' but there is no booking facility. Visitors are expected to contact the service providers direct or book via their travel agent or tour operator.

Visitors are asked to register by providing their full contact details and choosing a username and password. This gives them access to tourism statistics and reports as well as their travel organizer. Through this logging procedure the DMO can monitor visitor interests, which will enable them to improve the quality of their database and to undertake personalised CRM activities.

The template mini sites for regional and local destinations within Mexico are an excellent feature. Each follows the same structure and provides useful search facilities.

Turespaña – http://www.tourspain.es

The site has a high level of content and clearly indicates that it is targeted at different segments with sections dedicated to leisure travel, business travel and adventure travel. Links to regional or local DMO sites are not provided but local destination content is detailed.

This is an attractive site, with a simple style used consistently throughout. Short, guided tours on the area are available on key themes with pictures and audio commentary.

From the homepage, various browsing options are proposed either by choosing a travel type or by using the menu to access specific information. Eventually all merge into one detailed menu (with sub-menus), which is available on every page enabling smooth navigation. The link to 'home' leads to the tunnel page and not the homepage, which is aggravating.

Interactive search facilities are in use. The user first clicks on the category they wish to search, an interactive map enables them to select a region and a drop down menu function allows selection of criteria to narrow the search further. Booking facilities are not provided and accommodation search results display the provider's address, telephone and fax numbers so the user can make contact directly to make a booking.

No customer profiling information is collected, but the user is asked for their choice of preferred language (Spanish, English, German, French) to enter the site from the tunnel page and their country of origin if they choose to view a newsletter with news relevant to their market.

The site makes good use of an interactive map as part of the search facility enabling users to select a specific destination while actually locating it on the map. This is very useful when visitors are not familiar with the geography of the country and the names of local/regional destinations.

Switzerland Tourism – http://www.myswitzerland.com

The site contains very good content and has a number of interactive functions including forums, chat and searchable databases (accommodation, events, attractions etc). The site acts as a portal to DMO sites within Switzerland and only provides a general description of destinations, directing visitors to the more local sites for further information.

It is an attractive site, which provides a number of opportunities for the user to visually experience the destinations using animated pictures, Webcams and video. The site is very easy to use with simple and visible menus across the top and down the side of every page.

The site makes extensive use of multimedia throughout, including a virtual tour with an audio message promoting the destination. An interactive map is available to search by destination (country/region) and interactive databases with drop down menus are used to search the directory. The site provides online booking for hotels through Switzerland Destination Management (SDM).

The site has a tunnel page in which visitors are asked to specify which country they are travelling from before they enter the homepage. At other points in the site (e.g. registration to MySwitzerland folder / newsletter) visitors are asked for further details regarding their profile.

The most notable features of the site are the extensive use of multimedia and interactive functionalities: virtual tours, Web cams, forum/chat, interactive search database, and online brochure.

Tourism Authority of Thailand – http://www.tourismthailand.org

The site contains good general content and destination information but does not really provide detailed directory searches for many categories of products or services. Search facilities for accommodation and restaurants are available but repetitive searches at the time of the evaluation did not return any results. It does not provide links to DMO sites but contact details are available. The depth of information provided for the different categories of product is not consistent.

The design of the tunnel page and homepage is different from the rest of the site, which also suffered from a relatively slow download speed. It is relatively easy to navigate through the site with one of two menu bars: one with the different sections and the other which could be considered as a 'Guidance menu bar' with contact, site map, search and link to home (which leads to the tunnel page).

Each destination featured has its own sub-homepage (designed similarly) with a search available through clicking on a category from a drop down list. There is a user-friendly interactive map showing major city destinations and leading visitors to the destination sub-homepage but it is regrettable that this function is only available from the 'about TAT' section.

No personal information seems to be gathered about users except on the tunnel page where they are asked to select their preferred language to enter the site.

Lack of content was the main problem with this site, after a wide variety of searches using the interactive database facility, no results were returned.

British Tourist Authority (BTA) US Gateway – http://www.visitbritain.com

The site contains a very good level of content, using a simple but detailed structure. BTA uses different gateways for different target markets, all accessing the same data content, but presented in different ways to match the needs of the market. BTA's US gateway offers a real-time text chat facility with travel consultants in the US contact centre. The site offers 3 different options to browse the site: by geographical area, by type of information, by type of traveller (mature, family, student and gay & lesbian) clearly defining their main target segments.

The design look and feel of each BTA gateway is similar in most cases. The site offers a good balance between text information and photographs of the destination. It is easy to navigate through the site, with a consistent, simple but detailed menu available on every page.

The site does not offer on-line booking but provides an efficient search facility that enables users to quickly find the information they want. Generally e-mail and site links are provided, users can also contact the BTA call centre. GPS level interactive mapping is available, enhancing the ability to locate accommodation, attractions, events and TICs.

Throughout the site users are asked to supply personal details in response to key questions that enable BTA to gather personal profile and preferences data, eg to enter the homepage (country of origin only), to order a brochure, to enter a competition. On a random basis, users are also asked to provide their contact details if they agree to participate in a short survey at a later date with the chance to win British prizes.

The provision of different gateways tailored to their targeted market needs is of particular interest.

Turismo Andaluz – http://www.andalucia.org

The site contains good content as well as very detailed and enhanced interactive search facilities covering a wide range of products (shops, accommodation, events, activities, attractions, car rental). It also provides online booking not only for accommodation but also car rental, some attractions, golf courses and some events.

The site is attractive. Most of the site is available in four different languages. However, the 'reservation centre' section (from which you access the online booking search engine) and the special featured products section ('Star Offers') are only available in Spanish. This is unfortunate in that it will limit the use of this to domestic users and international Spanish speaking visitors.

The site is easy to use with a simple main menu consistently used throughout the site. It offers two methods of searching the database: one with an information orientated search and the other with the objective of making a booking. Online bookings are powered by the 'Sistema de reserves Séneca' (central de reserves turísticas de Andalucía). Visitors can either book online or complete a reservation e-mail and send credit card details separately by phone/fax.

Visitors who are sending feedback/comments from the site are asked to answer a few key questions in order to find out more about their profiles and preferences. This is not compulsory. Full contact details are required to register in order to be able to book online.

Edinburgh & Lothians Tourist Board – http://www.edinburgh.org

The site provides good access to the destination's directory of products and services with interactive search capabilities. There is a 'Kid's section' that acts as a mini-site enabling children to explore the destination and an interesting 'What's new Section' that provides a search by category using a drop down menu.

This is an attractive site, which maintains a good balance between editorial and pictorial information about the destination. It is easy to use with a menu frame available on every page. The menu system is in two sections: one down the left hand side and one across the top of the screen.

The site has an online shop, for the purchase of a limited selection of books and maps. Online booking is not available but users are encouraged to contact the providers direct. Generally, e-mail links are provided and in some cases, pre-defined reservation forms enable visitors to reserve a room and ask the provider to contact them to finalise the booking. Different options are available for accommodation search: price, rating, alphabetical order or using a very detailed search function combining all factors (location, type, rating, price, facilities).

As part of the introduction in the 'contact us' section, users are asked to participate in an online survey with key questions to identify user profiles and preferences. This is not compulsory.

New York State Division of Tourism – http://www.iloveny.com

The site does not contain detailed editorial about the destination. It acts more as a gateway to the state, providing links to more regional/local DMO sites, and a platform to search the state product directory. All sections are available for use by both international and domestic tourists, but the site seems primarily targeted to domestic visitors with one section, 'international visitors', providing an itinerary guide publication in 6 different languages.

The design look and feel is consistent throughout the site. Results returned from a database query are displayed in a search engine-like format (listing results with title and brief summary). Users can then click on each item to view more detailed information, which only consists of text. No images are displayed, which is disappointing.

The site uses a detailed but simple menu consistently throughout the site that makes navigation very easy. The homepage also contains a menu of links to other NY State sites. Users have the option of searching the database by category or using an interactive map to search by region. Clicking on a region links to that region's sub-homepage from which the user can further search by category. Once a particular product is found, there are further interesting functions eg locating it on a map (full GPS), planning the route to it, and searching for other products nearby (by category and distance).

There is a basic travel planner that enables users to save items of interest to view at the end of their site visit but if they want to print or e-mail it they need to use their browser.

Visitors are asked for personal details (full contact details) to personalize the travel planner and receive e-mail updates on travel opportunities. This is optional as visitors can use the trip planner without registering first. The site provides an e-mail form for users who wish to make an enquiry or order a brochure, at which they are also asked their opinion of the site and how they heard about it.

Notable features include the chance to locate your chosen product on a map and search for other products nearby.

Ontario Travel, TraveLinx – http://www.travelinx.com

The site is very functional, with detailed database searches for the different categories of product. It is very much a platform to encourage bookings in Ontario providing different options for accommodation, packages and tours in the way of online booking, call centre or online reservation request form (someone will call back within 24 hours to confirm the booking).

The site provides a consistent look and feel. There is good interactive map (province level, county level, city level). Visitors can also move the cursor over different areas to obtain a brief description before they choose to click on it for detailed information.

The site is very easy to use, with a simple main menu and detailed sub-menus available on every page. Search functions are very detailed with a good range of criteria to choose from (date, location, name, type, services, facilities, activities, amenities) yet are very easy to use and have appropriate guidance.

Users can search for a destination using either an interactive map or a drop down menu that allow selection of a region/city. Each destination has its own sub-homepage from which a list of products is available. Users can also search directly by category (accommodation, events, attractions search).

As part of the brochure request section, visitors are asked to give details about their preferences in a comment box (interest, travel plan, time of year, destinations chosen etc). Users have to 'make the effort' of writing all those details, when perhaps providing a choice of answers would increase the chance of getting answers.

The most notable feature of this site is the way the booking options are integrated into the DMOs overall services, e.g. call centre, real-time on-line booking and online reservation request.

Commonwealth of Pennsylvania, '100% Pure Pennsylvania Experience' – http://www.experiencepa.com

This is the main site of a network of nearly twenty '100% Pure Pennsylvania Experience' sites. It acts as a gateway to sites promoting the state by theme (Fall, Winter, Hunt & Fish, Haunted, Heritage regions, Civil War, Thrills, Fairways, Scenic routes, Railways, Shopping, Keystone ride). It also links to local DMO sites and contains functionality such as search facilities by category, travel planner and tools.

It is an attractive site with a quick movie promoting the destination or a special theme available. The site contains a main menu across the top (nature & outdoors, arts & entertainment, historic places, accommodation & dining) with colour coding that is used on those section's mini-sites. There is also a resources menu with main links. The main menu is not always available throughout the site and on some occasions, users are constrained to using the 'back' button in the browser.

The site provides quite detailed product search facilities with many different criteria to choose from. A link to 'Travelocity' is available for booking. Useful functions are available to enhance the information about each products e.g. nearby tourism products (restaurants, campground, accommodation, attractions etc) as well as a 'map it' function in co-operation with MapQuest, which provides GPS functionality and driving directions.

Visitors can register as a 'preferred visitor' if they want to customize the site and gain full access to the travel planner functionality (schedule in calendar).

Azienda per la Promozione Turistica del Trentino – http://www.trentino.to

This site has good content with an interesting approach promoting Trentino as a double – summer and winter - destination. Each 'season' has its own sub-homepage from which users can search and plan.

The site provides visual experiences of the destination with a photo gallery, flash movie, Web cams and panoramic images from which you can zoom in and out. The access is optional and does not interfere with the download speed of the site.

There are many ways to browse the site and three different types of menu available: top level menu, 'season' menu and a menu of the different categories (accommodation etc) that is a bit confusing. The site provides a search facility for many product categories. The accommodation search is the most detailed as it enables the user to specify a considerable number of criteria. Visitors can reserve accommodation by completing the online booking request form.

Visitors are asked to take part in an online survey before posting a message in the guest book. This enables APT to learn more about their visitors' personal interests and preferences. They also gather personal details as part of the brochure request form.

This site employs an interesting promotion/marketing approach with two clear ways in which to search for destination information, summer and winter.

Wallonie Bruxelles Office de Promotion du Tourisme – http://www.belgium-tourism.net

This site distinctly promotes two geographical areas Bruxelles and Wallonie. Visitors can search either Bruxelles or Wallonie's databases as each has its own separate sub-homepage. They are virtually two separate sites within one, and both have identical templates and functionality.

This distinctive choice of promoting what is one part of Belgium into two separate destinations can be slightly confusing for visitors. Nevertheless, a consistent template is used for both sub-homepages with a different colour for each. The site has a tunnel page from which visitors can select their language. This leads to a homepage from which they can access either the Bruxelles or Wallonie sub-homepage. The homepage has a main menu giving access to sections common to both geographical areas (Help/brochures/links section) and each sub-homepage has its own menu enabling the user to browse for destination information by product category.

Both sub-homepages offer the same functionality. Users can search product databases using an interactive map to select a district and then search by category. They can also search directly by categories. Users have good access to the database with access to accommodation, attractions, activities, events, database as well as general services such as TIC, embassies etc.

In order to view online brochures in PDF format, users have to register. The registration process involves supplying full contact details and a quick poll asking users how they found the site (from a search engine, a mailing, magazine etc).

The site has an interesting feature entitled 'Suggestions' which allows the user to search a database of suggested visits by type (cities, parks & gardens, discoveries) with a description, comments, practical information and recommended brochures for the visits.

Turisme de Barcelona – http://www.barcelonaturisme.com

The site contains a good level of content and is available in 4 different languages. The information on the homepage is a little spread out and the layout and navigation are slightly confusing.

The main menu bar contains general navigation tools (home, back, exit) as well as content tools (games, gifts). There are two options for browsing for destination product information through the site. The first one is to use the central menu on the homepage with icons for each category, which leads users to the category homepage where they have to click on an icon representing an arrow to go to the next page within the category. The second option is to click on 'index' within the menu bar which acts as a site map with the main menu and submenu. Users can then click to go directly to the subsections. The navigation isn't easy and this is aggravated by the fact that the download speed is very slow.

An interactive product database search (with drop down menu to select criteria) is available for accommodation, events and restaurants. The rest of the products are available on a list basis. Links to the online booking site are provided for accommodation booking.

Only contact details of users who wish to request information are gathered. No other personal information or user profiles are required.

The site suffers from slow download speeds and has rather complicated and confusing navigation.

Budapest Tourism Office – http://www.budapestinfo.hu

The site has good destination content and detailed products database search facilities. It is an attractive site with a simple but detailed structure. Nice photographs and live Webcams provide a good visual experience of the destination throughout the site. Photographs can also be viewed by categories on the 'Photos Album' section corresponding to the menu entry.

The site is very easy to use with a menu situated on the left side of the screen and available consistently throughout the site. It provides a comprehensive database search capability for restaurants, events and accommodation enabling visitors to define many criteria in order to find the products that match their needs. Information on other products is also available but on a listing basis. The site provides on-line booking facilities via Travelport.hu using the Hungarian Reservation System.

Under the section 'Your opinion', BTO has designed an on-line customer survey and asks visitors questions to define their profile, as well as questions on their opinion on the homepage and on Budapest as a tourism destination. This is not compulsory and no special incentives are proposed to encourage visitors to complete the questionnaire.

The site provides a very detailed search facility for restaurants (by location, type of restaurants, type of cuisine, facilities, services, type of live music, price, date). For each accommodation establishment a good location map (full GPS) is available via Travelport.hu. A large-scale map is provided with the establishment noted in red in order to locate it within the global area, visitors can then zoom in to a street level location map.

Canberra Tourism & Events Corporation – http://www.canberratourism.cam.au

This site is rich in content providing good access to the products and services database. Two similar versions of the site are available but dedicated to two different target audiences: one for general travellers and one for schools and groups. The site also gives access to sections (sub-homepages) dedicated to the Media and MICE sectors.

The design of the site is very different from traditional DMOs site. It is database driven and uses drop down menus to display the information available. A new narrow window, containing the information selected, appears for each sub-section. The site is poor in visual illustrations except in the 'send a postcard' section where visitors can e-mail photograph of the destination as e-postcards.

The site is easy to use. The fact that 'link to home' and 'list of content' is not available on each page is not problematic as the information selected is contained within a separate window, which the visitor only needs to close to go back to the homepage and re-initiate his search.

Most of the content of the site is database driven and is accessible via drop down menus. A products and services database is available featuring accommodation, packages, events, attractions, activities, shops, list of airlines, car rentals etc. More in depth search facilities are available for accommodation and a street level location map is available for each establishment. On-line booking request are available for packages and accommodation. Links to on-line tickets booking sites for theatre, sport/cultural events are also provided.

In the feedback section, Canberra Tourism & Events Corporation asked visitors to complete an on-line survey including questions on how they found out about the site, their comments on the site and suggestions to improve it. Visitors are asked whether they wish to receive a reply from that e-mail and also if they wish to be added to their mailing list. This is the only opportunity visitors have to join a mailing list.

The site has adopted a rather unusual design providing access to products and destination information using a drop down menu format for each category.

Wonderful Copenhagen – http://www.visitcopenhagen.dk

This site contains good content. It is dedicated to leisure travellers but also provides access to sections dedicated to the media, MICE and the travel trade.

It has a simple yet attractive design, and provides a good visual experience of the Destination with short videos about Copenhagen and Denmark (requires MediaPlayer), 360 degrees photos panorama and photo galleries.

The site is very easy to use and has adopted a simple menu (with submenu for details of the sections) situated on the right side of the screen and available consistently throughout the site. Visitors can also use the index (which acts as a site map) that lists alphabetically all the information/themes featured within the site.

The site gives access to a wide range of products from the product database. There is an especially detailed search facility for accommodation and events. A street level location map is available for each accommodation establishment. The accommodation database is powered by HORESTA via www.danishhotels.dk. Visitors can reserve accommodation by completing on-line booking form and have the option of providing their credit card details if they wish to guarantee their reservation. Visitors can also apply for the Copenhagen card (which gives free entrance and discounts to some of Copenhagen products) and Guide and transport package (for special tour/visits).

Wonderful Copenhagen does not gather personal details from their visitors, except when they complete an on-line reservation form and are asked to provide their personal details.

The site contains an especially good Photo Gallery section providing information on each attraction / site featured in the photographs.

London Tourist Board – http://www.londontown.com

This site is rich in content and is a detailed guide to London acting as an on-line directory of virtually all aspects of tourism of interest to travellers e.g.accommodation, events, shopping, entertainment, night life, restaurants. LTB claims that, in September 2000, Londontown.com was the most visited destination Website in the world with 603,455 unique visitors in one month.

The framework colour scheme is a bit too dark but more colours are used within the pages with colour code by categories. Each category has its own homepage with search facility, featured / preferred providers, articles etc. The site also contains many additional tools such as street level location map for accommodation establishments, popular attractions, the possibility to e-mail a postcard or a personalised map.

Despite the fact that there are a lot of features on the homepage, the site is relatively easy to use as the menus clearly detail the categories covered. Nevertheless, the number of different menus used (one for general tools, a detailed one for products, and another for main themes) can be a bit confusing. Some of the sections are under construction so some internal links are not working.

The site provides interactive search facility for accommodation, restaurants and conference facilities and list-type search by categories and subcategories for other type of products (events, attractions, tours). Users can book online to any of the establishments that enable it through their own or a third parties, reservations engine. Visitors can send an online reservation request for tours, restaurants etc. A London map guide can also be purchased online.

On various occasions visitors are asked to register, e.g. to post messages on the message board and to join the mailing list but only e-mail addresses are collected. LTB obtains an indication of where visitors are travelling from in the tunnel page as a log in procedure. Visitors have the opportunity to have a personalised shopping itinerary sent to them by answering 20 quick questions about their interests. LTB encourages visitors to complete an on-line survey by giving them the chance to win a prize if they participate.

When visitors first renter the homepage, a windows appears with special offers with up to 60% reduction on luxury hotel rooms. Visitors can click on the 'check availability' button and a smaller window appears with a message during the search process saying that the system is searching and checking availability in all the hotels taking part in the programme. Visitors can see the names of the hotels as they are being checked. The site also contains a detailed shopping search facility and in-depth guide and description of shops.

Paris Convention & Visitors Bureau – http://www.paris-touristoffice.com

This site is rich in content and provides a comprehensive information guide to Paris as well as links to other regional DMOs site within France. It is visually attractive using photographs and other multimedia elements to help make the site lively and interesting (e.g. there is a 360 degree panoramic view of Paris from 450 feet up).

The navigation is easy, and uses rollovers to display sub-menus from the main menu headings. A detailed site map is available listing all the different features developed within the each section of the site.

The site provides good access to a wide range of products/service from a database: accommodation, events, museums and monuments, restaurants, conventions and trade shows, transports, tours and practical information. The accommodation and museums and monuments as well as events search facilities is especially detailed. The entries for accommodation establishments are very detailed and informative. Information includes useful tools such as an access map (street level with 1bis.com), closest metro, RER, train section, area and distance from the centre of Paris.

Visitors are asked to register if they wish to receive the Paris CVB newsletter but only need to provide their e-mail address to do so. Paris CVB has designed an on-line customer survey that visitors can complete if they wish to but no incentive to encourage them to do so is offered.

The site contains a good link section called 'Paris on the Internet' with search by category available. The site also has a good magazine (report of the month) with pictures and a detailed article on the theme of the month.

Vienna Tourist Board – http://info.wien.at

This site provides access to the products and services database but does not provide destination information itself but links to other relevant sites that do and opens them in a new window. This has some impact on the usability of the site as users are not held within the main site.

The site is easy to use with the menu consistently available on every page of the site on the left side of the screen. Colour is also used to define each section, and assist with readability.

An interactive database search is available for accommodation, events and tours. Booking facilities are available via WienHotels.com. Visitors have the option of using the real time online booking system or sending a reservation request. Both are sent directly to the hotel. They can also choose to phone the call centre. Other products such as tickets for transportation, theatre, musicals can be booked via the organizer sites or company.

Visitors can subscribe to the VTB newsletter by providing their e-mail address, but no further personal details are obtained. Users can also download an events programme by month and print it.

Zurich Tourism – http://www.zurichtourism.ch

Zurich Tourism clearly states that the aim of its site is to provide information to both leisure travellers/visitors and business travellers and provide hotel reservation and these three functions are depicted on the home page with relevant illustrations.

The look and feel of the homepage is different to the rest of the site. The homepage adopts a very simple design with only the essential features: a general tools/features menu at the bottom, a list of all the theme/products covered within the site (accessible via a drop down menu facility) and at the centre photographs of the destination.

Notwithstanding that, the site is easy to use and has a consistent design and style throughout with a detailed menu on the left of all the screens. The site provides on-line booking for accommodation as well as the possibility to send an online reservation request for packages. Links to third party site for event ticket booking is provided.

Visitors need to register and obtain a username and password to be able to book accommodation online and order brochures. Contact details are captured at this point.

The 'Virtual Zurich' section provides a 360 degrees city tour of the destination starting with a map showing the different attractions and monuments. Visitors can view a virtual tour for each individual elements featured.

Consumer Websites evaluation - Reference Table

Some of the functions are rated level, 1, 2 or 3 according to the degree of sophistication present. Other more straightforward functions are just noted as present, or not. The following table details how each function has been analysed and explains the scoring used for the three levels.

FUNCTIONS & SERVICES OFFERED BY THE SITE				
	Y/N	Level 1	Level 2	Level 3
Generics				
Flash introduction		no skip facility	skip facility	+quick to download & instructive
Location context		within the site	within the homepage	as part of intro.
Logging procedure	Y/N			
Language selection		at least English	up to 3	more than 3
Logo/brand	Y/N			
Menu	Y/N			
Travel Information				
Culture/History info	Y/N			
Climate info	Y/N			
Travel essentials info	Y/N			
Transport info	Y/N			
Itineraries/tours info	Y/N			
Travel insurance info	Y/N			
Image gallery		Up to 10	Up to 30	More than 30
Maps		Static	Interactive	Full GPS
Tips/FAQ		Up to 5	Up to 10	More than 10
Links to DMOs	Y/N			

General Information

Company/organisation info	Y/N			
Contact details	Y/N			
Employment opportunities	Y/N			
Privacy statement, disclaimer terms & conditions, copyright	Y/N			
Info on the design of the site	Y/N			
On-line security transactions info	Y/N			
Warranty & return policy	Y/N			
Research data/customer survey	Y/N			
Links to other corporate sites	Y/N			
External links to related sites	Y/N			

Special features

Visitors comments...	Y/N			
Weather report/forecast		global	Localised	+ special interest
News/report/magazine	Y/N			
Newsletter	Y/N			
Chat/newsgroup	Y/N			
Postcards		up to 5	up to 10	more than 10
Other				

Design & functionality

Top level menu	Y/N			
Sub menus	Y/N			
List of content on every page	Y/N			
Link to homepage every p.	Y/N			
Site map	Y/N			
Use of Internet protocols consistently	Y/N			
Use of flash	Y/N			
Use of java applets	Y/N			
Use of animated gifs	Y/N			
Multimedia		Photos	livecams	Video / Virtual tours
Textual description of dest.	Y/N			
News	Y/N			
Special/last minute offers	Y/N			
Exchange rates (converter)	Y/N			
Job status tracking & amendments facility	Y/N			
Search facility – by key words	Y/N			
Search facility – by category		Up to 3 categories, with up to 3 criteria	Up to 3 categories, with more than 3 criteria	More than 3 categories
Search explanation/guide	Y/N			
Contest/prize	Y/N			
Registration (club, newsletter)	Y/N			
On-line brochure	Y/N			
Links to advertisers / banners	Y/N			
Links to partners	Y/N			
Local time	Y/N			
Date	Y/N			
List of awards to the site	Y/N			
Online customer service		Text Chat	Call-back button	Voice over IP
E-mail form for enquiry		e-mail link	pre-defined form	+ key questions
Request form for brochure		e-mail link	pre-defined form	+ key questions

Products Search/list

Accommodation		list	search - up to 3 criteria	more than 3 criteria
Flight		list	search - up to 3 criteria	more than 3 criteria
Car Rental		list	search - up to 3 criteria	more than 3 criteria
Packages		list	search - up to 3 criteria	more than 3 criteria
Attractions		list	search - up to 3 criteria	more than 3 criteria
Activities		list	search - up to 3 criteria	more than 3 criteria
Events		list	search - up to 3 criteria	more than 3 criteria
Restaurants		list	search - up to 3 criteria	more than 3 criteria
Tours		list	search - up to 3 criteria	more than 3 criteria
Tours operators/travel agents		list	search - up to 3 criteria	more than 3 criteria

Conference facilities		list	search - up to 3 criteria	more than 3 criteria
Local services & businesses		list	search - up to 3 criteria	more than 3 criteria
Shop & retail		list	search - up to 3 criteria	more than 3 criteria
Product Information end points				
Contact details	Y/N	Postal/tel./fax only	+ e-mail or Web	+ e-mail + Web
Multimedia		1 Photo	Few photos	+ video/Web cams
Availability		for accommodation	For 2 products	more than 2 pdts
Rates	Y/N			
Textual description	Y/N			
Facilities	Y/N			
Quality accreditation from governing body	Y/N			
Booking facilities				
Completion of e-mail/fax form (reservation enquiry)	Y/N	for 1 product	for 2 products	more than 2 pdts
Real-time on-line booking and confirmation	Y/N	for 1 product	for 2 products	more than 2 pdts
Link to 1/3 party site(s) for bkg	Y/N	for 1 product	for 2 products	more than 2 pdts
Call Centre		Call centre number	"Call me back" button	Voice over IP
Contacting provider direct		Phone/fax	+ E-mail or Web	+ E-mail +Web
On-line registration				
During booking procedure		Only enter e-mail	+ full contact details	+ key questions
To enter competition/draw		Only enter e-mail	+ full contact details	+ key questions
To create personal brochure		Only enter e-mail	+ full contact details	+ key questions
To shop		Only enter e-mail	+ full contact details	+ key questions
To access chat/forum		Only enter e-mail	+ full contact details	+ key questions
To subscribe to newsletter		Only enter e-mail	+ full contact details	+ key questions
To Join club		Only enter e-mail	+ full contact details	+ key questions
Other				
On-line Shop				
Clothes	Y/N			
Souvenirs	Y/N			
Books	Y/N			
Maps	Y/N			
Minimum total order value	Y/N			
Other Web sites				
Site dedicated to the Tourism industry	Y/N	Section on the site	Sub-homepage	Separate site/URL
Site dedicated to MICE	Y/N	Section on the site	Sub-homepage	Separate site/URL
Site dedicated to media	Y/N	Section on the site	Sub-homepage	Separate site/URL
Site dedicated to travel trade	Y/N	Section on the site	Sub-homepage	Separate site/URL

DMOs abbreviation used in tables

National DMOs Websites

NATIONAL DMOs	Abbreviation
Canadian Tourism Commission	CTC
Caribbean Tourism Organisation	CTO
German National Tourist Board	GNTB
Egyptian Tourist Authority	ETA
Japan National Tourist Organisation	JNTO
Tourism Malaysia	TM
Mexico Ministry of Tourism	MMT
Tourism New Zealand	TNZ
Turespaña	T
Switzerland Tourism	ST
Tourism Authority of Thailand	TAT
British Tourist Authority – US gateway	BTA

Regional DMOs Websites

REGIONAL DMOs	Abbreviation
Turismo Andaluz	TA
Edinburgh & Lothians Tourist Board	E&LTB
New York State Division of Tourism	NYSDT
Ontario Travel - TraveLinx	OT
Commonwealth of Pennsylvania, '100% Pure Pennsylvania Experience'	CoP
Azienda per la Promozione Turistica del Trentino	APTT
Wallonie Bruxelles Office de Promotion du Tourisme (OPT)	OPT

Local DMOs Websites

11 Local DMOs	Abbreviation
Turisme de Barcelona	TB
Berlin Tourismus Marketing GmbH	BTM
Budapest Tourism Office	BTO
Canberra Tourism & Events Corporation	CT&EC
Wonderful Copenhagen	WC
London Tourist Board	LTB
Paris Convention & Visitor Bureau	PC&VB
Singapore Tourist Board	STB
Tourism Vancouver	TV
Vienna Tourist Board	VTB
Zurich Tourism	ZT

Note:
Please note that :
the mark "-" in the table indicates that the function is not present.
the mark "N/A" indicates that the function is non applicable to the DMO.

Detailed table evaluation of Consumer Websites (1/5)

FUNCTIONS & SERVICES OFFERED BY THE SITE (first page)					
Organisation	CTC	CTO	GNTB	ETA	JNTO
Generics					
Flash introduction	-	-	-	-	-
Location context	Yes – 1	Yes – 1	Yes – 1	-	-
Logging procedure	-	-	-	-	-
Language selection	Yes – 2	Yes – 3	Yes – 2	Yes – 1	Yes – 3
Logo/brand	Yes	Yes	Yes	Yes	Yes
Menu	Yes	Yes	Yes	Yes	Yes
Travel Information					
Culture/History info	-	Yes	-	Yes	-
Climate info	Yes	-	-	Yes	Yes
Travel essentials info	Yes	Yes	Yes	Yes	Yes
Transport info	Yes	-	Yes	Yes	Yes
Itineraries/tours info	Yes	-	Yes	Yes	Yes
Travel insurance info	-	-	-	-	-
Image gallery	-	-	Yes – 1	Yes – 2	-
Maps	Yes – 1	-	Yes – 2	Yes – 1	Yes – 2
Tips/FAQ	Yes – 3	-	Yes – 2	Yes – 2	Yes – 3
Links to DMOs	Yes	Yes	Yes	-	Yes
General Information					
Company/organisation information	Yes	Yes	Yes	-	Yes
Contact details	Yes	Yes	Yes	-	Yes
Employment opportunities	-	-	-	Yes	-
Privacy statement/disclaimer/terms & conditions/copyright	-	Yes	Yes	-	Yes
Information on the design of the site	-	-	-	-	-
On-line security transactions info	-	-	-	-	Yes
Warranty & return policy	-	-	-	-	-
Research data/customer survey	-	-	-	-	-
Links to other corporate sites	Yes	-	Yes	-	-
External links to related sites	Yes	Yes	Yes	Yes	Yes
Special features					
Visitors comments…	-	-	-	-	-
Weather report/forecast	-	-	Yes – 2	Yes – 2	Yes – 2
News/report/magazine	Yes	-	-	Yes	-
Newsletter	Yes	-	Yes	Yes	-
Chat/newsgroup	-	-	-	Yes	-
Postcards	Yes – 3	-	-	Yes – 3	-
Other				Section for kids, recipes	
Design & functionality					
Top menu	Yes	Yes	Yes	Yes	Yes
Sub menus	-	-	-	Yes	-
List of content on every page	Yes	Yes	Yes	Yes	-
Link to homepage every page.	Yes	Yes	Yes	Yes	Yes
Site map	-	-	Yes	-	-
Use of Internet protocols consistently	Yes	Yes	Yes	Yes	Yes
Use of flash	-	-	-	-	-
Use of java applets	-	-	Yes	-	-
Use of animated gifs	-	Yes	Yes	-	-
Multimedia	Yes – 3	Yes – 1	Yes – 3	Yes – 1	Yes – 1
Textual description of dest.	Yes	Yes	Yes	Yes	Yes
News	Yes	-	Yes	Yes	Yes
Special/last minute offers	Yes	-	-	-	-
Exchange rates (converter)	-	-	Yes	-	-
Job status tracking & amendments facility	-	-	-	-	Yes

Search facility – by key words	Yes	Yes	Yes	Yes	Yes
FUNCTIONS & SERVICES OFFERED BY THE SITE (second page)					
Organisation	**CTC**	**CTO**	**GNTB**	**ETA**	**JNTO**
Search facility – by category	Yes – 3	-	Yes – 2	Yes – 1	Yes – 3
Search explanation/guide	-	-	Yes	Yes	Yes
Contest/prize	-	-	-	-	-
Registration (club, newsletter)	Yes	-	Yes	Yes	Yes
On-line brochure	Yes	-	-	-	-
Links to advertisers / banners	-	-	-	Yes	-
Links to partners	Yes	-	Yes	Yes	Yes
Local time	-	-	-	-	-
Date	-	-	-	-	-
List of awards the site	-	-	-	-	-
Online customer service	-	-	-	-	-
E-mail form for enquiry	Yes – 3	Yes – 1	Yes – 2	Yes – 1	-
Request form for brochure	-	Yes – 3	-	-	-
Products Search/list					
Accommodation	Yes – 2	-	-	Yes – 2	Yes – 3
Flight	-	-	-	Yes – 1	Yes – 2
Car Rental	Yes – 2	-	-	Yes – 1	-
Packages	Yes – 2	-	-	-	-
Attractions	Yes – 2	-	-	Yes – 1	Yes – 3
Activities	-	-	Yes – 1	Yes – 1	Yes – 3
Events	Yes – 2	-	Yes – 3	Yes – 1	Yes – 3
Restaurants	-	-	-	Yes – 1	Yes – 3
Tours	Yes – 2	-	Yes – 1	Yes – 1	Yes – 1
Tours operators/travel agents	Yes – 2	-	-	Yes – 1	Yes – 1
Conference facilities	-	-	-	-	-
Local services & businesses	-	-	-	Yes – 1	-
Shop & retail	-	-	-	Yes – 1	Yes – 3
Product Information end points					
Contact details	Yes – 3	-	Yes – 3	Yes – 3	Yes – 3
Multimedia	-	-	-	Yes – 2	Yes – 1
Availability	-	-	-	-	Yes – 1
Rates	Yes	-	-	Yes	Yes
Textual description	Yes	-	Yes	Yes	Yes
Facilities	-	-	-	Yes	Yes
Quality accreditation	-	-	-	Yes	-
Booking facilities					
Completion of e-mail/fax form	-	-	-	-	-
Real-time on-line booking and confirmation	-	-	-	-	Yes – 1
Link to 1/3 party site(s) for bkg	-	-	Yes – 1	Yes – 1	-
Call Centre	Yes – 1	-	-	-	-
Contacting provider direct	Yes – 3	-	Yes – 3	Yes – 3	Yes – 3
On-line registration					
During booking procedure	N/A	N/A	N/A	N/A	Yes – 2
To enter competition/draw	N/A	N/A	N/A	N/A	N/A
To create personal brochure	Yes – 1	N/A	N/A	N/A	N/A
To shop	N/A	N/A	N/A	N/A	N/A
To access chat/forum	N/A	N/A	N/A	Yes – 1	N/A
To subscribe to newsletter	Yes – 3	N/A	Yes - 3	Yes – 1	N/A
To Join club	N/A	N/A	N/A	N/A	N/A
Other	-		-	-	-
On-line Shop					
Clothes	-	-	-	-	-
Souvenirs	-	-	-	-	-
Books	-	-	-	-	-
Maps	-	-	-	-	-
Minimum total order value	N/A	N/A	N/A	N/A	N/A
Other Web sites					
dedicated to tourism industry	Yes – 3	-	Yes – 3	-	-
dedicated to MICE	Yes – 1	-	-	-	Yes – 2
dedicated to media	Yes – 2	-	Yes – 1	-	-
dedicated to travel trade	Yes – 2	-	Yes – 3	-	-

Detailed table evaluation of consumer Websites (6/10)

FUNCTIONS & SERVICES OFFERED BY THE SITE (first page)					
Organisation	**TM**	**MMT**	**TNZ**	**T**	**ST**
Generics					
Flash introduction	-	Yes	-	-	-
Location context	Yes – 1	Yes – 1	-	Yes – 1	-
Logging procedure	-	Yes	-	Yes	Yes
Language selection	-	Yes – 2	Yes – 3	Yes – 3	Yes – 3
Logo/brand	Yes	Yes	Yes	Yes	Yes
Menu	Yes	Yes	Yes	Yes	Yes
Travel Information					
Culture/History info	Yes	Yes	Yes	-	-
Climate info	Yes	Yes	Yes	Yes	Yes
Travel essentials info	Yes	Yes	Yes	Yes	Yes
Transport info	Yes	Yes	Yes	Yes	Yes
Itineraries/tours info	-	Yes	Yes	Yes	Yes
Travel insurance info	-	-	-	-	Yes
Image gallery	Planned	Yes – 3	-	Yes – 3	Yes
Maps	-	Yes – 2	Yes – 2	Yes – 2	Yes – 3
Tips/FAQ	Yes – 3	Yes – 3	-	-	Yes – 2
Links to DMOs	Yes	Yes	Yes	-	Yes
General Information					
Company/organisation information	Yes	Yes	Yes	Yes	Yes
Contact details	Yes	-	-	-	Yes
Employment opportunities	-	-	-	-	-
Privacy statement/disclaimer/terms & conditions/copyright	-	-	Yes	-	-
Information on the design of the site	-	Yes	Yes	Yes	-
On-line security transactions info	-	-	-	-	Yes
Warranty & return policy	-	-	-	-	-
Research data/customer survey	Yes	Yes	Yes	-	-
Links to other corporate sites	-	-	Yes	-	-
External links to related sites	Yes	Yes	Yes	Yes	Yes
Special features					
Visitors comments...	Yes	-	Yes	-	Yes
Weather report/forecast	-	-	-	-	Yes – 2
News/report/magazine	-	-	Yes	-	-
Newsletter	-	-	Yes	Yes	Yes
Chat/newsgroup	Yes	-	Yes	-	Yes
Postcards	-	-	Yes – 3	-	Yes – 3
Other	Games...		Screensaver	guided tour, game	
Design & functionality					
Top menu	Yes	Yes	Yes	Yes	Yes
Sub menus	Yes	Yes	-	Yes	-
List of content on every page	-	Yes	Yes	Yes	Yes
Link to homepage every p.	-	Yes	Yes	Yes	Yes
Site map	-	Yes	Yes	Yes	-
Use of Internet protocols consistently	Yes	Yes	Yes	Yes	Yes
Use of flash	-	Yes	-	Yes	Yes
Use of java applets	Yes	Yes	-	-	-
Use of animated gifs	Yes	Yes	Yes	Yes	Yes
Multimedia	Yes – 1	Yes – 1	Yes – 1	Yes – 3	Yes – 3
Textual description of dest.	Yes	Yes	Yes	Yes	Yes
News	Yes	-	Yes	-	Yes
Special/last minute offers	-	-	Yes	-	Yes
Exchange rates (converter)	Yes	-	-	Yes	-
Job status tracking & amendments facility	-	-	-	-	Yes
Search facility – by key words	-	Yes	Yes	Yes	Yes

FUNCTIONS & SERVICES OFFERED BY THE SITE (second page)					
Organisation	**TM**	**MMT**	**TNZ**	**T**	**ST**
Search facility – by category	Yes - 2	-	Yes – 1	Yes – 3	Yes – 3
Search explanation/guide	-	Yes	Yes	-	-
Contest/prize	-	-	-	-	-
Registration (club, newsletter)	-	Yes	Yes	-	Yes
On-line brochure	Yes	Yes	Yes	-	Yes
Links to advertisers / banners	-	-	-	-	Yes
Links to partners	-	Yes	-	Yes	Yes
Local time	-	Yes	-	-	-
Date	-	-	-	Yes	-
List of awards the site	-	-	-	-	-
Online customer service	1 planned	-	-	-	-
E-mail form for enquiry	Yes – 1	Yes – 2	Yes – 2	Yes – 2	Yes – 2
Request form for brochure	-	-	-	-	-
Products Search/list					
Accommodation	Yes – 3	Yes – 1	Yes – 2	Yes – 3	Yes – 2
Flight	Yes – 1	-	Yes – 2	-	-
Car Rental	Yes – 1	-	Yes – 2	-	-
Packages	-	-	Yes – 2	-	-
Attractions	-	Yes – 1	-	Yes – 3	Yes – 2
Activities	Yes – 1	-	Yes – 2	Yes – 3	Yes - 2
Events	Yes – 1	Yes – 1	Yes – 2	Yes – 3	Yes – 3
Restaurants	-	-	-	-	-
Tours	-	Yes – 1	Yes – 2	Yes – 1	Yes – 2
Tours operators/travel agents	-	Yes – 1	Yes – 2	Yes – 1	-
Conference facilities	-	-	-	Yes – 2	-
Local services & businesses	-	-	-	-	-
Shop & retail	-	-	Yes – 2	-	-
Product information end points					
Contact details	Yes – 1	Yes – 2	Yes – 3	Yes – 3	Yes – 3
Multimedia	-	Yes – 1	Yes – 1	-	Yes - 2
Availability	-	-	-	-	Yes - 1
Rates	Yes	-	-	Yes	Yes
Textual description	-	-	Yes	Yes	Yes
Facilities	Yes	Yes	-	Yes	Yes
Quality accreditation	-	-	-	Yes	Yes
Booking facilities					
Completion of e-mail/fax form	-	-	-	-	-
Real-time on-line booking and confirmation	-	-	-	-	Yes – 1
Link to 1/3 party site(s) for bkg	-	-	Yes – 2	-	Yes - 2
Call Centre	-	-	-	-	Yes – 1
Contacting provider direct	Yes – 1	Yes – 2	Yes – 3	Yes – 3	Yes – 3
On-line registration					
During booking procedure	N/A	N/A	N/A	N/A	Yes – 2
To enter competition/draw	N/A	N/A	N/A	N/A	N/A
To create personal brochure	-	Yes – 2	Yes – 1	N/A	Yes - 3
To shop	N/A	N/A	N/A	N/A	-
To access chat/forum	-	N/A	-	N/A	-
To subscribe to newsletter	N/A	N/A	Yes – 1	N/A	Yes - 3
To Join club	N/A	N/A	-	N/A	N/A
Other	-	to access stat...	to post testimonials		To post items in forum
On-line Shop					
Clothes	-	-	-	-	Yes
Souvenirs	-	-	-	-	Yes
Books	-	-	-	-	-
Maps	-	-	-	-	Yes
Minimum total order value	N/A	N/A	N/A	N/A	N/A
Other Web sites					
dedicated to tourism industry	-	Yes – 1	Yes – 3	-	-
dedicated to MICE	-	-	-	-	Yes – 2
dedicated to media	-	-	-	-	-
dedicated to travel trade	-	-	-	-	-

Detailed table evaluation of consumer Websites (11/15)

FUNCTIONS & SERVICES OFFERED BY THE SITE (first page)					
Organisation	**TAT**	**BTA**	**TA**	**E&LTB**	**NYSDT**
Generics					
Flash introduction	-	-	-	-	-
Location context	Yes – 1	Yes – 3	Yes – 1	Yes – 1	-
Logging procedure	Yes	Yes	-	-	-
Language selection	Yes – 3	Yes – 3	Yes – 3	-	-
Logo/brand	Yes	Yes	Yes	Yes	Yes
Menu	Yes	Yes	Yes	Yes	Yes
Travel Information					
Culture/History info	Yes	-	Yes	-	Yes
Climate info	Yes	Yes	Yes	Yes	Yes
Travel essentials info	Yes	Yes	-	Yes	-
Transport info	Yes	Yes	Yes	Yes	Yes
Itineraries/tours info	Yes	Yes	Yes	Yes	Yes
Travel insurance info	-	Yes	-	-	-
Image gallery	-	Yes – 3	-	-	-
Maps	Yes – 2	Yes – 3	Yes – 2	Yes – 1	Yes – 3
Tips/FAQ	Yes – 2	Yes – 3	-	Yes – 2	-
Links to DMOs	-	Yes	-	Yes	Yes
General Information					
Company/organisation information	Yes	Yes	-	-	-
Contact details	Yes	Yes	Yes	Yes	Yes
Employment opportunities	-	-	-	-	-
Privacy statement/ disclaimer/terms & conditions/copyright	Yes	Yes	Yes	Yes	Yes
Information on the design of the site	-	Yes	-	-	-
On-line security transactions info	-	-	Yes	-	-
Warranty & return policy	-	-	Yes	-	-
Research data/customer survey	Yes	Yes	Yes	Yes	
Links to other corporate sites	Yes	Yes	-	-	-
External links to related sites	Yes	Yes	Yes	Yes	Yes
Special features					
Visitors comments...	-	Yes	-	-	-
Weather report/forecast	-	-	-	-	-
News/report/magazine		Yes	-	-	-
Newsletter	-	Yes	-	-	Yes
Chat/newsgroup	-	-	-	-	-
Postcards	-	Yes – 3	-	Yes – 3	-
Other				Kids' section	
Design & functionality					
Top menu	Yes	Yes	Yes	Yes	Yes
Sub menus	-	-	-	-	-
List of content on every page	Yes	Yes	Yes	Yes	Yes
Link to homepage every p.	Yes	Yes	Yes	Yes	Yes
Site map	Yes	-	-	-	-
Use of Internet protocols consistently	Yes	Yes	Yes	Yes	Yes
Use of flash	-	-	Yes	-	-
Use of java applets	-	-	Yes	-	-
Use of animated gifs	Yes	Yes	Yes	Yes	-
Multimedia	Yes – 1	Yes – 1	Yes – 1	Yes – 1	Yes – 1
Textual description of dest.	Yes	Yes	Yes	Yes	Yes
News	-	Yes	-	Yes	-
Special/last minute offers	-	Yes	Yes	Yes	-
Exchange rates (converter)	-	-	-	-	-
Job status tracking & amendments facility	-	-	-	-	-
Search facility – by key words	-	Yes	Yes	-	-

FUNCTIONS & SERVICES OFFERED BY THE SITE (second page)					
Organisation	TAT	BTA	TA	E&LTB	NYSDT
Search facility – by category	Yes – 3	Yes – 3	Yes – 3	Yes – 3	Yes – 3
Search explanation/guide	Yes	Yes	Yes	-	-
Contest/prize	-	Yes	-	-	-
Registration (club, newsletter)	-	Yes	Yes	Yes	Yes
On-line brochure	-	-	-	-	Yes
Links to advertisers / banners	-	Yes	-	-	-
Links to partners	Yes	Yes	Yes	-	Yes
Local time	-	-	-	-	-
Date	-	-	-	-	-
List of awards the site	-	-	-	-	-
Online customer service	-	Yes – 1	-	-	-
E-mail form for enquiry	Yes – 1	Yes – 2	Yes – 1	Yes – 2	Yes – 3
Request form for brochure	-	Yes – 3	Yes – 2	-	Yes – 3
Products Search/list					
Accommodation	Yes – 3	Yes – 2	Yes – 3	Yes – 3	Yes – 3
Flight	-	Yes – 1	Yes – 2	-	Yes – 2
Car Rental	-	Yes - 2	Yes - 3	Yes – 1	Yes – 2
Packages	-	Yes – 2	-	-	-
Attractions	-	Yes – 2	Yes – 3	Yes – 2	Yes – 2
Activities	Yes – 1	Yes - 2	Yes - 2	Yes – 2	Yes – 2
Events	Yes – 2	Yes – 2	Yes - 2	Yes – 2	Yes – 2
Restaurants	Yes – 3	-	Yes - 2	Yes – 1	-
Tours	Yes – 1	Yes - 1	Yes – 1	Yes – 2	Yes – 1
Tours operators/travel agents	-	Yes – 1	-	-	-
Conference facilities	-	-	Yes – 1	Yes – 2	Yes – 2
Local services & businesses	-	-	Yes – 2	-	Yes – 2
Shop & retail	Yes – 1	-	-	Yes – 2	-
Product information end points					
Contact details	Yes – 1	Yes – 3	Yes – 3	Yes – 3	Yes – 3
Multimedia	Yes – 1	-	Yes – 1	Yes – 1	-
Availability	unavailable	-	Yes – 3	-	-
Rates	unavailable	Yes	Yes	Yes	Yes
Textual description	Yes	Yes	Yes	Yes	Yes
Facilities	unavailable	Yes	Yes	Yes	Yes
Quality accreditation	unavailable	Yes	Yes	Yes	-
Booking facilities					
Completion of e-mail/fax form	-	-	Yes – 3	-	-
Real-time on-line booking and confirmation	-	-	Yes – 3	-	-
Link to 1/3 party site(s) for bkg	-	Yes – 2	-	-	-
Call Centre	-	Yes – 1	-	Yes – 1	Yes – 1
Contacting provider direct	unavailable	Yes – 3	Yes – 3	Yes – 3	Yes – 3
On-line registration					
During booking procedure	N/A	N/A	Yes – 2	N/A	N/A
To enter competition/draw	N/A	Yes – 3	N/A	N/A	N/A
To create personal brochure	N/A	N/A	N/A	N/A	Yes – 2
To shop	N/A	N/A	N/A	Yes – 2	N/A
To access chat/forum	N/A	N/A	N/A	N/A	N/A
To subscribe to newsletter	N/A	Yes – 1	N/A	N/A	Yes – 2
To Join club	N/A	N/A	N/A	N/A	N/A
Other			Feedback - 3		
On-line Shop					
Clothes	-	-	-	-	-
Souvenirs	-	-	-	-	-
Books	-	-	-	Yes	-
Maps	-	-	-	Yes	-
Minimum total order value	N/A	N/A	N/A	-	N/A
Other Web sites					
dedicated to tourism industry	-	Yes – 3	-	-	-
dedicated to MICE	Yes – 3	Yes – 2	-	Yes – 2	-
dedicated to media	-	Yes – 2	-	-	-
dedicated to travel trade	-	Yes – 2	-	Yes – 2	-

Detailed table evaluation of consumer Websites (16/20)

FUNCTIONS & SERVICES OFFERED BY THE SITE (first page)					
Organisation	**OT**	**CoP**	**APTT**	**OPT**	**TB**
Generics					
Flash introduction	-	-	-	-	-
Location context	-	-	Yes – 1	-	-
Logging procedure	-	-	-	Yes	Yes
Language selection	-	-	Yes – 2	Yes – 3	Yes – 3
Logo/brand	Yes	Yes	Yes	Yes	Yes
Menu	Yes	Yes	Yes	Yes	Yes
Travel Information					
Culture/History info	Yes	-	Yes	-	Yes
Climate info	Yes	Yes	-	Yes	Yes
Travel essentials info	Yes		-	Yes	Yes
Transport info	Yes	Yes	Yes	Yes	Yes
Itineraries/tours info	Yes	Yes	-	-	Yes
Travel insurance info	-	-	-	-	-
Image gallery	-	-	Yes – 2	-	-
Maps	Yes – 2	Yes – 3	Yes – 2	Yes – 2	-
Tips/FAQ	-	-	-	-	-
Links to DMOs	Yes	Yes	Yes	Yes	Yes
General Information					
Company/organisation information	-	-	Yes	-	Yes
Contact details	Yes	Yes	Yes	Yes	Yes
Employment opportunities	Yes	-	-	-	-
Privacy statement/ disclaimer/terms & conditions/copyright	Yes	Yes	Yes	Yes	-
Information on the design of the site	-	-	Yes	-	-
On-line security transactions info	Yes	-	-	-	-
Warranty & return policy	Yes	-	-	-	-
Research data/customer survey	-	-	Yes	-	Yes
Links to other corporate sites	-	Yes	-	-	-
External links to related sites	Yes	Yes	Yes	Yes	Yes
Special features					
Visitors comments...	-	-	Yes	-	-
Weather report/forecast	-	Yes – 2	Yes – 3	-	-
News/report/magazine	-	Yes	Yes	-	-
Newsletter	-	Yes	Yes	Yes	-
Chat/newsgroup	-	-	-	-	-
Postcards	-	-	Yes – 3	-	-
Other		Screensavers			Games, screensavers
Design & functionality					
Top menu	Yes	Yes	Yes	Yes	Yes
Sub menus	Yes	-	-	-	Yes
List of content on every page	Yes	-	Yes	Yes	Yes
Link to homepage every p.	Yes	-	Yes	Yes	Yes
Site map	Yes	-	Yes	-	Yes
Use of Internet protocols consistently	Yes	Yes	Yes	Yes	Yes
Use of flash	-	-	Yes	Yes	Yes
Use of java applets	Yes	-	-	-	-
Use of animated gifs	Yes	-	-	Yes	Yes
Multimedia	Yes – 1	Yes – 3	Yes – 3	Yes – 1	Yes – 1
Textual description of dest.	Yes	Yes	Yes	Yes	Yes
News	-	Yes	Yes	-	-
Special/last minute offers	Yes	-	-	-	-
Exchange rates (converter)	-	-	-	-	-
Job status tracking & amendments facility	Yes	-	-	-	-
Search facility – by key words	-	Yes	Yes	-	Yes

FUNCTIONS & SERVICES OFFERED BY THE SITE (second page)					
Organisation	**OT**	**CoP**	**APTT**	**OPT**	**TB**
Search facility – by category	Yes – 3	Yes – 3	Yes – 3	Yes – 3	Yes – 3
Search explanation/guide	Yes	-	-	-	-
Contest/prize	Yes	-	-	-	-
Registration (club, newsletter)	Yes	Yes	Yes	Yes	-
On-line brochure	-	Yes	-	-	-
Links to advertisers / banners	Yes	-	-	Yes	-
Links to partners	Yes	-	Yes	Yes	Yes
Local time	-	-	-	-	-
Date	-	-	-	-	Yes
List of awards the site	-	-	-	-	-
Online customer service	-	-	-	-	-
E-mail form for enquiry	Yes – 2	Yes – 1	Yes – 3	Yes – 1	Yes – 2
Request form for brochure	Yes – 2	Yes – 2	Yes – 3	Yes – 2	Yes - 2
Products Search/list					
Accommodation	Yes – 3	Yes – 2	Yes – 3	Yes – 3	Yes – 3
Flight	-	-	-	-	-
Car Rental	Yes – 1	-	-	-	-
Packages	Yes – 3	-	Yes – 2	-	-
Attractions	Yes – 3	Yes – 3	-	Yes – 3	Yes – 1
Activities	Yes – 3	Yes – 2	Yes – 2	Yes – 3	Yes – 1
Events	Yes – 3	Yes – 3	Yes – 1	Yes – 3	Yes – 3
Restaurants	-	Yes – 2	Yes – 1	-	Yes – 3
Tours	Yes – 3	Yes – 2	-	Yes – 3	Yes – 1
Tours operators/travel agents	-	-	-	Yes – 2	Yes – 2
Conference facilities	-	-	-	-	-
Local services & businesses	-	-	-	-	-
Shop & retail	Yes – 2	Yes – 2	Yes – 1	-	Yes – 2
Product Information end points					
Contact details	Yes – 3	Yes – 3	Yes – 3	Yes – 3	Yes – 3
Multimedia	Yes – 1	-	Yes – 1	-	Yes – 2
Availability	Yes – 3	-	-	-	-
Rates	Yes	-	Yes	-	Yes
Textual description	Yes	Yes	Yes	Yes	Yes
Facilities	Yes	-	Yes	Yes	-
Quality accreditation	-	-	Yes	Yes	Yes
Booking facilities					
Completion of e-mail/fax form	Yes – 3	-	Yes – 1	-	-
Real-time on-line booking and confirmation	Yes – 3	-	-	-	-
Link to 1/3 party site(s) for bkg	-	Yes – 3	-	Yes – 1	Yes – 1
Call Centre	Yes – 1	Yes – 1	-	-	Yes – 1
Contacting provider direct	Yes – 3	Yes – 3	Yes – 3	Yes – 3	Yes – 3
On-line registration					
During booking procedure	Yes – 3	N/A	Yes – 2	N/A	N/A
To enter competition/draw	-	N/A	N/A	N/A	N/A
To create personal brochure	N/A	-	N/A	N/A	N/A
To shop	N/A	N/A	N/A	N/A	N/A
To access chat/forum	N/A	N/A	N/A	N/A	N/A
To subscribe to newsletter	N/A	Yes – 3	Yes – 1	Yes – 1	N/A
To Join club	N/A	N/A	N/A	N/A	N/A
Other		Customised travel planner - 3	post message - 3	View brochures (PDF) – 3	
On-line Shop					
Clothes	-	-	-	-	-
Souvenirs	-	-	-	-	-
Books	-	-	-	-	-
Maps	-	-	-	-	-
Minimum total order value	N/A	N/A	N/A	N/A	N/A
Other Web sites					
dedicated to tourism industry	-	-	-	-	-
dedicated to MICE	-	Yes – 3	-	-	-
dedicated to media	-	-	Yes 1	-	-
dedicated to travel trade	-	-	Yes – 1	-	-

Detailed table evaluation of consumer Websites (21/25)

FUNCTIONS & SERVICES OFFERED BY THE SITE (first page)					
Organisation	**BTM**	**BTO**	**CT&EC**	**WC**	**LTB**
Generics					
Flash introduction	-	-	Yes – 2	-	-
Location context	-	-	Yes – 1	-	-
Logging procedure	Yes	-	-	-	Yes
Language selection	Yes – 3	Yes – 2	-	Yes – 2	Yes – 2
Logo/brand	Yes	Yes	Yes	Yes	Yes
Menu	Yes	Yes	Yes	Yes	Yes
Travel Information					
Culture/History info	Yes	Yes	Yes	-	-
Climate info	Yes	Yes	Yes	-	-
Travel essentials info	Yes	Yes	Yes	-	-
Transport info	Yes	Yes	Yes	Yes	Yes
Itineraries/tours info	Yes	Yes	Yes	Yes	Yes
Travel insurance info	-	-	-	-	-
Image gallery	Yes – 2	Yes – 3	-	Yes – 2	-
Maps	Yes – 2	Yes – 3	Yes – 3	Yes – 3	Yes – 3
Tips/FAQ	-	-	-	-	Yes – 3
Links to DMOs	-	Yes	Yes	Yes	-
General Information					
Company/organisation information	Yes	Yes	Yes	Yes	Yes
Contact details	Yes	Yes	Yes	Yes	Yes
Employment opportunities	-	-	-	-	-
Privacy statement/disclaimer/terms & conditions/copyright	Yes	-	Yes	-	Yes
Information on the design of the site	-	-	-	-	-
On-line security transactions info	Yes	Yes	-	-	Yes
Warranty & return policy	-	-	-	-	-
Research data/customer survey	Yes	Yes	Yes	-	-
Links to other corporate sites	-	-	-	-	Yes
External links to related sites	Yes	Yes	Yes	Yes	Yes
Special features					
Visitors comments…	-	-	-	-	-
Weather report/forecast	-	-	-	-	-
News/report/magazine	Yes	-	Yes	-	Yes
Newsletter	-	-	-	-	Yes
Chat/newsgroup	-	-	-	-	Yes
Postcards	-	-	Yes – 3	-	Yes – 3
Other	Game				Email a map
Design & functionality					
Top menu	Yes	Yes	Yes	Yes	Yes
Sub menus	Yes	-	Yes	Yes	-
List of content on every page	Yes	Yes	-	Yes	Yes
Link to homepage every p.	Yes	Yes	-	Yes	Yes
Site map	-	-	-	Yes	Yes
Use of Internet protocols consistently	Yes	Yes	Yes	Yes	-
Use of flash	-	Yes	Yes	-	-
Use of java applets	-	-	-	-	-
Use of animated gifs	Yes	Yes	Yes	Yes	Yes
Multimedia	Yes – 1	Yes – 2	Yes – 1	Yes – 3	Yes – 1
Textual description of dest.	Yes	Yes	Yes	Yes	-
News	Yes	-	-	-	Yes
Special/last minute offers	Yes	-	-	Yes	Yes
Exchange rates (converter)	-	-	-	-	-
Job status tracking & amendments facility	-	-	-	-	-
Search facility – by key words	Yes	Yes	Yes	-	-

FUNCTIONS & SERVICES OFFERED BY THE SITE (second page)					
Organisation	**BTM**	**BTO**	**CT&EC**	**WC**	**LTB**
Search facility – by category	Yes – 2	Yes – 3	Yes – 3	Yes – 3	Yes – 3
Search explanation/guide	-	Yes	Yes	-	-
Contest/prize	Yes	-	-	-	-
Registration (club, newsletter)	-	Yes	-	-	Yes
On-line brochure	-	-	-	-	-
Links to advertisers / banners	-	-	Yes	-	Yes
Links to partners	Yes	-	Yes	Yes	-
Local time	-	-	Yes	-	Yes
Date	-	-	Yes	-	Yes
List of awards the site	-	-	-	-	-
Online customer service	-	-	-	-	-
E-mail form for enquiry	Yes – 1	Yes – 1	Yes – 1	Yes – 1	Yes – 2
Request form for brochure	Yes – 2	-	-	-	Yes – 1
Products Search/list					
Accommodation	Yes – 3	Yes – 3	Yes – 3	Yes – 3	Yes – 3
Flight	-	-	Yes – 1	Yes – 1	Yes – 1
Car Rental	-	-	Yes – 1	Yes – 1	Yes – 1
Packages	Yes – 1	-	Yes – 2	-	-
Attractions	Yes – 1	Yes – 3	Yes – 2	Yes – 3	Yes – 2
Activities	-	-	Yes – 2	-	-
Events	Yes – 3	Yes – 3	Yes – 2	Yes – 3	Yes – 2
Restaurants	-	Yes – 3	-	-	Yes – 3
Tours	Yes – 1	Yes – 2	Yes – 2	Yes – 2	Yes – 2
Tours operators/travel agents	-	-	Yes 1	-	Yes – 1
Conference facilities	-	-	-	-	Yes – 2
Local services & businesses	-	-	-	-	-
Shop & retail	-	-	Yes – 2	-	Yes – 2
Product Information end points					
Contact details	Yes – 3	Yes – 3	Yes – 3	Yes – 3	Yes – 3
Multimedia	Yes – 1	Yes – 2	-	Yes – 1	Yes – 2
Availability	Yes – 1	Yes – 1	-	-	Yes – 1
Rates	Yes	Yes	Yes	Yes	Yes
Textual description	Yes	Yes	Yes	Yes	Yes
Facilities	Yes	Yes	Yes	Yes	Yes
Quality accreditation	-	Yes	-	Yes	Yes
Booking facilities					
Completion of e-mail/fax form	Yes – 3	-	Yes – 2	Yes – 1	Yes - 2
Real-time on-line booking and confirmation	Yes- 1	Yes – 1	-	-	Yes – 2
Link to 1/3 party site(s) for bkg	-	-	Yes – 2	-	-
Call Centre	Yes – 1	Yes – 1	Yes – 1	Yes – 1	Yes – 1
Contacting provider direct	Yes – 3	Yes – 3	Yes – 3	Yes – 3	Yes – 3
On-line registration					
During booking procedure	-	Yes – 2	N/A	N/A	-
To enter competition/draw	Yes – 2	N/A	N/A	N/A	N/A
To create personal brochure	N/A	N/A	N/A	N/A	N/A
To shop	N/A	N/A	N/A	N/A	-
To access chat/forum	N/A	N/A	N/A	N/A	Yes – 1
To subscribe to newsletter	N/A	N/A	N/A	N/A	Yes – 1
To Join club	N/A	N/A	N/A	N/A	N/A
Other					Kids log in
On-line Shop					
Clothes	-	-	-	-	-
Souvenirs	-	-	-	-	-
Books	-	-	-	-	Yes
Maps	-	-	-	-	Yes
Minimum total order value	N/A	N/A	N/A	N/A	-
Other Web sites					
dedicated to tourism industry	-	Yes – 1	-	-	-
dedicated to MICE	Yes – 2	-	Yes – 2	Yes – 1	Yes – 3
dedicated to media	Yes – 2	-	Yes – 2	Yes – 1	Yes – 2
dedicated to travel trade	Yes – 2	-	-	Yes – 1	-

Detailed table evaluation of consumer Websites (26/30)

FUNCTIONS & SERVICES OFFERED BY THE SITE (first page)					
Organisation	**PC&VB**	**STB**	**TV**	**VTB**	**ZT**
Generics					
Flash introduction	-	-	-	-	-
Location context	-	Yes – 1	-	-	Yes – 1
Logging procedure	-	Yes	-	Yes	-
Language selection	Yes – 2	Yes – 3	Yes – 2	Yes – 3	Yes – 2
Logo/brand	Yes	Yes	Yes	Yes	Yes
Menu	Yes	Yes	Yes	Yes	Yes
Travel Information					
Culture/History info	-	Yes	-	-	Yes
Climate info	-	Yes	Yes	-	Yes
Travel essentials info	-	Yes	Yes	-	-
Transport info	Yes	Yes	Yes	Yes	Yes
Itineraries/tours info	Yes	Yes	Yes	Yes	-
Travel insurance info	-	-	Yes	-	-
Image gallery	Yes – 3	Yes – 3	Yes – 3	Yes – 2	-
Maps	Yes – 3	-	Yes – 3	Yes – 1	Yes – 1
Tips/FAQ	Yes – 3	Yes – 3	Yes – 3	-	-
Links to DMOs	Yes		Yes	Yes	Yes
General Information					
Company/organisation information	Yes	-	Yes	Yes	Yes
Contact details	Yes	Yes	Yes	Yes	Yes
Employment opportunities	-	-	Yes	-	-
Privacy statement/ disclaimer/ terms & conditions/copyright	-	Yes	Yes	-	-
Information on the design of the site	Yes	-	Yes	Yes	-
On-line security transactions info	-	-	Yes	Yes	-
Warranty & return policy	-	-	Yes	Yes	-
Research data/customer survey	Yes	-	Yes	Yes	-
Links to other corporate sites	-	Yes	Yes	Yes	-
External links to related sites	Yes	Yes	Yes	Yes	Yes
Special features					
Visitors comments...	Yes	Yes	-	Yes	-
Weather report/forecast	-	-	Yes – 1	-	-
News/report/magazine	Yes	-	-	-	-
Newsletter	Yes	Yes	-	Yes	-
Chat/newsgroup	Yes	-	-	-	-
Postcards	Yes – 2	Yes – 1	Yes – 3	-	-
Other		Screensavers, recipes...			
Design & functionality					
Top menu	Yes	Yes	Yes	Yes	Yes
Sub menus	Yes	-	-	-	-
List of content on every page	Yes	Yes	Yes	Yes	Yes
Link to homepage every p.	Yes	Yes	Yes	Yes	Yes
Site map	Yes	Yes	-	Yes	-
Use of Internet protocols consistently	Yes	Yes	Yes	Yes	Yes
Use of flash	-	Yes	Yes	-	Yes
Use of java applets	-	Yes	Yes	Yes	Yes
Use of animated gifs	Yes	Yes	-	-	Yes
Multimedia	Yes – 3	Yes – 3	Yes – 3	Yes – 1	Yes – 3
Textual description of dest.	Yes	Yes	Yes	Yes	Yes
News	Yes	-	Yes	Yes	-
Special/last minute offers	-	Yes	Yes	Yes	Yes
Exchange rates (converter)	Yes	-	Yes	-	-
Job status tracking & amendments facility	-	-	Yes	-	-
Search facility – by key words	Yes	Yes	Yes	Yes	Yes
FUNCTIONS & SERVICES OFFERED BY THE SITE (second page)					

Organisation	PC&VB	STB	TV	VTB	ZT
Search facility – by category	Yes – 3	Yes – 2	Yes – 3	Yes – 3	Yes – 3
Search explanation/guide	-	Yes	Yes	-	-
Contest/prize	-	-	-	-	-
Registration (club, newsletter)	Yes	Yes	-	Yes	Yes
On-line brochure	Yes	Yes	Yes	-	-
Links to advertisers / banners	Yes	-	Yes	-	Yes
Links to partners	Yes	Yes	Yes	Yes	Yes
Local time	Yes	-	-	-	-
Date	Yes	-	-	-	-
List of awards the site	-	-	-	-	Yes
Online customer service	-	Yes – 1	-	-	-
E-mail form for enquiry	Yes – 1	Yes – 1	Yes – 1	Yes – 2	Yes – 1
Request form for brochure	-	Yes – 2	-	-	Yes – 2
Products Search/list					
Accommodation	Yes – 3	Yes – 3	Yes – 3	Yes – 3	Yes – 3
Flight	Yes – 1	-	Yes – 2	-	-
Car Rental	Yes – 1	-	Yes – 1	-	-
Packages	-	Yes – 1	Yes - 2	Yes – 1	Yes – 2
Attractions	Yes – 3	Yes – 2	Yes – 2	Yes - 1	Yes – 2
Activities	-	-	Yes – 2	-	Yes – 2
Events	Yes – 3	Yes – 2	Yes – 2	Yes – 3	Yes – 3
Restaurants	Yes – 2	-	Yes – 2	-	-
Tours	Yes – 1	Yes – 3	Yes – 1	Yes – 3	Yes – 1
Tours operators/travel agents	Yes – 1	-	Yes – 2	-	-
Conference facilities	-	-	Yes – 2	-	Yes – 1
Local services & businesses	Yes – 2	-	Yes – 2	-	-
Shop & retail	Yes – 1	Yes – 1	Yes – 2	-	Yes – 1
Product Information end points					
Contact details	Yes – 3	Yes – 3	Yes – 3	Yes – 3	Yes – 3
Multimedia	-	Yes – 1	Yes – 1	Yes – 1	-
Availability	-	-	Yes – 1	Yes – 1	Yes – 1
Rates	Yes	Yes	Yes	Yes	Yes
Textual description	Yes	Yes	Yes	Yes	Yes
Facilities	Yes	Yes	Yes	Yes	Yes
Quality accreditation	Yes	-	-	Yes	Yes
Booking facilities					
Completion of e-mail/fax form	-	-	-	Yes – 1	Yes – 1
Real-time on-line booking and confirmation	-	-	Yes – 2	Yes – 1	Yes – 1
Link to 1/3 party site(s) for bkg	Yes – 3	Yes – 2	-	-	Yes – 1
Call Centre	-	-	-	Yes – 1	Yes – 1
Contacting provider direct	Yes – 3	Yes – 3	Yes – 3	Yes – 3	Yes – 3
On-line registration					
During booking procedure	-	N/A	-	-	Yes – 2
To enter competition/draw	N/A	N/A	N/A	N/A	N/A
To create personal brochure	-	-	-	N/A	N/A
To shop	N/A	N/A	N/A	N/A	N/A
To access chat/forum	-	N/A	N/A	N/A	N/A
To subscribe to newsletter	Yes – 1	Yes – 3	N/A	Yes – 1	N/A
To Join club	N/A	N/A	N/A	N/A	N/A
Other			Personalise site		To order brochure
On-line Shop					
Clothes	-	-	-	-	-
Souvenirs	-	-	-	-	-
Books	-	-	-	-	-
Maps	-	-	-	-	-
Minimum total order value	N/A	N/A	N/A	N/A	N/A
Other Web sites					
dedicated to tourism industry	-	Yes – 3	Yes – 2	-	-
dedicated to MICE	-	Yes – 3	Yes – 2	Yes – 3	Yes – 1
dedicated to media	-	-	Yes – 2	-	Yes – 1
dedicated to travel trade	-	Yes – 3	Yes – 2	-	-

Appendix B – Technical glossary and abbreviations

Technical Glossary

active server pages*	A specification for a dynamically created Web page with a ASP extension that utilises ActiveX scripting (usually VB Script or Jscript code). When a browser requests an ASP page, the Web server generates a page with HTML code and sends it back to the browser.
animated GIF*	A type of GIF image that can be animated by combining several images into a single GIF file. It is extremely popular as it is supported by nearly all Web browser and tend to be quite a bit smaller that other animation files such as Java applets.
ASP*	Application service providers. Third-party entities that manage and distribute software-based services and solutions to customers across a wide area network from a central data centre.
banner***	Advertisement in the form of a graphic image on the Web. Most banner ads are animated GIFs.
B2B**	Organisation's sales and marketing efforts aimed at other companies, not end consumers
call centre	An operational department within an organisation that handles all the telephone enquiries from customers or those seeking information on products and services.
chat* (Text chat)	Real-time communication between two users via computer. Once a chat has been initiated, either user can enter text by typing on the keyboard and the entered text will appear on the other user's monitor.
chat room*	A virtual room where a chat session takes place. Technically, a chat room is really a channel, but the term *room* is used to promote the chat metaphor.
cookie*	A message given to a Web browser by a Web server. The browser stores the message in a text file called *cookie.txt*. The message is then sent back to the server each time the browser requests a page from the server.
CRM	Customer relationship management and/or marketing. An approach to marketing, based on the principle that knowledge of, and relationship with, customers is key to maximising sales opportunities, particularly through repeat purchase. See Section 1.4 for further discussion.
CRS	Computer or central reservation system. The GDSs used to be called airline CRSs but now the term CRS usually refers to a reservation system internal to an organisation.
download	The transfer of electronic data from a third party computer to your own.
DMO	Destination Marketing Organisation – also sometimes called Destination Management Organisation. An organisation that is most probably a tourism authority that has, amongst its responsibilities, the task of promoting its destination and operating information services and, in some cases, reservations.

DMS	Destination management system. The technical infrastructure that supports the business activities of a destination marketing organisation. See Chapter 3 for further discussion.
domain name*	A name that identifies one or more IP addresses, used in URLs to identify particular Web pages. Every domain name has a suffix that indicates which top level domain it belongs to (e.g. .gov, .edu, .org, .com…)
dpi	Meaning 'dots per inch'. This refers to the resolution of an image, the greater the number, the sharper the image.
e-business	Electronic business. The process of doing business with partners or customers electronically. This includes e-marketing, processing business transactions electronically; integrating business processes electronically, transferring payments electronically; and delivering services electronically. See Section 1.3 for further discussion.
e-commerce	Electronic commerce. The term used to refer to conducting commercial transactions online.
e-marketing	Electronic marketing. Exploits the Internet and other forms of electronic communication to communicate in the most cost-effective ways with target markets and to enable joint working with partner organisations, with whom there is a common interest.
e-procurement***	Purchasing which takes place between companies using services such as the Internet, Electronic data Interchange or Electronic File transfer. Two companies, one the supplier and the other the purchaser, transmit inquiries, orders, invoices, payments etc, directly through their computer systems.
extranet	The connection of two or more intranets across the Internet.
flash*	A bandwidth friendly and browser independent vector-graphic animation technology. As long as different browsers are equipped with the necessary plug-ins, Flash animations will look the same.
gateway page	A Web page specifically designed as an entry point into a Web site.
GDS	Global distribution system. The term given to the global airline booking systems such as Amadeus, Galileo, Sabre and Worldspan.
GIS*	Geographic information systems are tools used to gather, transform, manipulate, analyse, and produce information related to the surface of the Earth. This data may exist as maps, 3D virtual models, tables, and/or lists.
homepage	The page designed as a starting point to further explore a Web site.
host***	A computer open for access to other computers. A host site is where an ISP provides the location of a Website.
HTML	Hypertext Markup Language. The script language in which Web pages are written. For example, before a phrase and after the phrase would make it appear in a bold font on a Web page.
IDTV	Interactive digital television. Television programming that is transmitted in digital rather than analogue format and that also has a return path so that the viewer can respond to on-screen prompts for information.

intranet	An Internet style system that is only available to users within a single organisation.
IP address*	An identifier for a computer or device on a TCP/IP network. The format of an IP address is a 32-bit numeric address written as four numbers separated by periods. Each number can be zero to 255. For example, 1.160.10.240 could be an IP address
ISP	Internet service provider. A telecommunications company that provides its customers with access to the Internet and other related services.
java applets*	Small Java applications that can be downloaded from a Web server and run on your computer by a Java-compatible Web browser, such as Netscape Navigator or Microsoft Internet Explorer.
kiosks****	Computer terminals linked to a DMS and used by the public to access tourism-related information and transactional services
link	Text or image on a Web page that, when the mouse cursor is placed over it and the mouse button is "clicked", takes the user to another Web page.
meta-tag	Words serving a special purpose that are part of a Web page but that are not displayed. For example, a 'description' meta-tag will hold descriptive text that will be displayed within many search engines.
multimedia	Referring to a mix of electronic media such as text, static images and video.
online	Typically used to describe being connected to the Internet but can mean being connected to any remote computer or computer device.
PDF***	Portable Document Format. Platform independent file format created by Adobe. Created for offline reading of brochures, reports and other documents with complex graphic design. When you download a PDF file, you get the entire document in a single file.
portal	Most often used to describe a Web site used by people as an entry point to the Web. This might be your Internet service provider's home page or a search engine. IDTV services are now trying to also position themselves as portals to the online world.
protocol	A common basis of language by which computers can pass data between themselves across computer networks. The protocol of the Internet is IP – Internet protocol.
resolution	The degree of detail that can be seen on a computer monitor. Usually measured in pixels - the number of squares on-screen. Most computer monitors have a resolution of at least 800 pixels across the screen by 600 pixels down the screen, i.e. 800 x 600.
search engine /directory	A Web site that allows the visitor to conduct a search for Web pages containing words that are of relevant interest. For example, Yahoo!, Lycos, Excite, AltaVista.
splash page	Sub-homepage within a main site

3G*	3G is a specification for the third generation (analogue cellular was the first generation, digital PCS the second) of mobile communications technology. 3G promises increased bandwidth, up to 384 Kbps when a device is stationery or moving at pedestrian speed, 128 Kbps in a car, and 2 Mbps in fixed applications.
unique visitors	The number of people visiting a Web site regardless of the number of pages they view.
URL	Uniform Resource Locator. A URL is the common term used to denote a Web site address.
WAP*	The Wireless Application Protocol is a secure specification that allows users to access information instantly via handheld wireless devices such as mobile phones, pagers, two-way radios, smartphones and communicators.
Web	Short name for the World Wide Web, also referred to as WWW. The Web is that part of the Internet that is made up of Web sites.
Web browser	A software application used to view Web sites. The two most popular are Microsoft Internet Explorer and Netscape Navigator.
Webmaster*	An individual who manages a Website. Depending on the size of the site, the Webmaster might be responsible for any of the following: making sure that the Web server hardware and software is running properly, designing the Web site, creating and updating Web pages, replying to user feedback, creating CGI scripts, monitoring traffic through the site.
Web server*	A computer that delivers (*serves up*) Web pages. Every Web server has an IP address and possibly a domain name.
WYSIWYG*	Pronounced "wizzy-wig", stands for *what you see is what you get*. A WYSIWYG application is one that enables you to see on the display exactly what will appear when the document is printed. WYSIWYG is especially popular for desktop publishing.
XML	Extensible Markup Language. An advanced version of HTML that will allow Web sites to pass data back and forth to software applications as if the site was directly connected to the software in use.

*   *Source: Webopedia (http://Webopedia.Internet.com)*
**   *Source: Responsive Database Services, Inc's library*
          (http://www.rdsinc.com/library)
***   *Source: Enterprise Ireland's glossary of terms (http://www.enterprise-ireland.com)*
****   Source: Impact Through IT – Practical Guidelines for England's Tourism
Organisation on the Use of Information Technology

Other Abbreviations (as used in Part C)

ABC	Activity-Based Costing
AMS	Agency Management Systems
ASTA	American Society of Travel Agents
CLIA	Cruise Lines International Association
DIS	Destination Information System

EIP	Enterprise Information Portal
ERP	Enterprise Resource Planning
ESP	Expert Searching and Pricing
GPS	Global Positioning Satellite
IBE	Internet Booking Engine
IT	Information Technology
MRO	Maintenance, Repair, and Operation/Overhaul
PDA	Portable Digital Assistant
PMS	Property Management System
SCM	Supply Chain Management
SME	Small and Medium-Sized Enterprise
TCP/IP	Transmission Control Protocol/Internet Protocol
TIA	Travel Industry Association
TO	Tour Operator

Appendix C – Suggested reading

Here are a few suggestions for those who want to stay abreast of the latest news about online competition and innovative solutions.

The following Web Sites provide **News and Cases on Information Technologies and Tourism**:

Tourism Industry – General	Tourism Industry – Sectors
www.twcrossroads.com	www.eyefortravel.com
www.etourismnewsletter.com	www.hospitalitynet.org
www.webtravelnews.com	www.hotelmarketing.com
www.infotec-travel.com	www.hotels-online.com
www.t-ti.com	www.str-online.com

The following research groups regularly publish **surveys of tourism e-business markets and practices**:

Dedicated to tourism e-business research/consulting	Generalists with many e-tourism publications
www.phocuswright.com	www.forrester.com
www.genesys.net	www.jup.com (Jupiter Media Metrix)
www.garrett-comm.com	www.emarketer.com
www.horwath-consulting.com	www.gartner.com

These sites offer e-business and e-commerce **News and Cases** from a managerial viewpoint:

- www.thestandard.com: News, Company Listings, Who's Who, Metrics and Research, etc.
- www.cyberatlas.com: News, Trends and Statistics, Research, Tutorials, Technology, etc.
- www.ecommercetimes.com: Articles, News, Case Studies, Research, etc.
- www.ciomagazine.com: Articles, e-business Resource Centre, Case Studies, etc.
- www.wsrn.com: Companies by Industry Segments, Company Profiles and News, etc.

These books define key concepts on e-business **Strategies, Applications, and Management**:

- Alan Afuah and Christopher Tucci, (2000), Internet Business Models and Strategies: Text and Cases, New York, McGraw-Hill Higher Education (www.mhhe.com)
- Ravi Kalakota and Marcia Robinson, (2001), E-Business 2.0: A Roadmap for Success, 2nd edition, Reading, Mass., Addison-Wesley/Pearson Education (www.awl.com)
- Efraim Turban, et al., (2000), Electronic Commerce: A Managerial Perspective, Englewood Cliffs N.J.: Prentice-Hall/Pearson Education: www.prenhall.com/turban

The following Web sites list e-business and e-commerce **Courses, Programs, and Conferences**:

- *http://dossantos.cbpa.louisville.edu/ISNET/Ecomm/*
- http://portal.brint.com/cgi-bin/getit/links/Business/E-Commerce/Education/Centres/
- http://dir.yahoo.com/Computers_and_Internet/Internet/Conferences_and_Events/

Finally, some **Industry and Research Associations** Web sites list tourism and technology events:

- Tourism Industry Association of America (www.tia.org)
- Pacific Asia Travel Association (www.pata.org)
- International Federation for Information Technology and Travel & Tourism (www.ifitt.org)

Appendix D – Bibliography for Part C

[1]   F. Frangialli, "A Vision, Three Worksites, A Strategy,". Madrid, 2001.

[2]   B. Kleindl, "Competitive dynamics and new business models for SMEs in the virtual marketplace," in *Journal of Developmental Entrepreneurship*, vol. 5, 2000, pp. 73-85.

[3]   R. Monk, "Why small businesses fail," in *CMA Management*, vol. 74, 2000, pp. 12-13.

[4]   P. Weill and M. Broadbent, *Leveraging the New Infrastructure: How Market Leaders Capitalise on Information Technology*. Boston: Harvard University Press, 1998.

[5]   Gartner/cPulse, "Gartner/cPulse Report: Net Users Favor Niche Travel Sites," *www.ecommercetimes.com*, 2000.

[6]   Forrester, "Online Travel Service Breeds Loyalty," Forrester.com 11 July 2001 2001.

[7]   Jupiter Media Metrix, "Research Report: Corporate Travel Energizing Online Market," *www.ecommercetimes.com*, 2001.

[8]   D. Lake, "Web Travel Takes Off," *The Industry Standard*, vol. http://www.thestandard.com, 2001.

[9]   PhoCusWright, "The Online Travel Marketplace 2001-2003: Forecasts, Business Models, And Best Practices For Profitability," PhoCusWright.com July 11th, 2001 2001.

[10]   Jupiter Media Metrix, "Europeans Move Travel Planning Online," *CyberAtlas*, 2001.

[11]   Ipsos-Reid, "Internet Transforming Canadian Travel Habits," *CyberAtlas*, 2001.

[12]   G. Evans and M. Peacock, "Small is Beautiful? ICT and Tourism SMEs: Comparative European Survey," in *Information and Communication Technologies in Tourism 2000*, D. R. Fesenmaier, S. Klein, and D. Buhalis, Eds. Vienna: SpringerWienNewYork, 2000, pp. 497-508.

[13]   T. Mullen, "Travel's Long Journey To The Web," in *Internetweek*, vol. Issue, 2000, pp. G103-106.

[14]   D. Schuette, "Turning e-business barriers into strengths," in *Information Systems Management*, vol. 17, 2000, pp. 20-25.

[15]   B. Kienan, *Small business solutions E-commerce*. Redmond, Wash.: Microsoft Press, 2000.

[16]   T. R. Lituchy and A. Rail, "Bed and breakfasts, small inns, and the Internet: The impact of technology on the globalization of small businesses," in *Journal of International Marketing*, vol. 8, 2000, pp. 86-97.

[17] Canadian Travel Press, "Net Numbers," *Canadian Travel Press,*, vol. 33, pp. 12, 2001.

[18] T. Kemp, "Online Travel Takes Off Despite Poor Economy," *http://www.Internetweek.com/story/INW20010517S0003*, 2001.

[19] eyefortravel.com, "GetThere Gets Wyndham,"., 2001.

[20] A. Petrone, "Convenience And Price Key to Consumer Loyalty," *Canadian Travel Press,*, vol. 34, pp. 1 & 27, 2001.

[21] J. Ott, "Airlines Dig for New Tools, Seek Online Travel Partners," in *Aviation Week & Space Technology*, vol. 153, 2000, pp. 62-64.

[22] eyefortravel.com, "Marriott Hotels In View,"., 2001.

[23] L. S. Tillett, "Tools Personalise Travel Shopping,",, 2001.

[24] M. Whitford, "Mapping it out," in *Hotel and Motel Management*, vol. 215, 2000, pp. 30.

[25] eyefortravel.com, "New Look for HotelRes.com,"., 2001.

[26] hotel-online.com, "Webvertising Powers Destination Site With iHotelier System," *Hotel.Online Hospitality News Headlines*, 2001.

[27] www.conferenceboard.ca, "TRAVEL FORECAST 2000: Twenty-One Questions for the 21 st Century,"., 2000.

[28] L. McConnell, "B&Bs And The Internet: Not Just An Online Reservation System Anymore," *CTX News*, 2001.

[29] eyefortravel.com, "Real Time Access to 500 hotels Across India,"., 2001.

[30] L. S. Tillett, "Site Gives View Of A Room: Marriott.com update includes more personalization and support for customer preferences," *http://www.Internetweek.com/ebizapps/ebiz111300-2.htm*, 2000.

[31] D. Buhalis, "Information technology for small, and medium-sized tourism enterprises: adaptation and benefits," *Information Technology & Tourism*, vol. 2, pp. 79-95, 1999.

[32] eyefortravel.com, "Tailor-Made Internet Reservation & Marketing Solutions for the Lodging Industry by RoomsNet,"., 2001.

[33] eyefortravel.com, "Leapnet Developments,"., 2001.

[34] M. Bush, "Internet will not replace traditional reservation systems," in *Hotel and Motel Management*, vol. 215, 2000, pp. 31.

[35] Canadian Travel Press, "GDS Hotel Booking Up," *Canadian Travel Press,*, vol. 33, pp. 14, 2001.

[36] eyefortravel.com, "Travelocity Birthday Developments.,"., 2001.

[37]   eyefortravel.com, "TRUST International, Member Of Bertelsmann Group, Strengthens U.S.,"., 2001.

[38]   eyefortravel.com, "HotDeals Goes Mobile,"., 2001.

[39]   eyefortravel.com, "More French Offerings from Laterooms.com,"., 2001.

[40]   Eyefortravel.com, "goStay Launch by Netpace,"., 2001.

[41]   Eyefortravel.com, "Zoho Adds Budget Tracking and Inventory Management Applications to Online Procurement System,"., 2000.

[42]   eyefortravel.com, "HotelTools ASP Rollout,"., 2001.

[43]   eyefortravel.com, "Headquarters Plaza Signs With Synxis For Leading Edge Reservations And Electronic Distribution Services," *http://www.eyefortravel.com/index.asp?news=16227&src=nwsltr*, 2001.

[44]   eyefortravel.com, "Newtrade Technologies Inc. Announces Appointment of Barry Gleason as Vice-President, Sales and Marketing," *http://www.eyefortravel.com/index.asp?news=16369&src=nwsltr*, 2001.

[45]   eyefortravel.com, "Yatra Solutions for Arizona Businesses,"., 2001.

[46]   eyefortravel.com, "'More Hospitality E-Procurement' – Aberdeen Group,"., 2001.

[47]   www.hotelsmag.com, "E-Commerce: The Pace Picks Up," in *Hotels*, 2000.

[48]   E. Ngonzi, "Hospitality eProcurement - Will the Industry Take Advantage of These Internet Models and Strategies,",, 2000.

[49]   www.eurhotec.com, "Telefonica And Sol Melia to Create Hotel Sector B2B e-commerce Portal with Barcelo, Iberostar and BBVA,"., 2000.

[50]   J. L. Caro, A. Guevara, A. Aguayo, and S. Galvez, "Increasing the quality of hotel management information systems by applying workflow technology," *Information Technology & Tourism*, vol. 3, pp. 87-98, 2000.

[51]   eyefortravel.com, "Wireless Access for Bass Hotels Brands,"., 2001.

[52]   eyefortravel.com, "Turn-Key Web Marketing Approach for Florida Hospitality Industry,"., 2001, pp. 5/2/2001.

[53]   eyefortravel.com, "Movenpick Operates IDeaS Solution,"., 2001.

[54]   eyefortravel.com, "IDeaS for Mandarin,"., 2001.

[55]   eyefortravel.com, "Does The Room Have Net Access?,"., 2001.

[56]   Canadian Travel Press, "High-Speed Service Offered By Toronto Hotel," *Canadian Travel Press,*, vol. 33, pp. 9, 2001.

[57]   eyefortravel.com, "Curbside Check-In at Wyndham Hotels,"., 2001.

[58]   eyefortravel.com, "Cutting The Paperwork,"., 2001.

[59]   eyefortravel.com, "Utell To Represent Park Place,"., 2001.

[60]   eyefortravel.com, "Worldspan First To Offer Integrated Hotel Rate Range Functionality; Marriott Signs As Launch Customer,"., 2001.

[61]   eyefortravel.com, "Banners Banned On Travelclubhouse Site,"., 2001.

[62]   eyefortravel.com, "Concierges Needed For Global Site,"., 2001.

[63]   eyefortravel.com, "Nexion Selects Lanyon's DigitalQueue Technology to Automate Travel Ticketing Process,"., 2001.

[64]   eyefortravel.com, "Avendra Procurement Client Base Expands,"., 2001.

[65]   eyefortravel.com, "IDeaS for Park Hyatt Tokyo,"., 2001.

[66]   eyefortravel.com, "MICROS Interface for Wyndham Hotels,"., 2001.

[67]   eyefortravel.com, 'The Consortium' Hospitality Business Model,"., 2001.

[68]   eyefortravel.com, "New Check-Rate Online Product Helps Hotels Search Multiple Travel Sites For Easy, Real Time Online Rate Comparitives,"., 2001.

[69]   eyefortravel.com, "New Web Performance Tool,"., 2001.

[70]   M. G. Echo, "Tad Smith, futurist," in *Management Review*, vol. 88, 1999, pp. 64.

[71]   J. Galloway, "Booking Travel on the Internet," *http://www.astanet.com/news/article_bookingtravel.asp*, 2001.

[72]   S. Khan and D. Rosato, "Web to cut travel agents by 25%," in *USA Today*, 2000, pp. 01A.

[73]   Eyefortravel.com, "IDC eTravel Research Update,"., 2001.

[74]   J. Sharkey, "Rosenbluth, a trend spotter among travel agents, believes it has found a new one," in *New York Times*. New York, 2000, pp. C.14.

[75]   ASTA, "ASTA Releases Results of 2001 Service Fees Report," *http://www.astanet.com/news/index.asp#Spring*, vol. Los Cabos, Mexico, 2001.

[76]   W. B. Schatzman, "Ready for takeoff," in *Best's Review*, vol. 101, 2000, pp. 81-82.

[77]   M. Goldstein, "The great Web site shakeout," in *Successful Meetings*, vol. 49, 2000, pp. 27.

[78]   M. Dunbar, "Dot.coms No Immediate Threat To Agents," *Canadian Travel Press*,, vol. 32, pp. 6, 2000.

[79]   A. Diba, "An old-line agency finds an Online niche," in *Fortune*, vol. 141, 2000, pp. 258.

[80]   eyefortravel.com, "New Latin American Sites,"., 2001.

[81]   B. Mowat, "Tips To Protect Your Investment Online," *Canadian Travel Press,*, vol. 32, pp. 2 & 22, 2000.

[82]   M. Villano, "That's the ticket," in *Cio*, vol. 13, 2000, pp. 210-224.

[83]   J. Slater, "On the move," in *Far Eastern Economic Review*, vol. 163, 2000, pp. 34-36.

[84]   vacation.com, "Vacation.com,",, 2001.

[85]   P. Richer, "The Battle of Brand," *Travel Trade Gazette e-commerce Articles*, 2000.

[86]   T. Wilson, "Sabre, Ariba Build B-To-B Marketplace For Travel, Hospitality Industries," *http://www.Internetweek.com/story/INW20000301S0004*, 2000.

[87]   eyefortravel.com, "Jetour Streamlines Processes,"., 2001.

[88]   eyefortravel.com, "Expedia ESP,"., 2001.

[89]   C. Belman, "Are You Keeping Current with Technological Advances? - Maintaining pace requires a collective effort from the top down," *ACTA Voyage*, pp. 32-34, 2001.

[90]   ASTA, "ASTA Puts The Emphasis On Education With Diverse New Offerings," *http://www.astanet.com/news/*, 2001.

[91]   ASTA, "ASTA 2001 World Congress," *http://www.astanet.com/conference/cg01_seminars.asp#Technology*, 2001.

[92]   Canadian Travel Press, "Online Training Offered By CLIA," *Canadian Travel Press,*, vol. 32, pp. 9, 2000.

[93]   Canadian Travel Press, "Free Amex Service," *Canadian Travel Press,*, vol. 33, pp. 4, 2001.

[94]   eyefortravel.com, "VacationCoach introduces Me-Print Technology to Help Online Travel Sites Move Beyond Airline Tickets and Into More Complex Travel Products,"., 2001.

[95]   T. Kemp, "Travel Sites Take Off: Technology fuels success, but independent sites face threat from airlines," *http://www.Internetweek.com/ebizapps01/ebiz052101-2.htm*, 2001.

[96]   Canadian Travel Press, "New Tool Helps Agents Create Travel Agendas," *Canadian Travel Press,*, vol. 33, pp. 10, 2001.

[97]   eyefortravel.com, "Amadeus Launches Travel Assistant Web Site: Provides On-line Itineraries and More for Amadeus-Powered Travellers and Travel Professionals in North America," *http://www.eyefortravel.com/index.asp?news=16370&src=nwsltr*, 2001.

[98]   Canadian Travel Press, "TravelBestBuys Provides New Agency Sales Option," *Canadian Travel Press,*, vol. 33, pp. 1 and 27, 2001.

[99]   B. Mowat, "Software Package Creates Desktop That Connects Agents And Operators," *Canadian Travel Press,*, vol. 33, pp. 16, 2001.

[100]   eyefortravel.com, "Students Travel Habits Uncovered,"., 2001.

[101]   A. Leary, "Going it alone," in *Asian Business*, vol. 36, 2000, pp. 18.

[102]   B. Rosier, "Saga's portal to target affluent 'grey' market," in *Marketing*, 2000, pp. 11.

[103]   K. W. Sudeikis, "Have Passion, Will Travel," *http://www.astanet.com/news/article_havepassionwilltravel.asp*, 2001.

[104]   D. Murphy, "Web travel takes off," *Marketing - London*, pp. 43-44, 2000.

[105]   Government of Australia, "Case Studies of Tourism DotComs,", vol. http://www.isr.gov.au/sport_tourism/tourismdotcom/Appendices/casestudies. html, 2001.

[106]   L. Del Rosso, "Perspective: Turning Web lookers into off-line bookers," *www.twcrossroads.com*, 2001.

[107]   eyefortravel.com, "Uniglobe.com launches new "Travel Shop" and announces ten affiliate partners," *eyefortravel.com*, 2000.

[108]   eyefortravel.com, "Uniglobe Expands Fare Offerings," *eyefortravel.com*, 2000.

[109]   CIO Magazine, "That's the ticket," *CIO Magazine*, vol. http://www2.cio.com/archive/061500_ticket_content.html, 2000.

[110]   B. Sharak, "Agencies Move To The Web," *http://www.eyefortravel.com/index.asp?news=6969*, 2000.

[111]   J. Sharkey, "Last week's stock debacle may point to a consolidation in the online booking business," in *New York Times*. New York, 2000, pp. C.8.

[112]   C. Rosen, "Internet shatters travel model," in *Informationweek*, vol. 816, 2000, pp. 56-60.

[113]   P. Sontag, "Forecasting The Industry 2001," *Canadian Travel Press,*, vol. 33, pp. 27, 2001.

[114]   www.ntaonline.com, "Tour Operators,"., 2000.

[115]   www.eyefortravel.com, "No turning back : Tour operators and e-commerce,"., 2000.

[116]   www.eyefortravel.com, "No turning back: Tour operators and e-commerce,"., 2000.

[117]   www.hotel-online.com, "The Changing World of E-Travel,"., 2000.

[118]   P. Richer, "The Death of the Brochure," *Travel Trade Gazette e-commerce Articles*, 2000.

[119] P. Richer, "Creating Content," *Travel Trade Gazette e-commerce Articles*, 2001.

[120] www.serverworldmagazine.com, "New Channels for Travel Industry,"., 2001.

[121] www.atemiami.com, "Advanced Technology Enterprises, Inc.,"., 2001.

[122] www.ibm.com, "GTI Tours delivers perfect getaways with DB2-based extranet,"., 2001.

[123] eyefortravel.com, "Local Solution for Hawaii,"., 2001.

[124] Canadian Travel Press, "Logibro Amadeus Team Up," *Canadian Travel Press,*, vol. 33, pp. 14, 2001.

[125] 203.111.122.76/about/newsroom.html, "Viator Builds Technology Bridge Connecting Tour Operators and Global Distributors,"., 2000.

[126] www.freesun.be, ""Gradient Solutions" uses new technologies to cut the costs of travel distribution by 75% unique intranet solution connects old technology to new,"., 2001.

[127] G. Jewell, B. Williamson, and K. Kärcher, "The Airtours Cruise Intranet: Streamlining the distribution of information, knowledge and money," *Information and Communication Technologies in Tourism 1999 - Proceedings of the International Conference in Innsbruck, Austria - Enter 1999*, pp. 337-346, 1999.

[128] www.ustoapackagepower.com, "Instant smarts,"., 2000.

[129] Travelink.co.uk, "Travelink product details,"., 2001.

[130] www.pegsinc.com, "Pegasus Systems Enters the European Tour Operator Market through Agreement with U.K.-Based Mirror Image Communications,"., 1999.

[131] eyefortravel.com, "SCS Solars Moves Tourtek into Chile,",. 2001.

[132] www3.ncr.com, "Travel Unie,"., 2000.

[133] www.unexplored.com, "Unexplored Travel Network Finalizes Acquisition Of Resort Automation To Offer Call Centre And Online Inventory Solutions,"., 2000.

[134] eyefortravel.com, "MEDiARO.com Launches First Dynamic Travel Exchange in Asia Pacific in FinderPlus,"., 2000.

[135] Asiatravelmart.com, "Asiatravelmart.Com Gains Competitive Advantage With Egain's Solutions,",. 2001.

[136] A. Lupton, "Tour Operator Built Success By Getting On The Net Early," *Canadian Travel Press*, vol. 32, pp. 16 & 26, 2000.

[137] G. McKenzie-Wilson, "Web-based tour operator and handling agent," *www.ecommerce-scotland.org*, 2001.

[138]   M. Pittini, "Italy's largest tour operator migrates its booking system to the Web and saves costs," *www.ibm.com*, 2001.

[139]   Microsoft, "Advanced Self-Help Reservation System Accommodates Online Travel Customers," *www.microsoft.com*, 2000.

[140]   K. Rice, "Online travel companies exploit the Web with a human touch," *www.webtravelnews.com*, 2000.

[141]   M. Beaunoyer, "Joane Tétreault, de Skylink - Une passion pour le professionnalisme," *Le magazine L'agent de voyages*, vol. 6, pp. 4, 2001.

[142]   L. McNeill, *Travel in the digital age*. London. U.Kk: Bowerdean Publishing Company Ltd., 1997.

[143]   D. Buhalis, "Information Technology for Small and Medium-Sized Tourism Enterprises : Adaptation and Benefits," *Information Technology & Tourism*, vol. 2, pp. 79-96, 1999.

[144]   P. Sheldon, *Tourism Information Technology*. London, U.K.: CABI Publishing, 1997.

[145]   J.-M. Godart, "Using the Trip Planning Problem for Computer-Assisted Customisation of Sightseeing Tours," in *Information and Communication Technologies in Tourism 2001 - Proceedings of the International Conference in Montreal, Canada 2001*, K. W. W. Pauline J. Sheldon, Daniel R. Fesenmaier, Ed. New York: SpringerWienNewYork, 2001, pp. 377-386.

[146]   U. Gretzel, Y. Yuan, and D. R. Fesenmaier, "White Paper on Advertising Strategy and Information Technology in Tourism,". Urbana-Champaign, 2000, pp. 48.

[147]   A. Creed, "The Real Way To Travel In Style," *Newsbytes*, 2000.

[148]   J. Mallory, "Rand McNally TripPlanner," *Newsbytes*, 1995.

[149]   eyefortravel.com, "Travelago Offers Free Online Promotion For Hawaii Businesses," *http://www.eyefortravel.com/index.asp?news=16270&src=nwsltr*, 2001.

[150]   eyefortravel.com, "Satellite Photography Through AOL," *http://www.eyefortravel.com/index.asp?news=16260&src=nwsltr*, 2001.

[151]   S. Dennis, "Netherlands - Libertel Taps Signalsoft For M-Location Services," *Daily News*, 2000.

[152]   eyefortravel.com, "GORP.com Names America's Best Beaches," *http://www.eyefortravel.com/index.asp?news=16265&src=nwsltr*, 2001.

[153]   S. Elmy, "Wireless Travel Guides," *Canadian Travel Press,*, vol. 33, pp. 4, 2001.

[154]   Y.-H. Cho and D. R. Fesenmaier, "A Conceptual Framework for Evaluating Effects of a Virtual Tour," in *Information and Communication Technologies in Tourism 2000 - Proceedings of the International Conference in Barcelona, Spain, 2000*, D. R. Fesenmaier, S. Klein, and D. Buhalis, Eds. Vienna: SpringerWienNewYork, 2000.

[155] H. Pechlaner and L. Osti, "Reengineering the Role of Culture in Tourism's Value Chain and the Challenges for Destination Management Systems - The Case of Tyrol," in *Information and Communication Technologies in Tourism 2001 - Proceedings of the International Conference in Montreal, Canada.* New York: SpringerWienNewYork, 2001, pp. 300-301.

[156] S. Tufts and S. Milne, "Museums - A Supply-Side Perspective," *Annals of Tourism Research*, vol. 26, pp. 613-631, 1999.

[157] B. Ebiri, "Napster freaked the music industry, and Web entertainment had some ups and downs. What does the future hold?," *Yahoo! Internet Life*, 2001.

[158] S. Elmy, "Le Louvre On Le Web," *Canadian Travel Press*,, vol. 33, pp. 4, 2001.

[159] P. Paolini, T. Barbieri, P. Loiudice, F. Alonzo, and et al., "Visiting a museum together: How to share a visit to a virtual world," in *Journal of the American Society for Information Science*, vol. 51, 2000, pp. 33-38.

[160] PC Magazine, "Smithsonian Institution," *PC Magazine*, 2001.

[161] A. A. Goodrum and K. Martin, "Bringing fashion out of the closet: Classification structure for the Drexel Historic Costume Collection," in *American Society for Information Science. Bulletin of the American Society for Information Science*, vol. 25, 1999, pp. 21-23.

[162] S. Ditlea, "Digital deep space," in *Technology Review*, vol. 103, 2000, pp. 108-109.

[163] L. J. Goff, "IT's a Zoo at New York's Wildlife Conservation Society," *Computer World*, 2001.

[164] M. Misek, "Art and technology? Zuma Digital, the Guggenheim, and the Premises of a paradox," in *E Media Professional*, vol. 12, 1999, pp. 28-29.

[165] eyefortravel.com, "Timberland Forms Alliance With Gorp.Com: Bringing the outdoor playground online for outdoor enthusiasts world-wide," *http://www.eyefortravel.com/index.asp?news=16049&src=nwsltr*, 2001.

[166] J. Kelly, "Looking to sports for development dollars," in *The American City & County*, vol. 115, 2000, pp. 20-21.

[167] T. Sullivan, "At your Web service," *The InfoWorld.com Network*, 2001.

[168] Canadian Travel Press, "Web Site Designed For Divers," *Canadian Travel Press*,, vol. 32, pp. 14, 2000.

[169] G. Evans, "Networking for Growth and Digital Business: Local Urban Tourism SMTEs and ICT," in *Information and Communications Technologies in Tourism 1999*, P. J. Sheldon, K. W. Wöber, and D. R. Fesenmaier, Eds. Wien: Springer-Verlag/Wien New York, 1999.

[170] eyefortravel.com, "Travelocity and TravelCLICK Team Up,", 2001.

[171] eyefortravel.com, "Viator Partners With Travelocity To Offer Booking For Destination Activities World-wide," *http://www.eyefortravel.com/index.asp?news=16048&src=nwsltr*, 2001.

[172]   G. A. Lyons, "Developing Rural Tourism Destinations: Implications for, and of, Information Systems," in *Information and Communication Technologies in Tourism 2000 - Proceedings of the International Conference in Barcelona, Spain 2000*, D. R. Fesenmaier, S. Klein, and D. Buhalis, Eds. Wien: Springer, 2000, pp. 241-242.